The poems and written addresses of Mary T. Lathrap ... with a short sketch of her life

Mary Lathrap, Julia R Parish

Nabu Public Domain Reprints:

You are holding a reproduction of an original work published before 1923 that is in the public domain in the United States of America, and possibly other countries. You may freely copy and distribute this work as no entity (individual or corporate) has a copyright on the body of the work. This book may contain prior copyright references, and library stamps (as most of these works were scanned from library copies). These have been scanned and retained as part of the historical artifact.

This book may have occasional imperfections such as missing or blurred pages, poor pictures, errant marks, etc. that were either part of the original artifact, or were introduced by the scanning process. We believe this work is culturally important, and despite the imperfections, have elected to bring it back into print as part of our continuing commitment to the preservation of printed works worldwide. We appreciate your understanding of the imperfections in the preservation process, and hope you enjoy this valuable book.

Mary T. Lathrap

THE

POEMS AND WRITTEN ADDRESSES

OF

MARY T. LATHRAP

President of the Michigan Woman's Christian Temperance
Union for Fourteen Years

WITH A

SHORT SKETCH OF HER LIFE

INTRODUCTION BY
FRANCES E. WILLARD

CHARACTER SKETCHES BY
LADY HENRY SOMERSET   PROF. A. A. HOPKINS
DR. L. R. FISKE, Etc.

COMPILED AND EDITED BY
JULIA R. PARISH
State Corresponding Sec'y of Michigan W C T. U

PUBLISHED IN THE INTEREST OF THE
WOMAN'S CHRISTIAN TEMPERANCE UNION
OF MICHIGAN

PREFACE.

BY the kindness and generosity of Dr. C. C. Lathrap, her husband, we are enabled to put in book form many of the written words of Mary T. Lathrap. He and members of the family have spent much time and bestowed much labor in collecting this material and putting it into the hands of the editor. He has also given the financial aid necessary to the publishing of a work of this kind by advancing funds to meet the expense of publishing. It is his wish that all profits arising from the sale of this volume shall go into the treasury of the Woman's Christian Temperance Union of Michigan, at the head of which Mrs. Lathrap stood for so many years.

The work herein published comprises but a small fraction of her wonderful labor, for the majority of her addresses, sermons, and Bible readings were given without being written. This is a fact much to be regretted, for her written work gives a very inadequate idea of the real work which she did in her busy life. No hand but hers could fill out what she left only in skeleton form, and no one would presume to undertake such a task.

In her intense earnestness she scattered with a lavishness seldom seen, rare gems of thought, the products of her fertile brain, but she was too eager for the end to be accomplished to preserve these even for her own use, and the world is the loser. It was her intention to retire from official life in the near future, and to complete her public work by issuing three volumes,— one of poems, one of sermons, one of addresses. But the only hand that could perform that task is stayed, and these words herein contained are published for the sake of perpetuating the noble work which she has done.

JULIA R. PARISH.

CONTENTS.

	PAGE.
PREFACE	3
INTRODUCTION	7
MARY TORRANS LATHRAP	11
HER PUBLIC LIFE	15
CHARACTER SKETCHES	19
THE CLOSE OF A BRILLIANT CAREER	28
INCIDENTS AND REMINISCENCES	35
EARLIER POEMS	42
MISCELLANEOUS POEMS	197
LATER POEMS	232
MISCELLANEOUS	264
ANNUAL ADDRESSES	281
ADDRESSES BEFORE THE WOMAN'S COUNCIL	413

ILLUSTRATIONS.

MARY T. LATHRAP	*Frontispiece.*
MRS. HANNAH TORRANS	14
DR. C. C. LATHRAP	40
MARY T. LATHRAP	120
LATHRAP HOME, JACKSON, MICH.	184
MARY T. LATHRAP HALL, HACKLEY PARK, MICH.	280

INTRODUCTION.

GREATNESS does not happen, achievement is no accident; the broad river that blesses the plains is the outcome of innumerable springs, rivulets, and brooks far up among the hills. It took generations of Christian culture to poise that comely head and face full of the fire of intellect above that symmetrical and perfectly proportioned figure, and to furnish forth the amplitude of personality that we think of whenever to our mind's eye she stands forth once more whom we shall never see again on earth, our queen of Prohibition orators,— Mary T Lathrap.

Nothing is more rare than such a combination of the logician and the poet as was fused in the alembic of her unique mentality. She could handle a syllogism and a group of iambics with equal skill, a gift as rare as it is coveted. The daintiest fancies waited upon her pen as readily as the most solid arguments. Without the advantage of collegiate training she marshalled her mental forces like a skilled strategist Born and bred on a crude farm in the early days of Michigan, earning her own bread from the beginning of her teens; going to Detroit to study in the public schools, and afterward teaching in those schools; writing for the country press when but fourteen years old, and working her way single-handed to the highest recognition as an artist in words and a statesman in speech, her life from its small beginnings to its magnificent close is an epic of American independence and individuality. Her marriage in 1864 to a man of genial nature and independent fortune furnished her an environment from which the need of self-support was soon eliminated, so that she could give herself to the work that most strongly drew her mind and heart.

The hidings of her power were an inheritance from her strong, sturdy, Scotch-Irish Presbyterian ancestry What she owed in nature and in nurture to that brave old Roman, her mother, who at ninety-eight years still survives, we can hardly overestimate. She had as much rarer gifts than are lavished on the cradles of crowned heads and the nobility, as her perception of truth was more clear and her ability to harness it to the chariot of language was more conspicuous. It is easy to see that she owed nothing to fortuitous circumstances. But the virility of her mind, the fresh upspringing that kept a scintillant light in her eyes, and a keen, wise smile on her lips, came to her from an ancestry whose wits had been sharpened and whose consciences developed through generations of study in which the textbook had been the word of God. The sense of duty and the pressure of destiny were supreme factors in their problem of life, and they passed on to her such a make-up as confirmed the impressions that had been worked into the warp and woof of their own characters throughout many a generation. Nor can I think the life of a pioneer family in the western wilds is ill adapted to the best results of character. The emigrant woman whom some of us saw perched on a load of wood near Puget Sound, and who in reply to our expressed admiration of the country, doggedly said, "It's a first rate place for men and horses but terrible hard on women and oxen," stated a foundation principle But the children of the pioneer mother have everything to gain from their close union with the heart of Mother Nature, which gives them a strong physique and a poetic way of looking at the world, while they gain an untold advantage from the necessity of developing their own resources to which they owe that strong flavor of individuality which is one of the most attractive qualities in character, and cannot be had in a strong measure by those who have all their lives been catered to by

"All art yields and nature can decree."

Her manner of working reminded me of Emerson's great lines,—

"The hand that molded Peter's dome,
And grooved the aisles of Notre Dame,
Wrought with a sad sincerity,
Himself from God he could not free."

And under the quip and pleasantry, the sarcasm and irony, under the lambent light of her perpetual humor, all who read her writings or listened to her polished utterances, felt that indeed Mary T. Lathrap, "wrought with a sad sincerity." She could not free herself from God; it was the glory of her life that she lived under the constant consciousness of his presence and his power. She made more votes "for God and Home and Native Land" than any other woman of her time. She added jewels of epigram to the White Ribbon vocabulary.

MARY TORRANS LATHRAP.

MARY TORRANS LATHRAP was born on a farm, twelve miles from Jackson, Michigan, April 25, 1838, and her childhood was spent amid the hardships of pioneer life. She was educated at Marshall, where she lived during her girlhood days. Though receiving only a common-school education, an after course of reading and study fitted her for her future brilliant career. When about fourteen years of age she wrote for various papers under the *nom de plume* of "Lena."

When ten years of age she was converted, but was not allowed to enter the Presbyterian Church until nearly eighteen, she being deemed too young. Her mother was a strong Scotch-Irish Presbyterian, who was a noble example of a godly woman, and her precepts were an inspiration to her young daughter.

Mary Torrans taught in the public schools of Detroit from 1862 until 1864, when she married Dr. Carnett C. Lathrap, then assistant surgeon in the Ninth Michigan cavalry. One year later they removed to Jackson. Dr. Lathrap being a member of the First M. E. church, his wife united with that church by letter, where they were honored and loyal members.

Though brought up in the Presbyterian Church, where the voice of a woman had not been heard, she felt that life would be a failure unless she could preach the gospel. Her ability was soon recognized, and the quarterly conference of the Methodist Church granted her a license to preach. She also became prominent as a lecturer. In 1865 she organized a night school for colored children in Jackson, which was attended by adults as well, and three nights during the week for three years she maintained it, bearing most of the expense herself. She organized the Ladies' Aid Society of the First M. E. Church in 1866, and was always a leading worker in the Woman's Foreign Missionary Society. For many years she was conference secretary. In 1881 she was elected president of the Michigan

W. C. T. U., a position which she filled for fourteen years, and until her death in January, 1895, with remarkable power.

As secretary of the Ladies' and Pastors' Union her labors were rewarded. Mrs. Lathrap always felt a deep interest in her own sex, and through her influence was secured the establishment of the State industrial school for girls at Adrian.

Through her temperance and evangelistic work she became widely known. Thousands have been converted under her teachings, and her unwavering fidelity to all that is good and noble endeared her to the hearts of men and women all over this broad country.

Although Mrs. Lathrap has lectured so many years, she left comparatively few addresses which are complete. It was her hope to continue in active work for ten or fifteen years longer, then spend her remaining years compiling these, together with her Bible readings, but she was not granted this desire, and the world has lost much that was valuable. Several manuscripts are finished, but the majority awaited the only hand and heart which could complete them. Her style of speaking and writing, combining the logical with the poetical, was so original and scholarly that no one could reproduce her sermons and words. This is a matter of deepest regret.

HER HOME LIFE.

She was a devoted wife, a loyal, affectionate daughter, and a loving aunt, in her home which was such a bright, cheery one. It was touching to see the aged mother,— ninety-eight in June, 1895,— every evening after tea come to Mary and kiss her good-night, and to note with what affectionate simplicity and reverence and respect the daughter returned the kiss. The child spirit was still in her heart. Her husband was in sympathy with her in her work, and among the things asked for at daily prayers, he always prayed with unction for the temperance work and the temperance workers. National as well as Michigan temperance workers owe much to Dr. Lathrap, as well as to the nieces who have done so much to make the home in Jackson a welcome one for weary and often discouraged people.

Dr. C. C. Lathrap writes thus of his beloved wife : —

"The world knows Mrs. Mary T. Lathrap as a poet, a reformer, a lecturer, and a preacher of righteousness. She was also a lovely wife and companion. She loved her home as the dearest place on earth, and often spoke of it as 'my home, my beautiful home. I love it and all its associations.' She went out from it to do her work at the call of duty, which to her was the call of God ; and as soon as it was done, she turned toward home for comfort, rest, and love

"It was most perfect in all its appointments. She was skilled in all the art and science of housekeeping The cooks have often said : 'If she will but put one of her fingers into the bread or cake, it will make it perfect.'

"She was a close student, an indefatigable worker ; always busy She very seldom took a drive unless it was to go and see a shut in sufferer, or on business in connection with some of her many lines of work.

"She did much work among the poor, the suffering, and sorrowful Many a poor girl has been able to finish her term at school because of her open purse While she had no time to sew for herself, she made over many hats, bonnets, and dresses for the poor

"She had a keen appreciation of all the virtues and gifts, and a broad mantle of charity for the faults and failings of those about her. She usually read her poems and written articles to those at home, and she had no audience more appreciative, for all were very proud of her and loved her dearly.

"In her last illness her patience and fortitude were very remarkable. She was so sweet, so kind, and so trusting. Her faith in God was so strong ; there was no 'dark river' for her to cross — It was all light She talked familiarly of her going home and the friends she would meet When she heard of Mary Woodbridge being stricken, she said ' Mary and I may go arm in arm into heaven '

"For years it has been understood that if she went home first, her mother Mrs. Hannah Torrans, now ninety eight years old, was to remain with me

"For several days before going she held no conversation regarding the things of this life, but spoke freely and confidently of the life that is just beyond A few hours before her departure she called for me, and said to me and those about her, 'It is all right It is all right ' These were her last words, and a noble soul was promoted to the triumphant host above "

Three nieces, the Misses Emma, Florence, and Augusta Knight thus speak of her —

"We early learned to love her, and that love grew stronger with each passing year. Although her journeyings from home were frequent, always the days on which she departed were sad ones. The members of the family allowed no engagement to take them away until they had seen her to the carriage door Her home comings were real red-letter days. Business, so far as could be, was laid aside, and all the little home happenings were discussed. Her work drew largely on her strength and time, but she was never so busy as to forget her home duties, ever ready to counsel and advise. No project, however small, was considered settled until she had passed judgment upon it. Her co-laborers will miss her, but only those privileged to sit at her own fireside can know of the irreparable loss there."

She was given to merriment and innocent mirth when at home, and enjoyed simple, homely joys and pastimes with the zest of a child. Her home was beautiful, and she often said she did not like to leave it ; it was so pleasant and restful

MRS. HANNAH TORRANS.

Her mother, Mrs. Hannah Torrans, *née* Hopkins, was born in the north of Ireland, June 15, 1797. Her parents were of the old Scotch Covenanter and Presbyterian stock, her father being for many years a leading elder in the Presbyterian Church. At the age of twenty-eight she was united in marriage with Mr. David Torrans, and in 1830 they emigrated to America, arriving in Quebec in May of that year.

From thence they removed to Whitehall, N Y, where they remained seven years In 1837 they removed to Concord, Michigan. A few years later they removed to Marshall, Michigan, from which place Mr. Torrans went west as a railroad contractor, where he died.

Mrs Torrans is the mother of seven children, three of whom are now living,— John, William, and Mary. One daughter, deceased, was the wife of Hon Wellington R Burt, E Saginaw, with whom Mrs Torrans made her home after her husband's death, until after the war, when she removed to Jackson, and since that time has been a member of the Lathrap family. She has always been a woman of more than ordinary mental power Her education was limited, for when she attended school, it was not thought necessary for a girl to study arithmetic or writing. She did learn to write, however, and in her later years has become quite proficient as a letter-writer.

Her faculties are still almost unimpaired, and although near-sighted in her early years, her sight is such now that she reads without the aid of glasses. She has kept pace with current events and lives in the present. She brought up her children in a religious manner. She had always been a member of the Presbyterian Church until she went to Jackson, when she united with the Congregational Church, there being no Presbyterian Church in the city at that time.

June 15, 1895, she celebrated her ninety-eighth birthday, and notwithstanding her great age, she is vigorous still.

She has lived nearly a century, and has been a noble example of motherhood. Hers has been a life of unusual strength, and she bequeathed to her youngest child, Mary, that strength which made her such a power for good

HER PUBLIC LIFE.

MRS. LATHRAP'S fame as a lecturer spread from her Michigan home to every part of the United States. She spoke in nearly every State in the Union and in every large city. The press notices concerning her are unanimous in placing her among the most brilliant, witty, logical speakers of her time. Even when they were not willing to concede the right of the cause which she vindicated, they confessed the superior merit of her logic. Whenever she held a series of revival services, hundreds and in many cases thousands flocked to hear her. Among the many press notices we quote the following:—

"She is a woman of large brain, strong reasoning powers, and intuitive knowledge of the springs of human character, and withal she has a woman's sensitiveness, appreciation, and affection. Apart from any question of sex, as she stood on the platform, speaking with power and inspiration such as is rarely listened to, we were compelled, in the exercise of honest judgment, to decide that neither the clergymen on her right or on her left were her equals in force, logic, eloquence, or in the actual weight of brain. We may, therefore, be permitted to ask why, being their superior, she should by any law of church or modern society be hindered from the full exercise of her exceptional oratorical and logical powers? If anybody can give us a sound reason for putting up the bars to keep Mrs Lathrap out of any field which she may choose to enter and adopt as her life work, we will change our present views on that subject."

"We do not hesitate to say that for literary style, rhetorical finish, elegant antithesis, and logical grip, the speech of Mrs Mary T. Lathrap made at the First Congregational church, last evening, was a masterpiece. We doubt if a speech so well worth hearing has been made in Springfield by a man in ten years."—*Daily News, Springfield, Ill*

"It is difficult to analyze Mrs Lathrap's oratorical power. It is essentially masculine in breadth and logic, and yet never for a moment does the woman disappear. Her title —'The Daniel Webster of Prohibition'— was first given her by Gov. St. John, and was quickly accepted by her platform associates."—*Editorial Bureau Record, New York.*

"It is simply impossible to put into print the magnificent address of Mrs Lathrap delivered last night"— *Standard, Belvidere, Ill*

"It is doubtful if such an address has ever been delivered from the platform in Chicago by a woman. It was eloquent from beginning to conclusion, scathing, earnest, persuasive, and denunciatory in turn."— *Chicago Journal.*

"Mrs Lathrap, of Michigan, waked up that audience with an oratorical cyclone set to music She was epigrammatic, dramatic, and most emphatic She was argumentative, witty, rhetorical, sarcastic, and pathetic "— *Washington Correspondent Advocate, Nashville, Tenn*

"For putting the truth down on the heart, and brain, and conscience, Mrs Mary T. Lathrap stands out unexcelled and rarely equaled. Her logic and eloquence are irresistible God bless her!"— *C. H. Mead*

"I believe there is no man or woman living, the superior of Mrs Mary T. Lathrap in the discussion of the temperance question. While she is a great logician and noted for depth of thought, she has a pithy way of putting things and a poetical use of language seldom found combined. She is a great and good woman "— *George W Bain*

"Mrs. Mary T. Lathrap has no superior on the temperance platform, among men or women, in this or any other country."— *Frances E Willard.*

Eulogies from the press are too numerous and too lengthy to be quoted in a sketch so brief as this one must be. She gained the title —"The Daniel Webster of the Temperance Reform"— early in her public career, and right worthily she held it to the last.

Like all positive natures she did not escape the attacks of partisan papers, and was accused of "being in the pay of the Prohibition party." The editor of one paper says of one address, "It was simply a political Prohibition harangue." Notwithstanding these criticisms she never faltered or yielded one iota of what she believed to be right.

Prof. Samuel Dickie says. Her three chief characteristics were clearness, conscience, and courage. She carried points by clearness of argument and by womanly, persuasive eloquence In the star chamber of her conscience the question was not, Is it policy? but, Is it right? She was loyal to the cause of Christ and the church. Her heart was sore and she grieved over the fact that the church has not yet come to its proper place on the questions of reform "

Those who advocated the perpetuity of the liquor system and kindred evils, feared her vigorous assaults upon their methods. She was fearless in the utterance of what seemed to her to be the truth. In conversation with a friend after the heated campaign for constitutional prohibition in Michigan, in 1887, she said, "I often thought when traveling during those anxious weeks, that I was taking my life into my own hands."

As president of the Michigan Woman's Christian Temperance Union for fourteen years, she showed wonderful ability both as a leader in thought and as master of details. She never hesitated to adopt a bold policy nor stopped to ask concerning its popularity. She grasped the work in its entirety, she saw future results with a quick, strong, almost inspired vision. She carried minute details with as much fidelity as she planned larger things, for no duty was small to her. As an executive officer she was firm and just, even to those whose views did not always harmonize with hers in methods of work

She was a wise counselor, an impartial executive officer, a true friend, a safe adviser, always true to every member of the Executive Board, whether absent or present. She put the work first and the worker second   The cause went ahead of the individual. Her deep conviction and clear vision as to the importance of the work to be done were so emphasized in her activity that a casual observer lost sight of her gentle traits which were underneath all. She could be touched into pity and sympathy as readily as she could be roused into heroic action. That rare combination of strength and gentleness was blended in her in an unusual degree, but not always recognized.

Her spiritual life has been an inspiration to thousands, her sermons and Bible readings have been wonderfully honored of God and listened to with eagerness by the multitude   Her logic was as keen as a surgeon's knife, her eloquence was like a beautiful strain of classic music. She was a matchless leader in thought and execution.

We quote a sentence or two from some of the members and ex-members of the Michigan State Board —

"She could deal with hard, cold facts in a most uncompromising manner, or she could fashion a poem so touching and so tender as to stir the pathos of the coldest nature." - *Mrs A S Benjamin*

"Flowers of speech were always hers, and every convention was made bright by them"— *Mrs. C. H. Johnson.*

"I never met so charming a hostess — hospitable, gracious, she was also at times frolicsome as a girl. It was in her home that the beauty and symmetry of her character were delightfully revealed."— *Mrs. Jennie Voorhies*

"Her efficient and faithful work for the advancement of her sex will cause many to arise and call her blessed."— *Annie Andrus*

"As with all deep natures, there were lovely tenderness and sweetness and the holy of holies in the temple of Mrs Lathrap's character to those who had entered in — a wonderful vision "— *Julia D Stannard.*

"The last State Convention has left with me a lovely memory of our president, to be cherished till we meet again."— *Catharine Birrell*

"On every hand her production of thought from the printed page will be an inspiration to urge us on to higher and grander work for our cause than we have ever achieved in the past."—*Irene Smith Clizbe*

"The home, motherhood, fatherhood, and the cause of humanity in general, have all been raised to a higher plane by her example and eloquent words."—*Charlotte E. Brown.*

"To me she was a help and strength."—*Mrs. R. A. Campbell*

"Prophetic in vision, brave in speech, eloquent in portrayal, a two edged sword to the enemy."—*Mrs P. J. Howard.*

"Her satire and wit, launched at shameless, conscienceless cowards, where moral boldness should be found, were as keen and direct as well-aimed poniard thrusts"—*Mrs. C. C. Faxon.*

"I learned many lessons from her noble life that will follow me through all my days."—*E. N. Law*

"Mary T. Lathraps's words and influence will live on, blessing humanity through those who have been brought to Christ through her tender pleadings"—*Emma A. Wheeler.*

"To her judicious counsel and untiring energy, I attribute much of the growth of the State society during the years of my presidency."—*Mrs B. B. Hudson*

Her audiences listened to her words and acknowledged their power, even if they refused to accept her views. She held them from the beginning to the end of her addresses, which were often from one and a half to two hours in length. While she was skilful in appealing to men's reason, she was powerful in her appeal to conscience; and the climax of her masterful addresses was usually reached by the way of conscience rather than by the way of cold argument. Strong argumentative power warmed by an impassioned appeal made her efforts brilliant, pathetic, and winning

CHARACTER SKETCHES.

AS A LEADER IN THE WOMAN'S CHRISTIAN TEMPERANCE UNION.

By Frances E. Willard, in "Michigan Union"

IT has been nobly said by a great thinker that "the only wealth is life." By this computation what riches melted away from the White Ribbon movement when, in this world of chance and change, Mary T. Lathrap was no more alive! The riches of the W. C. T. U., as its leaders have said a thousand times, consist in the women who have cast in their lot with us, and on the round earth no woman of greater power than the president of "Michigan, my Michigan," has ever done so. She has been from the first the central figure in our great debates, uniting the grasp of a man's mind to the electric intuition of a woman; she has been one of the century's most vivid illustrations of the fact that in intellect there is no sex. No woman among us was less self-seeking; none had retained more of that fresh, girlish enthusiasm which made her company delightful in the rare hours off duty that we know. None had a more radiant eloquence, nor had any a wing so swift and white in the realms of poesy. I had learned to lean on her; to love her I had no need to learn. From the day I saw her first (and it was the first day of the convention at which our national society was organized, in 1874), she always stood to me for power purposely consecrated to the highest uses, power original, immense, and wisely guided to the wisest ends. She has traversed the United States and Canada, as carefully searching for prohibition votes as Diogenes traversed the streets of Athens, lamp in hand, searching for an honest man. Her commanding figure, her face radiant with intellect, her attitude of equipoise and dignity, but instinct with vigor and vitality; the rythmic movement of her beautiful hand, the flashing smile, the scintillating dark blue eyes — how plainly we can see them all! In the long laborious years I have always felt that no keener sickle was at work in the great harvest field, and none came back to us more richly laden with the spirit of our splendid "peaceful war."

Wherever Mary Lathrap went, a broad path of light flashed out over the darkness of average opinion and mediocre purpose. When she represented the White Ribbon movement at the great council of women in Washington, in 1889, it seemed to me that no woman living could have equaled the lofty and inspiring view she gave our society, its genius, history, and method. No one has given us a greater number of golden sentences than she has coined in the rich mint of her racy, philosophic, and original forms of speech. It is beautiful to admire as we have admired her; indeed hardly less delightful than to be worthy of such admiration and loyal pride as every White Ribboner felt in the richly endowed personality of Mary T. Lathrap. She has made a record brilliant as a star and enduring as the granite of old Scotia whence came her sturdy ancestry. She had the wit of that Irish race, a strain of whose blood was in her own; she had the broad, bright outlook of the great West where she was reared; she had the generous, sisterly sympathy of the movement that swept her into its deep current and bore her on to fame and death.

AS A POET.

By Lady Henry Somerset.

I have always held Mary Lathrap in special affection and warm admiration. She was ever to me a figure that towered strong in her accomplishments, and above even the gifted comrades in the White Ribbon work. Her songs are an inspiration to her English sister, and her written words have touched thousands who never heard her eloquent voice.

Mrs. Lathrap's muse was like the rock from which may burst forth the bright refreshing water when smitten by the rod of Moses. She was so preoccupied with her pulpit and platform work that she did not in later years especially put forth her blossoms of song save under the sweet south wind of a friend's appeal. For instance, we owe the ode on President Garfield's death to the earnest request of Miss Willard; the poem at the laying of the corner stone at the World's Temple to the insistence of Mrs. Carse; and the White Ribbon hymn that has now gone around the world to Anna Gordon's plaintive request for help in her difficult endeavor to edit a book for the children that should be worthy the romance and poetry of the temperance reform. Hardly any writer of modern times has given us a song that has made a deeper impression on philanthropic work. At the great demonstration in Queen's Hall before five thousand persons, and in Royal Albert Hall before ten thousand, a group of sorrowful little children from the slums stood on the platform and sang,

"There's a shadow on the home."

Their pitiful cry was jubilantly met by a procession of children bearing aloft the white ribbon in long fluttering lines and advancing rapidly to the platform from their places of concealment while they sang,

"We are coming to the rescue,
We are coming in our youth;
The homes we build to-morrow,
Shall be shrines of love and truth."

This produced an effect, the deepest and the most helpful that I have ever witnessed in a public assembly. As we watched that bright procession bearing aloft their ribbons, and heard the fresh gush of their childish voices as they came to the platform and surrounded the group of sorrowful faced children while they waved their white banners and sang the chorus,

"We are coming to the rescue
Of Purity and Right,
And for a winsome token,
We wear the ribbon white,"

tears were in all our eyes and smiles on every lip. Miss Willard turned to me and whispered, "I cannot help believing that Mary Lathrap sees all this with us and rejoices as we do in the good that is done by her beautiful song."

While it is true that in her youth Mrs. Lathrap wrote a poem entitled, I think, "A Woman's Answer," which was so good that Elizabeth Barrett Browning was thought to be the author, and it was included in a collection of her poems, I can but think that in its far-reaching influence for the uplifting of humanity this song of "Ribbons White" will prove to be the crowning inspiration of her great life; for it has gone from London, the heart of the world, to ten thousand cities, towns, and villages where, with the pageantry I have described, it will be reproduced in the hearing of uncounted myriads who will be helped by it to the concept of a pure life and hallowed home.

AS A PREACHER.

By L. R. Fiske, LL D

During her early womanhood Mrs. Lathrap shrank from appearing before the public as a speaker. Presenting herself for membership in the church of which the writer was pastor, she sought to exact a pledge that she should not be called upon to take part in any of the meetings held. But becoming deeply interested in some special efforts put forth to lead young people to Christ, she gradually overcame the timidity which had held her back, entering into the active work of the church and showing an ability for spiritual leadership which soon brought her into marked prominence. Before she was fully aware of the change that was taking place, Providence had led her on to the very door of the ministry. It was the heart much more than the judgment that influenced her action — a love for souls, more than a deliberate conviction of personal fitness for the work of preaching the gospel Results soon proved that the voice which reached the will through her awakened spiritual life was not a delusive one. Almost immediately the public recognized in her a divinely called and able minister of the gospel.

Intellectually Mrs Lathrap was a commanding figure. Indeed her whole being was in an extraordinary degree symmetrical. Rather above the average physically, her mental life, including intellect, heart, and will, measured fully up to her bodily stature. Perhaps it would be a better putting to say that in the unusual vigor of her womanly nature there seemed to be a completely rounded personality.

To make the ideal preacher there must be several factors blending in the unity of the being While in some respects least important, yet by no means unimportant, there is the bodily presence In the case of Mrs. Lathrap the physical was a fitting medium for the mental As she stood before an audience, there was a strength of character manifested in the face, a largeness of the soul speaking through the eyes, an intellectual mastery appearing in the poise of the body, which always impressed the people and won attention at the very beginning of her sermons. As she proceeded, the earnestness of a soul breathing out intense desires for the salvation of the people, could be read in the features of the face, and the deep soul life inspired gestures calculated to make more profound the convictions awakened. Her voice was clear, her utterances physically decisive and comparatively rapid, and there was a dignity as well as a grace of demeanor that always secured for her more than a respectful hearing. The physical never stood in the way of the mental, but rather seemed to be a perfect channel for the message that came from the soul. She could easily be heard by audiences of two or three thousand persons, without any straining of the voice or manifestation of painful effort, and indeed without impairing the womanly quality of her voice.

She was a strong preacher. I think the word *strength* properly characterized her sermons. It is often said that woman quite naturally speaks beautifully, but that we may expect less of intellectual might than grace of diction. While her productions may be charming, we must turn to man for logic and vigor of thought Mrs Lathrap was a poet. It was easy for her to create poetical conceptions,—they sprang up in her mind spontaneously,—but they were not winged fancies, they always rested back on sharp intellectual discernment They were the clothing of thought, not a substitute for thought. Not less vigorous were the blows she struck for right, not less weighty were the truths she uttered because the armor was polished She was eminently an acute and logical thinker Hence as a preacher she did not talk about a subject, she unfolded it. Her expositions of Scripture were clear and full, and she always brought truth to the audience as food for reflection. She was a masterful logician. The defensive armor she would wrap around the soul of the Christian believer was thoroughly interlaced as a shield of faith, so that the darts of the evil one could not penetrate it, and when she made an assault upon the realm of darkness, she employed all needed weapons for the complete demolition of the kingdom of wickedness.

More than this, she was a bold preacher. She struck directly at sin in every form in which it made its appearance. All wrong was hateful in her eyes, and its overthrow was the end at which she aimed It never occurred to her to propose a compromise. Logically she could not stop short of the complete eradication of evil from the human heart There was, therefore, no covering up, no passing around, but the most determined blows for its extirpation To the sinner she spoke with a directness and point that was difficult to evade, to the Christian she brought a salvation that would save to the uttermost Neither in the teachings of Scripture nor the demands of logic did she find a stopping-place this side of the complete healing of the soul from the disease of sin

Hence, in a very eminent degree was she an evangelical preacher. She conceived sin to be a crime against God, not a mere misfortune in the life. She treated the sinner, therefore, as a rebel against the divine government, holding up before him his guilt, and pleading with him to turn from his evil ways. She exhorted him to flee from the wrath to come, for not only was there guilt, but impending ruin She preached to the believer a full salvation. Not only did Christ die to redeem all men, but wholly to save each soul from the thralldom and power of sin. Logic is always lame when it necessarily limits the work of grace to a partial salvation God wishes to heal all the diseases of the soul, and this work he is able to do when the surrender is complete She conceived that God was dishonored by the doctrine that in his plans of human salvation he stopped short of the entire eradication of moral evil, making provision only for a partial restoration of the divine image. Only two possible reasons could be assigned for limitations in his plans,—either that his power was restricted, or his mercy partial, neither of which could be harmonized with the infinitude of his being. The divine law is infinitely sacred ; God's justice is absolute, but also is his mercy without bounds. Hence it was natural that she should proclaim a gospel that was able to save even to the uttermost. In an unlimited sense did she conceive Faber's words to be true —

> "There is welcome for the sinner,
> And more graces for the good,
> There is mercy with the Saviour,
> There is healing in his blood"

Such conceptions of the divine plan adequately expressed, necessarily impart strength to a sermon Truth came to Mrs Lathrap round and full, not maimed and halting Possessing in a degree beyond most people the power of verbal utterance, she dealt in great principles, so that the vigor of which I have spoken was vigor of thought expressed in language fitted to carry the truths uttered. While her discourses were not devoid of poetic imagery,— rather abounding in it,— their greatest merit consisted in the breadth of her conceptions and the invincible logic with which her arguments were framed. Such sermons are not evanescent, but bear fruit long after they are spoken.

It might be supposed that with such a type of intellectuality there would be but little room for the emotional. It is a common notion that the intellect and heart act in an inverse ratio There is indeed a sentimentality that contains within itself but little of clear, guiding thought. This is often found in inferior minds. But there is a wealth of heart that grows out of a wealth of intellect, the emotional nature being profoundly stirred because of the majesty of truth which the intellect encloses. Mrs. Lathrap's reasonings were not formal and cold, but glowed with the warmth of a loving, deeply sympathetic heart. She saw the peril of the sinner, and longed to save him. Eternal death appeared to her an awful doom. The folly of the people absorbed in temporal concerns, forgetful of eternal interests, deeply moved her. The utterly irrational procedure of the great mass of men putting earth before heaven, the gratification of the senses before the spiritual life, stirred most profoundly her emotional being. The heart always kept company with the intellect in the contemplation and discussion of every theme. Her sermons glowed with a fervor that showed the deepest interest in those to whom she spoke. Her appeals to the sinner came from a heart aching for their rescue, and her exhortations to the church members betrayed an anxiety that they should not fail to obtain the wonderful good a loving Father was holding out to them. Solicitude, marked her words, and all her reproofs — and not infrequently were they uttered — were not spoken to wound, but to heal.

It is not strange, therefore, that her labors were very effective in revival services. As the Methodist Church made no provision for women in the pastorate, her special opportunity was in evangelistic work. For several years she conducted services of this nature in different places, and in some of our largest cities. Many were reached by her warm, forcible, and eloquent appeals. There are hundreds of people living to-day who were brought to Christ through her instrumentality. Few ministers of the gospel possessed that admirable poise of the intellectual and emotional so well fitted to meet all the demands of the sacred desk. Cold thought will not save, neither will fervor without truth.

The foregoing analysis of the personal qualities of Mary T. Lathrap, appearing in her public ministrations as a preacher, bear out the assertion made earlier in this chapter, that her life was eminently symmetrical. As stated, there was a physical presence fitted to impress an audience, a voice full and round while it was penetrating, an utterance displaying force and energy of life; a deep mental penetration and comprehension of truth; a poetic gift that charmed, united with logical blending of thought which carried conviction to the mind of the hearer. With all this there was a wealth of emotion which, accompanying the truth, opened the way to the heart, so that the conscience was reached, and the best conditions supplied in connection with the work of the divine Spirit, for the salvation of the souls of men. Mrs. Mary Torrans Lathrap was a great and successful preacher.

AS A POLITICIAN.

By A. A. Hopkins.

When we come to write of Mrs. Lathrap as a politician, we must discard altogether the lower meanings of a partially degenerate term. Associated with her memory, in the minds of all who have made a study of political things, and who knew in what spirit these were regarded by her, the term *politician* is uplifted to the noblest plane of pure *civics*. In this better atmosphere a definition given by the new Standard Dictionary well befits the word, and renders it appropriate as applied to her,—"One skilled in political science or administration; a statesman."

Mrs. Lathrap was skilled in political science; but it was rather through her clear, keen, unerring womanly instincts, her native grasp of underlying principles, than through mere study of rudimental or partisan ways and means in politics. To her heart's core she was a patriot, and under all and above all she was a Christian. She stood everywhere, in the discussion of public questions, upon the high levels of Christian patriotism and intelligence. Her woman's thinking would have found fair interpretation in this language of Dr. J. G. Holland, applied to his own sex, and quoted by the "Standard" to emphasize its definition: "The more the Christian gentleman knows, the better *politician* he will make, and in him, and in him only, will scholarship come to its finest issues in politics."

She craved and pleaded and prayed for the highest Christian knowledge to inspire the people of this republic as to the purpose of government, and the gifts of citizenship, and the responsibilities attaching thereto. "The realm of politics," to use a phrase often on her lips, was the realm of consecrated brain, of devoted heart, of loyal life, of honest manhood, brought to their unfailing best. A few sentences in the "Life of General Clinton B. Fiske," culled from a few pages contributed to that volume by Mrs. Lathrap, will illustrate how she felt and thought:—

"Great masses of our people leave their political thinking to party leaders, orators, and writers, so any campaign lifts or lowers the standards of patriotism, loyalty and integrity, according as the ideals and arguments are high and worthy or the reverse."

"One mission of the Prohibition Party and its leaders is already proven, in lifting public thought once more from this low level of strife for spoils, to the high realm of principle, thus compelling public attention along patriotic channels"

"General Fiske's speeches were not alone remarkable for the absence of what makes up the average political tirade, but for the presence of all that brings manhood to its best, in the interest of home and country"

"He was a typical American, an ideal statesman, a pure patriot, conducting a model campaign."

It was on the platform, as an advocate of true political development, and pleading for the proudest patriotic ideals, that Mrs. Lathrap revealed in full measure her endowments as a stateswoman. She had mastered the philosophy of government, as a man must, to be a statesman, as a woman may, by her own demonstration, given the superlative qualities of head and heart essential to such mastery Many times men said of her, with entire realization of what their words meant: "She ought to sit in the United States Senate!" She would have been the intellectual peer of any man who ever sat in that body during her lifetime. She would have been a sure stimulus to higher moral standards of political faith, to grander national ambitions, to sublimer utterances of statesmanship She would have done more than any senator has done since Charles Sumner, in a just and wise patriotism, inspired by the divinest influences of civilization, to fix "the attitude of government" (adopting her most familiar phrase) as it should be forever determined and maintained in behalf of the supreme Right and against the selfish Wrong.

THE CLOSE OF A BRILLIANT CAREER.

IN the winter of 1893 Mrs. Lathrap first made known to some of those in official relation with her in the Michigan Woman's Christian Temperance Union that she was disturbed about the condition of her health. She sought the best medical aid that the State afforded, and her physicians gave her much encouragement; but she felt that her work was drawing to a close, and this conviction never left her

In the autumn of 1893 she said to the writer, while sitting in the Chicago National W. C. T. U. Convention, "I feel that I am coming to the end. I cannot rid myself of this impression." She was ill for the most part of the winter of '94, but carried on the convention program work with the aid of her corresponding secretary. When the corresponding secretary left her home where the preparations had been made for the convention to be held in a few weeks, Mrs. Lathrap said as she bade her good-by, "Once again and often you have been a great comfort to me." She stood in the door and watched her guest to the last, with that far-away look that had become so habitual to her.

Never did she seem so gentle, so thoughtful for our highest interest, as at this last convention. Some of her winsome and beautiful sayings seemed prophetic of the "going away" soon to be Some of these are quoted below, and we are indebted to the faithful recording secretary of the Michigan W. C. T. U., Mrs. C. H Johnson, for preserving so many of her words for us. "Forgetting the things that are behind, let us reach forward unto the victories yet to be, since the battle is not ours but God's." In the memorial exercise, she said · "Do not think of me as sick, think I am well; thoughts are things"

In her prayer at the close of the memorial service, she said · " Help us to lift our eyes from the beautiful grasses, as we go out to think, not of death, but of eternity. The way lies on before only a little way for some of us. We thank thee for eternal, boundless love; comfort those who stay"

At one of the morning devotional exercises she said: "I have made up my mind for the rest of my life to give up my life more fully to God. Let us be holy women, have a higher ideal than we ever had. I thank you with all my heart for the atmosphere of love and sympathy you have put around me the past year. Let us be higher, purer, holier women, nearer to God than we have ever been before. Make your local union a center of spiritual power. I some way think the morning lingers just over the hill. Christ will not let this evil go on much longer. The Lord has brought me back, and I hope to do better work."

Her closing words when the convention adjourned were: "We have come to the end of our program, to the closing moments of our convention. Thanks for all the strength, all the pleasure you have been to me. Pray God that all together this year, we may make this work a power as it never has been before. Be holy women, more given to God than ever before. Pray for all officers, for a fresh baptism of the Holy Spirit."

The following letter, written on a sick bed to the members of the State Board then present at Lathrap Hall, Hackley Park, reveals her tender and ever thoughtful interest in her co-workers

"JACKSON, July 23, 1894

"DEAR SISTERS. I confess to a sharper heart ache these days than has come to me all these months of sickness. I want to be at Hackley Park so much. I longed to be there yesterday to do my part. I want to be there our day and hear John G. Wooley's apostolic message. I long to spend these days at the Hall with my sisters in Christ, my comrades in the great battle for all things pure, the beloved gray-haired girls to whom my soul is knit. I do not worry about the work. I thought when I read the last *Michigan Union* [State paper of the Michigan W. C T U], and examined the program, with its promise of such good things, that I needed you all so much more than you needed me; and I feel it this morning though I long to be with you. I hear the wind in the tall trees, and see again the soft light through the leaves, the gleam on the lake, and I hear its music on the sand until the tears will come, as I lie here still a prisoner of pain, shut away from you all.

"I hope you will have a delightful sojourn and enjoy every hour. I am trying to be both brave and patient, and in the strength of Christ am succeeding, I trust, in a measure at least. I often think I ought to be perfectly well, so many are praying for me. Some time, while you tarry together, if you feel drawn to it, will you not make special prayer for me. It seems that God will hear you, as perhaps no others, and send help from our sanctuary in the woods. My physicians think I am improving, but I have many downs on the way which seems very long

"I send you my greeting and my love. Let me know about everything. I trust our plans were well made, and that profit and pleasure will come to all God be with you Yours ever,
"MARY T. LATHRAP"

In letters to the corresponding secretary she says: "I still camp where both worlds are in view. . . . I am some discouraged. I fear my health is not coming back as soon as I had hoped; but we shall see."

August 24, 1894, she says:—

"I am forced yet to be very much of an invalid . I had the loveliest letter from Miss Willard two days ago that one woman ever wrote to another, and in the same envelope one from Lady Henry. The latter wrote me about the singing of my hymn, 'The Battle Song of the Y's,' at Queen's Hall Mother has been very sick for a week, she is very feeble, and I think it doubtful if she is ever down stairs again She is so anxious to go and be with the Lord Love to all the family and a heap for you, my right hand in these trying days"

After Miss Willard's return from a two years' sojourn in England, she says:—

"When I came home, after two years of absence, and learned that our great heart was an invalid, it seemed as if an eagle had been stung by some cruel hunter's relentless shaft As time went on, and I heard more and more of her great sufferings and greater fortitude, she grew more dear to the comrade who had loved her always. I do not think that any human being has been so constantly in my thought for the last six months as Mary Lathrap. Often in the night-watches among the Catskill mountains or on the swift trains, or in the great assembly, her presence has been with me and my heart has been lifted up for her in prayer. It came to be a custom with me as I did this to place in fancy a loving kiss on that imperial brow. One day last summer I wrote her just what I have here stated. She was a woman brave, strong, and self-contained I had never dared to say as much to her before, nor did I feel certain that she would receive such an avowal with the tenderness I felt in making it, but a few days later a letter in the hand that had grown tremulous came back from her, so beautiful, so rich in all womanly softness and devotion, that I shall cherish it all my life as one of the sweetest and most sacred communications ever made to me. Some sentences I shall disclose to those her tender 'gray haired girls,' as she called them, in the last days, and those younger ones who have joined the army and marched with us through storm and stress —

"'Dear Frances Willard: I cannot make any suitable reply to your letter which reached me some days ago. The tears come when I think of it, and I feel no woman ever wrote so graceful a tribute to another I rejoice that it has been mine to stand with you in some of the storms, as well as the sunshine, of the battle for God and home and native land. . Nothing could exceed the sweetness of word and action on the part of my sisters of the White Ribbon What a gathering it will be when we meet on the other side and go no more out forever . . . I have much I would like to say, but cannot now; if my work is done, I rejoice that my best years were given to such a cause, and in such a company. . I bless you from my heart for your words, so full of fragrance, they seem the well-weighed values of a comradeship which shines like beaten gold. I hope it may be my joy to see you at Cleveland, but only the Lord our leader knows

"'Yours now and forever,

"'MARY T. LATHRAP.'"

August 13, 1894, Lady Henry Somerset wrote to her as follows:—

"It is impossible to spare your great gifts from the warfare. I have so hoped that some day you would extend your campaign to England. We should give you such a welcome, and your white ribbon sisters would make the old country home-like for you. Your beautiful hymn, 'There's a Shadow on the Home,' was sung at our great annual gathering at Queen's Hall. Men and women bowed their heads and wept as the band of ragged gutter children wailed out the song that was evidently true; and hearts were uplifted by the glad prophecy that rang out from the white-robed child choir that filled up the great auditorium, bearing aloft the white ribbon, and singing, 'We are coming to the rescue'

"Your words have so often been to me an inspiration that I know you will let me thank you for them"

October 26, 1894, the writer of this sketch spent a few hours at Mrs. Lathrap's house. We talked of our State work as she found strength. She had been confined to her bed since the early part of July and was very weak physically, but her brilliant mind was active, and her faith in God was triumphant. As I entered the room, bearing a basket of flowers, sent to her from the Fourth District Convention, she said, after the greeting: "The chariot is swinging low for me, these days, dear. I am looking out upon two worlds." Later in our interview she said, "I sometimes fear we have lost the way, or else my work is done; for the vision of the work closes. I doubt the wisdom of our taking the platform on political issues, such as silver and tariff, rather than on the moral part of the question."

In reply to a question concerning an alliance with men's societies, she said, "In an alliance of men and women, the men's views always gain the ascendency. I do not approve of organic union. I feel, though, that there should be something besides adhesion in our relation to the Prohibition Party."

When I bade her good-by, she said, "Keep this thought on the mast-head,—that it is the work and not the worker that should be promoted. It is such a little thing when only honor to the women is sought." Her good-by was tender and thoughtful; even in her suffering she tried to spare others from grief. She spoke freely of "going away," and requested her husband and the nieces to give to each of the members of the State Board a souvenir from among her belongings. This wish was carried out, and each member of the Board cherishes the gift, and, most of all, the tender thought back of it. In speaking of her illness she said "I feel grieved that this should come to me. I had such a sweet compact with the Lord years ago, that I had looked for long life. I cannot make it seem right" As she said that, I thought of the piece of statuary on exhibition at the World's Fair, called "The Angel of Death and the Sculptor." A sculptor with chisel in one hand and up-raised mallet in the other, was represented as making a form, the outline of whose features already appeared in a block of marble, and just above stood the Angel of Death with hand closed over the hand that held the chisel, as if staying him in any further work.

The startled, anxious look on the sculptor's face, the work only in outline, the beautiful figure seen to the artist's vision in the unfinished marble, plead with an "eloquent silence" for more time The relentless expression on the face of the angel revealed the fact that the marble thought must be wrought out by other hands, and I thought, Who shall make such masterful strokes as our Mary in the unfinished work of the temperance reform.

She saw the battle still raging and longed to be again in the conflict, but as her sickness and suffering were prolonged, her vision turned from earth's conflict to heaven's victory. She laid down earthly weapons of warfare calmly and with resignation, and met with patience and trust and courage "the last enemy," though she endured great physical suffering During these months of sickness her husband gave her his constant attention, and every material comfort was supplied to her with unsparing hand.

The two nieces in the home were loving, careful, and faithful, and the nurse tended her patient with an affectionate interest.

Nothing that money could purchase was left untried, but for all medical skill or faithful care she grew weaker day by day, and Jan. 3, 1895, with her vision of the eternal world bright, and with this message to her friends on earth, "It is all right," repeated many times during the last hours of life, she fell asleep without a struggle. She died of universal neuralgia. She had given instructions to the family as to how she should be clad, and many other details concerning the funeral service, and her requests were carried out even to the smallest detail.

Her remains lay in state at her home Saturday, January 4, from 1 to 4 P. M., but scores of friends came at all times to see them. She was clad in a tasteful black dress, on her heart the bow of ribbon white with flowers, also flowers on the lining of the casket. It was a beautiful casket, trimmed in white and lavender. By her special request there was no crape—no black of any kind. The room in which she lay was bright and sunny, as were all the rooms about the house. There was no suggestion of death about the house, only the lifeless form. The triumphant smile that was natural to her, abode still upon the features.

The floral offerings were rich and numerous

A committee of ten from the Jackson Union acted as a guard of honor; also a committee from the State Prohibition Club. At 1 o'clock, January 7, relatives, guards of honor, and State officers gathered for a brief home service and proceeded thence to the M. E. church for a public service.

Four pure white horses, caparisoned in delicate black net and with white ribbons waving over their heads, carried the precious burden Their very step and carriage symbolized a victorious going away, and as they took their place as leaders of this long train of carriages, nearly all of which were drawn by white horses, we thought of the victorious soul's glad "sweeping through the gate" Jackson never witnessed so long a line of carriages as this in honor of a departed citizen.

The M E. church, of which she was a member, was beautifully decorated, all in white, and with nature's most rare gifts of flower and plant. It was crowded to its utmost, and the street for a long way was thronged with people who could not get in.

The Jackson *Morning Patriot* said:—

"Never was greater sorrow witnessed at the First M E church than yesterday at the funeral services of Mrs Mary T Lathrap, and yet, mingled with all this sadness was a feeling of triumph over the glorious life closed to earth, but leaving a memory dear to all

The seating capacity of the church was not large enough for the many who assembled to do honor to the deceased, and a large number stood during the entire service, which lasted two hours. The services were most impressive and solemn, and affected many to tears.

Telegrams and messages of sympathy were received and read from all parts of the United States The secular and religious press of the country had given columns in honor of Michigan's fallen leader. The Industrial Home for Girls at Adrian had the flag at half-mast while she lay cold in death in her home.

Brief addresses were made at the public service in the church by L. R. Fiske, LL D., president of Albion College, Dr. Callen and Rev. John Graham, her pastors; Mrs Jane M Kinney, National Superintendent of penal work in the W. C. T. U., Mrs. Julia R Parish, State Corresponding Secretary of the Michigan W. C. T U ; Hon. Samuel Dickie, Chairman of the National Prohibition Committee

The remains were laid to rest in beautiful Mt. Evergreen, just out of the city of Jackson, in a lovely part of the cemetery.

After the brief burial services, members of the State Board, her "gray-haired girls," and other State workers, each plucked a rose and threw it upon the uncovered casket, and each took away a flower from the profusion scattering about We left the beautiful spot, Mt. Evergreen, to wage our peaceful war, and as we had turned from the turmoil for a few brief hours to pay our last tribute to our promoted leader, we thanked God for the inspiration that we had received from her leadership.

Every detail of this last rite was just as she would have had it The entire plan was carried out in a way that suggested life, and life only. The beautiful hands are folded, the silent reaper has stayed their further work, but in the hearts of two hundred thousand White Ribboners in the nation a name will live as long as the cause for which we labor lives — and that name is Mary T. Lathrap.

ADDENDUM.

Miss Anna Gordon went from Boston to Jackson and back again as a token of her great love for Mrs. Lathrap, to attend the funeral and to carry and read the messages from Frances E. Willard, President of the World's and National Woman's Christian Temperance Union, and from Lady Henry Somerset, President of the British Woman's Temperance Association. These elect ladies were unable to be present, and it was fitting that Miss Gordon thus represent them, as she stands in official relation to both the World's and the National Woman's Christian Temperance Union.

The messages are among the character sketches in this volume.

Editor.

INCIDENTS AND REMINISCENCES.

BEFORE the funeral service for Mrs. Lathrap a woman from the country drove in several miles and begged the privilege of seeing the remains This privilege was readily granted, and the woman related the following, in substance . —

"My husband was a drinking man and our home was poor and desolate. I had little to encourage me to live It was reported that a woman was to speak in the schoolhouse, and my husband with a sneer said, 'Let's go and hear what that woman will say anyway,' and we went.

"He soon became interested in Mrs. Lathrap's sermon, and listened to every word When the services were over, he and I lingered in the vestibule, and as she came down the aisle, he said, 'I wonder if she will speak to me.' She shook hands with me, and then turning to him said, 'My brother, you look as if you were having a hard time serving the devil O come to the Lord and be saved. Will you kneel here with me and seek the salvation of your soul?' The man, deeply moved, consented, and they knelt in the vestibule on the dirty. floor, and she prayed, he yielded and was converted. Now, we have a happy, prosperous home, my husband is a sober, industrious, Christian man, and I want to see her face once more"

The poem, "A Woman's Answer to a Man's Question," went through the papers entitled, "A Woman's Question," and was credited to several other authors Notably among these, was Elizabeth Barrett Browning. To one of these papers Mrs Lathrap wrote as follows —

"DEAR EDITOR: I am moved once more to claim another bit of my brain estate. The poem published in the April *Union* entitled, 'A Woman's Question,' was written, not by Elizabeth Barrett Browning, but by Mary T. Lathrap When first set afloat, it was 'A Woman's Answer to a Man's Question,' and was written in reply to a man's poetic unfolding of what he conceived to be a woman's duty "
"M T L"

A brother preacher, after listening to one of Mrs Lathrap's philippics, ejaculated, "Lord, give us more back-bone."

"Mrs. Lathrap made the 'fur fly' in her fearless and faithful denunciation of the practice of bringing liquor on the sly into Ocean Grove, and the prevalence among otherwise decent people of using tobacco She pleaded on her own behalf for a breath of God's pure air down along the beach, unmingled with the smell of cigar smoke. The people approved by spontaneous plaudits, wishing her to 'lay on' and 'spare not' Her chief rebuke was aimed point blank at some of the preachers."

Mrs. Torrans says "Mary was one always devoted to books, study, and writing; she always was hunting out the reason of things"

The ease with which Mrs. Lathrap picks up her Democratic and Republican antagonists and pitches them out of the window and clear over the fence is enjoyable, for it was done deftly, gently, without a suggestion of the slugger, or a word that was not an honor to the lips that spoke it She gives some mighty solid chunks of reason for the ground taken by the Prohibitionists.—*Daily News, Springfield, Ill*

Mrs. R A. Campbell relates the following· "I once told Mrs. Lathrap, after hearing one of her grand sermons, that I believed I could live a true Christian life if I could hear her preach once in three months. I afterward heard her refer to the remark as a source of strength to her, she having forgotten who it was that made it. She often said, 'Do not save all the flowers until the people are dead.' I personally, among many pleasant recollections, had a *whole wreath* of flowers bestowed upon me by her. Coming in during the session at the Chicago Convention, after an absence of two years from the State, she quietly slipped her hand into mine saying, 'As welcome as roses in June.'"

[*Plain Dealer* Special, Wellington, O.]

In Wellington there is a society of temperance women, . . . and these ladies wanted a public meeting in the interest of temperance — not a political Prohibition meeting to make votes for Prohibition candidates. They engaged Mrs Mary Lathrap, of Michigan, to deliver a temperance address. . . . The next thing in order was to find a place wherein to hold it. Since the removal of the old town hall, there is no suitable place for holding public meetings except the church. Mrs Lathrap being an ordained Methodist preacher, and the Methodist church being pledged by discipline to temperance and to Prohibition even, what more natural than for these ladies to go to the house of their friends in search of a place to hold a temperance meeting?

Their committee accordingly waited upon the trustees of the church with a petition that Mrs. Lathrap be allowed the privilege of speaking on temperance in the church. But when these temperance Esthers touched the top of the scepter, it was not held out unto them, and it pleased not the trustees to grant their petition, and in language of holy writ the trustees said substantially:—

"Thou foolish woman, seest thou not our mourning and what is happening to the G. O. P.? How that the G O. P is full of heaviness and sore distressed because of the wicked Prohibitionists? And how that the G. O. P. is neither for nor against probibition? And how the G. O P is trying to ride two temperance nags at once, and is even now split almost in twain with much straddling? Moreover, we bethink ourselves of how Parson Burchard slopped over, and what assurance have we that Parson Mollie Lathrap won't come and do likewise? While, therefore, we roll temperance under our tongues, as a sweet morsel, and are grieved over the abomination of the liquor traffic, yet we dare not have a temperance lecture in our church, for fear it might make votes for Parson Leonard [Prohibition candidate.] Nevertheless we bid you temperance ladies God-speed in your noble work."

The temperance ladies turned Mrs. Lathrap over to the Prohibitionists for whom she gave an outdoor lecture

[O. P H. in Nashville *Advocate*, Washington City, April 2, 1890]

Mrs. Lathrap, of Michigan, waked up that audience with an oratorical cyclone set to music. 'She was epigrammatic, dramatic, and most emphatic. She was argumentative, witty, rhetorical, sarcastic, and pathetic.

Mrs. Lathrap's synopsis of a lecture given by Mrs. ——— against the enfranchisement of women is as follows ·—

Women should not vote because —

1. They cannot sing base.
2. It would degrade them, and ruin the country.
3. They do n't know what the ballot means.
4. They are so contrary they would not vote like their husbands and fathers
5. Men do n't like to have them.
6. The women are so mean in New Jersey.
7. Men would have to rock the babies
8. If women make clubs trumps, they would have to play clubs
9. Women have all the property rights, etc , that men have now
10. The ship of State would swamp with women aboard.
11. The elective franchise has the effect of making women ride horseback without side saddles in Wyoming.
12. Men do n't like it.
13. The ivy can't grow without clinging to the oak
14. Women will have to stand up in street and railway cars.
15. Men will be afraid to marry, and most women want to marry real bad. It is not right to live single.
16. Men do n't like it.

Remarks · If Mrs. ——— is honest in her sentiments, why do n't she stay at home, sing treble, and cling around somebody?

Mrs Emma A. Wheeler, for eight years the State corresponding secretary, says· "After my mother died, and my husband's business kept him from home, she wrote, 'You are alone a good bit, that is a fact, and I do n't quite like to have it so I think you need chirking up a bit in some way. I wish you could travel with me for two months this summer, and see how it goes.' A frequent expression of hers was, 'God bless our women.' Among a large package of letters I find one written while speaking in the West Virginia campaign, in which she says 'I feel a bit tired these days, not quite the vim I would like I wish I could rest a year.'

"After directing what articles should be sent from Michigan to be placed in the corner stone of the Temple, she wrote : 'Where will we all be when the records are opened.' In her merry moods (and she had them often, for she was of a sunny disposition) she was child-like in her mirth. These playful moods were oftenest seen in her own home, where I have spent many happy hours."

FIRST PUBLIC WORK.— Mrs. Lathrap read her first missionary letter on the "Women of India" in the Jackson Church. She says: "I was unwillingly 'tugged' out on the seas of all lands, thus entering on my work for the Woman's Foreign Missionary Society Within four miles of this church I preached my first six sermons, in the little Congregational church at Michigan Center. It was in this building I was licensed to preach the gospel after such profound religious experiences as yet lie in the great silence between God and my own soul

---

AN early schoolmate says: "In our ten-year-old check-apron days, no schoolmate was so dear to me. Her sturdy independence and utter fearlessness of the pupils, who assumed airs of superiority, used to fairly awe me. She had an utter abhorrence of any sort of sham or pretence, and on play-ground and in school room she considered honor and self-respect far above any advantages of wealth or position.

She was leader in composition and debate. Four months my junior, she seemed the elder, and led while I followed.

LATHRAP HALL AT HACKLEY PARK.— In 1893 the Michigan Woman's Christian Temperance Union built a beautiful hall for educational purposes in our work at Hackley Park, near Muskegon, Michigan; and by vote of the annual convention held in Muskegon in that year, the hall was named Mary T. Lathrap Hall in honor of her. She put time, thought, and money into this work. She spared no effort to make it a house beautiful; and the persistency and care with which she looked after all of the details was a surprise to those who thought they knew already about her wonderful painstaking. The building was dedicated, Aug 1, 1893, by Mrs. Lathrap, who said, among other things, "The hour of consummation has come; let the struggle cease. We dedicate this hall to God and Home and Native Land." To-day the House Beautiful stands a substantial structure, a White Ribbon home, another powerful agency for waging our peaceful warfare.

Lathrap Hall stands, sheltered on the one side by a wooded hill, and facing Lake Michigan on the other side, a fitting type of her in whose honor it is named — sheltered by the everlasting God but bravely facing stern realities as relentless as the ceaseless ebb and flow of the waves of Lake Michigan. Nestled under the shelter of the hill, Mary T. Lathrap Hall is in a beautiful location for Michigan W. C. T. U. Educational headquarters.

LATHRAP CHAPEL, at Harriman, Tenn., now in process of erection, will seat 1500 persons, and is named in honor of Mrs. Lathrap, who was one of the University trustees. No more fitting or beautiful monument could be erected to her memory.

[Extracts from letters to Emma A. Wheeler.]

JACKSON, MICH., Nov. 4, 1890.

. . "The battle is going on as I write. I wonder how far ahead our cause will go to-day. It is *slow*, is it not?"

AUBURN, July 11, 1890.

. "I want to send a floral offering to Coldwater, Saturday, to the new-made grave of General Fisk. What a loss to the church, to the country, and to me; he has been such a good, true friend since the years when I worked with him in New Jersey."

[Copy of letter to Mrs. Fisk. When General Fisk was nominated for President on the Prohibition ticket.]

COLDWATER, MICH., May 22, 1888.

"DEAR MRS. FISK. I have been thinking of writing you for many days, and feel like saying to you some things I have on my heart. The eyes of all this country are turning toward General Fisk, and already I believe he is the choice of a million voters, with more to follow if no mistakes are made; and I solemnly believe the choice is not so much *human* as *divine*.

"I have wondered these days, when your husband's name is on our lips and in our prayers, if we have thought of you as much as we should. I sat one day with Mrs. St. John, in an art gallery in Rochester, while she told me of the trial days when her husband was candidate, and she said, 'You did not care for all I felt about it, and I was angry at you.' But the temperance people *did care*. They saw the sacrifice, and see it yet. But I replied, 'If you had sat in the convention at Pittsburgh and seen the choice come down upon Governor St. John, you would not have dared to raise an objection; you would have felt that these things are not of human contriving.' And she answered, 'Well, perhaps you are right, but it has all been so hard.'

"I remember some things I heard you say in the campaign in New Jersey. I remember my feeling about you and the general while in your elegant home those few hours; and I know there is nothing for him or for you of *honor* in the choice which has been foreshadowed now four years. I know a little of your feeling concerning the present situation. I swiftly guess at more, because I am a woman. I think I could think and say all you would utter of objection,—health, friends, money, the unspeakable unkindness of our political methods, all touching a home so sweet, and a life so royal as that of General Fisk. But, my friend, this nation is making history as grand as when Wendall Phillips was egged and hissed for the truth, and Sumner was stricken down in Congress. And, as God could not write the history of freedom for the slave, and emancipation from its wrong, for the nation, without Seward, Sumner, and Lincoln, no more can he write this new history without a group of men, of which just now your husband is the center. I *pray you see it this way*, for your own comfort. All these personal considerations are but small, measured by the destiny of a great people and the coming of Christ to his own in the world.

"You are very strong, so I make a strong appeal. *You* are needed, not only in slow consent for him to be the candidate of the prohibition party, but as the *best strength* at his side. I pray you be willing. It will be *almost* treason to your country, dear, to be otherwise. This is enough. Before you are tried with me for this, think, I write with eyes dim with tears. Be great, my friend.

"MARY T. LATHRAP."

EARLIER POEMS.

(Under Nom de Plume of "Lena")

TO ONE WHO WISHES FAME.

Thou wishest fame! in thy life sky afar
Shines there in glory that strange burning star,
Whose light has sometimes led the good man's way
Upward, but ah! more frequent led astray.

Thou wishest fame! ambition in thy soul
Bids thee toil onward to the distant goal,
And holds the dazzling prize before the view,
Fought for by many, gained by ah, how few!

But some there be now in the silent land,
Who long have slept with coldly folded hands,
Their names we breathe with bitter shame or pride,
They, they began to live the day they died.

All used a magic pen, a fadeless scroll,
Wrote their great heart-throb on the *human soul*,
Then died ; but each strong wave for good or ill
They raised, along time's shore, is washing still

They lived and died, but did the tide-like flow
Of their deep thoughts bring more of joy than woe?
Ask the long past, whose page has many a blot
It would not have, were some great names forgot.

And thou wouldst stand upon that dizzy height,
Around which rests a halo glory bright,
And wear the chaplet whose undying ray
Would glow undimmned when thou hadst passed away

But shouldst thou win the wreath, would it when worn
Prove one of roses, and without a thorn?
And would it be to an immortal soul,
The crowning top-stone to the purest goal?

No! thou mayest toil till on that brow of thine,
Thought, that strange sculptor, chisels many a line;
And find how poor a boon is empty fame,
And of how little worth a titled name.

No! let thine be a holier mission here,
To bless earth's erring, and earth's mourners cheer;
Then when thy hands are folded into rest,
No voice shall curse the name that many bless.

Marshall, Dec. 1, 1858

EVENING.

The meek stars are brightening up heaven's blue deep,
The low winds are rocking the flowers to sleep,
And the leaflet's soft, rustling melody seems
Like some echo that comes from a beautiful dream.

The evening has stolen the sunset's last hue,
And changed all the sky to a motionless blue,
Save where the white cloudlets their snowy fold fling
Across the deep azure, like angels on wing.

The lakelet throws back in its gentle unrest,
The light that falls soft on its billowy breast,
And it seems like another sky — calm, and as blue
As the one that bends o'er us — the stars shining through.

Each sound that breathed discord at length has grown still,
And quiet is bathing the vale and the hill.
All that breaks on the ear is a low, dreamy hum,
As sweet as the roll of the Indian drum.

As rose the pure incense from Israel's fires,
So the gold-tinted mist curls around the church spires,
And seems like that cloud — just waiting to bear
To the throne of " Our Father " the heart's evening prayer

Marshall, May 31, 1859.

TO MR. AND MRS. W. W. MOORE.

In memory of their boy WILLIE — whose path to Heaven was only ten years long — these lines are affectionately dedicated

A brow that was spotless as marble,
   Eyes that were gentle and true,
Lips that were brimfull of sweetness,
   A heart that was pure as the dew;
A form that our fond arms have folded,
   Dear hands that are cold as the frost;
The promise and hope of the future —
   These are the things *we* have *lost.*

A home in God's beautiful summer,
   A place 'neath the dear Saviour's eyes,
Where blossoms are rare and eternal,
   And never a single one dies;
A land free from darkness and sinning,
   Where the heart is ne'er saddened or pained,
Escape from life's possible burdens —
   These are the things *he* has *gained.*

So right in the night-time of sorrow
   Gleameth God's balance of gold,
Weighing the seen and the earthly,
   With that out of sight, and untold;
Weighing the gain and the losses,
   That hearts he has smitten, may see
That his love runneth all through the trial,
   And his way is the best that can be.

Willie's form lies asleep on the hillside,
    'Neath the sunshine and blossoms of spring;
But his soul is awake where the seasons
    No possible winter can bring.
Take comfort, sad hearts, in thy mourning,
    Heaven's nearer thee, now, than before,
Willie's steps light the way to the portal,
    Tho' he has passed in at the door.

Jackson, April 29, 1870.

"I HAVE NO MOTHER NOW."

      I see him now,
A half-veiled look of heaven upon his face,
    That heavenlier seemed baptized in recent tears,
And that peculiar shadow, brightness traced
    Alone where sorrows come with childhood's years
      Was on his brow.

      The sunlight shone
Down with a loving kiss upon the hair —
    That fell in gold-waves round the half-bent head,
As if it would replace a mother's care,
    That mother lain yestreen among the dead,
      To sleep alone.

      And low I bent
To kiss the upturned brow so pure and white,
    And called his name; but still the drooping lid
Shut close within the soul its wonted light,
    While on the silken lash a tear unshed
      Hung eloquent.

      The trembling tone
Was like a bird wail, O, so sadly sweet;
    In five short words the simple tale he told;
Told why his rosy cheeks with tears were wet,
    And why like dew upon his locks of gold
      They brightly shone.

And this the tale.
"I have no mother now;" he said no more,
　But I looked down upon the shadowed brow,
And then away into the years before,
　When he must weep e'en bitterer tears than now,
　　And sadder feel.

　　Through all the years
I thought how he must live and never know
　The warm caress a mother's hand can give,
And miss her blessing amid weal or woe,
　And missing these, still onward toil and live,
　　Without her prayers

　　I see him yet,
And hear the murmur of those music tones,
　"I have no mother now." May those sweet eyes
Keep still that upward look toward thy home,
　And their appealing blue lead to the skies,
　　Thy wandering steps.

Marshall, April 29, 1859.

[For the *Daily Citizen.*]

WHAT OF THE SHIP?

We thought that the day of our conflict was passed,
　That the day of our triumph had come,
We thought that the ship of the Union, at last,
　Had swept out from the breakers among.
We heard the boom, boom of the rock-fretted surf,
　As it struck on the dangerous shore,
While we sailed, as we thought, from the peril behind
　Out into the glory before.

We were out on the tide, at its uttermost flood,
　And a world stood to see if we failed;
While above all the human, the great eye of God
　Looked down on the right, as she sailed

High up at the mast-head our flag was afloat,
   All riven and torn by the blast;
But its motto of "*Freedom and Manhood to Man*,"
   Flashed out on the world as it passed

All this was but yesterday — vict'ry and song;
   Our foes bending suppliant knee;
And the race whose dark faces looked God-ward so long,
   Standing up where all manhood could see,—
All this was but yesterday! What of to-day?
   "The clouds return after the rain,"
Boom, boom! to our ears comes the sound of the surf,
   And we drift to the breakers again!

"Right about with the ship," cries Freedom on watch;
   "Away!" from the rocks and the sand
"Down with the helm!" but the call's disobeyed —
   On that helm lies a traitorous hand!
The pilot is false to the words written out
   Upon our sacred banner in blood,
He is false to the living, and false to the dead!
   False to justice, and honor, and God!
Tho' we're out on the tide, at its uttermost flood —
   Rocks are near us — then what shall we do?
Our pilot's great soul in those breakers went down,
   The man in *his* place *must be true!*

[For the *Advertiser and Tribune*]

THE DEED AND THE MEN.

Up, up to the curtains of darkness
   Leaped the tongues of the pitiless flame,
Mapping out on the sky of the evening
   A horror too deep for a name;
    Filling the air with a terrible gloom,
    Blotting from heaven the stars and the moon,
    Spreading its smoke far above like a pall,
    Below, busy wrapping a ruin round all.

Below were the dark, angry faces
  Of what God intended for *men ;*
But the hate in their eyes made them demons,
  And blotted out all, but revenge.
    The curses of passion went up to the sky,
    And through them, beside them, ascended the cry,—
    The cry of a great and terrible wrong—
    The wail of the weak — He who heard it is strong!

Below rolled the surges of passion,
  Above the calm heavens looked down ;
Below glared the human misdoing,
  Above, gloomed the infinite frown
    Below, rocked the billows of passion that night,
    Above, paused the angel of record to write ;
    Madly below did these hands light the flames,
    Sternly above wrote the angel their names.

The anger and tumult are over,
  The names and the deeds that were done,
Are connected forever and ever —
  They'll meet in a time that will come.
    They built in their madness a tower of shame ;
    The wrong and injustice are written in flame ;
    O did they think, in their rage 'gainst the weak,
    That God who will judge, willed the hue of the cheek ?

Detroit, March 12, 1863.

[For the *Advertiser and Tribune*]

"OUT OF THE DEPTHS WE CRY TO THEE."

Because in the past we were mighty,
  And our pathway was glory so long,
We forgot to look upward and God-ward,
  And thought all alone we were strong.
Faithless and sinning and proud were we ;
Now, " Out of the depths we cry to Thee."

Because of the splendid uprising
  Of hearts when our danger drew nigh;
Because of the oaths they recorded,
  For our country to dare and to die,
We still kept our pride — self-trusting were we;
  Now, "Out of the depths we cry to Thee."

Because that the tread of our army
  Had power to startle the world;
Because on the ocean no banner
  More proud than our own was unfurled;
The cause nor the help from Jehovah sought we,
  Now, "Out of the depths we cry to Thee."

Because that the shadow has deepened
  And our hands are too frail to bring light;
Because now our trial is bitter,
  We've learned to look up through the night;
We have found there is something stronger than we,
  And, "Out of the depths we cry to Thee."

Because man has failed when we trusted,
  And our sod has been sprinkled with gore;
Because of the brave hearts who left us —
  So many will come back no more —
In tears and our weakness more humble are we,
  And, "Out of the depths we cry to Thee."

Because Thou hast taught us our frailness,
  And told us Thy hand is so strong;
Because Thou hast promised salvation,
  Though Thy people forget Thee so long —
Now lowly, trusting, and hopeful are we,
  As, "Out of the depths we cry to Thee."

Detroit, April 30, 1863.

[For the Detroit *Advertiser and Tribune*]

FOR THOSE WHO ARE AFRAID.

Cannot conquer the South ! Are they stronger than we,
   That you 'd tamely submit to their treason ?
Call pride to your rescue, poor soul, if you 've lost
   The whole of your courage and reason.
Look over the strong and magnificent North,
   Will it bow before treason so humble ?
No, no ! better that every freeman should die
   Than that Freedom's proud temple should crumble

Cannot conquer the South ! Is it better than ours —
   The cause for which they are contending ?
Are honor and liberty, country and home,
   And our banner not worth the defending ?
Would you see their dark flag o'er your capitol wave
   While they hurl their proud scorn in your faces,
And rivet your chains as they claim their high right
   To rule the "*inferior races ?*"

Cannot conquer the South ! Are they braver than we ?
   Go stand where our fallen are lying,
Go ask for the hearts that *have died* for our cause,
   And those, just as brave, who are dying.
Go count ye the thinned ranks to-day in the field,
   Do their lips look like saying, " Surrender " ?
Do such daring and doing deserve for reward
   Your cowardly, pitiful slander ?

Cannot conquer the South ! Are they winners to-day ?
   Which flag is the brightest with glory ?
Mississippi flows onward unchained to the sea ;
   Ask its waters to tell you the story.
From Vicksburg and Hudson the shout of the brave
   With that from the eastward is swelling,
And Morgan's *repose* (?) is disturbed I presume,
   By the tale which the chorus is telling.

Cannot conquer the South ! Talk loud as you will,
  The guns at Fort Sumter speak louder ;
The flag over Charleston is proud, I admit,
  But the one that *will be there* is prouder.
Cannot conquer the South ! Yes we can, and we will,
  For true to our country her sons are ;
But before they come home, you who say that " they can't,"
  Had better go over to Windsor

East Saginaw, Aug. 21, 1863.

[For the *Expounder*]

VACANT CHAIRS.

I'm thinking how the temples of our nation rang to-day,
With the anthems of thanksgiving that have scarcely died away ,
How back to many homesteads the wandering feet have come,
And 'round the hearthstone gathers the grandsire and the son.

I am thinking how the bounties, by Nature's hand out-poured,
Have crowned with good and plenty, the gay and festal board ;
How love's dear light is burning, its language in each eye,
And hearts forget what may be in the hidden by-and-by.

I'm dreaming o'er the mem'ries, those amaranthine flowers
That fill with rarest fragrance these velvet-footed hours ;
But I turn from all the gladness of this and other years,
To think of what is filling too many eyes with tears.

There's an undertone of sadness in our song of praise to-day,
For a cloud has gathered o'er us, in the year just passed away ,
How much of joy is clouded by the hearthstones everywhere,
As shadowed eyes turn fondly toward the vacant chair.

There's war within our borders, and many homes are sad,
For lack of manly voices which last year made them glad ;
For lack of eyes now turning from the camp-fire's light to hide
The tears which show that *mem'ry* is stronger far than *pride*.

I ween the mirth was quiet by many boards to-day,
As the smile shone through the tear-drops, for soldiers far away;
And voices of thanksgiving sank lower to a prayer,
As eyes with wistful yearning fell on the vacant chair.

There's war within our borders, and there are homes to-night
From which its awful shadow has shut out all the light;
The loved and brave have perished in the battle's fiery rain,
And the chairs which they left vacant, will ne'er be filled again

There are hearts all o'er our country, too sad for songs of praise,
Whose light and joy are lying within a soldier's grave,
And other hearts whose gladness is darkened by the fear
Of what may be their portion before another year.

Some voices have sung anthems in the house of God to-day,
But more have bowed in silence, with saddened hearts to pray
That God would make up losses to the mourner, by his care,
And bring once more the loved ones to fill the vacant chair.

Thanksgiving Day, 1861.

[For the *Washington Post*.]

BREAKING OF THE ICE.

Under the winter moon they lay —
Frozen river, and frozen bay,
Stretching for miles and miles away.
    An ocean of silver
      With waves of gold,
    By the prodigal moonlight,
      Over it rolled,
As under their shackles of molten light,
The bay and river throbbed on that night.

Winter was old, a great round sun,
All day long, in the skies had hung,
Promising blossoms soon to come,
    Till the heart of the waters
        Had caught the light,
    And was singing of freedom
        Now, in the night,
Learning the song through its icy bars,
And chanting it up to the listening stars.

Skaters skimmed o'er the silver sea,
Idle argosies, winged with glee,
Heeding never the minstrelsy
    That was heard in the water's
        Impatient dips,
    As they lapped the fetters
        With hungry lips,
While hurrying onward, with muffled feet,
To pour their wrong in the heart of the deep.

Under the stretches of moonlight sweet,
Under the skaters' careless feet,
Under the icy, silvered sheet,
    The river was singing
        That old, old song
    The world has been singing,
        For ages long;
Defiantly asking in name of the right,
God's boundless freedom, God's loving light.

So, when the skaters all were gone,
Leaving the moonlight gleaming on,
I stayed yet by the shore alone,
    For the tale it was telling,
        Had power to hold
    Like that by the "ancient
        Mariner" told;
River and moonlight were holding me still,
And like the weird mariner, had their will

What could I do but choose to stay,
Hearing all the waters might say,
Hearing the booming miles away
    Of the great deep ocean,
      That's always free,
    As it sent its pulsations
      Far up to me,
Through the vein-like river, that felt the swell
Of its mighty heart as it rose and fell?

By and by from toward the sea,
Twixt the golden splendor and me,
Broad winged mists floated lazily;
    While a wind that was lonesome
      And wet with brine,
    ·Slowly moaned up the river,
      Bending the pines;
And the moonlight's wonderful sheen of gold
Grew pale and wan in the mists' gray fold.

Then pealed louder the wind's great bells,
Higher the heart of the river swelled,
Grayer the mist over all things fell;
    And up through the pauses
      There came the roar
    Of the surf as it trampled
      Along the shore;
And the shackles trembled on river and bay,
Trembled and loosened for miles away.

Trembled and loosened more and more,
Shrieked and parted from shore to shore,
Until the free waters, with maddened roar,
    O'er the chains that had bound them,
      Sang the glad song,
    The world will be singing
      Some day ere long;
When it, like the river, unbound and free,
Shall bury its chains in the fathomless sea.

For now, under many an icy creed,
Murmurs the world its terrible needs,
Looking for grander days and deeds ;
    But great waves of progress
      Boom on the shore ;
    The glad spring cometh,
      The wide world o'er ;
The wild surf may trample the sands for a night,
The mad winds ring loudly — morn bringeth light

God's time is coming — winter is old —
Fetters of iron nor chains of gold,
No more than the ice, can forever hold ;
    For the heart of humanity
      Sings in its might
    Of a beautiful morning
      God shall make light ;
But only the faithful who watch for the day,
Shall see how grandly the ice gives way

BISHOP CLARK.

What need hath he for praise whom God hath crowned?
    What use for tears, when all life's pain is o'er ?
    What need of anything from out our store
Of little treasures, with all heaven just found ?

What need have we to say how well he wrought !
    Since God hath said · " Well done, come to thy rest , "
    Since on the wondrous shores among the blest,
The kingly soul has found all things it sought ?

How poor the wreaths we weave, or songs we sing,
    To him whose brow is touched with fadeless glory —
    To him who listens to the angels' story,
At home among God's chosen priests and kings.

And yet, and yet, a stricken people stand
    Beside their hallowed graves with wond'ring grief ;
    For thrice the blow has fallen 'mong the chief,
And we are smitten sorely by God's hand.

First, from white fields his hands did bravely reap,
    Came back the tidings, "Thompson is no more,"
    Then, 'mid strange blooms upon a foreign shore,
Our precious Kingsley found a place to sleep

And now, before our cheeks are dry of tears,
    Another leader lays his armor down ;
    For *us* three graves — for *them* the starry crown,
And joy and glory, in God's endless years.

O stricken church ! that mourn your dead to-day,
    A wondrous glory gleams your sorrow through ;
    Departing feet have left the path for you
To heaven so bright, you cannot miss the way

Then onward bravely, up the shining road
    Toward the land that hath no death or loss.
    Remember that your great ones bore the cross,
Before they grasped the deathless palms of God

[For the Detroit *Tribune*.]

OUR HERO'S NATAL DAY.

The sleeper at Mt Vernon,
    Our hero, lives once more,
The altar fires of freedom
    Burn brightly as of yore ;
The patriot blood is stirring,
    In great, swift throbs to-day,
As our glad and grateful homage
    To our Washington we pay.

Foul traitors have polluted
    The spot on which he sleeps,
That hallowed shrine they've trodden,
    With sacreligious feet.

But the day of vengeance cometh,
   The soil that keeps his dust
Shall be as free as sunlight,
   For our country's God is just.

Ring out, glad bells, your pæan,
   On this his natal day;
Let music's grandest numbers
   Along our breezes play
Unfurl our flag and gather
   Beneath its folds with pride,
He bathed that flag in glory
   And freedom, e'er he died

What tho' the clouds are o'er us?
   They cannot quench the flame
That burns in freemen's bosoms —
   'T is deathless as his name,
Another year, and brightly
   Shall shine our clouded sun,
No shadow o'er our country,
   The land of Washington.

Detroit, Feb. 22, 1862.

[For the *Advertiser and Tribune*]

MAN'S WORK IN GOD'S WORLD.

Below us the evergreen valleys are lying,
   Around us all beauty is given,
Down near to our souls is the Infinite bending,
   And above — just above us — is heaven.

And this is man's dower — even mortal existence,
   Aglow with a beauty divine,
Where far, far above, waits a glory eternal,
   Where "lights unapproachable" shine.

But alas for the dark in the evergreen valley,
    Alas for decay on the hills,
Alas for the gloom on the wonderful mountains,
    Alas for the mildew that kills !

The earth and the air, to the height of our steeples,
    Is full of humanity's woe ,
The earth and the air, up as high as man reaches,
    Are damp with the tear-drops that flow.

Above, far above, looketh down the blue heavens
    Alit with mysterious stars ,
And almost we ken, as with still hearts we're gazing,
    That angels look down through the bars

Below, far below, the hoarse tumult is raging,
    As if Mercy from mortals had fled ;
Mad Passion drives on with his car o'er a highway —
    A highway all paved with the dead.

Man puts his proud heel on the heart of his brother,
    And smiles at the work he has done ,
And the wrongs that cry up to a pitying Heaven,
    Might blot from its arches the sun.

Around us the evergreen valleys are lying,
    Unto us all beauty is given,
Down near to our souls is the Infinite bending,
    And above, just above us, is heaven.

But the tumult goes on, man defying the Highest,
    And trampling on things all divine ;
Forgets in his rashness the vengeance that waiteth
    To come in Jehovah's good time.

Alas for my country, thy evergreen valleys,
    Are wet with a tide that is red,
Alas for thy hills for they shudd'ringly cover
    War's sacrifice, bloody and dread !

Alas for my country ; thine ensign of glory
  Thy sons have baptized with their blood,
Alas for us now, in the gloom of this darkness,
  If above, over all, was not God !

Detroit, Sept 10, 1862.

[For the *Expounder*]

RETROSPECTION.

Standing by the school-room window all the idle hour of noon,
Tapping off with listless fingers on the pane an olden tune,
Wandering, wandering ever backward, far into the heretofore,
Gathering up the pebbles lying all along on memory's shore ;

Through the ways I 've trodden over, where my footsteps yet are seen,—
Footsteps that e'er long will mingle ever more with what has been, —
Through the spots so sadly haunted only by an echo now,
I have wandered, only finding faded garlands for my brow.

From the low roof-tree whose shelter was above my youthful head,
From the trees and flowers I cherished — from their beauty I have fled ;
Trees and flowers will keep on growing, tended by another's care,
Sifting through their leaves the moonlight, as they did when I was there.

From the church whose quiet altar was an ever dear retreat,
Through the years whose passing sobered fast my childhood's restless feet,
And from friends who loved me truly, true in happiness and tears,
I have passed to tread another pathway through the vale of years.

Ties are broken ; I have drifted from the haven sweet of home
And across its hallowed threshold, stranger feet will go and come ;
And the dear ones who were gathered by the fires in days of yore
Now by fortune widely scattered, will, I ween, meet there no more.

All of this have I been thinking, in the idle hour of noon,
Standing, listless, at the window, humming o'er a pensive tune ;
And I thanked the great All-Father, that the parted ways will meet,
In the calm, eternal sunshine where He'll bring our wand'ring feet.

Detroit, March 1, 1862.

[For the *Detroit Tribune.*]

FORT DONALDSON AND VICTORY.

Our flag is afloat on the breezes to night,
  Our country's dear colors float free,
And the cannon's deep throat peals the victory won,
By her brave sons in old Tennessee.
  Our flag is afloat upon turret and spire,
    Hung out by the loyal and true,
  A nation's great heart at the sight of it beats,
    For it floats at Fort Donaldson, too

Our flag is afloat, e'en where treason's dark sign
  Has hung like a blot in the sky ;
And traitors have found there are thousands who'll stand
  By the flag of our country, or die.
  Our banner is out upon turret and spire,
    Hung out by the loyal and true,
  A nation's great heart at the sight of it beats,
    For it floats at Fort Donaldson, too

And music peals clear, through the gloaming to-night,
  Its pæan of triumph and pride ;
But our hearts, beating high in their victory and hope,
  Must sigh for the brave who have died.

Our flag is afloat upon turret and spire,
    Hung out by the brave and the true,
A nation's great heart at the sight of it weeps,
    For it floats o'er our fallen ones, too.

Our march is still onward, for down where the sea
    Breaks restless on Roanoke's strand,
The foul friends of treason our ensign must see,
    By the breath of their own breezes fanned,
    Our banner is out upon turret and spire,
        Placed there by the loyal and true,
    The heart of a nation beats high in its joy,
        'T is floating at Roanoke, too.

On, on to the Southward, till treason lies dead
    On the soil that is black with its stain;
On, on, till each spot, from the Lakes to the Gulf,
    Is bound in our Union again.
    Our banner is out where have fallen the brave,
        And unto the death were they true,
    O'er Roanoke's Isle and Fort Henry it waves,
        And now at Fort Donaldson, too.

[Written for the *Advertiser and Tribune*]

LIGHT THROUGH THE CLOUD.

Long time our country for her shadowed glory,
    Amid the murky, muffling clouds has wept;
Long time to God each breeze has borne the story
    Of her deep woe — but it is dark as yet

Long time upon her mountains and her valleys
    Has lain rich dew that came not from above,
Long time beside her desecrated altars,
    Brave hearts have laid their life to prove their love.

Long time in shadowed homes the wife and mother
    Have prayed for loved ones with each sobbing breath,
Loved ones that stand or fall, where war's wild voices,
    With their long shriek, talk never but of *death*.

Long time the calmer breath of prayers unnumbered
   Have pierced above the clouds that gloom our sky,
Prayers strong and pure, that bind our cause and country
   Unto the Power that rules and guides on high.

Long time the empty hands that gave their treasures
   Have held these earnest pleadings up to God,
And comes there yet no echo of his footsteps?
   Methinks of late somewhere his feet have trod.

   For the bugle notes have sounded
     The "Forward March" once more,
   And along Potomac's waters,
     Echo speaks it o'er and o'er;
   Strong as the tides of ocean
     Moved our columns as they shone,
   And by our hopes of heaven,
     They went not forth alone.

   They have met the foe, and round them
     Now falls the fiery rain,
   But God encamps about them,
     They shall not fail again;
   We'll welcome them as victors
     When the day of strife is o'er,
   And God will watch the sleepers,
     Who will come to us no more.

Detroit, May 12, 1864

[For the Detroit *Advertiser and Tribune*]

THE PARTING WITH SUMMER.

The beautiful feet of the summer,
   So late by the woodland and rill,
With slow, lingering movement are going
   Down the brown, southern slopes of the hills;
Her dreamy-eyed sister, the autumn,
Looks down at the summer-clad trees,
And, 'neath her cool breathing, a garment
   Of brown is put on by the leaves

A soft haze comes up from the valleys,
   And floats between landscape and sky,
And the sun, looking down through the lacework
   Of mist, has a tenderer eye
The azure of heaven grows deeper,
   More vivid the sunset's last glow,
And the clouds at the gates of the morning
   Have mingled some gray with their snow.

O 'er the fields and the slopes of the meadows,
   The swift-footed sunshine and shade,
In frolic are chasing each other,
   Far away to the dim forest glade.
There 's quieter light on the waters,
   A many-hued robe on the trees,
And the anthem the wild winds are playing,
   Runs down on the low minor keys.

It is beautiful, all, in its going,
   This wonderful, sweet summer time;
The leaflets glide down through the sunshine,
   As poet thoughts glide into rhyme.
Sweet Summer looks over her shoulder,
   And whispers once more her farewells —
I wonder if *Peace* will come with her
   When her feet are again on the hills.

Detroit, Sept. 24, 1863.

[For the *Advertiser and Tribune.*]

THANKFULNESS.

1 Sam 2.1-11.

My heart rejoiceth in the Lord,
   Exalted by his hand,
My mouth all full of thankfulness,
   Above my foes I stand

Because of my salvation,
   My heart and lips rejoice,
Do I, o'er all, in praises
   Lift up to thee my voice?

There is none holy as the Lord,
   And there is none beside,
Neither for us is there a rock,
   Like God, our shield and guide
Then talk no more so proudly,
   Let arrogance be still,
The Lord, a God of knowledge,
   Weighs all our acts at will.

Broken the bows of mighty men,
   Girt are the weak with strength;
And they who toiled and hungered long
   Are satisfied at length.
The Lord, he taketh life away
   And bringeth to the grave,
Or maketh them alive again
   Whom he desires to save.

The Lord, he makes the poor and rich,
   To all his power doth go,
He lifts the beggar from the dust,
   And lays the mighty low.
The poor he sets on glory's throne,
   While princes are forgot;
The pillars of the earth are his,
   The world man ruleth not

He keeps the feet of all his saints,
   By strength shall none prevail;
In darkness shall the wicked hide,
   His foes destroyed shall fail.
Out of the heavens his thunder speaks,
   And he shall judge the earth,
Exalting his anointed ones
   To glory and to worth.

Detroit, May, 1863.

[Written for the Monthly Association of Detroit Teachers.]

THE TEACHER'S MISSION.

BY MISS MARY TORRANS.

All writers have a preface, so must I,
But I'll not, like them, tell a modest lie
About how poor the work is I have done,
Because the thing is new and I am young,
But I will write because the powers that be,
Sans ceremonie, gave that task to me.
And I believe a great truth told one day
That those who govern well must first obey.
So, spite of looks vexatious on your part,
And spite of palpitations round my heart
I'll just believe in self-complacent pride,
Myself the admired, and you the edified.

The teacher's mission, what is it? and how
Can we best fulfil that mission now,
That we who write on human hearts may not
Leave there a line we'll ever wish to blot?
To-day, we mold them to what form we will,
To-morrow, they are adamant beyond our skill.
I might let fancy have her will to-day,
And soar on lofty wing her wildest way,
And tell how solemn is the work we do,
How grand a duty rests on me and you;
How much we hold the weal of human kind,
Whose hands sweep daily o'er the chords of mind.
But for awhile I'll fancy's wings control,
For tho' we're guiding human heart and soul,
Still, I remember,—'t will not be denied—
Our lofty mission has its humble side.
They gather round us with their restless feet,
These restless children that we have to teach;
They come from homes, some happy and some sad,
From hearthstones dreary, and from firesides glad;
Some trained at home to lovingly obey,
Others, neglected, early taught to stray.

I looked on teaching with a poet's eye,
To me 't was always grand and high,
A field of labor somewhat nearer heaven
Than most the work to human beings given,
A garden to make beautiful with care,
And to be watched with love that grows from prayer.
I sought my new school-room but few moons ago,
And found my dream as fleet as spring-time snow;
Not that I lost my beautiful ideal,
But daily practice made it grow more real
Some came with clothes and faces clean and bright,
And some presented but a sorry sight.
And looking o'er my portion of young minds,
I found each urchin humanly inclined,
They all could play a game of marbles well,
But found it far a harder task to spell,
And easier work by far to whirl a top
Than finding if the world turns round or not.
With restless spirit, chafing at control,
Children are children — same from pole to pole.
I've heard the theories, sounding and sublime,
For guiding up to fulness human mind,
Listened to words, both eloquent and new,
From hearts that to the work are leal and true.
But we all can tell others how to teach
Better than we can practice what we preach;
And theories, like stars upon the sky,
Are very fair and yet a trifle high.
There's daily labor, humble and unknown,
And cares uncounted by the looker on;
There's crosses lifted in our daily way
For which the gold of Crœsus would not pay
It may be pleasant human thoughts to till,
But not so pleasant bending human will.
A theory full often will take wings
Before the presence of some childish things,
And leave us face to face with simple fact
Where naught avails us but a host of tact
Talk as you will of all o'ermastering love,
The Spirit that rules all so well above,

But I have found where love will rule one Dick,
A dozen Toms and Harrys need a stick.
Could these romancing minds, for just one term,
Teach urchins who have got all things to learn,
Taken from homes where discipline's unknown,
And order is a thing forever flown,
They'd find, perhaps, as you and I have done,
That talk, like moonshine, fades in real sun.
I'd like to see them right among the troop
Of threescore boys, and see them scan the group
To find ideal diamonds in the rough,
Until their patience is just tired enough
To make them look to less of stilted thought
On those whose labors are with care so fraught;
I'd like to see them look with thought on faces
Most plainly traced with pancakes and molasses, .
And leading them by hands whose dusky dye
Shows adepts at mixing of mud pie
'T is very easy standing off one side
In self-complaisence, cool and dignified,
And tell poor teachers what they ought to do,
And when we fail, forsooth, as if 't were new;
To know responsibility is in our work,
From which we may not ever try to shirk.
'T is very easy teaching little things,
So easy managed that it only brings
Relief from *ennui*, and if you have pure
And philanthropic purposes, why then sure
Two-forty is enough for clothes and food —
They must be sacrificing who do good.
Just one thing more upon the lowly side
Of the grand mission that we name with pride.
I mean the gruffness of the sage papas,
And outraged love of overkind mamas.
The little cherubs must be made to mind,
Must learn a great deal in a little time,
Their minds and manners we must cultivate,
And put refinement in each heedless pate,
Must teach them what they ought to learn at home,
And have a nursery in each first-grade room,

And yet, forsooth, we must not ever tire
Or ever show one bit of human ire,
For if you just look crooked at the dears,
You meet with papa's growl and mama's tears,
Then if we speak a self-defensive word
They recommend us to our "honored Board"
Each parent thinks his children are the best,
They must be favored spite of all the rest,
And each one thinks his own so very smart
If they do n't learn, the teacher has no art,
When at their homes, a dozen times a day,
He 'd push the plague in anger from his way
And call them blockheads if some hard command
The heedless mischief failed to understand,
But we are teachers and must patient bear,
Not three, but three-score blockheads for our share.

But, teachers, there 's a holier side and true,
A loftier look of gladness left for you,
We sow to day, perhaps with weary hands,
The harvest comes apace, the promise stands.
There 's darkness in the little heart we guide,
But careful hands will find the "angel side",
Their feet are wayward, ever more astray,
But can be guided in the better way,
Out from the darkness to pure light,
Out from the ignorance which makes all night,
Up to a manhood noble and sublime,
Up to a womanhood blessing human kind,

Up to the pathway all the good have trod,
Up higher still, to purity and God.
We labor thankfully, with many fears,
But our reward is coming with the years.
What may lie now beyond our wisest ken,
Is hidden in the destinies of men.
These days are wax we mold to any cast,
But are eternal adamant when past.
The world needs earnest work from teachers now,
Because it needs uplifting from the slough

Of sinful darkness to the purer light
Of that celestial sun which has no night.
Our country needs our earnest work to-day,
Our schools will be guardians of her way,
Her shame or honor will soon rest on them,
And oh! our country needs more honest men,
More men who stand above mere mammon's nod,
Whose manhood knows no worship save its God.
If our dear land shall keep her upward way
The promise is encircled in to-day.
Our future men the *now* must educate
Or else our glory finds a wreck on fate.
Look at the specimens we sometimes meet,
From shining beavers down to kid-cased feet,
Got up by tailors with the barbers' aid,
Instead of being honest and self-made,
Society takes in these brainless foes,
And judges worth full often by its clothes.
O, I have wondered in indignant pride
How long mere money must be dignified.
How long 't will buy the counsels of the land
And place its honor in dishonor's hand,
If ever to us comes an honest age
Of honest men, 't would surely take no sage
To tell that round the children must be brought
That which shall rear them to unbiased thought.
This is no mawkish sentiment to me,
'T is what is possible, and what should be.
Unthinking pates dressed up in hat and curls,
But burlesque manhood and degrade the world.
Led here and there alike, to good or ill,
By just the force of some strong will
Without the power of self sustaining thought,
Are doing all alone the things they ought.
The years must find these children weak or strong.
In right's defence, or in destroying wrong,
The years will bring them work enough to do,
'T is ours to make them to this labor true.
I've spoke of rearing manhood up to power.
Has womanhood a less important dower?

A frail hand she has and yet its grasp
Has held and molded history in the past;
A lower voice, and yet its every tone
Has had a wider power than that of home,
'T were better for the world if woman stood
True evermore unto her womanhood.
Had we more women with their guiding spell,
And less of ladies, 't would be quite as well.
Our modern girls must learn to *parlez vous*,
The latest fancy dances must go through,
Play grand pianos with their useless hands
Until they catch some unspecting man,
And, like a moth, in fashion's tempting glare,
Destroy a life that might be true and fair
Accomplishments are good, but what's a blink
At this and that if we do n't learn to think?
And what are all things if the heart and eye
Go not beyond them with an earnest, Why?
Why tread the world so deaf to every sound,
When choirs of voices palpitate around?
Why blindly walk with eyes that do not see,
When every footfall covers mystery?
Why waste the vigor and light of youth,
In folly's way just side by side with truth?
We lose the strength and granduer of the mind
Because its truest use we fail to find.
And lose so many lessons, wisdom fraught,
Because we do not find the power of thought
Our pupils' future will be what our care
Shall make their pathway; it will lead them, where?
I 've tried to stand from theory apart,
And say what 's welling from an honest heart.
I love our work, and 't were enough for me,
Were I the teacher that I long to be,
Could I perform my duty just as well
As I desire, but have not power to tell.
We may grow weary often in our way,
But strength will come to clothe us every day.
Courage! Look upward with unfaltering eye,
The lives we bless will bless us by and by.

Courage ! There is an eye and hand above
Who knows each trial in our work of love,
And guardian angels hovering overhead,
Will garner up the sheaves when we are dead.

[Written for the Detroit *Tribune*]

A SUNSET ON DETROIT RIVER.

Through the air twixt earth and heaven
  Autumn spreads her veil unseen,
And the sunlight falling through it,
  Had a soft and tender sheen,
      Floating gayly, floating idly,
        In the golden sunset time,
      Rocked we gently to the rythm,
        Of the water's perfect rhyme.

Up the river with the sunlight
  Laughing at us from each wave,
Drinking in the wealth of gladness,
  That the hand of nature gave.
      Up the river, floating idly,
        In the sunset's golden glow ;
      On the west the clouds were crimson,
        On the east as white as snow.

Up the river where "Belle Island"
  Parts the waters with its green ,
Round and past its wave-locked beauty
  There we glided down the stream.
      Down the river, floating idly,
        With the river and the sky
      Both baptized in perfect beauty,
        Colored both with richest dye.

Down the river swept the steamer,
  Down the westward swept the sun ,
Of the faces then around me,
  I remember now but one.

> Floating gayly, floating idly,
> > I'm not certain but the skies
> Looked to me a little brighter,
> > For the glance of other eyes

Down the river toward the steeples
  And the noises of the town,
I'm not certain but I'd liked it
  Just a little farther down.
> > Down the river, floating idly,
> > > Gazing at the sunset's glow,
> > And with not a lesser pleasure,
> > > Looking at a face I know.

Down the river swept the steamer,
  Down the westward swept the sun,
And before I hardly knew it
  Had the grayer twilight come
> > Floating gayly, floating idly,
> > > I remember still the day;
> > And I wonder if the picture
> > > From one mind has passed away.

Detroit, March, 1862.

[For the *Advertiser and Tribune*]

IS IT A TIME FOR MIRTH?

Is it a time for mirth, when o'er us glooming
  Rolls the dark cloud and angry voice of war?
When from our skies the long, long gloom has driven
  Almost the only ray of hope's bright star?

Is it a time for mirth, when ties are broken,
  And lips all chiseled to a stony calm
Speak farewells that make hearthstones sadly dreary,
  And darken hearts that God-ward look for balm?

Is it a time for mirth, when all the wires
    That bring us tidings, now but tell of death?
When fear drifts into homes, e'en with the sunlight,
    And printed pages hush the very breath?

Is it a time for mirth, when pale hands weary
    Of the long conflict, and the bitter strife
Told over hearts that far from home's dear comfort,
    From some low couch of pain go into life?

Or when upon some field the day has reddened,
    Cold, marble faces at the nightfall lie
With no tear save the pitying dew of heaven,
    No watcher save the stars, so far and high?

They went from 'mong us, and we wept their going;
    Each roll-call finds some brave hearts missing there;
It seems to me Columbia's sons and daughters
    Have little time for anything but prayer

Is it a time for mirth, when Right and Freedom,
    The world's last hope, are in the field to-day?
When all we love, our country and her glory,
    Turns on the hour, for grandeur or decay?

'T is time for patient hope and earnest courage,
    A time for faith in Him who rules the earth,
A time for deeds and words, all strong and manly,
    But 'neath God's chastening, is it time for mirth?

Detroit, Feb. 17, 1863.

SHADOWS.

I have watched the twilight fading,
    Like a joy upon the wall;
And like a memory round me
    Have seen the shadows fall.

I have sat here, just remembering,
    Until the shadowy night
Stole silent o'er the threshold,
    As outward passed the light.

Upon the shores of Memory
    I have seen the ebb and flow;
And heard the mystic murmurs
    Of the waves of long ago

But the dream at last was broken
    By a footfall at the door,
And I looked and saw a shadow,
    As it lay upon the floor.

And it was but a shadow,
    For that light, familiar tread
Sought long ago, and early,
    The pathway of the dead.

But like some song, whose key-note
    The heart long, long has felt,
So I've treasured up the music
    Of that low and gentle step

And full often when the sunset
    Is just mingling with the night,
The darkness overlaying,
    And shutting out the light,

Then I hear the muffled footfall
    Come softly, as of yore —
Can you tell me why it pauses
    Forever at the door?

Marshall, Mich , 1859.

[From the *Jackson Citizen*, June 5.]

DIED.

At East Saginaw, May 18th, SARAH J., wife of W. R. Burt, and sister of Mrs. C. C. Lathrap, of this city.

We laid her away in her beauty —
    The fair, young mother and wife.
She who had done her duty
    And passed to an endless life.

We folded her white hands softly
    Over the heart at rest,
And clasping like palms of victory
    The green leaves over her breast.

We laid her away in her beauty,
    And she looked so rested at last,
Mid the silken folds of her coffin,
    We knew that all pain was past.

We wept as we looked upon her,
    But gazing, our tears grew dry.
For her, was the way all trodden;
    For her, all the night gone by.

For her, was the land of morning,
    The snowy robe and the palm.
For us, was the pain and the shadow,
    And the heart's great cry for balm.

She dwells in God's beautiful summer —
    God's endless, wonderful year —
But alas! for the feet that journey
    Without her, the pathway here.

Alas! for the motherless wee ones,
    Since *she* wakens not to their call.
Alas! for the strong heart that's smitten,
    Of him she loved better than all.

Alas ! for us *all* that have loved her,
   As the old pain comes back at the dawn,
When waking, we sum up our sorrow,
   "Another night she has been gone."

We laid her away in her beauty,
   But the last of such farewells shall fall,
When unto the "rest she has entered,"
   She welcomes the last of us all

[For the *Expounder*]

SO SOON!

IN MEMORY OF JAMES M PARSONS.

So soon from the weary marches,
   So soon from the toil and pain,
So soon from the sad, stern conflict,
   He comes to us once again.
He comes, for the battle's ended,
   A wonderful peace came down
As the soldier obeyed the order
   From the conflict to the crown.

He comes from his post of duty,
   Back to his home to-day,
And oh ! it is so much sooner
   Than we dreamed when he went away.
He went, with his young, strong manhood,
   All ready to do and dare ;
He comes with a strange, strange quiet,
   A hush on the brow so fair.

So soon, with his hands all folded
   Across in so calm a sleep,
It stirs not the eyelids laying
   Their fringe on the quiet cheek.

So soon is the work all finished,
  So soon have the dear feet trod
The path that leads through the shadow
  Out into the light of God.

What matters it that his going
  Was not where the loving band
Of his own, own home might watch him,
  On his way to the other land?
What matters it, when a better
  Than father or mother was there,
When round him the watching angels
  Gave more than a sister's care?

He sleeps, and our hearts are grieving
  O'er hopes that are unfulfilled;
He sleeps — and our hearts are crying
  Out after the heart that's stilled.
He sleeps — our passionate sorrow
  He only who smote can tell.
But can we, when looking upward,
  Still fail to say, "It is well"?

Farewell — in the night we linger,
  But the morning land is thine,
Through the shadows now between us
  We'll pass in our Father's time.
Farewell — tho' deep was our loving
  He loved thee better than we,
So sent his messenger saying:
  "Beloved come higher" to me.

Detroit, Jan. 24, 1863.

"AS THY DAY, SO SHALL THY STRENGTH BE."

Hark! a solemn voice is speaking
  To the dwellers here below;
Softly on the air 't is stealing,
  Like some harp-note, soft and low,

And its gentle words are breathing
   Hope and joy divinely free,
As 't is ever, ever whispering,
   "As thy day, thy strength shall be."

Listen, weary, way-worn pilgrim —
   Trav'ler o'er life's toilsome way,
Unto thee the promise given,
   "Strength sufficient for thy day."
Youth, whose fondest hopes are blighted,
   Hark! that sweet voice speaks to thee,
Tho' thy trusting heart be slighted,
   "As thy day, thy strength shall be."

Mortal, say, art thou earth weary,
   Has thy path been lone and dark,
Are thy future prospects dreary?
   Comfort comes unto your heart;
Our life-dream is not all pleasure,
   Sorrow there must mingled be;
But the promise faileth never —
   "As thy day, thy strength shall be."

Courage! faint one, know thy mission,
   Though thou here may suffer long,
Teach thy heart life's *sternest* lesson,
   How to "suffer and be strong."
Has thy past been full of sorrow?
   So thy future way may be;
As to-day, so on the morrow,
   "As thy day, thy strength shall be"

Mortal, hush thy heart's wild murmur,
   Draw not future's veil aside,
Let earth's trials make thee firmer —
   God is ever near thy side.
Though the wail of true hearts broken,
   On the air is borne to thee,
Yet remember God hath spoken,
   "As thy day, thy strength shall be."

Marshall, July 6, 1857.

[For the *Expounder*.]

LIFE.

What is life? is it an hour
  Of vain and idle dreaming?
Is this world a solemn real,
  Or a transient seeming?
Is our destiny a thing
  With which we here may trifle?
Or a deep and meaning charge,
  Teeming with the awful?

What is life? a widening stream
  Adown which we are floating,
But, is it no matter where
  Our strange journey's leading?
Every day a wave that bears
  Our frail life-boat farther;
Dare we, then, sweep heedless on,
  Never asking whither?

Is life naught, when every act
  Is a thing undying?
And our thoughts, swift winged as light;
  Through the world are flying?
E'en our heart's low, measured beat,
  Sets some other throbbing,
And the tear drops we let fall,
  Wake an echoed sobbing.

We're not writing on the sand,
  By the shifting waters,
But upon the fadeless scroll
  Of the *hearts of others.*
Angels from the "other shore,"
  Wonder much that mortals
Sport where falls the shadow
  Of eternity's dim portals.

Life's an anthem, and its strains
    Through *three worlds* are stealing,
And along the arch of each,
    Every note is pealing.
Death will speak the *amen* here,
    But beyond the river,
Shall the ceaseless anthem tell,
    Joy or woe *forever*.
Marshall, Jan. 31, 1859.

[For the *Republican*.]

AN ANSWER — TO MISANTHROPE.

Saddened heart amid life's shadows,
    Does thy lonely spirit stand,
Weeping o'er some wreck that sorrow
    Left for thee upon life's strand?
Into darkness hast thou wandered,
    Haunted by a bitter doubt,
Looking every way but *upward*,
    For some hand to lead thee out?

I will tell thee why we mourn,
    Often, o'er our darkened fate,
'Tis because our restless spirits
    Never, never learn to *wait*,
'Tis because in pride we question
    If our Father's ways are just,
Seeking ever for the *reason*
    Where He wills, that we shall *trust*.

If we trusted in *his* goodness
    'Mid the gloom of sorrow's night,
Waiting for his hand to lead us
    Through the darkness into light,
Tho' we still wept o'er our treasures,
    We would know a blow from Him
Came not save in love and mercy,
    Unto us, and unto them.

"Have I faith in a hereafter?"
  Yes, a strong o'ermastering faith,
Looking with triumphant glances,
  Far beyond the stream of death;
I have seen the *loved* and *gifted*,
  Midway of life's journey fall,
With their glorious course unfinished,
  They have died — but is that all?

What were *eloquence*, if dying
  With the *breath* upon the tongue?
What were *poesy's* wrapt numbers,
  If the lyre could be unstrung?
What were *knowledge*, if its fountains
  Only for an hour it gave?
What were *love*, if it were bounded
  By the *cradle* and the *grave?*

If the soul's unconquered longings
  Ne'er shall hope's fruition find,
To his most sublime creation
  Then has God been most unkind,
And if *all* men's meager portion
  Is a few years — then a spot
Where to sleep — is he not poorer
  Than the beasts, that reason not?

Yes, sad heart, there's a "hereafter,"
  Where the *reason* we shall see,
Why we're led to *light* through *darkness,*
  And through *pain* to *purity;*
Trust it — for of all the orphans
  'Neath the sun that shines above,
O, the loneliest and saddest,
  Is the one that *doubts* God's love!

Marshall, Jan. 20, 1861.

[For the *Expounder*]

DREAMS.

Bright are my dreams.
Not brighter are the beams that gild
   The far off Oriental hills,
Nor richer dyes, along the west,
   Glow as the day-god sinks to rest,
     His labor done

High are my dreams
Not higher are the stars that sleep
   Far up in yonder azure deep ;
Nor yet the beauteous orb of light
   That sweeps across the skies at night,
     With silent step

Grand are my dreams.
Not grander is the thunder's tone
   Rolling across yon bended dome ,
Nor more sublime the storm king's wrath,
   Leaving all desolate his path,
     As he rides on.

Wild are my dreams.
Wild as the wind-harp's thrilling chimes
   That roll so grandly through the pines
And deep as ocean's solemn roar,
As 'mong its caves, or on the shore
     Its waters break.

Calm are my dreams.
Just like the lakelet's silver breast,
   When all is still, and hushed to rest ,
Or like a river, broad and free,
   Majestic sweeping to the sea.
     In conscious might

'T is thus I dream
A mingled chain of wild and fair,
  A mystic web of colors rare,
Now bathed in Heaven's immortal light,
  Now dark and fathomless as night,
    A shifting scene.

    Still let me dream.
The chainless wing of thought shall bear
  My soul above all earthly care;
Till life's last dream my soul sweeps o'er,
And I awake to dream no more
    In bliss that 's real

[Written for the *Expounder*]

"MONEY MAKES THE MAN."

In this learned age of maxims broad and deep,
When men wake famous after one night's sleep;
When the forked lightnings, from the sky bro't down,
Carry the various news the earth around —
In these fast days of wonder and of steam,
Even society is one vast machine.

Words cannot tell the many parts that meet,
To make this mighty structure all complete,
Nor volumes give the rules that must be known,
E'er this charmed circle can become your home.
One thing we 'll speak of — just one simple fact
That guides the wheels and keeps them on the track;
'T is all important in the mystic plan,
So mark it well now — "Money makes the man!"

Talk not of homage humble worth should claim,
Proud lips will curl at mention of the name;
Nor yet of flowers, within some shaded place,
Whose beauty might some better station grace

No, you must have, or *seem* to have, a purse,
That spending much — for that is not the worse;
Your clothes the "latest cut" must all be made,
E'en tho' the tailor's bill is long unpaid.
Be sure you stop at the "first" house in town,
Altho' for board your trunk is levied on;
To be a pet, make all the show you can,
Keeping in mind that — Money makes the man!

And you, young man of fashionable life,
When you conclude to find yourself a wife,
Do n't choose a maid who ever used her hand,
Except to hold boquets or flirt a fan.
Young ladies, too, who would a husband gain,
Look out for *money* — never mind the brain;
For now-a-days, as all must understand,
Not intellect, but — *Money* makes the man!

'T is stubborn truth, tho' it should be denied,
Society is rife with silly pride,
And many a warm, aspiring soul is crushed
E'er manhood's noontide, even to the dust,
While many another who has dyed their soul
In sin, has glossed it with their glittering gold,
Indulging in the darkest, deepest guile,
Yet meeting in the throng the welcome smile,
Which proves it true — deny it if you can —
Not worth nor wit, but — *Money* makes the man!

But man's no less a man because he's poor,
Nor woman lovely less, tho' quite obscure;
No villain less the foe of good, tho' proud
He walks, the favored one of fashion's crowd,
And real worth, less noble sure is not,
If it be uncommended and forgot;
And just as bright is virtue's chaplet now,
Tho' it may rest above a poor man's brow,
For in the eyes of Him who hearts doth scan,
'T is *purity*, not — Money makes the man!

Alike for lofty and for lowly spread
The same sky's changing, shifting blue o'erhead ;
For poor and rich alike the flowers bloom,
And wave as sadly over both their tombs
Oh ! when within the " great beyond " we stand,
Not by his *money* will God judge the man !

Marshall, April 27, 1858.

[For the Marshall *Statesman*.]

ACTIONS — NOT WORDS.

Go, freeman, hang your banner out,
   Boast of its stripes and stars ;
Tell how it conquers on the sea,
   Tell of the fame it bears ;
Fling out its colors to the breath
   Of every passing gale,
Then stand beneath its folds and list
   Unto the bondsman's wail !

Go, rear your eagle to the sky,
   And glory in your might ;
Boast of your country strong and free,
   The world's great beacon light ;
Then bend 'neath freedom's chosen crest,
   Your brows in piteous shame,
For your free hills now echo back
   The clang of slavery's chain.

Go, dream your star of glory burns
   With light that will not fade ;
Dream that time's latest day shall find
   Its grandeur undecayed ;
Then look upon the glittering clouds
   That fill the darkening sky,
And shout the oldest words again,
   " To conquer or to die ! "

Your danger lies not at the South.
    Your foes are nearer home,
Where puny souls are cringing low
    For place, and place alone;
Where coward politicians crawl,
    To please the public throng.
Great heaven! that men should meekly bow
    And kiss the hand of wrong!

Your danger lies not at the South,
    For traitors' feet now tread
Upon the very soil where once
    Your noble grandsires bled;
And hearts as dark and false as hell,
    And hands that are untrue,
Are lightly trifling with the rights
    Entrusted unto you.

Yes, traitors stand on freedom's soil,
    And league with slavery's clan,
And here before your very face,
    Your own destruction plan;
And you have yielded inch by inch,
    Your sacred claims to them.
For shame! When will your actions prove
    The North has sterling men!

Then rail no more against the South,
    Until the Northern press
Shall plead the cause of freedom more,
    And party doctrines less;
Till bar and pulpit both are free
    From men who crush the weak,
Or what is worse, from craven tongues
    Too cowardly to speak!

Firm be the heart and strong the hand
    Your mission to perform;
Unflinching stand for human right
    And combat human wrong.

But yet let every deed you do,
   The golden rule fulfil,
For though you deal with freedom's foes,
   They are your brethren still.

Marshall, June 15, 1860.

[For the *Expounder*.]

SUNSET ON A LAKE.

Adown behind the woodland,
   In glory sank the sun,
And o'er the rippling waters
   A farewell halo flung.
And we *almost* heard the rustle
   Of the curtains in the west,
As their gorgeous folds were lifted,
   To wrap his couch of rest.

The lazy, floating cloudlets,
   In their journey paused awhile,
To bathe them in the glory
   Of the sunset's parting smile;
While the waveless sea of ether,
   He left in blushes still,
'Neath the parting kiss he gave it,
   As he sank behind the hill.

The fair, light-winged breezes,
   Stole the whisp'ring waters o'er,
And woke a quivering anthem
   'Mong the poplars on the shore.
There in a thrilling silence,
   That *none had dared to break*,
Each drew a memory painting
   Of that sunset on the lake

The moist eye, as we listened
   To the wave wash at our feet.
Told better far than language,
   The thoughts we *could not speak*.

The waters slept, and dreaming
    At their beauty-haunted side,
We lingered till the moonlight
    Flung its sheen upon the tide.

Then, as the bells of evening,
    With a distant, dreamy chime,
To the dashing of the waters
    Were softly keeping time,
We turned away — but ever
    The olden chord will wake,
As comes the memory whisper,
    Of that sunset on the lake

Marshall, March, 1859

[For the *Expounder*]

SNOW.

Soft as the fall of a beautiful thought,
    Or a leaf on the stream,
White as the robe by purity wrought,
    Bright as the flow of a dream.
Calm as a sleeping infant's breath,
Cold as the brow just touched by death,
Falleth in many a graceful wreath
    Gently, the beautiful snow.

Caught like a robe on the leafless trees,
    With diamonds in every fold;
Stepping like sprites where the fallen leaves
    Mingle their brown and gold.
Covering over the graves of the flowers,
And those *other* graves where gems of ours
We laid away in summer hours,
    Now resteth the gentle snow.

Falling to gladden the hearts of some,
  With the joys it has in store;
Falling to chill, in the hovel home,
  The souls of the suffering poor.
Melting to pearls on the brow of the glad,
Melting to tears on the cheek of the sad,
What gladdens the one, drives the other mad,
  Oh! coldly beautiful snow.

Bright as the clouds where the sun goes down,
  Is thy fall to the happy heart,
Cold as the world with its bitter frown,
  To the child of woe thou art.
But if thy coming shall cheer or chill,
One hand yet gathers the winds at will,
And the eye of the Sleepless is watching still,
  In pity, O, pitiless snow!

Marshall, Nov 16, 1859.

[For the Detroit *Advertiser and Tribune*]

SIC ITUR AD ASTRA.

EAST SAGINAW, AUG 5, 1862

I send you from my vacation sojourn, more lines on the *same subject*. I need make no apology — our hearts are all too full of our country's fate to wonder that we talk of it most of all It is hard to possess our souls in patience in this gloomy pause of affairs, and in my impatience I am half angry to see men placing *money* where *hearts* should be — between our country and her foe. Gold may help, but men must stand where men have fallen, and stand there without wishing to be Brigadier-Generals, so as to get more than a private's pay for their patriotism, ere our case is won.

  Yours, anti-strategy,
          LENA

The mournful sound of the muffled drum,
  The peal of the solemn bell
With the measured tread of many feet,
  Has spoken the soldier's knell.

It is over now — the soldier sleeps ;
    So soon is the sword laid down,
So soon for him did the order come —
    From the conflict to the crown

Tears are in eyes that are seldom dim,
    And the proudest cheeks are pale ;
Fairbanks has folded his arms in rest,
    And passed beyond the veil.
Not few are mourning beside his bier,
    But hundreds of hearts are bent,
As God rolls o'er us the solemn tide,
    Of his mournful providence.

We know how nobly was duty done,
    How needed the heart that fell ;
And must needs look up for a higher strength,
    Before we can say 't is well
And we know this too — O, hold it close
    To your heart with a sterner pride ,
Let it make you *act — the cause we love,*
    Is dearer because he died !

Close not the ranks, till that vacant place
    That he left shall speak its plea ,
Close not your ranks till avengers stand,
    To dare or to die as he.
Shall his sword rest long ? O, answer ye,
    Who loved him ye bore away ;
Have the calm, mute lips no deep reproach
    For you, if you dare to stay ?

His work is over — for country's sake,
    All, even life was given,
And his peace is won — the Christian went
    From wounds and strife to heaven
Your work's to do ! for our country drifts
    Toward the wrathful breakers yet ;
'T was *treason* that laid a Fairbanks low —
    Are ye *men*, if ye *forget?*

[Written for the *Expounder*]

THE ATLANTIC CABLE.

T' is done — from where mid-ocean's solemn organ rolls
   Its echoed anthem through its thousand caves,
The noble ships sweep on to either shore,
   While breathless thousands watched the rocking waves.

'T is done — no ruder gale than two proud nation's hopes
   Swept o'er those barks, upon the swelling tide;
Each wave that bore them on its billowy crest,
   Bade them "God speed," with its low murmuring glide.

'T is done — the electric chain its fiery belt has clasped
   Around two nations, and has made them one,
Man's intellect has taken a daring flight,
   And shouts its triumph o'er the laurel won.

The sons of Genius, not content that thought
   Should leave its tracery e'en on heaven's height,
Or bear away to "isles unknown to song,"
   The dazzling splendor of the noon-day's light,

Has in the mid-realm, with the world shut out,
   Conceived a newer and a stranger scheme;
And living hands have made the wonder real,
   That erst seemed but fantasy's wildest dream.

Atlantic's waters are not stirred alone,—
   Now, by the motion of its ebb and flow
Each wave now trembles with a thrilling thought,
   As its swift shaft glides onward far below.

And the glad shouts, a people's joy proclaim,
   And to the world the victory proudly tells,
While from far England's "dasied shores" there comes
   The tide-like echo in its wave-like swells

As age on age rolls to oblivion's sea,
   It leaves the trace of some great action done,
And ne'er till time shall grow gray haired and die,
   Shall the *last* trophy of the mind be won.

Marshall, Aug. 13, 1858.

[For the *Expounder.*]

IN MEMORIAM.

I will not say, "Weep not for him,"
   For tears are holy now,
But weep them with a deep-hushed heart,
   And low-bent, reverent brow.

I will not say, "Mourn not for him,"
   When gathering round the bier,
But mourn with awe, remembering
   That heaven has come so near

I will not say, Sigh not above
   The calmly-pillowed head,
Our hearts are human, and must throb
   With anguish o'er the dead.

The dead? Oh! when the lofty stars
   Melt out in yonder sky;
When morning loops night's drapery back —
   Do *they* in fading, *die?*

And when o'er day's great "sleepless eye,"
   Falls evening's fringed lid,
Is there one ray of glory lost
   Because its beams are hid?

Nor is *he* lost, tho' now he sleeps
   The slumber we call *death;*
And all that makes it this to us,
   Is that we miss his breath.

He only sleeps, the years have passed,
   That unto him were given,
His upward path has reached a height
   From which he stepped to heaven.

Marshall, Jan. 12, 1860.

THE WORKS OF THE YEARS.

Some things have grown into beauty,
   And some things have gone to decay,
New ones are taking the places
   Of the old that have faded away.
And here 'mid the multiplied changes,
   In scenes that were one day so dear,
Half way 'twixt the tear-drop and smiling
   I sum up the work of the years.

In the ways that the past has made holy
   The foot of the stranger I see,
And the home they call theirs is all fragrant
   With wonderful mem'ries to me
Ah, wide are the pathways that meet us
   Strewn thick with life's sunshine and tears,
With a height now and then, where our vision
   May measure the work of the years.

The church, where far back in my childhood
   I learned the old story and blest
Stands yet, but its gray revered elders
   Have passed to a marvelous rest,
And some in youth's bloom were laid by them
   To sleep, amid heartbreak and tears,
While others pass into their places —
   And such is the work of the years.

Sad ? yes, were that all of the story,
   But time has a wonderful hand
That may fashion our souls into beauty,
   If we will, that our lives shall be grand

We may gather up glory from ashes,
    And strength from our sorrow and fears,
Till bearing us safe to God's heaven,
    Shall be the last work of the years.

Marshall, Nov. 16, 1875

[For the *Advertiser and Tribune.*]

LABOR AND REST.

There are groves where the cool shadows linger,
    Where the breezes are freighted with calm,
And streams thread the plain with their silver,
    Each ripple the note of a psalm;
A land where life's tumult is over —
    Its sorrow, and longing and grief —
A land where the spirit's unresting
    Is bathed in a wonderful peace;
        But not here — no, no! 'tis not here!

Not here, where life's battle is raging,
    And shadows drift into our way;
Where success or defeat must be written
    At the close of every day.
The cry of the great world is onward
    And on, without pausing to rest;
But the toiling will one day be over,
    And the heart of the weary be blest!
        But not here — no, no! not here!

Not here is a moment for sighing,
    There's work for the humblest to do;
And 'tis all of our Father's ordaining,
    Ere rest, must the toil be passed through.
All round us the saddened are crying,
    'Neath crosses they need help to bear,
And hearts to be blest and uplifted,
    By kindness, and pity, and prayer
        Rest not here — no, no! not here!

There are wandering feet to be guided
  From sin to the beautiful way,
And sad, lonely eyes to be lighted
  By gleams from a perfected day,
Our own lives, each day, to be chiseled,
  To symmetry, God-like and pure,
So the work that in time we are doing
  Shall on through the ages endure.
    Rest not here — no, no! not here!

Then scatter the sunlight — what matter,
  Tho' you have but little of light —
Your words and your deeds may outblossom,
  As stars, in *another's* dim light.
At the end of life's rock-waste is lying,
  A wonderful, beautiful land,
The rest, and the peace, and the glory
  Will come to your spirit like balm
    Rest not here — no, no! not here!

Detroit, June 25, 1863.

THE NIGHT BEFORE ELECTION.

There's a battle for to-morrow, then, freemen, cool your brain,
This is no time to trifle, there is too much to gain;
For ere to-morrow's sun has set below the western sky,
At Michigan's free ballot box, the *wrong* or *right* must die.

There's a conflict for to-morrow, and though no man may fall,
Yet something there may perish that is dearer than thy all,
Then question your heart deeply, in the sight of God to-night,
See that your hand to-morrow makes sure the blow for right.

Down on the field of battle *our* soldiers wait the day.
If you are false or faltering, what will our brave ones say?
Their manhood's *all* is given — shall they toil on alone?
While that for which they're dying, is voted down at home?

Our State's brave sons are battling against our country's foe,
But all her enemies are not where Southern breezes blow ;
For you will meet to-morrow what's worse than they, now mark !
Assassins at the ballot box, stab Freedom in the dark.

Our soldiers look toward you with confidence and pride,
The blood of many speaketh, from fields where they have died.
Then dare you, dare you falter ? O, withered be the hand
That casts a vote to darken the shadow of our land.

No compromise with treason, no tenderness for those
Whose love for dark oppression has deluged us with woes,
No men who call *them* brethren, who 've dimmed our banner's stars,
No men save those who 'd crush them beneath the heel of war.

The night before election ! O freemen, cool your brain,
Compute your country's peril, and what you have to gain ;
Question your heart in silence before high heaven to-night,
And may the God of nations protect and speed the right !

Detroit, Nov 3, 1862

[For the *Citizen*]

ELECTION.

'T is the morning of election , O freemen, cool your brain,
There 's a battle to be fought, and a victory to gain ;
If victory be defeated at the setting of the sun,
God knows if that misdoing can ever be undone.

'T is the morning of election ; O freemen, stop an hour
To calm all idle passion, to calculate the power
Of the little white-winged ballot, whose yes or no shall be
The ring of blight or blessing in the counsels of the free

'T is the morning of election ; O freemen, stop to pray,
The maddest waves of passion break at your feet to-day ;
To-day God lays the future in your free, untrameled hand ;
To-morrow he may judge you if you fail to understand

'T is the morning of election; O freemen, dare to say
You believe all men are equal in the sight of Heaven to-day;
Fling off the chains of prejudice, and with your own right hand
Give justice and the glory of manhood unto man

'T is the morning of election, dark faces look to you —
Of men who did their duty when they wore their coats of blue;
God remembers all the valleys their blood and tears have wet,
And he shall judge you, freemen, if you shall dare forget.

'T is the morning of election; there is duty to be done,
And some shall do that duty, blind, staggering — drunk with rum;
Mad hands will cast the ballot, when brain and soul are lost
In the power of this demon, O freeman, count the cost.

Is it best to license rum? Have not souls enough gone down?
Enough of hapless women yet worn the martyr's crown?
Enough of homes been blighted, enough of lone graves filled?
The future 's what you make it — the past was as you willed.

'T is the morning of election; O freemen, cool your brain;
There 's a battle to be fought and a victory to gain
The crown of yew or laurel waits Michigan to night,
Your hands shall crown her, freeman; may God defend the right!

[For the *Daily Citizen.*]

A SCENE.

These city streets are full of wrong and sorrow —
  Dark, bitter things that never see the light,
Black crimes against the human race and heaven,
  Are shut from us by walls, and hid by night.

But *some* infernal things walk right among us,
  Beneath the blaze of God's own blessed sun,
Come from below, with hell's own mark upon them,
  And men endure it — letting them pass on.

These fiends stalk near us, often on a sudden
   They strike a blow, and all that's pure goes down;
A soul is lost — a manhood crushed forever,
   We sigh or censure, while the curse moves round.

Why write I thus? — Because a piteous victim
   Lay 'neath my feet a wreck, but yesterday;
I do not know what monster bought his manhood,
   And gave him *rum*, but God will sure repay.

He lay upon the street, the hot sun pouring
   On the limp form, unpitied save by few,
Scorned by the throng that should have wept above him;
   He was a soldier, in our country's blue.

The drooping face was brown with weary marches,
   Through storm and danger 'neath the South sun's glow.
The life God willed to spare through every battle,
   Some demon dared to wreck with one swift blow.

This is not man — I've seen these veteran heroes,
   For whom a world stands with uncovered head,
In those blue coats that every heart should rev'rence,
   Lie on these streets degraded, *worse* than dead.

O men in power! what worth have hollow welcomes?
   Defend from *rum* our noble boys in blue;
If some are weak, 't is you who should defend them,
   When did they fail America or you?

Jackson.

[For the *People's Press*]

CLOUD-LAND.

Gazing off into the cloud-land
   Tinted with the sunset's glow,
Watching waves of gold and purple
   O'er the silent ether glow;
Gazing on the clouds that grandly
   Climb the arches of the sky,
And upon those fleecy idlers
   In their beauty gliding by;

Much I wonder who are dwelling
  On those far, etherial shores,
And whose feet, unseen, are treading
  O'er those amethystine floors.
Much I wonder if the spirits
  Of the loved ones, upward flown
From those bright, mysterious regions,
  On us are still looking down

Tell me, are those snowy cloudlets
  Only shadows on the sky?
May they not be angel pinions
  Seen by us while passing by?
Coming in the twilight shadows
  Nearer to us than by day,
With a silent benediction
  On us as they pass away?

Gazing off into the cloud-land
  Tinted with the sunset hue,
Seem they not like gauzy curtains,
  Letting half the glory through,
Till we almost see beyond them
  Through the vistas, long and grand,
And the heavy folds of darkness
  Drop from evening's silent hand?

Marshall, December, 1860.

[For the *Detroit Tribune*]

LINES,

Written on Seeing a Piece of Statuary.

Western clouds with sunsets gleaming
  Looked like ocean's tinted shell;
Down to earth, the quiet gleaming
  With the saintly snow-flakes fell —
Half in cloud and half in sunlight
  Died the day of which I tell.

In that hour I crossed the threshold
  Of a church all gray and dim,
Where the quaintly colored windows
  Let a solemn halo in,
And I held my breath to listen,
  Half expecting spirit hymns.

Just outside, the restless surges
  Of a human tide swept on.
But within, baptized in silence
  As if into marble grown,
Knelt one figure at the altar,
  Silent, motionless, alone

In the shadows stood the organ,
  Like the oracle of old,
Silent now, and from the altar,
  In her eyes a woe untold,
Looked the grief-enshrouded Mary
  At our Saviour, still and cold

Wordless woe in every feature,
  Save the gulf of sorrow told
In the great, sad eyes so haunted,
  By the anguish in the soul;
Love unfathomed, woe unmeasured,
  Gave the face a power untold.

There was solemn, God-like grandeur
  In the dead Christ's deep repose,
As if Death *himself* were kinder,
  And, more rev'rent than his foes,
He had touched the brow in pity,
  Taking thence its shade of woes

It was only sculptured marble
  That I stood entranced beside,
But a *human* love and sorrow
  Spoke the mournful mother's eyes;
And the *other;* words divine —
  "I so loved the world," I died.

Detroit, March 5, 1862

[For the *Expounder.*]

THE FAITH OF CHILDHOOD.

Turn backward, turn backward, O tide of the years
    And just for an hour give back
The buds and the blossoms of earth that have died
    In the heat of my life's dusty track ,
Turn backward life's pages of sorrow and pain,
And give me the faith of my childhood again.

Roll backward, roll backward, O pitiless stream —
    O relentless, unpitying time —
And give me once more the unquestioning trust
    That I had when life's morning was mine
Take the chill from my heart and the throb from my brain,
And give me, O give me *beliefs* once again !

Turn backward, O time, I'm so weary to-night ,
    Life's pathway so long and so drear
Stole slowly the light that once shone in my heart,
    Leaving less of its gladness each year.
Turn backward, turn backward, O time, is it just
To take all our joys, leaving only distrust?

O, once I had faith in the good and the true,
    I little knew then that deceit
Walked abroad in the garments of honor and truth,
    Telling lies with smiles passing sweet,
Till I woke in amaze from my beautiful dream
To find that the fairest are not what they seem.

Turn backward, turn backward, if just for an hour,
    O time, make me once more a child,
With all of the confidence lost since the days
    When bright stories of fairies beguiled
I know that experience teaches us well,
But O, what bright visions dissolve neath her spell !

In vain do I call to the pitiless years
  That have borne my bright childhood away ;
In vain do I plead for the trust and the faith
  That have died upon life's desert way,
The chill and the scorn of my heart yet remain,
And childhood's sweet trusting comes not back again

Marshall, January 1861.

[For the *Expounder*]

A SONG.

When the quiet lake is sleeping
  With the moonlight on its breast,
And the nightingale is chanting
  Love-hymns by its leafy nest,
When the gentle flowers are bathing
  'Neath the starlight in the dew,
And the violets look sleepy,
  With their half shut eyes of blue ;

When the graceful willow bendeth
  Down to wash its robe of green
From the dust the day threw on it,
  In the sweetly singing stream,
And the breeze hangs *almost* silent,
  On the trees it's ceased to woo,
Lifting now and then a leaflet,
  Just to let the moonlight through,

Then I think of one who wandered
  At my side long, long ago,
Till one felt no joy or sorrow,
  That the *other* did not know ;
Till *each heart* became an altar,
  Love the *priest* who waited there,
And we gave to him our offerings,
  Knelt and gave them with a prayer

But at last there came a shadow,
   Love the hallowed shrine forsook,
And *her* post beside the ruin
   Memory in silence took.
Erst we laid there bud and flower,
   Meet to deck affection's shrine,
Now the dry and withered garlands,
   Mournful Memory, are *thine*.

Tho' the same sky's o'er me bending,
   That we looked upon before,
Yet methinks *less bright it seemeth*
   Than it did in days of yore;
And the flowers have lost their fragrance,
   And the stream its olden tone,
For we've parted now *forever*,
   And I look on them — *alone*.

Marshall, March 24, 1859

[Written for the *News*.]

AUTUMN RAIN.

There's a sad, sad voice in the autumn rain,
        Mournful rain;
As it beateth slowly against the pane,
        Window pane.
And the wind sings by with a conscious breath,
And seems like a messenger whispering death,
As the flowers bend with a drooping eye —
        Bend and die.

What gives such a sadness unto the rain?
        Autumn rain;
For it sobs like a human heart in pain,
        A heart in pain;
Does it know its drops with a chilly tread
Lie cold on the beauty that now is dead?
Does it know the beautiful must decay?
        Passing away.

Sure the summer rain had a merry tone,
    A laughing tone ;
Its patter made melody all its own,
    Yes, all its own ,
The flowers looked up when it came from the skies,
And the drops for mischief fell right in their eyes,
And sparkled in brightness like mimic tears,
    Joyful tears.

Then tell me, why is it this autumn rain,
    Mournful rain,
Chills my very heart as it sweeps the pane?
    Dripping pane.
Is it that it sighs o'er a summer fled,
O'er the graves where more than flowers lie dead ;
Is it that memory lendeth a strain
    To the sobbing rain?

O where are the hopes of the bright spring tide ?
    Sweet spring tide.
With the summer blossoms they too have died,
    Yes, they have died
They have fled away , will their bloom come back?
Will they bless again as I tread life's track?
Or, by and by on some other shore
    Bloom evermore?

Sob on,— it is well,— O passionate rain ,
    'T is well, O rain,
Tho' the flowers now faded may bloom again,
    Will bloom again ;
Some things that have died with the summer's light,
Some things that have fled with the summer's flight,
Will never, no, never, come back again,
    Sob on, O rain !

Marshall, Oct. 30, 1860.

[Written for the Gratiot *News*.]

'NEATH THE WILLOW.

In a cool and quiet valley,
   Where the echoes ever sleep,
And the brooklet always murmurs
   Dreamily its music sweet,
There's an ever mournful willow,
   And an ever solemn pine,
And beneath them in the shadows,
   Sleeps a treasure once called *mine*.

There the sunshine's always paler,
   And the moonlight's mixed with shade,
For to me 'tis ever twilight
   In the spot where she is laid.
And the winds sing measured numbers
   Through the long and bending grass,
Breathing weird and mystic dirges
   For the lost one as they pass

Low the willow's slender branches
   Bend to touch the passing wave,
Scatt'ring oft like fairy fingers
   Crystal drops upon the grave.
And the sad-eyed violets hold them
   In their blue like a mourner's tear;
While the white-robed lillies watch them
   Like a group of angels near.

Clearly twined the myrtle wreath
   O'er the spot a pall of green,
And its pale and tender blossoms
   Fleck it o'er with azure sheen.
Close the ivy leaves are lying
   Softly on the snowy stone,
Veiling from cold eyes the record,
   Keeping it for *mine* alone.

In a far, eternal city
    Where the day is ever bright,
Where no pain or sorrow enters,
    Where there is no death nor night;
There, amid unfading glory
    Shall I clasp the form divine
Of the sleeper 'neath the willow,
    In the shadow of the pine.

Marshall, Mich., August, 1860.

[For the Saginaw Valley *Republican.*]

NO MORE.

No more beneath the linden,
    Or in a maple grove,
Or by the laughing streamlet
    Where oft we used to rove,
Shall we ever, ever wander,
    As we did in days of yore,
To listen to the music
    Of the ripple on the shore

No more the swaying rushes,
    Or the waves of wind-swept grass
Shall whisper old romances
    Unto us as they pass;
Nor the green, caressing fingers
    Of the swaying wildwood tree,
Bend low to touch thy forehead
    As if 't were blessing thee

Thou 'rt still beside the streamlet
    Where oft we used to sit,
And o'er the turf still lightly
    As of old the shadows flit;
But now above thee bending
    Waves not the linden bough,
But ah! the shivering willow
    Is weeping o'er thee now.

Marshall, July 6, 1860.

INK-DROPS.

The summer blooms are fading
   Upon the lawn and lea,
And I'm thinking as I'm gazing,
   Have they bloomed their last for me?

A darker hue has fallen
   Upon the hill and vale,
While now and then a leaflet
   Floats downward through the gale.

With bounding heart at spring-time
   I loved each bud and stem,
But now when they are drooping,
   I'm drooping, too, with them.

I've had such wild, gay visions
   Of a mission that was mine;
But, perchance, its glad fulfilment
   Lies in another clime.

I have watched the mystic webbing
   That my loom of life has done,
The threads of light and shadow
   It mingled one by one;

And wondered if it gathered
   Those hues of deepest night,
Only to make the seeming
   Of the gayer tints more bright.

Sometimes a thread is broken,
   And a mar is left to tell
Where some fond hope lies buried,
   Or some one cherished fell.

Perhaps 't is almost woven,
   This strangely-mingled web;
Perhaps the weaver holdeth
   E'en now the closing thread.

Marshall, Mich., 1859.

[For the *Expounder*.]

WAVE WHISPERS.

A thrilling of winds through the forest,
    A murmur of waves on the shore,
A gleam from the spray kissed by sunlight,
    While dancing the silver sands o'er;
Wave music, with low bird-songs blended,
    I heard, as I stood on the shore.

The tiny waves rolled to the shoreward,
    And laughingly broke at our feet,
And then with a light, graceful motion,
    Played softly their own bright retreat;
The sands and the waves met as gently
    As warm lips of friends when they greet.

Along by the shore, the bright waters
    Lay shallow upon the white sand,
But I saw them grow deeper and darker
    As they glided away from the strand;
And they danced not so gay 'neath the sunlight,
    As when they were close by the land.

And this was, methought, but a picture,
    The mapping of life's changeful wave
From the time our life-boat's in motion,
    Till it reaches its haven — the grave,
And the soul seeks those mystical borders
    Where rolls immortality's wave.

In the blush of life's beautiful morning,
    We launch our frail barque on the tide,
Where dances the sunlight of pleasure,
    And joy like a phantom doth glide;
But soon drifts our light into shadow,
    And our treasures are scattered full wide.

"Bound outward," the current grows swifter,
   And paler the light that had hung
Like a halo upon the bright ripples,
   To list to the song that they sung;
For now through the gathering shadows
   Its half stolen glory is flung.

A murmur of winds in the forest,
   A music of waves on the shore,
A gleam from the spray kissed by sunlight,
   As 't was dancing the silver sands o 'er;
I thought it like life, and was thankful
   'Twas as bright on the opposite shore.

Marshall, 1859.

THE ERRING.

The latest goal of the suffering soul
   Is wearily reached at last;
     And the brow is cold,
        And the throbless breast
     Of marble-like mold
       Is hushed into rest,
   And the long life struggle 's past.

There are lines of woe on the brow of snow,
   Though the brow is young and fair;
     And the eye once bright,
       Like a shadowed sun
     Has veiled its light
       E'er the noon had come,
   And the spell of peace is there.

Gone from the stain that darkened her name;
   Gone from a cold, careless world,
     Whose heartless neglect
       Made that beautiful soul
     A dark mournful wreck,
       And *it* from the goal
   That 't was long seeking for hurled.

Scorn her not now, the stain on her brow
  Fled 'neath the death-angel's hand ;
    Her bitter soul-cry
      Wailed upward to Heaven,
    And down from the sky
      Came, "Thou art forgiven,"
  Soft as a wave o'er the sand

The way was dark, and her frail life bark
  Was rocked by a storm-lashed deep,
    While a false light shone
      But to lead astray,
    And she turned aside
      From the "better way,"
  While angels bent down to weep.

Then, O how cold to the shuddering soul
  Grew the misty way she trod,
    While her sad heart beat
      Like a muffled drum,
    A long, last retreat
      For the weary one,
  From the world, away to God

Down through the night came a holy light
  From the rifted clouds above,
    And a murmur sweet,
      From the nearing shore
    She was soon to reach,
      Swept the waters o'er ;
  One note from a strain of love

Now the voyage is past — at last, at last,
  The boat has touched the strand,
    While the jewel flown
      From the casket frail,
    Now has found a home
      Safe "within the veil,"
  The veil of the silent land.

Marshall, November 6, 1858.

[Written for the Gratiot *News*]

WE MET AND PARTED.

Where the broad and sweeping river
Onward flows, and on forever,
Going but returning never —
    There we met.
Golden was the bright October,
And, tho' summer's bloom was over,
Gorgeous tints with those more sober,
    Mingled yet

Past us, swift and unreturning,
Rolled the waves in glory burning,
As the sun its broad face turning,
    Looked on them
And we watched the shadows creeping,
Watched them as the day retreating
Was the evening half-way meeting,
    Like a friend.

For a while we stood together —
Looking less upon the river
Than we looked upon each other,
    In that hour.
And we thought less of the picture,
Mapped before our eyes in nature,
Than we did of the dim future
    To be ours.

'Neath the evening skies we parted,
Vowing as the hot tears started,
To be true and honest hearted
    To the last.
But the words you then repeated
Vanished with the years that fleeted,
Leaving mockeries that cheated,
    In the past

Marshall, September 1860.

OCTOBER.

Sad October's mournful song
Rolls the woodland aisles along,
And her hand sweeps o'er the keys
Of the organ mid the trees —
     Waving trees.

Leaflets falling one by one,
Tell the frost-king's work begun;
And the swaying, wind-kissed grass
Withered as his footsteps passed —
     Swiftly passed.

Summer's "upper deep" of blue
Changed to Autumn's shifting hue;
Painted clouds go floating fast,
Each more fleeting than the last —
     Fading fast.

All the grove-choir, one by one,
Followed the receding sun,
As their temple's green grew dim,
Slowly died their sweet-voiced hymn —
     Woodland hymn.

And the flowers, bright summer's pride,
And her offspring, too, have died,
When the mother fled the wild,
Left she there no orphan child —
     Lonely child?

Now the grand old forest, too,
Has a robe of varied hue,
Golden tint and sober gray,
Gorgeous emblems of decay —
     Sad decay.

Autumn's in the woods again,
Through its arches thrills her strain,
As she sweeps the quivering keys
Of the organ mid the trees —
     Dying trees.

[For the Detroit *Tribune*]

GOD O'ERHEAD.

Home of Freedom ! God protected,
   Since the lone, sea-beaten rock
Grew so hallowed 'neath the footsteps
   Of a wandering pilgrim flock ;
Since their lofty adoration
   Borne to heaven on wings of air,
Bathed our country's hour of dawning
   With the holy spell of prayer.
      Now and *then* thy hills are free,
        God has kept a watch o'er thee —
           Watch o'er thee.

Favored land ! Jehovah guided
   Through thy weakness, up to might;
Leading thee in safety onward
   From the darkness into light.
'T was a pathway rough and stormy,
   That our father's footsteps trod ;
But at last the heroes conquered,
   Through their motto, " Trust in God "
      Favored land ! by them made free,
        God has ever watched o'er thee —
           Watched o'er thee

Land of freemen ! hope of nations !
   Freedom's day-star in the west,
Giving 'neath thy starry banner,
   Liberty to the oppressed.
On thy soil our homes are clustered,
   'Neath thy sod our heroes sleep,
And the altar fires of worship
   Brightly glow on every steep.
      Homes and altars both are free,
        God yet keeps a watch o'er thee —
           Watch o'er thee.

Land beloved! our fathers' glory,
   And the shrine that holds their dust,
Shall the swelling notes of freedom,
   Ever on thy hills be hushed?
No; all foes to thee shall perish,
   For with lifted hands we vow,
Never shall the sun in heaven
   See thy hills less free than now.
      Glorious still thy fame shall be,
      God himself is watching thee —
         Watching thee

WEARY.

I'm weary of loving what passes away,
I'm tired of trusting what's sure to decay,
I'm worn out with weeping o'er dreams of the past
That blossomed and faded, too gorgeous to last.

I'm weary of mourning o'er joys that are gone,
And hoping and yearning for something to come;
I'm tired of thinking of that which is o'er,
And listening to waves on the future's dim shore.

I'm sad mid the wrecks of my beautiful dreams,
That fade in their glory like day's dying beams;
Hope veils half the light of Futurity's brow,
And leaves me to shudder in helplessness now.

The flowers I gather will fade in my clasp,
They die but the sooner the tighter my grasp;
The pleasures I sought upon Life's morning strand,
Slip away from my hold like a handful of sand.

I know that God's sunlight is flooding the earth,
I know that the waters are laughing with mirth,
I know that God's flowers are decking the sod,
But they've withered along by the pathway I've trod.

I know that God's music is flooding the air,
I know all his works are surpassingly fair,
But the heart of Humanity's erring and weak,
For aye sorrow-muffled must painfully beat.

I'm weary, so weary, of losses and tears;
I'm so weak as I look down the swift coming years,
That sometimes I long for a sleep without dreams —
A land where the glory unfadingly beams.

I'm tired of trusting what passes away,
I'm weary of loving what's sure to decay,
But though for awhile the heart sadly may sigh,
There's joy, rest, and love which will come bye and bye.

Marshall, June, 1860.

LAURELS AND IMMORTELLES.

TO THE MEMORY OF CHARLES D. MC NAUGHTEN.

He has solved it — life's wonderful problem —
  The deepest, the strangest, the last;
And into the school of the angels
  With the answer forever has passed.

How strange, that in spite of our questions,
  He maketh no answer, nor tells
Why so soon were Yale's honoring laurels
  Displaced by God's own immortelles.

How strange he should sleep so profoundly,
  So young, so unworn by the strife,
While beside him, brim-full of hope's nectar,
  Untouched stands the goblet of life.

Men slumber like that, when the evening
  Of a long, weary day droppeth down;
But he wrought so well, that the morning
  Brought for him the rest and the crown.

'T is idle to talk of the future,
  And the rare " might have been," 'mid our tears ;
God knew all about it, yet took him
  Away from the oncoming years.

God knew all about it — how noble,
  How gentle he was ; and how brave,
How brilliant his possible future —
  Yet *put him to sleep* in the grave.

God knew all about those who loved him,
  How bitter the trial must be ;
And right through it all, God is loving,
  And knows so much better than we.

So, right in the darkness be trustful ;
  One day you shall say ; *It was well :*
God took from his young brow Earth's laurels,
  And crowned him with Death's immortelles.

AIR CASTLES.

Dear Editor, now tell me,
  While enjoying your cigar,
Did you ever with the smoke wreath
  Build castles in the air ?
Now you need not say you have not,
  For I know it is a fib ;
And, in spite of Coke or Blackstone,
  I rather think you did.

Well, to-night I have been building
  A chateau fair and grand,
By a music-murmuring river
  In a gorgeous summer land,
Where the noontide light falls softened
  Through the linden and the palm,
And the idle air is freighted
  With the odors of the balm.

And O, such waves of music
   Enchant the very breeze,
Till in silentness to listen
   It hangs upon the trees;
And the flowers tremble with it
   Like a human heart with sighs,
Till the dew-drops sparkle in them
   Like tears in human eyes.

And 'round my dream-built castle
   Bright birds on golden wing
In the mellow sunset glory
   Their liquid carols sing;
And, mingled with their music,
   The streamlet's silver fall
With a far-off dreamy cadence
   Makes an undertone to all.

And there is not a shadow
   To make the scene less bright,
And the happy hearts there gathered
   Have never known the blight
That the world flings o'er the gayest
   And the strongest of us all,
Till our hearts are cold and silent
   As a face beneath a pall.

There love is ever faithful,
   And friends not bought or sold
By the honey-dew of praises,
   Or the magic ring of gold.
There *right* not *might* is victor,
   And *truth* alone is strong;
The even scales of justice
   Are never held by *wrong*.

Dear Editor, I've told you
   Of my chateau fair and grand;
Too far away to reach it
   Is that gorgeous summer land,

And yet we love to wander
    Through the dream-built halls we rear,
Who knows but we may find them
    When we 've done dreaming here?

Marshall, 1861

SHIPS AT SEA.

Over the ocean the great white ships,
    Spreading their banners, go and come,
Sailing away where the calm wave dips,
    Or when 't is lashed to snowy foam.

Out from the harbor we see them go,
    Fading away from sight and shore;
Then turn we sadly, but cannot know
    Whether our eyes shall see them more.

Over the ocean they gaily ride,
    Bearing a freight of many things —
Satins and jewels and gold for some;
    Often to others a corpse they bring.

Some that are borne by the gentlest gales,
    Gallantly steer in port at last;
Many, dismantled with ragged sails,
    Barely out-ride the wild, mad blast.

What could we do who watch our ships,
    But for the hope that falls like balm,
Of a port where the bright wave dips
    Evermore in God's wondrous calm?

And so we all have our ships at sea;
    We send them out across the main.
Freighted with precious hopes they be,
    Oft we ask, Will they come again?

Some that we sent have crossed the tide,
   Some are just lessening on the sight ;
Others are out on the sea so wide,
   Battling with storms in a starless night.

And some we watched with a beating heart
   Sail long ago from a sunny shore,
Have sent no tidings from any port,
   And we know only, they'll come no more.

THE WIND.

Rattling at the casement,
   Sighing in the grass,
Tossing withered leaflets
   'Gainst the window glass ;
Roaring in the chimney,
   Moaning in the trees ;
Wild the pranks it playeth —
   Ever restless breeze.

Sweeping round the corners ;
   Stealing, drear and cold,
In through crack and crevice
   Of the hovels old,
Where the poor are battling
   With a bitter fate,
While their hearts are throbbing,
   Sad and desolate.

Playing witch-like dirges ,
   Singing solemn chimes
Through the sounding branches
   Of the grand old pines.
Waking weird-like voices ;
   Strange the strain it weaves,
Mad the pranks it playeth —
   Ever restless breeze.

Bringing back the faces
   Far away and dead;
Bringing back the music
   Of the voices fled.
Till, beneath its magic,
   Round us quickly throng
Those who went to heaven,
   Or who've wandered long.

Knocking at the casement,
   Knocking at the heart,
Making far-off echoes,
   Making tear-drops start,
Leaving all enchanted
   With the song it weaves;
Strange the power it wieldeth—
   Ever restless breeze

Marshall, 1861.

A QUESTION.

Suggested by reading the title of a book, which contained an argument against the immortality of the soul.

If man is not immortal, vain sophist, tell me why
The soul's poised wings forever are stretching for the sky,
And why the restless spirit chafes so beneath the chain
That from its upward soaring would bring it back again

Can you tell me why those murmurs through the windings of
   the soul,
Like a deathless strain of music will ceaseless rise and roll?
And why those wild, deep yearnings for something undefined
That steal uncalled, unwished for, into the busy mind?

Why is it, when we're happy, and the soul is flooded o'er
With joy's entrancing sunshine, that the thoughts will upward
   soar?

MARY T. LATHRAP.

And when some low hung shadow with woe our bosoms fill,
Why is it that each thought and prayer and look is upward
   still?

The roused soul, when 't is shining out through the speaking
   eye,
Has a half-veiled look of heaven, that cannot, will not die;
And the heart's low-measured beating is ever keeping time
To the solemn roll of ages; where light eternal shines.

If man is not immortal, then throw a fetter 'round
The pinions of thy spirit, to drag and hold it down,
Chain all thy aspirations, for fear thy soul shall rise,
To claim a long existence beyond the changing skies.

List not unto the breezes; they 'll hymn it to thy soul,
List not unto the waters, 't is in their stately roll.
And look not, look not upward, lest the deep, unfathomed sky
Should echo from its arches, "The soul can never die."

But most of all, be careful to drown the solemn tone
That speaks from out thy bosom when thou art all alone.
Quench all those mighty askings, for a higher power to save,
And take thy meager portion, a few years — then a grave.

Tis vain; thou canst not do it, those voices will be heard,
And by immortal longings the spirit will be stirred.
And to stay it in its soarings, is to stop an angel's flight,
And hurl a star to darkness from the diadem of night.

Marshall, 1859.

A POETICAL LETTER.

   Through the leafy trees that cluster
      Lovingly around my home,
   In a gorgeous, golden shower,
      Rays of moonlight glory come.

Softly chirps the busy cricket,
   While the testy katy-did
Sings within her secret temple,
   By some friendly leaflet hid;
And I hear the waters falling
   Down beside the silent mill,
While within the willow near it,
   Gaily sings the whippoorwill.

With the muse's favoring presence
   On this charming night I'm blest,
And if you will kindly listen,
   I will do my very best.
As for news, that's out the question,—
   We'er so dignified at M———
That there's not the least excitement,
   Save 'mong office-seeking men.
But we had a grand convention
   Here on Saturday the last,
And our "Wide-awake" procession
   Showed that "Douglas dieth fast."
I, of course, am strong for Lincoln
   (Woman's always with the right),
And, of course, I heard the speeches
   That the great men made at night.

All the crowded street was glowing
   With the lamplight o'er it flung;
As the Wide-awakes were marching
   To the sound of fife and drum.
Many a graceful evolution
   Brought them to the Court house square,
And a sight well worth the seeing
   Was the concourse gathered there.
Then the steps between the pillars
   Made a grand impromptu stand
And the men that night upon it
   Were an honor to the land.

First, there was a spicy speaker
   Made a speech a minute long;
Then I think 't was Walbridge followed,
   And each word was keen and strong,
Then a moment's pause we waited
   For another to appear;
When we looked, "Our Blain" was bending
   Graceful to the greeting cheer,
Then there followed keen sarcasm,
   Wit as sparkling as the dew;
And, all pitiless, he riddled
   Poor "non-intervention" through
Every argument he uttered,
   And the logic, clean, and sound,
Came like light unto the listener,
   Clothed in words that weighed a pound.
When he closed, they sung a ditty
   Which was much less grave than gay,
And the chorus asked the question,
   Who would bet on Stephen A.
I did hear one poor disciple
   For the "Little Giant" shout,
But I knew the old rye in him
   Had quite turned his senses out.
But a truce to this description
   May the palm of victory
Only into hands be given
   Who are true to Liberty.

There is not a word of gossip;
   No one's stole another's wife;
And within our quiet city
   Old Dame Rumor's lost her life.
Our "improvements," called "internal,"
   Are a school-house in each ward,
And they,'re laying out "God's acre"
   That by beauty, woes debarred.

If we do n't have much excitement,
    I am sure we 'er not in fault,
For we lack the pines for lumber,
    And, alas! we lack the salt

Well, dear editor, I 'm thinking
    You are weary by this time;
I presume you 're awful sleepy
    O 'er this dosey, prosey rhyme;
So I 'll stop before the moonlight
    Leaves the window of my room;
For its rays are gliding outward,
    As now inward glides the gloom.
With good wishes by the barrel
    Till to you again I write,
Please remember that in friendship
    I am ever yours, good night.

Marshall, Aug. 1860.

HEART MYSTERIES.

O! hast thou felt within some by-gone hour
Thy heart's great deeps stirred by mysterious power,
When from the soul-harp rose so strange a note
It held each thought in awe-struck silence mute?

Perhaps 't was when a rosy kiss, the day
Left on the brow of night — then passed away —
When queenly silence in night's regal car
Fastened her foldless curtain with a star

That hour of hush, when to the charmed ear
Comes voiceless music that we *feel*, not *hear*,
When all without fades in unreal maze,
And to the world within we turn our gaze.

You 've known such times; they come with awful power,
Unveiling life's great mystery in an hour

Then gleams of light from heaven's high lattice dart,
And moments stamp long years upon the heart,
A spell surrounds us, deep and uncontrolled;
Beneath its teaching we grow strangely old.

There is a world within, that's rarely trod,
Save by the feet of angels and of God,—
A temple from whose shrine may ever rise
Devotion's breath, like incense to the skies.
And hours there are — it is no idle dream —
When heaven seems nearer than 't is wont to seem,
When those dark spirits, that on wings of night
Would keep from us each gleam of heavenly light,
Lose all their power to lead the soul astray,
And flee from us on raven plume away.

O, then, beneath the spell of holy thought,
The very air around seems glory-fraught,
Almost we catch from heaven some angel's note,
As through the solemn ether down it floats,
And, bending o'er us with a noiseless sweep,
Spirits their watch in breathless silence keep,
Wondering that minds so like their own should stray
So far from God and purity away,
And folding back the curtain that hath kept
The unspoke secrets of our beings' depth,
They bid us gaze in reverence and prayer,
Upon the mysteries that lie folded there.

Just for an hour, perchance, we take the view,
Then closed again each well-kept avenue,
The troubled water sinks once more to rest,
As if no ripple ever swept its breast.

O! we may gaze on what things *seem* to be,
But the deep-moving *why* we cannot see;
Thesh ruing waters of the whirlpool hide
The rocks beneath, that fret the angry tide.

So every heart keeps mysteries deeply sealed,
And in its depth lies many a spring concealed.
The many chords by heavenly wisdom strung,
Tremble and thrill beneath the touch as one.
Then lightly tread; the smallest action done
Spreads still in widening circles ever on;
A *breath* may wake the prelude to a song
Whose notes eternal ages shall prolong,
Or on time's ocean chance a wave to make
That on eternity's far shore shall break.

August 2, 1858.

THE STRIPES AND STARS FOREVER.

There's sorrow in the nation's heart, a cloud upon her sky,
And the murmur of a tempest on the breeze is passing by;
For traitors have insulted our banner's sacred folds,
And sought to dim the glory that the stars must ever hold,—
  The stars that long have floated
   On the gales of every sea,
  The flag that nations honor,—
   The emblem of the free.

'Tis not the hands of strangers that have laid our banner low,
'Tis those who've sworn to honor, that have now become its foe;
Unholy hands have broken the compact of our sires,
And kindled deep in loyal hearts all freedom's wonted fires,
  Till again the watch-word ringeth
   Through the North from sea to sea,—
  The stars and stripes forever
   Shall wave above the free.

Each patriot heart springs upward with devotion deep and strong,
Indignant to fling backward the insult and the wrong,
For Lexington and Bunker Hill our land cannot forget,
And in the spirit of her sons our sires are living yet.
  Once more they wake the anthem
   Round the shrine of liberty,—
  The stars and stripes forever
   Shall wave above the free.

Down with the hand that dares to blot one star from off the blue
Where they have gleamed so long, the pride of honest hearts and true,
And withered be the tongue that speaks one word against the oath
That linked so long in hallowed bonds the North unto the South!
  Come, rally round your olden shrine,
   And let your song still be
  The stars and stripes forever,—
  Our flag and liberty.

False to the lofty freedom our fathers fought to save;
False to the trust they gave us when they found a soldier's grave.
Would not their blood cry upward unto the throne of God,
 f treason went unpunished in the land the Pilgrims trod?
  Yes, rally round your standard,
   Ye loyal hearts and free,
  And rear aloft your banner —
  The banner of the free.

We have gloried in the Union we deemed so true and strong,
The chain that bound our people, and made them one so long;
But they trample on the compact — the compact sealed in blood—
And break with hands unholy the ties of brotherhood.
  They raise another banner
   Where the stars and stripes should be,
  And with the dust dare mingle
  The emblem of the free.

In the past we called them brethren, and the memory brings regret,
But Columbia's flag and honor to her sons are dearer yet;
And the children of the heroes who unfurled it first, shall stand
With their very lives to guard it from treason's daring hand.
  There are heroes yet to rally
   Round the standard of the free,
  And swear our banner ever
  Shall float on land and sea.

On, freemen, to the rescue! By the glittering names that shine
Upon the hist'ry's pages, defying even time,
By all our love of freedom, and by our nation's God,
Swear that our nation's colors shall float upon her sod

> Our Scott wears deathless laurels;
> Once more his voice shall be
> A spell still leading onward,
> Through all to victory.
>
> There's sorrow in the nation's heart, a cloud upon her sky,
> But the murmur of the tempest will into silence die
> For the hands of those who loved it' and those who prize its worth,
> Shall fling the spangled banner to the gales of South and North.
> Then rally round the stripes and stars
> Ye sons of liberty,
> And protect the folds forever
> Now waving o'er the free

Detroit, April, 1861.

ASLEEP.

TO MR. AND MRS. E., OF HECTOR, N. Y.

> Asleep where the straying sunshine
> Falls with a holier glow;
> Asleep where the waving willow
> Bends *so lovingly low*,
> Asleep where the moonlight's footstep
> Touches the dewy sod,
> Is resting the bright, sweet presence
> That went so soon to God.
>
> It came like a strain of music
> From a harp and hand unseen,
> That strange and unutterable music
> That *sometimes* is heard in a dream.
> But the song is here finished forever,
> For e'er the soft prelude was done,
> The string, by its quivering sweetness
> Was broke — and the melody gone.
>
> It seemed like a wandering zephyr
> Escaped from the groves above,
> Upon each restless pinion
> Bearing a weight of love;

Or, like a star that had wandered
   Awhile from its azure way;
But the zephyr went back to heaven,
   And the light soon died away.

We watched, and our hearts ceased throbbing
   Neath the weight of a terrible fear;
And we only knew that our hearth-stone
   Grew suddenly dark and drear;
And we did not know that the angels
   Around us a vigil kept;
We only knew that the beautiful
   Too strangely and silently slept.

We laid him to rest 'mong the flowers —
   Our bud that had withered so soon —
Where the wind-kissed leaves as they quiver
   Sing a low lullaby tune.
As we bend in our desolate sorrow,
   Over the place of his rest,
We feel that until we look upward
   There's naught but a *memory* left.

We know that the beautiful sleeper
   Is a link 'twixt us and the sky;
We know that heaven came nearer
   When they told us our darling must die;
And oft when the moonlight so holy
   Falls on the flowery sod,
Come whispers that tell us our loved one
   Has only gone back to his God.

TO DELIA H ———.

Dost thou ask why my muse is silent
   And all silent the pen so long?
Dost miss then the voice of the warbler,
   And listen in vain for her song?

That thou askest in questioning wonder
    Why the lute of the minstrel is still,
Dost thou dream that its music, dear Delia,
    Can ever be wakened at will?

Sometimes through the soul's lighter measures
    Such grand undertones can be heard;
That the spirit in listening silence
    Forgets to express them in words.

And sometimes too sad for expression
    Are the thoughts that well up from the soul,
Tho' the strain might be bright, it would glitter
    With tears that were scorning control.

And sometimes so wild and so bitter
    Is the wail of the passionate heart,
Its deep, scornful sadness might startle
    The dignified world to remark.

Then ask not in questioning wonder
    Why the lute of the minstrel is still;
It thrills to the surges of feeling
    And cannot be wakened at will.

1859.

LINES.

Written on being charged with stealing my poetry

Yes, critic, you are right, every song that I have sung
Has been stolen from the labor of another hand and tongue;
The beauty that has glided in the measure of my rhyme
Was written out before me by another pen than mine.

Yes, critic, I acknowledge it; I own it all to you,
Some were stolen from yon heaven with its overarching blue,
And from the moon that walketh in her regal beauty there,
And light that stealeth downward from the bosom of a star.

Yes, I've stolen from the wind when it whispered to the leaves
Something that made them tremble and thrill upon the trees;
And from the flowers springing where the angels' feet have trod,
And blushing in the beauty that was given them by God.

And, doubter, I have stolen from the anthem of the storm
When the thunder rolled in heaven like a tocsin of alarm;
And from the rain when surging upon the driving blast,
Or like a benediction falling on the thankful grass.

And the poem of the waters as they ripple to the shore,
My wrapt and silent spirit has oft stolen o'er and o'er;
While the deep psalm of the river when rolling to the sea,
I have taken, tho' its grandeur belongeth not to me.

I have snatched the thoughts that sunset has painted on the west
When day's lordly king in glory sank to the ocean's breast.
I have caught bright wreaths of fancy from the colors that adorn
The hill-top and the meadow at the coming of the morn

Yes, critic, and I've copied, too, the sobs of human woe
From hearts where every sorrow had been felt that mortals know.
I have written out the tear-drops that, unheeded by the throng,
Were wept by spirits broken 'neath the cruel hand of wrong.

I have set to words the dirges over dreams forever fled,
Over graves where hopes lie buried and aspirations dead,
Over flowers of human feeling by cold unkindness killed,
And wrecks of deep affection by dark suspicion chilled.

Yes, often I have stolen from the holy and the true;
For earth has much of beauty, if we bring it into view.
And much there is of goodness in this world by mortals trod;
For man tho' weak and erring is still the work of God.

Yes, critic, you are right, I have written not a line
But what was penned before me by an intellect divine.
I've stolen but the margin marks from nature's volume deep,
And, critic, I've confessed it; will you my secret keep?

March, 1860

COMPLAINING.

This world is not a wilderness;
   'T is not a veil of tears;
I hate these endless murmurings
   About life's dreary years —
As if unerring Wisdom here
   Had made a grand mistake,
And given to his noblest work
   Such bitterness of fate.

This world is not a gloomy vale
   Of darkness, woe, and death,
Where sighs and tears must float for aye
   On every passing breath,.
I hate the selfish hearts that pine,
   The selfish tongues that croak;
It seems too much like finding fault
   With God's own handiwork

I know there's sometimes cause for tears,
   And so there's need of rain;
But is the earth less beautiful
   When sunlight smiles again?
I know that shadows often drift
   Between us and the light,
And so the clouds oft hide the sun,
   But does it shine less bright?

This world is not a wilderness,
   And man is not a slave
To storms of ceaseless sorrowing
   That follow to the grave

We have no time for murmuring ;
   Life is a solemn fact,
And those who do the pining here
   Are not the ones that act.

Then, though the swift years bring thee care,
   There are sadder hearts than thine ;
There are weaker ones that shudder now
   In rougher blasts of time.
Pray for the erring and the weak ,
   Go, crush the sad heart's sigh,
And when thy work is done, thou 'lt find
   That thine own cheek is dry.

Then mourn not that the path we tread
   .Lies sometimes through the shade ;
Remember, thou art finding fault
   With what God's hand has made
This world is *not* a wilderness
   Unto the loving mind
That labors with an earnest will
   For God and humankind.

1860

TRIAL.

   How oft our wearied feet
Turn sadly away from the path we tread,
While the aching heart and the weary head
   Some place of resting seek.

   But still that search is vain ;
Our rest cometh not till our work is done ;
Our rest cometh not till the race is run,
   And life's far goal we gain.

   Were life a gladsome thing,
Where were the fruits we gather from tears ?
Where were the moments in which we live years,
   And those high thoughts they bring ?

And shall we backward start?
Teaches not trial a lesson sublime?
Writeth not suffering a heavenly line,
Deep on the patient heart?

Tho' future years bring woe,
Chiseling the thought-lines deep on the brow,
Making the closed lips firmer than now,
And deeper the spirit's flow;

Still, know no thought of fear;
For great is the soul that can suffer long,
And in its suffering, be firm and strong,
Though all the way be drear.

Then nobly struggle on,
Gathering from trial an armor of strength,
Winning the laurel of triumph at length,
And the high praise, "Well done."

1859.

WAVE WHISPERS.

A thrilling of winds through the forest,
A murmur of waves on the shore;
A gleam from the spray kissed by sunlight
When dancing the silver sands o'er —
Wave music with low bird songs blended,
I heard as I stood on the shore.

The tiny waves rolled to the shoreward,
And laughingly broke at our feet,
And then, with a light, graceful motion,
Played softly their own bright retreat,
The sands and the waves met as gently
As the lips of dear friends when they greet.

Along by the shore the bright waters
  Lay shallow upon the white sand,
But I saw them grow deeper and darker
  As they glided away from the strand,
And they danced not so gay 'neath the sunlight
  As when they were close by the land.

And this was, methought, but a picture —
  The mapping of life's changeful wave,
From the time our life-boat 's in motion
  'Till it reaches its haven, the grave,
And the soul seeks those mystical borders
  Where rolls immortality's wave.

In the blush of life's beautiful morning
  We launch our frail barques on the tide,
Where dances the sunlight of pleasure,
  And joy, like a phantom, doth glide ;
But soon drifts our light into shadow,
  And our treasures are scattered full wide.

Bound outward, the current grows deeper,
  And paler the light that had hung
Like a halo upon the bright waters,
  To list to the song that they sung ;
For down through the gathering shadows
  Its half stolen glory is flung.

A murmur of winds in the forest,
  A music of waves on the shore,
A gleam from the spray kissed by sunlight,
  As it dances the silver sands o'er ;
And I thought it like life, and was thankful
  'Twas as bright on the opposite shore.

1859.

JUDGE NOT.

Stop! On thy lip let that dark slander die,
  And die there all unspoken,
Let that half-uttered thought forever lie
  In silence deep, unbroken.
How dar'st thou breathe such bitter, bitter words,
  When they will wrong another?
Who bade thine evil eye and wicked heart
  Judge thus thy erring brother?

Stop, lest that word another's fame to blight,
  The wayward lip shall blacken.
Sometime thou may'st be as he is now,
  By all the world forsaken.
Then dare not crush an upward struggling soul,
  That battles now its foemen,
Nor wake within the heart, perchance just calmed,
  Again the slumbering demon.

Art thou all pure from error and its stain?
  Then pity those less holy.
Has thy weak soul sin's "clankless" fetters felt?
  Then learn to be more lowly.
Hope not to win the erring back to truth
  By cold and cruel scorning;
Pour on the spirit's deeply troubled pool
  Some low, sweet, gentle warning.

Perhaps unto that wayward soul has come
  The "peace be still" from heaven,
If thy harsh words awake again the storm,
  Hopest thou to be forgiven?
If thou hast sought and found "the better way,"
  Then gently lead him thither,
And save the soul that now along life's road
  Hastens so madly — whither?

Judge not! That spirit's struggles are not known,
  Save to "the pitying heaven;"
His boat braved fiercest storms e'er 't was at least
  From virtue's moorings driven
O! had temptation's storms around thee swept,
  Wouldst thou have stood unbending?
Or, like him, weary with protracted strife,
  Have fallen while contending?

Shame on thee, that thy lips should lightly tell,
  A brother's frailties ever!
Beware, lest in his heart thy hand shall break
  Some strained chord forever.
Till thou hast driven from thine own soul's depths
  The plague spot and the staining;
Dare not, as thou dost hope for pardon, speak
  The frailties of the erring.

Marshall, Aug 26, 1858.

AN INDIAN LEGEND.

Far, far away, where the sun goes down,
And the beetling crags of the mountains frown,
Where the rivers sweep with a graceful flow,
Unruffled save by the light canoe;

Where the forest grand with its stately trees
Tells the solemn roll of the centuries,
And the calm, deep voice of the Western wave
Sings the ceaseless hymns of mighty praise;

There the Indian lives as proudly free
As the peerless bird that roams o'er the sea,
Through the forest bounds, or his light canoe
Like a feather sends o'er the lakes so blue.

In that far-off land of the setting sun
There dwelt a maid some moons agone;
A peerless star was that chieftain's child —
The proudest rose of the forest wild

Her proud, dark eye had a midnight look,
And her voice was clear as the running brook,
Her step was free as the bounding doe,
And wild as her ebon tresses' flow.

'Tis said that the angels loved the maid,
And sang to her in the forest glade,
Till her eyes had a dreamy, far-off look,
And her heart became like a sealéd book

One night, they say, when the evening star
Hung its pale lamp out in the skies afar,
That she wandered down from her wigwam door,
To the lakelet's sandy, wave-kissed shore.

She wandered out, but she came not back,
They sought her long in the forest track,
Then said she'd gone with the angel band,
To dwell for aye in the "better land"

She wandered out — and they tell the tale
How music stole on the evening gale,
And o'er the water the low strains crept
From wave to wave like the moonbeams' step

They say, when the year brings that eve around
There comes o'er the lake the same sweet sound,
Which floats for awhile the waters o'er,
Then dies with the waves on the other shore.

1859.

RHYMES.

Hearts are burning,
Throbbing, yearning,
Vainly turning
    Everywhere;
Searching, seeking,
That which, fleeting
And retreating,
    Mocks their care.

Looking wistful
For the truthful
And the faithful
   Among men;
Finding ever
That the treasure
Mocks endeavor,
   And is vain.

Vows are spoken
To be broken,
And each token
   But deceives;
While to-morrow —
Sad to-morrow —
Brings him sorrow
   Who believes.

Proud hearts beating,
Sad hearts weeping,
Wrong is keeping
   Watch o'er right;
Crushing slowly
All that's holy,
Pure, and lowly
   Into night.

Hearts are throbbing,
Wildly sobbing,
While we're robbing
   Them of love,
This we smother
From each other,
While our brother
   Needs our love.

Dark oppression,
Cold ambition,
And suspicion
   Bring a blight

On each feeling,
Closely sealing
And concealing
   All the light.

Words of cheering
For the erring
And the sorrowing
   Are denied,
None are praying
For the straying,
All are wrapping
   Them in pride.

Deeds of loving,
Words forgiving,
Might make heaven
   Here below,
But our blindness
And unkindness
Makes much darkness
   For us now.

Vainly wailing
Human failing,
Bitter railing
   Others' sin;
And forgetting
While regretting,
We're neglecting
   Worse within.

When will duty
Be more mighty,
And sweet pity
   Make mankind
Far more gentle,
Firm and faithful,
Strong and truthful
   To his kind?

1860.

LOST FRIENDS.

We can leave the dead in the hands of God,
    But the living that are untrue —
How the heart will pine for the olden love
    That in by-gone days we knew.

We can leave the dead in the hands of God
    And bend to our Father's will
As we look away to the shining shore,
    And feel that they love us still.

But hearts that have turned from our own away,
    Forgetting the sacred past —
How our spirits sit in the Upas shade
    That their cold neglect has cast.

How we mourn the missing link from the chain
    That bound together so long,
And weep when we find how fragile a thing
    It was we had deemed so strong.

We must meet them still in the busy throng
    'Neath the gaze of mocking eyes,
And cover the sorrow that floods the soul
    With a well-wrought mask of lies.

While meaningless words of meaningless things
    We must force our lips to speak,
With a calmness that's terrible mockery
    To hearts just ready to break.

And false, false smiles — those perpetual lies —
    On the calm, schooled lip must glow,
While the waters cold of a slighted love
    So mournfully surge below.

We can leave the dead in the hands of God,
    They have only passed from view;
But spare our hearts from that bitter pang
    For those who have proved untrue.

1860

L. C. M.

"He came to the village church,
  And sat by the pillar alone,"
While over his bright young head
  The rippling lamplight shone.

And the downcast lid half-veiled
  The eye with its fathomless blue,
As if he feared that his soul
  Too plainly was looking through.

The fair locks were swept back
  From the pale and motionless brow —
He seemed like a pictured saint,
  And seems so to memory now.

And I gazed on the stranger's form
  As he sat from the rest apart,
And felt that the sad, sweet face
  But mirrored a deep, pure heart.

He seemed like some wandering one
  From a brighter and holier sphere,
Who lingered, the prayers and the songs
  Of earth's erring children to hear.

1860.

A TRIBUTE TO WILLIAM G——.

Another link is broken
  In the lessening household band,
Another the angels have welcomed
  To his home in the "better land."
O, silent tears are falling,
  And the mourners' hearts beat low,
As to the churchyard's silent shade
  They bear him, sad and slow.

He has come from the far-off eastern land
   Back to his boyhood's home;
But where are the kindred that gathered with him
   Long ago, 'round the old hearthstone?
Some o'er the wide earth wander now —
   And hark! while the breezeless air,
As it sighs o'er the grave with a solemn tone,
   Whispers, "And some lie there."

Yes, he has come, and the friends that he loved
   Have gathered to greet him now;
But a deep, unbroken silence rests
   Upon his marble brow.
Unheeded our greeting, the long dreamless sleep
   Is unbroke by the voices of love;
From the still sleeper's eye, earth has faded away, —
   He has gone to his bright home above.

Ever fading away, now another has gone,
   From the lessening household band,
His sire, and mother, and sister he's joined
   In their home in the "better land."
Link after link of the bright golden chain
   From the rest on earth is riven,
But weep not, a few more rolling years
   Shall make it complete in heaven.

O then, bear the gifted away to his rest,
   Where the bending willow weeps;
Let the fragrant wild flower mark the spot
   Where the lost one calmly sleeps.
Hope's finger is pointing away to the skies,
   And her voice has a soothing spell,
As her low-whispered words, "Ye shall meet again,"
   Mingle softly with our farewell!

Marshall, May 4, 1857.

ONE YEAR AGO.

Sweet memory's voice is falling
   Soft on my listening ear,
And the story she is telling
   Is to my heart most dear.
Now from her harp is breathing
   In tones half sad, half gay,
The memories that cluster round
   One year ago to-day.

The knell of time is telling
   A fleeting twelve-month gone,
Since first we met as strangers
   Amid the city's throng.
But as the weeks have fleeted
   With an ever noiseless flow,
We have spent glad hours together
   Since one little year ago.

And time still onward winging
   With a swift and silent flight,
Oft from the past is bringing
   Some visions of delight
The future we vainly question,
   Fate shuts out every ray,
And none can tell what waits us
   A twelve-month from to-day.

But the eye of faith still brightens
   And it turns to heaven's blue dome
And sorrow's burden lightens,
   For there's a happy home.
When to that home in heaven
   We upward take our way,
Our thoughts shall love to linger
   Round a year ago to-day.

Oct. 9, 1856

SONG OF THE EARTH-WEARY.

Father, take home thy child,
One only boon my soul doth wildly crave,—
A dreamless rest within a quiet grave,
A heart all hushed, to throb no more with pain,
Eyes closed in silence ne'er to wake again
    To earthly grief so wild

I know the world seems fair,
But mocking echoes from the joys that flew
Swift as the sunlight steal the diamond dew,
And gathering shadows, misty, cold, and dark,
That cast their twilight ever round the heart,
    Whispers of nought but care.

Tho' morning's sky be bright,
Calm and serene in its unclouded blue
As the bright sun climbs its high arches through,
Yet e'er his beams shall fade along the west,
The dark storm-cloud may wrap his couch of rest,
    Veiling his beams in night

Earth's flowers all sweetly bloom,
But ah! the fairest hides the secret thorn
By which the hand of him who plucks is torn;
The close wrapped bud conceals a living death,
Withering its beauty like a poison breath,
    Within itself a tomb.

The plaintive murmured song
Of the bright river in its graceful sweep,
Falls on the ear like music wildly sweet;
Yet if the surface with the sunlight glow,
Still there's a current cold and dark below,
    Hidden, silent, but strong.

Love's dream, too, knows decay;
Awhile the soul-harp's wildly thrilling strain
Pours out those notes we ne'er forget again,
And the deep fountains of the heart burst forth
As if to gladden every spot of earth;
But O! it will not stay.

An hour the song may flow;
Then one rude touch will shatter every wire,
And hush the notes of that strange magic lyre.
Affection's tide checked in its onward roll
Flows back an icy wave upon the soul,
And Hope's star sets in woe.

The world is dark to me;
For early round me gathered clouds of gloom,
For early in my heart joy found a tomb;
And haunting shadows from the gloomy past,
Make all the future seem a shrouded path,—
A shadowed destiny.

Grant me the boon I seek;
Earth's flowers are fading, and the joys I clasp
Turn all to ashes in my straining grasp;
I would not linger where each broken tie
Makes me but yearn, like all I love, to lie
In death's undreaming sleep

June 16, 1858

THE OLD HOME.

The sunlight steals in through the pane
And lies aslant the floor;
The vine climbs up toward the roof
Just as it did of yore.

Upon the lawn the stately elms
  Point still unto the skies,
The graceful willow bendeth yet
  Beneath its weight of sighs.

Beside the path the roses grow,
  As in the past they grew ;
The violets still look a prayer
  From out their eyes of blue.

The same old spot — yet not the same —
  The walls are browner grown,
And moss has covered all the roof
  Since I was last at home.

Change has been busy all these years,
  And here I stand once more,
And only list to echoes where
  Were voices sweet before.

Upon the shores of memory,
  The waves of long ago
Are breaking ever ceaselessly,
  And murmuring ever low.

There murmurs with the shadows drift
  In through the open door,
And each are hyming what *has been*
  But will be, nevermore.

1860

TO THE FRIEND OF MY CHILDHOOD.

I knew thee in my childhood,
  But ever potent time
Had well nigh stole the image
  Once treasured in my mind ,

Yes, time has dimmed the picture
  And thrown its veil across,
And now and then a golden link
  From memory's chain was lost.

But there are names and voices
  That in other days were dear,
That among the heart's immortals
  Grow brighter year by year ;
Unmarred by weary distance,
  Undimned amid the strife,
They burn like love-lit beacon fires
  Along the path of life

And tho' I had forgotten
  Thy once familiar face,
There are things I do remember
  Change never can erase.
Thy name was ever music
  In the chimes of days gone by,
And words you wrote on my young heart
  Know not what 'tis to die.

July, 1860

LIFE IN THE COUNTRY.

O ! beautiful spot where the hill and the vale
  Are blooming with mullen and thistle,
While over the hills comes the low, gentle sound
  Of the cow-boy's unmusical whistle

The moonbeams fall soft on that cobble-stone wall
  Beside which those pigs are reposing,
While calmly I sit on this half-rotten log,
  This eloquent poem composing.

Those cows over there, Gray would call " lowing herd,'
  And sing of their voices so mellow,
Well, perhaps they did low in the days that he wrote,
  But *those* animals, certainly bellow.

Those sheep in the road add their share to the sounds
   That evening of quiet is cheating.
Their utterance I'm sure's an unqualified ba-a,
   Instead of a soft, gentle bleating.

There's a lake just in sight, and its waters lie there
   As calm as the slumber of childhood;
But alas, all around it is growing marsh hay
   Instead of a shadowy wildwood !

The brook that runs by, in the days that are past
   May have had some romance in its winding,
But a Yankee mill-dam has now sobered its song,
   And turned its attention to grinding.

O life in the country ! O rural retreat !
   No wonder I'm growing poetic;
For if streamlet and lake fail to waken my muse,
   Those mosquitos would make me romantic.

O beautiful spot ! I must bid thee adieu ;
   Farewell to thy pigweed and clover,
May no one who enters these hallowed abodes,
   Ever fail all thy charms to discover.

Spring Arbor, July, 1860.

MEMORIES.

The storm king's car sweeps o'er the skies,
   But I heed not the blast,
I'm wandering through the grand old aisles
   Of the past, the holy past

I'm living o'er in one short hour
   Those fleeting by-gone years,
With all their many joys and woes,
   With all their hopes and fears.

I rove again the sunny spots
   I knew in childhood's hours,
And sport along the mossy bank,
   And cull the woodland flowers.

I stand amid the youthful throng —
   That gay and happy band —
Meet the bright glances of those eyes,
   And clasp the friendly hand.

The glorious summer of my life,
   And autumn's later ray,
Like some half sad, half pleasant dream,
   Has come and passed away.

And as fond mem'ry's magic tone
   Chimes sadly through my soul,
The wild emotions of my heart
   Yield not to stern conrtol.

I call to those I loved in youth,
   And ask, "O where are they?"
A mocking echo only comes,—
   "They all have passed away."

Gone, all gone! The silent grave
   Has claimed them for his own,
And with the storm, and with the past,
   I'm left alone, alone.

Marshall, Aug 6, 1857.

TO J——.

Could I appoint thy earthly lot,
   I would not seek for thee
A name 'mongst men, that dieth not,
   Tho' it thy right should be.

I'd seek no laurel wreath to twine
   Around thy noble brow,
Displacing thus the charm of mind
   Which is its glory now ;

Nor yet upon some far-off isle,
   Would seek for thee a home
Where joy should every hour beguile,
   And leave to sorrow, none.

Nor would I give to thee the gold
   Before which thousands bow,
For that might make thy heart grow cold —
   Make thee less kind than now.

But I'd give thee the good man's fame,
   Brightest of all on earth ;
And willing hearts should gladly bend
   In homage to thy worth.

A happy home, and trusty friends
   Should make thy life more bright,
Who'd love thee well in sunny hours,
   But *best* in sorrow's night.

I'd give thee joy ; yet bitter drops
   Would kindly mingle there,
Lest thou shouldst love this world too well,
   Forgetting one more fair.

But my best gift should be a home
   In yon bright land for thee,
And the unwithering crown of life
   From heaven's own laurel tree.

Dec. 30, 1857.

RESTING.

Folded are the hands in whiteness,
Closed the eyes o'er all their brightness,
Hushed the heart amid the lightness
    Of its throb.
Silent, too, the bird-like warble,
And the pearly brow is marble,
But the soul, a bright immortal,
    Is with God

Grief's wild passion could not save her,
And a lowly bed we made her,
And beneath the willows laid her
    Down to sleep,
Where the breezy anthems quiver,
Where the willows kiss the river,
And the waters whisper ever
    Dirges sweet.

O GIVE ME THE WOODS.

O give me the woods, the budding woods,
  In the gentle time of spring,
When her dantiest robe o'er tree and shrub
  With a noiseless hand she flings,
When the warbling notes of the birds do float,
  As from their southern home
To their place of rest in the olden nest,
  On gladsome wing they come.

O give me the wood, the shady wood,
  In the balmy summer-time,
When voices sweet in the charmed retreat
  Blend in a dreamy chime.
And the murmur low of the streamlet's flow
  Has ever a charm to the eye,
Seeming to say as it floats away,
  I go, good by — good by.

O give me the wood, the gorgeous wood,
   In the fading autumn-time,
When the fitful breeze as it sighs through the trees
   Breathes ever a solemn rhyme.
O! strange is the song that echoes along
   Through the forest aisles so dim,
Like the anthem grand of some spirit band
   Or the organ's wildest hymn.

O! give me the wood, the dreary wood,
   When winter, old and hoar,
In his snowy shroud with many a cloud
   Comes from some ice-girt shore.
O! there is a charm in the wind and storm,
   Like the echoes wild and deep
That rise and roll through some convent old
   Where the dead undreaming sleep.

O! give me the woods, the grand old woods,
   Where a fairy-land it seems;
And I dwell while there in a charmed air
   And lose myself in dreams.
Art thou weary of life and its ceaseless strife?
   Then go to the tuneful wood;
In that retreat let the heart grow meek
   As ye list to the voice of God.

Oct. 20, 1857.

TO A BEAUTIFUL PICTURE.

I've dreamed of such a being,
   With just such glorious eyes,
Where a shoreless sea of meaning
   Forever hidden lies.

I have dreamed of such a forehead,
   So broad, and marble fair,
With just such loving tresses
   Of clinging, clustering hair.

And when I've dreamed of angels,
    The bright, and the divine,
I've seen the sweet expression,
    And a smile like unto thine.

But as I gaze so sadly
    Upon each pictured grace,
I feel that I'm not dreaming
    When looking on thy face.

You came to us in beauty,
    Our frail and cherished flower,
Just lingered till we loved thee—
    Then died in autumn's hour.

But still the gentle presence
    That we fondly called our own,
Is loved and wept as sadly
    As when she first went home.

1859.

THE TWO SONGS.

'T was Sabbath morn, and from the sky
    The sunlight drifted down,
And with a glory bright and sweet
    The vale and hill-top crowned.

'T was early spring-time, and the breeze
    Sang now a softer strain,
While far away the waterfall
    Murmured its low refrain.

When close beside my window rose
    A warble clear and sweet,
Just like the laugh of waters where
    Two wandering streamlets meet.

'T was spring's sweet warbler, and upon
   A twig it graceful hung,
And out upon the floating gale
   Poured forth its Sabbath song.

It was a song of praise — no sigh
   For errors unforgiven ;
No upward, yearning cry of woe
   Unto a pitying heaven

No supplication from a soul,
   Grown weak from cherished sin ;
Each trill seemed but the quivering note
   From joy's exquisite string.

      *   *   *

'T was later on that Sabbath morn,
   And glittering throngs were bowed
Beneath the lofty domes they 'd reared
   In which to worship God.

And waves of melody swept out
   Upon the Sabbath air,
As with the organ's tide-like swell
   Arose the anthem there.

The strain was deeper, grander, far
   Than that bird song had been,
But there was less of thrilling joy
   In that grand, rolling hymn.

The little songster's psalm had not
   That undertone of pain,
Like the low sob of dying winds
   That murmur after rain ;

But with the other song of praise
   Was heard the low, deep sigh,
And upward, with a yearning look
   Was turned the tearful eye ;

And this, methought, the lesson taught
   By thee to me, sweet bird,
That *human hearts must weep and pray*,
   For human hearts have erred ;

That sin has mingled sorrow's tone
   With every song we raise,
While purity has made thy life
   One long, sweet hymn of praise.

1859

MIDNIGHT.

From yonder tower the solemn bell has tolled
   Another requiem to departing time ;
Along the charmèd air the notes have rolled,
   Then died, as dies some sweet, some far-off chime.

A silence strange and deep has cast its spell,—
   A silence felt within the inmost soul,
Forth from whose realm there comes no voice to tell,—
   Things to be dreamed, but never to be told.

The air seems burdened with the gathering wings
   Of spirits from some strange and far-off home,
Coming on swift, but noiseless plume, unheard to sing
   Unto our heart of hearts their holy song

The pale, meek stars with milder radiance shine,
   And a deep hush pervades the host on high,
In whispering groves, silent the wind-harp's chime
   Hushed as weird midnight wrapt the solemn sky.

Strange, holy hour, thine is no time for tears ;
   Thy grandeur doth reprove such weakness now.
And 'tis no time for hollow smiles nor fears ;
   Before a holier shrine our spirits bow.

The soul bounds upward with an eager joy,
    Bursts all its fetters, breathes its native air,
Revels in dreams unmixed with earth's alloy,
    Free for an hour from sin and toil and care.

Ambition's voice is hushed, and pleasure's tones
    Dare not to tempt us with their winning power;
Passion's unholy tide grows sweetly calm,
    And midnight gives to thought a lofty hour.

Dec. 1857.

A FRAGMENT.

Time's pulse beats slower, and with muffled tread
    The movements come and go,
Like some lone watcher bending o'er the dead
    In silent, tearless woe.

Time's wing half pauses in its onward sweep
    Across the vale of years,
As if to give hushed hearts a time to weep —
    A time for prayers and tears.

Silence has grown more silent; nature's pulse
    Throbs with a noiseless beat;
As if some spectral army, hushed and mute,
    Were on a long retreat.

The trailing robe of darkness sweeps so low
    It hides its fringe of light,
And the low wind hides in its heavy folds,
    Seized with a strange affright.

The past unlocks her halls, and from their shade
    Comes forth the long gone by,
Like a bowed train of mourners darkly clad,
    To watch the old year die

New Year's Eve, 1859.

A VALENTINE.

I've watched thee, as across thy brow
    There swept some shade of feeling,
And seen within thy softened eye
    A dreamy halo stealing.

I've seen the smile upon thy lip,
    By shadows followed slowly,
Until beneath the mingled charm
    Thy face grew almost holy.

I've seen thy deep and earnest eye
    Lit by some strange illumine,
As if with something far away
    Thy spirit was communing,

And wondered if you always wore
    That mask of airy lightness,
And if no solemn wave of thought
    E'er comes to quench its brightness.

I've wondered if thy soul's deep chords
    Awoke no deeper measure,
Whose great, grand tones cannot be drowned
    In lighter strains of pleasure.

I've wondered if thy heart was bound
    To pleasure's paths of beauty,
Ne'er waking to the clarion call
    Of stern and lofty duty;

And thought if that strange mask was off
    That makes us all deceivers,
And in our *seeming*, not our *real*,
    Making the world believers,

That slumbering down within thy soul
    Are deeps no line can measure,
And that would prove, if rightly stirred,
    Unto the world a treasure;

Thy future's page, unwritten still,
    Will tell to me the story,
And may it be a blotless book,
    Traced bright with lines of glory.

February, 1859.

THE LAST PAGE OF A LIFE.

I am sitting in the moonlight and its glory round me falls,
While the past, like some lone night bird, ceaseless to my spirit calls;
All unheeded has the sunset mingled with the sober gray,
All unheeded on the heavens, faded out the twilight ray,
Till the moon shone through the ether with a calm and holy look,
And the sky lay out before me like the pages of a book.
But I heeded not their beauty; memory's spell was all too deep,
As I thought of one, who sometimes weary grew and fell asleep;
I was then a child, but round me such an awe his presence threw
That my heart bent hushed before him, as the flowers 'neath the dew.
I would sit and gaze for hours, as I vainly wondered why
Suff'ring threw such nameless glory in that unforgotten eye —
Wondering at his strength in weakness, and the lofty look he wore,
Wond'ring at the silent patience with which all he meekly bore.
And my childish thought grew deeper when I listened to his tone,
    For each word seemed like a heart-throb, and they strangely thrilled my own;
But to-night, when I am looking backward through the arch of years,
I know why that voice had power thus to wet my cheek with tears;
Now I know that strong soul battled with an anguish stronger still,
And I know that hidden sorrow had subdued that mighty will.
And I know, for I have suffered, that he battled to the last,
Then with one long, quivering shudder, slowly yielded to the blast;
O, there is a solemn grandeur in a lofty spirit bowed —
Mighty even in its weakness death itself can scarcely shroud.

True, there's grandeur in the courage with which sorrow's storms are met,
But a lofty soul when conquered has a something nobler yet.
Tho' life's victories bathe in glory the o'ermastering human mind,
It is in life's desolation that the human seems divine;
This it was that gave such magic to that tall and graceful form,
That hushed heart that throbbed so gently had been riven by the storm;
Now I know full well he perished, like a pine struck down in pride;
Then my glances went no deeper, and I only knew he died.
I remember well our parting, tho' I knew not 't was the last;
I remember how he gently took my hand within his clasp;
I remember, too, the feelings that his measured words awoke,
I remember e'en his pauses had an eloquence that spoke.
'T was a dreamy day in summer, and the sleepy leaves just stirred
As from far the gentle rustle of the coming breeze was heard.
Long I stood entranced beside him with a mist-enshrouded eye,
And I felt that face was changing, but I dared not question why;
Still I lingered in the silence, till the evening's coming gloom
Drifted in across the threshold — drifted in across the room,
Then his voice amid the shadows whispered low the last good-night,
And I turned away and left him, in the solemn, calm twilight.
Well I knew my childish spirit had grown strangely saddened there,
And I knelt to say "Our Father," feeling all the need of prayer.
But I did not know "another" stood unseen beside that form,
Till a face was changed to marble in the shadows of the dawn,
Till two eyes from which the glory had died out were softly closed;
Till two folded hands forever on the throbless breast reposed.
Swift and strong the years have traveled down the avenues of time,
And my path has many mile-stones since that hand last lay in mine,
But that face is unforgotten that in childhood was so dear,
And beneath the touch of mem'ry, grows more perfect every year
Now, sometimes, when I am sitting with the moonlight on the floor,
When I almost see the glory shining on the "other shore,"
All unheeded is the moonlight, or the night bird's clear refrain,
Or the wind that's ever sighing like a human heart in pain,
As I listen, half unconscious, for the voice that singeth now
With the throng that won through suffering, fadeless laurels for the brow.
1860.

HERE AND THERE.

The stars look down from yonder sky;
The winter winds wail mournful by,
    And I am sad to-night,
Thinking of those I love so well,
Dearer to me than words can tell,
As memory with her witching spell
    Around me throws her light.

O, what a happy band were we!
In childhood's hours so glad, so free!
    But now all this is past.
We're parted now, each rolling year
Broke some link in the chain so dear,
Scattering the loved, one there, one here,
    To meet the world's cold blast.

Grief we've seen in its wildest storms,
The world we've met in its rudest forms,
    And met them all alone;
For we're parted now, one here, one there,
Denied by fate to kindly share
Each others joys, or e'en their care
    To soothe with kindly tone.

Some, away in the boundless West
Have sought awhile a home and rest
    Where strangers round them dwell,
And in the city's throng there be
Some who dwelt 'neath the old roof tree
And sported in days of yore with me —
    Days we remember well.

We've learned the lesson, nor studied long,
Learned to "suffer, and yet be strong;"
    And now within each eye
The laughing light of other days
Has changed to a deeper, sadder gaze,
And often quenched in tearful haze,
    When sorrow's clouds float nigh.

And ah ! upon each well-loved brow
There rests a thoughtful shadow now,
    In place of light before ;
We try in vain the olden song,
The words die away on the voiceless tongue
And from the yearning heart is wrung
    One strain — 'tis " Nevermore."
1856.

THE DESERTED VILLAGE.

A city deserted! How strangely still
Falls the chastened light on the untrod hill,
And muffled seems even the laugh of the rill,
    As gliding along
It kisses the wheel of the motionless mill,
    With a sighing tone.

Echoes lie sleeping in every nook,
But wake at the sound of a human foot,
And fly to the meadows across the brook,
    And hide away
Till gone are the eyes that came to look
    On beauty's decay.

The soft, green moss has daintily thrown
Its velvet sheen o'er each paving stone,
And undisturbed it has ever grown,
    For gone are the feet
That trod them once   The busy throng
    Are *all* asleep.

And the homes that were once by love made bright
Are dark and cold.   Ah, no more the light,
Nor the holly bough of the festal night,
    Shall deck the walls ;
For decay is there, and the mildew's blight
    Makes dim the halls.

The ivy climbs round the old church door;
Steals in at the cracks to trail on the floor,
And seems half conscious that nevermore
    The Te Deum long
Shall roll through the aisles, as in days of yore,
    From the low-bowed throng.

They say, sometimes when the day grows dim,
And through each crevice the shades drift in,
That unseen hands sweep the organ grim,
    Till the very breeze,
To list to the strange and holy hymn,
    Hangs mute on the leaves.

Lonely and still; but the mists dim fold
As it upward glides with a graceful roll
And is turned by the sunlight's kiss to gold,
    Rests softly there
O'er the ruined homes and gardens old
    Like a silent prayer

Marshall, 1859.

VOICES.

There are voices sweet in the echoing wood,
    And tones by the streamlet's shore;
A musical chime thrills on every breeze,
    Then dies, and we hear it no more.

They tell us of eloquence and of its power
    As it sweeps like a spell o'er the soul,
But give me the language that hath not a word,
    Yes, give me its magic control.

There's a voice in the spring-time, telling of life —
    Of a life that is glorious and free,
That speaks of a spirit unfettered by sin,
    And tells us of what we may be

There's a voice in the summer; sweetly it steals
   O'er the spirit and hushes the best;
Those wild storms of sorrow that deluge the soul,
   And tells to the weary of rest.

There's a voice in the autumn, sadly it takes
   A low thrilling dirge for its lay,
And sings of the beautiful, lovely, and fair,
   As they're passing forever away.

Then the hoarse tones of winter, chillingly drear,
   Tell of no fairy dream life,
But that in earth's warfare, if heroes we'd be,
   That each must take part in the strife

We stand where the murmurs of varied tones
   In unceasing harmony blend —
God's wordless preachers, hymning to man
   The love of his Father and Friend.

There's a voice in the streamlet, and far deeper tones
   In the rolling psalm of the sea;
The palm in its pride and the violet sweet,
   O man, have a lesson for thee.

August, 1859.

TWILIGHT.

Twilight, sweet and soul-subduing,
   Bridal of the day and night,
When the hand of evening mixes
   Into gray the shade and light.

Twilight day's sweet afterthinking,
   And the sunset's backward look,
Nature's pause just ere she closes
   With night's clasp her picture book.

Twilight days' soft benediction
    E're she seeks the western hill,
Twilight evening's gentle prelude
    Whose refrain is, " Peace be still."

Twilight time when mem'ry's paintings
    Are unveiled within the heart,
When the by-gone scenes and faces
    Once more into being start.

Time when foot-falls once familiar
    Throng around the hearth once more,
As they did e'er their last echo
    Died upon the " other shore."

Twilight-time, when stars are lighted,
    Holy altar-fires in air,
As through nature's vast cathedral
    Rolls the universal prayer.

1859.

" We must have something above ourselves, or we are lost."— *A Sermon.*

Something beyond us, with all our powers,
Something above us, for high desires,
Something more sure than these hearts of ours.

Something higher toward which to reach,
Something deeper our souls to teach,
Something better for us to seek.

A lofty model our spirits need,
A stronger trust than a bending reed,
A better light than a human creed.

Something above and beyond the throng
Of cruel passions that lead us wrong,—
An anchor that's stedfast, sure, and strong.

Some one mighty in whom to trust,
Something stronger than human dust,
Something above us, or we are lost.

A calmer calm on which to rest,
A bosom unruffled and undistressed,
A refuge strong for the soul oppressed.

We're utterly weak, with all our pride,
And human wisdom's a dangerous guide
Over the rocks to eternity's tide.

We're utterly weak, and scoff as we may,
There are places along in our checkered way
Where the proudest and strongest soul must pray.

And, God be thanked, we have something high
On which we may ever with faith rely,
And find forever a full supply.

A God above us for steadfast trust,
A Saviour that's near to pity us,—
With such an anchor we are not lost
Marshall, 1860.

TO THE SONGSTER OF SHAKER GLEN.

O lute of the glen, there's a charm in thy numbers,
   A spell in thy slenderest strain.
Has the harp of "St. Israfel" woke from its slumbers
   To thrill with its magic again?
Or, has some stray seraph from bowers elysian
   Sat down for awhile by the sea,
And touching her harp in some pause of her mission
   Sent melody floating to me?

Ah! well might I think thee some spirit immortal,
  By the sweep of thy glorious song.
Ah! well might I think thee a being celestial
  While borne by thine eloquence on,
Were it not for the undertones, sad and complaining,
  The notes that have voices of woe,
That tell of a heart that is panting and longing
  As hearts must forever below.

O bird of the glen! I have listened enchanted,
  My heart has oft thrilled to thy tone,
Each note of thy melody seems ever haunted
  With echoes of something that's gone
Ah! well do I know that the strong hand of sorrow
  Makes deeper the thoughts of the brain,
Ah! well do I know that the heart's grand emotions
  Come forth in baptisms of pain.

And thus, when thy heart-songs so free and defiant
  Are hymning their lessons to me,—
Those anthems whose grand and magnificent marches
  Seem caught from the roll of the sea,—
I wonder full oft if the minstrel has measured
  Each line by the passionate throb
Of a heart that its deep desolation has treasured
  From all but a pitying God

O lute of the glen, let thy magical numbers
  Still cheer in the battle of life,
As they tell the worn spirit by earth cares encumbered,
  Of strength to be won in the strife.
O bird of the glen, still soar on thy pinions
  Of matchless and beautiful song;
Teach weak hearts that tremble thine own lofty lesson,—
  To suffer and yet to be strong.

October, 1860.

I CANNOT FORGET THEE.

No, I cannot forget thee, while the ever holy past,
Its dreamy lights and shadows around my spirit casts,
The dear old by-gones whisper unto my spirit yet,
No, No, I still remember, I never can forget.

You ask me if the hours we spent in days of yore,
On the haunted wings of memory come to my soul no more;
You ask me if the murmur of their music quivers still
With a power to wake the heart-strings to their softest, sweetest thrill.

Do the restless waves of ocean forget to ebb and flow?
Do the peerless stars of heaven through the ether fail to glow?
Have the leaflets ceased to quiver to the music of the breeze
As it steals with wayward motion among the forest trees?

When the waves have all grown silent, and the stars forget to shine,
When the grave no more shall echo to the spirits of the wind;
And when the day-god ceases on the world to rise and set,
Then I may learn the lesson thyself to quite forget.

But now each hour of musing will bring back olden days,
Till their scenes all float around me like a soft vermillion haze
I view each olden pleasure, in mem'ry's mirror shown,
And listen to the murmur of thy well-remembered tone.

No, I cannot forget thee, while the ever holy past
Its dreamy lights and shadows around my spirit casts;
For each scene is deeply dwelling within my spirit yet,
And till mem'ry's power shall wither, I never can forget

December, 1858.

THE VOICES OF THE WIND.

O, I love the wind, the sighing wind,
  As it murmurs softly by,
With a low, sad note like a broken lute,
  Or some lonely heart's vain sigh;

As it floats along with its shivering song,
    O it ruffles the fount of tears,
And we 're held awhile by its witching wile
    At the grave of by-gone years

O I love the wind, the wailing wind ,
    It speaks to the child of care
With a wordless speech that the heart can reach,
    And stills the tumult there.
Then, then, I dream of some strange, wild scene,
    And a light my soul doth cheer ;
And a voice I find, in the careless wind,
    That others never hear.

O I love the wind, the reckless wind,
    When longings fill my breast
For the end of strife, and a noble life
    In the far-off land of rest.
For well we know while here below
    We sigh in vain for peace,
While the air that now strays o'er the brow,
    Is fraught with human grief.

Yes, I love the wind, the wild, wild wind ;
    It suits my wayward mood,
As it rolls along with its spell-like song,
    And dies in the dark-arched wood.
O, there is a charm in the wrathful storm,
    Its echo my heart doth wake ;
And I list entranced to the magic chants
    The weird wind-voices make.

Hast thou ever stood in some dark, arched wood
    And heard a far-off sigh,
Till louder it broke, and the forest shook
    As it onward passed thee by ;
Then softly and still, like the harp's last thrill
    At the close of the minstrel's lay,
Or the murmur sweet, of the distant deep,
    It died on the ear away ?

1858.

ALONE.

I'm sitting here alone to-night,
   With thoughts so wild and sad
That, with their ever-restless woe,
   Have almost drove me mad.
O heaven! if ever sorrow here
   Could for our sin atone,
'T would be when we had fully learnt
   The meaning of *alone*.

My past, with all its wasted dreams,
   Comes clutching at my heart —
An ever moaning, restless woe
   That never can depart.
There was a gleam of light, just once,
   Shot through the shudd'ring gloom,
A hand soon dashed its brightness out,
   And hope then found a tomb

Why is it that on all I love
   There ever falls a blight?
Why is it that each ray fades out
   To leave a darker night?
Why is it that beside me stands
   An ever present fiend,
Who, when I try to grasp some joy,
   Forever glides between.

O, save me, Father! in this storm
   That desolates my soul,
O, save me from those dreadful doubts
   That scorn my weak control!
O, pity me! I madly drift
   Along a seething tide;
O God, through all this shuddering dark,
   In mercy be my guide.

September, 1860.

A PETITION.

Pity, Lord, our human weakness,
    Be to us unfailing strength ;
Guide our erring footsteps ever,
    Bring us to our home at length.

Pity us ; for thou hast sorrowed,
    Thou hast wept ; O wipe our tears,
Thou who knowest all our frailty,
    Pity us, and soothe our fears.

1860.

"WE SHALL KNOW HEREAFTER."

When some fair young flower fadeth
    In the quiet woodland shade,
Or the buds we've nursed and tended
    In their gentle beauty fade,
Then we sigh in pensive sorrow
    O'er the sweets so early lost,
Sad that anything so lovely
    Could be blighted by the frost.

When we see an old tree dying
    Slowly in the solemn wood,
To decay the proud strength yielding
    That a century has stood,
We look on, and sadly wonder
    At the mighty wreck of time,
As its potent finger traces
    Sure destruction, line by line.

But when some proud forest monarch,
    Lifting its great arms to heaven,
As if conscious of its greatness
    By a sudden bolt is riven,

Then we stand in breathless silence
   Where the shattered ruin lies,
Watching with almost a shudder
   As its massive verdure dies.

Thus, when gentle human flowers
   Pass away, we gently weep;
And we mourn when old age closes
   Time-dimmed eyes in dreamless sleep;
But when death, like sudden darkness,
   Falls on manhood's early light,
Then we stand and vainly question
   Why the noontide's quenched in night.

Yes, we wildly, madly question,
   But our own impatient "Why?"
With an ever-mocking echo
   Comes alone as our reply.
And the heart beats on in anguish,
   Years of woe in every throb,
Till our all in conscious weakness
   We have rendered back to God.

September, 1860.

BY-AND-BY.

We tread the checkered vale of years,
Bedew life's flowers with our tears,
We watch our high, glad hopes decay,
Our wild, bright visions pass away;
Then whisper as we hush each sigh,
"They'll blossom for us by-and-by."

We look in eyes with love all bright,
And bless them for their thrilling light,
Nor dream we they can ever change
Until the tones grow cold and strange;

O! then at what a fearful cost
We learn to *smile* when all is lost!
And crushing back the heart's great cry,
Say, "We'll be happier by-and-by."

We say farewell with husky tone
To those whose hearts have blest our own,
And with each word a sob, we pray,
"God bless the loved ones far away."
Then wipe the unshed tear-drops dry,
And say, "They'll come back by-and-by."

We leave that sacred spot — our home —
And wander through the world alone,
Till round the old familiar spot
Our very names are quite forgot.
We turn from where bright hearthstones glow,
To think of one left long ago;
Our proud lips quivering as we sigh,
"We'll go back sometime, by-and-by."

We stand from other men apart,
And fold the shadows round the heart,
As some of love's own chosen few
Have dared to doubt that we are true.
We lay in mem'ry's burial urn
The broken trust; and sadly turn
From all with but one bitter cry,
"They'll know us better by-and-by."

We watch death's snow drift o'er the cheek,
When hearts loved madly cease to beat,
While the "dark angel" folds his wing,
And slowly severs string by string.
We lay them in their breathless sleep
Where slender willows bending weep,
Then kneel in anguish where they lie,
And, sobbing, murmur, "By-and-by."

Yes, by-and-by, the hopes will bloom;
Yes by-and-by the joys will come;
And by-and-by a home be found
Where only deathless flowers abound
Then, then, upon that other shore
We'll clasp the loved and lost of yore,
And nevermore will hush the cry
Of our sad hearts with, "By-and-by."

Marshall, September, 1860.

[Written for the Detroit *Tribune*].

UNDER THE LINDEN.

Come, dear sister, sit beside me in the twilight calm and still,
As the velvet-slippered shadows creep across the window-sill,
And I'll turn a page in mem'ry, that a sorrow penciled o'er,
With a record that has saddened in the clouded heretofore.

First I'll paint to thee a picture, 't is an island far away,
Where the gorgeous-tinted flowers know not autumn-time's decay,
Where strange birds of wond'rous plumage, and of wond'rous minstrelsy,
Mingle music with the moonlight, floating o'er a summer sea.

There within a quiet valley, where the fountain's bubbling song,
Just beneath the linden's shadow, murmurs sadly all day long,
There's a grave, that now for heaven doth a priceless jewel keep,
And the head-stone saith, " He giveth unto his beloved, sleep."

Long ago, before life's dawning lost its rosy flush to me —
Met I first the one now sleeping 'neath the graceful linden tree,
Long ago when first the shadows fell upon the path I trod,
All my young heart's love went upward with its idol unto God.

I could see the white brow growing whiter still as days went by,
I could see a light unearthly glowing in the calm, blue eye,
But I shut the fear that shadowed from the portal of my heart,
And drove back the gloomy phantoms that would sometimes upward start.

Then they spoke of gentle breezes on a far-off Southern shore,
That would bring the wasted vigor to the manly form once more.
Crushing back the tears, I whispered words of hope and earnest cheer,
And we parted with our heart-strings quivering with unspoken fear.

And he sought the fabled sunlight of the far-off Southern clime,
Sought the perfumed gales that whisper through the myrtle and the vine —
And I watched, and hoped, and waited till the winter days were gone,
Till the spring-time brought its flowers, and the days were growing long.

Then there came a waif of tidings from the island of the sea,
Freighted with a woe that darkened every ray of hope to me;
For the perfumed gales were sighing through the flowers above his head
And the ocean sang a requiem on the shores where slept my dead.

I can never tell how weary passed that mournful summer by,
How I shut away the sunlight, how I wildly prayed to die,
But the sorrow worked its healing; for when autumn days were past,
I looked upward through the darkness, and a peace came down at last.

Years have passed. I count the milestones by the paths I've trodden o'er,
And the shadows linger round me of the saddened heretofore;
But some blossoms are the sweetest where the shadows deepest fall,
And some hearts amid the darkness are developed most of all.

Now full oft I dream it over, and the light will round me shine
From the eyes that long have slumbered 'neath the trailing ivy
    vine,
And a hope comes o'er my spirit in the twilight calm and still
Of a union where no shadow falls to darken or to chill.

1861.

ACHANS.

My heart is far too sad to-day
    For anything but tears,
And words slip off my pen as hot
    And bitter as my tears.
My Country! O the cloud is dark
    That hangs above thee still,
The silver lining's hid from sight,
    The storm is dark and chill.

I can forgive the ruthless hands
    That tore our banner down,
I can forgive the impious feet
    That trod it to the ground,
I can forgive the minds whose work
    Has bro't these waves of woe,
Who laid their grasp upon our land,
    And sought its overthrow.

I can forgive the hands all wet
    And red with brothers' gore —
Forgive them while for slavery's sake
    They madly cry for more;
And I can look on darkened homes
    Their crime made desolate,
And yet amid the maddening storm,
    Can keep my heart from hate.

But when, right here where freedom's air
  Is pouring o'er the brow,
I see men standing all in league
  With Southern traitors now,
May God forgive me if the storm
  Within me scorns control,
And I, forgetting his commands,
  Should hate them from my soul.

To think these serpents dare to crawl
  Among our honest men,
And hiss their hate at loyal words,
  And plot in secret den!
I can forgive the South the deeds
  Which they in madness do,
But, *traitors* upon Northern soil,
  I've only scorn for you.

My heart is far too sad to-day
  For anything but tears.
When treason's rife where patriots meet,
  'Tis time for saddest fears.
Yet trusting in our Country's God,
  My sad soul to his hand
For justice and for care commit
  Thy cause, O chastened land.

East Saginaw, August, 1862.

SPEAK KINDLY.

Speak kindly; every gentle word
  Makes glad some sorrowing one;
They'll bless thee till life's latest hour
  For that one friendly tone.
There's many a fount of kindness
  In this world so seeming cold,
And flowers of human sympathy
  One kind word may unfold.

Then remember, O remember,
  Each gentle word endears,
And give not to earth's travelers
  Another cause for tears.

If, darkened by an angry frown,
  Thine eye shall lose its light,
Some one may look on thee to whom
  That frown may be a blight
There's many a wail of sorrow,
  Borne on the breeze to heaven,
Wrung from some heart that's bleeding yet
  From wounds by harshness given.
Then remember, O remember,
  Each gentle word endears,
And give not to earth's travelers
  Another cause for tears.

O! gently speak to him who strays
  From virtue's path — a tone
Of earnest love and gentleness
  May win the wanderer home.
Speak kindly, true, a cold, harsh word
  Is spoken in a breath,
But it may be unto some heart
  The poisoned arrow — *death*.
Then remember, O remember,
  Each gentle word endears,
And give not to earth's travelers
  Another cause for tears.

October, 1857.

THE WANDERER'S GRAVE.

    'T was the holy hour of twilight;
With hushed hearts they stood around his couch,
And looked upon the dying youth.
It was not a group of kindred dear
That gathered there, to watch o'er him
As life's faint, fitful light was waning.

    No mother's hand
In that lone hour smoothed back the curls
From the damp forehead, on which death's seal
Was all too plainly set. No father's form
Bent in still agony o'er his son,
Forcing each sigh and tear-drop back,
Lest at his grief the dying one be sad.
No sister there clasped his cold hand
In speechless sorrow; no brother knelt
In mighty grief too deep for tears

    Far, far from home,
Away from kindred and the love
That all untiring, watched his childhood;
Amid strange faces and strange forms,
He lay   Anon his mournful eye
Would sadly wander o'er the group
That stood around him, then his gaze
Would rest upon the calm, blue sky,
Where the stars, those holy sentinels,
Watched o'er him as he passed away.

    At last his eye,
Dimmed by the gathering shade of death,
Brightened with heaven-born luster;
His pale lips parted, and he spoke·
"I'm dying now, soon the scene will end,
And I be numbered with the throng
That once have lived. Life's long, troubled dream
Is over, and I go; but ere
Unbroken silence stills my voice
I crave a boon, deny me not."

"When I am dead,
Cut ye from off my brow a curl
And send it to my mother. Tell her
That it was taken from a forehead
Cold and pale; tell her with my last tones
I blessed her; and my last prayer
Was for the loved in my far-off home.
Tell ye my kindred how I longed
To die with them around me. But ah!
It could not be. Send ye to them
My long and last farewell, burdened
With deep, thrilling tenderness.
And now to all, farewell." His voice
Died away in plaintive whisperings,
Low they bent, that they might catch the last
Fond word he breathed. But to their ears
Came but the words—"Mother, Home, and Heaven."

He spoke no more
They held their breath as flickeringly
The lamp of life went out. So soft and still
The silver cord was broken, that
Long they gazed upon his marble face
Ere they were 'ware that he was gone,
And that they stood around the dead.

Now, far away
Toward the setting sun he sleeps
They laid him where the grand old woods
Cast their long shadows, where the song
Of forest birds makes thrilling music.
And oft the stranger pauses while
Passing by the spot; stops long to gaze
Upon the lonely mound, and asks
Who the sleeper is, and listens
With mournful brow to the sad story
Of the stranger youth, and tears fall
Often from the traveler's eye
Upon the "wanderer's grave."

May 25, 1857

LET ME KISS HIM FOR HIS MOTHER.

[A touching story is told of a youth who left his home in Maine and went to seek his fortune in New Orleans. While there he was attacked by the yellow fever, and died. At his funeral, just as the coffin was being closed an old lady stepped forward and said, " Let me kiss him for his mother "]

"Let me kiss him for his mother;"
   And the words were low and sweet
As the winding sea-shell's murmur
   In the ocean's dim retreat.
Upon the air they lingered
   Like moonlight on a stream,
And thrilling as the echo
   Of music in a dream

"Let me kiss him for his mother,"
   The last, low spoken prayer,
With the hushed "Amen," still lingered
   Upon the silent air
When the low request was spoken,
   And the trembling lips were pressed
Upon that pale, still forehead,
   So cold in its deep rest.

He had left the home of childhood,
   In the far-off Northern clime,
And sought the sunny region
   "Of the myrtle and the vine."
But there he met " the shadow
   That even manhood fears,"
And the blight of the destroyer,
   Fell on his youthful years.

He had left the home of childhood;
   While on his bright young head,
The richest, deepest, blessing
   Of a mother's prayers was shed
But the brow made almost holy
   By that mother's last caress,
Was pale and cold as marble,
   In the still outline of death.

They had watched him as the glory
    Went out in either eye,
And heard him often whisper
    Of home, and days gone by;
Thoughts of the loved and cherished,
    With murmured words would blend,
And every prayer was laden,
    With the name of some dear friend.

At last the voice grew silent,
    And the sufferer "fell asleep,"—
A slumber that for wakening
    Was far too still and deep.
Then all the sleeper needed
    Was done by stranger hands;
And finished the last offices,
    That man can do for man,

When one whose locks were frosted,
    With the roll of many a year,
By a tender, holy action,
    Baptized that lonely bier.
Methinks the angels lingered,
    As they heard that low request,
And gazed with wondering silence,
    Upon that last caress.

"Let me kiss him for his mother,"—
    That simple act of love
Won yet another jewel
    For the crown she'll wear above.
In deep, thrilling words of blessing
    Will the mother speak of one
Whose tears and lips touched softly,
    The cold brow of her son.

"Let me kiss him for his mother;"
    And the speaker turned away
As they bore him to the shadow
    Of the bending cypress tree

As the anthems of the breezes
    Through the low-bent branches thrill,
 "Let me kiss him for his mother"
    They seem to echo still.

Jan. 3, 1859

"GIRLS, TAKE CARE."

When you see a young man in some loafers' retreat,
Or lounging forever on some box in the street,
Or in a saloon now, taking a glass,
Then talking so cute of the ladies that pass;
Tho' he sail down the street with so killing an air,
He deserves our contempt, so beware, girls, beware.

When you see a young man in the evening around
With not the best company that can be found,
Overseer in general of people's affairs,
Forgetting his own while attending to theirs;
Tho' he talk long of truth with eloquent eyes,
Take care, girls, take care, he looks well in disguise.

Much as we admire the bright crimson rose,
The color looks bad on a gentleman's nose,
When you find such a one, look out, for his face
Speaks much; tho' his mustache is curled with such grace,
He should not a thought or a wish ever share,
O, then, of one like him, beware, girls, beware.

Mark well that young man who, on Sabbath, would dare
To stroll through the street as he puffs his cigar;
Whose feet never tend to the still house of prayer,
Or actions speak loud that his thoughts are not there.
While in kindness his follies you mantle from view,
Yet gently, but firmly reject him from you.

Then trust not your hopes with the world's fast young man;
For just as secure is the frail rope of sand.

Names traced on the shore by the sea's shifting tide
Will as long as their vows of affection abide.
If your brow and your heart you would still keep from
    care,
Of a gentleman loafer, beware, girls, beware.

May 22, 1858.

LITTLE MARY

Death stole amid the golden curls,
    And shut the sweet blue eyes,
And hushed the little throbbing heart,
    Then took her to the skies.
We twined the sunny, sunny curls,
    Like bands of shining gold,
Around the little marble brow
    So spotless — but so cold.

And then the gentle "flowers made room" —
    Made room for her to sleep,
And o'er that spot of hallowed ground
    They watchful vigils keep.
Our little bud so gently nursed
    Within an earthly bower,
Will in its native air of heaven
    Bloom to a lovely flower.

June, 1859.

DO YOU REMEMBER?

A river rolling to the west
    Beneath a calm October sun,
While, softly on its tranquil breast,
    Some frost-dyed leaves were floating down;

The steeples of a city bathed
    In golden glory, like a robe,
As, listening to the hum of life,
    We by the sweeping waters stood?

LATHRAP HOME, JACKSON, MICH.

A little parlor where the light
   Danced as in play the carpet o'er,
A window where the moon at night
   Crept in to lie upon the floor;

A table where familiar books
   By careless hands were scattered round,
A mantle where two marble saints
   With folded hands were looking down;

A lounge beneath a little clock
   That ticked too soon the hours away,
Where oft we sat and painted life,
   And quite forgot that joys decay;

A door that opened to the east
   Where low good-nights were softly said,
And only heard by listening stars
   That blossomed in the blue o'erhead;

A chamber where I listened oft
   Until a footstep died away,
Then, with a name upon my lips,
   By love made sacred, knelt to pray;

A door upon whose threshold once
   Our tones grew husky, and tears fell,
As, thrilling up from heart to lip,
   Came love's own passionate farewell.

I've sketched the picture; once t'was real;
   'Tis but a memory to day,
But mem'ry clothes in deathless light
   The joys that pass so soon away.

We met and loved and parted once,
   You know we never met again;
Perhaps you have forgotten all,
   But are you happier *now* than *then?*

October, 1860.

FOR AN ALBUM.

TO L. S.

Friends have prayed that all thy pathway
   Might be rich with sun and flower,
They have wished a golden future
   For thee, till life's latest hour.
Shall I then pray Heaven to give thee
   Something different for thy dower?

I'd not wish that thy life journey
   Through a shadowed way should lie,
But I would not have the sunshine
   Always bright before the eye;
For, if earth were free from sorrow,
   What would lead us to the sky?

I'll not wish that friends may always
   Be unto thee tried and kind;
I'll not wish that love may ever
   Round thy happy heart entwine;
For if friendship were immortal
   Would we seek for love divine?

I'd not wish for thee a future
   Free from every cloud and tear,
For the rainbow never cometh
   When the bending skies are clear,
And the soul looks ever upward
   In the time of doubt and fear

'Tis not that I do not love thee,
   That I'd mingle shade with sun,
But our feet are sure to wander
   When life's rougher paths we shun
And this world is not for resting,
   That comes when our work is done.

I would have thy soul, dear Libbie,
   Strong when clouds are darkening o'er;
I would have thy heart grow holy
   In life's struggle evermore;
Then there 'll be eternal sunshine
   For thee on the other shore.

May, 1860

ON THE HILLSIDE.

On the hills the sunset glory
      Slowly dies;
Fadeth, too, the gold and crimson
      Of the skies.
On the pond the water lilies
      Sleepy look,
Sung to rest like floating fairies
      By the brook;
And the creeping shadows darken
      Down within the vale,
And the breeze has stopped to hearken
As, within her temples oaken,
      Chants the nightingale.

Looking downward through the ether,
      Gleam the stars,—
Light that comes from heaven's lattice
      Through its bars,—
Something lies against the heavens
      We call clouds;
But perhaps 't is watching angels
      Earthward bowed.
Bend they over us to listen,
      Pitying our fears;
For, tho' in the blue so distant,
Something on the flowers glisten —
      Glisten just like tears.

And the moon all calm and holy
    Rises now,
Veiling with soft clouds the glory
    Of her brow.
On the lake each bright beam dances
    With the wave,
But upon the hill it shudders
    O'er a grave,—
O'er a grave where softly sleepeth
    One just laid to rest,
O'er the willow tree that weepeth
And the pure white urn that gleameth
    On his silent breast.

Spring-time's grass is not yet growing
    On the mound,
And our teardrops still are flowing
    O'er the wound.
Tho' "thy will be done" is trembling
    On the tongue,
Still the look of wistful yearning
    Is not gone.
The uplifted eye will wander
    Even from the skies,
With a deeper look and fonder
To the hallowed hillside yonder
    Where the lost one lies.

Sadly weeping to remember
    That dear brow,
Tho' he wear a crown in heaven,
    Fadeless now ;
Wildly longing for the music
    Of the tone,
Thus from sounds of earthly discord
    Early flown ;
Wondering that the grave can sever
    Even strongest bands,
Mourning, though their toil is over,
That we've lost the clasp forever
    Of those slender hands.

Moonbeams on the willows quiver
  Silently,
Breezes turn the long leaves over
  Daintily,
And the violets are drooping
  Their blue eyes,
O'er the spot where our lost treasure
  Pillowed lies.
And a star has bloomed in heaven
  Just above the spot,
And this message it has given
To the mourning hearts and riven,—
  "Pray, but murmur not."

May 4, 1860.

"WINNING WAYS."

I live beneath a luckless star,
 Or else was born too late,
For sure it is I've ever trod
 The darkened side of fate;
Nature, though lavish in her gifts,
 A partial hand displays,
And she, for some one says 't is so,
 Denied me "winning ways"

'T is true, perhaps, she gave me brains,
 But that's a wretched dower
When gold or brainless self-conceit
 Still hold the seat of power,
And so I must be luckless still,
 As I've been all my days,
I wonder if 't is just because
 I have no "winning ways"?

I think I have some little grace,
 Tho' beauty was denied,
But it may be my self-esteem
 Gives me too much of pride.

Perhaps the only reason why
    My good luck still delays
Is just because, as some one says,
    I have no "winning ways"!

I've tried to say that black was white
    And think the evil good;
I've tried to bend to fashion's rules
    And see things as I should;
But all is vain; I cannot be
    What I am not, for praise,
And so am forced to think they're right
    About my "winning ways."

I've thought of half a dozen things
    I'd like to undertake,
But always at the very first
    I made some grand mistake;
I cannot learn the taking style,
    And every hope decays,
For some one says, and some one knows,
    That I've no "winning ways!"

I know I lack the honeyed phrase
    That's always sure to win;
I know that speaking honest truth
    To some, is mortal sin.
And O! this saying what you think
    Will not do now-a-days,
And being what you are will take
    From you your "winning ways."

Then if 'tis not a luckless star
    That rules my adverse fate,
Perhaps it would not be in vain
    My style to cultivate.
But as my fortune such a mood
    Of frowning still displays,
Will some one tell me how I can
    Improve my "winning ways?"

April, 1860.

THE ADIEU.

Go, the dream at last is broken,
Go, and take each fond love-token
  Thou didst give to me,
For the chord thy hand didst sever
Is a tuneless thing forever,
And its music waketh never-
  More for thee and me.

Go; for all respect is blighted,
And the love so coldly slighted
  Turns my heart to stone
Pride each tender thought concealing
And each soft emotion sealing,
Leaves in all the range of feeling,
  Scorn for thee alone.

Go, my lips shall never chide thee,
For though good or ill betide thee,
  This revenge is mine;
Filling every hour of sadness,
Haunting every hour of gladness,
Memory shall goad to madness
  Every thought of thine.

Go; I will not wish thee sorrow;
Mem'ry from our past will borrow
  Grief enough for thee
When thou think'st the spell is broken,
Than shall some word lightly spoken,
Or the sight of some old token,
  Whisper still of me

If thou canst crush all regretting,
Thy life-task will be forgetting
  All the joys of yore.
Farewell! all the wrong's forgiven,
But the heart that er'st was riven
Proudly takes what once was given
  Back forevermore.

1859.

A FAREWELL.

Every sunshine has its shadow,
    Every joy its throb of pain,
And the word that makes us linger
    Must be spoken now again;
Though it hush the heart's high measure
    To a sadder, deeper tone,
Though it veil in misty shadow
    Eyes that erst so brightly shone.

Yes, the sound will make us linger
    Fondly o'er the happy past,
O'er the days that came and fleeted
    Like our dreams, too bright to last
Here as schoolmates we have gathered,
    Seeking pearls from wisdom's mine,
Sadly now we bring our offerings
    As we leave our hallowed shrine.

Loving be the tribute rendered
    To our teacher as we part,—
She whose gentle hand has guided
    Wayward mind and wayward heart.
Though our thoughtless ways have saddened,
    Casting shadows on her brow,
Yet each heart's fond benediction
    Rests in blessing on her now.

Golden hours have o'er us fleeted,
    In this spot so dear to all,—
Hours that in the far-off future
    Shall come back at mem'ry's call.
Is it strange, then, that our faces
    And the clasping hands both tell
How the chords of sweet affection
    Thrill beneath to-day's farewell?

Some are here in childhood's morning,
   Some almost on manhood's verge,
Or on womanhood's are listening
   To the future's ceaseless surge.
All untrod the pathway lieth,
   Has it more of shade than light?
Has it more of thorns than roses?
   Has it less of bloom than blight?

"Farewell!" trembling lips have spoke it,
   Trembling lips must speak it now;
Farewell! loving hearts have wept it
   As they whispered some deep vow.
This be ours,— that life's great battle
   Shall be nobly fought and won
Till we win the fadeless laurel,
   And the Master's praise, "Well done"

Farewell, like the dying music,
   Of the wind among the flowers
Passes now the closing moments
   Of these happy, happy hours.
Farewell! softly, sadly breathe it;
   We its magic power can tell
As in prayerful love we whisper,
   "Teacher, schoolmates, friends, farewell."

1860

FATHER, I LOOK TO THEE.

   Father, I look to thee,
     Thou only true;
   In mercy pity me,
     Friends I have few.
   Do thou in mercy be
     All that I need to me;
   Help me to trust in thee
     All my life through.

Saviour, I look to thee,
  Thou only One,
Changeless and constant be
  Till life is done ;
Be thou my guide and friend,
  On thee would I depend
E'en to my journey's end,
  Trust thee alone.

Jesus, I look to thee ;
  Human hearts fail,
And every hour I see
  Their love is frail
Comfort my saddened soul,
  Its erring trust control,
Round me thine arms enfold,
  Shield from the gale.

Father, I look to thee ;
  Pity thy child,
Out on the stormy sea
  Tempest-tossed, wild ;
Take thou my yearning heart,
  To me thy grace impart,
Thou who so changeless art,
  True, undefiled.

1861

TO W. M. C. ON THE DEATH OF HIS LITTLE DAUGHTER.

There's one more link now safe within
  Thy household chain once riven,
There's one less tie on earth for thee,
  One more for thee in heaven.

I have no heart to bid thee now
  Thy sorrow to restrain ;
No heart to bid thee check the flow
  Of tears that fall like rain.

I do not know as I should come
   With any words of mine
To comfort when I cannot sound
   A grief so deep as thine.

'T is almost mockery to tell
   Another how to bear
Some crushing woe in which our hearts
   Have only pity's share.

And when I think your love's last flower
   Is laid beneath the sod,
I feel that I can only leave
   Your grief and you with God

I know you loved her far beyond
   Your power or mine to tell,
And you will find it hard to say,
   "He doeth all things well."

I know God loved her, and he took
   The spirit he had given;
But does not love shine through the stroke
   That binds so close to heaven?

1861.

IN MEMORIAM.

Yes, drape your flag in sable, it is fitting, it is well,
The flutt'ring crape hath eloquence a nation's grief to tell
The silent symbol speaketh what words can never say
Of the heart-throb of a nation o'er her great ones passed away.

Yes, drape your flag in sable, for the heart so young and brave,
Who first upon the altar of the right its life-blood gave,
Let his name be now a watch-word to bid our people rise
And avenge the wrong that calleth for such costly sacrifice

O, it is well to cover with the ensign of our woe,
The dear and chosen colors that on our breezes flow ;
'T is well to weep ; for tear-drops shame not proud manhood's eye,
When for our nation's honor, such men as Ellsworth* die.

Yes, drape your flag in sable, a statesman, too, has gone,
The Patriot with the Soldier is asleep, his life-work done ;
The eagle eye is shrouded, and the massive brow is cold ;
The tongue of eloquence no more shall listening senates hold.

Yes, drape your flag in sable, for upon a silent breast
A guiding hand now lieth in still, unbroken rest.
The master-mind at noontide of its splendor passes o'er
Time's narrow bound'ry, and its power the land shall feel no more.

A nation stands in silence, like a mourner o'er her dead,
O'er worth and power and glory from her counsels lately fled ,
'T is well to feel our weakness, when the noontide of life's day
Beholds a Douglas† falter, and grow weary by the way.

Yes, drape your flag in sable, it is fitting, it is well
That the banner both defended, should a people's sorrow tell
O'er the hero who from labor so early went to rest ,
O'er the statesman calmly sleeping in his own belovéd West.

* Assassinated at Alexandria, Va , May, 1861 ; Col of Fire Zouaves.
† Died at Chicago, June, 1861.

June, 1861.

MISCELLANEOUS POEMS.

AFTER-GLOW.

The day gloomed softly to its close,
　The sunset struck the sea,
And up the valleys slowly crept
　The night-fall's mystery.

We sadly said, "The day is done,
　The golden day of days;"
And through the gateways of the west
　Sailed out our argosies.

We turned our eyes toward the east,
　The sky was gray and cold;
Once more we said, "The night has come
　Upon our day of gold"

We looked again toward the west,
　And saw through tears, but lo!
A radiance lay on hill and sea,
　The day's sweet after-glow.

　　　*　　*　　*

We close a year of toil and faith
　When many wrought as one,
The ways divide, we softly say,
　"The sunset time has come."

We turn away, with halting feet,
    To other toil, but know
Upon life's uplands softly shines
    The day's sweet after-glow.

A THOUGHT OF SUMMER.

The year is fair, the year is sweet,
And Nature's ministry complete.
The graceful tree-tops idly swing,
The summer birds are on the wing;
And ladened with a rare perfume
Is every wandering breeze of June.

The far-off stable hills abide,
And guard the valleys cool and wide.
Across the green the rivers run,
Like silver ribbons in the sun;
With low wish-wash they onward flee,
Swift-footed seekers for the sea.

Fair skies of June with radiant glow,
Bend over all their blue and snow
With clouds that sweep the upper air
Like angels, winged to answer prayer.
And yet the tender summer skies
Keep close their secret from our eyes,
And never open any door
Into the land we would explore

Ah! fields of summer, sweet with balm!
Ah! skies of summer, far and calm!
Across your beauty yet doth break
The cry of hearts that long and ache.
O! give the world some perfect strain,
To heal its discord and its pain;
For though the year is fair and sweet
Your ministry is not complete

A WOMAN'S ANSWER TO A MAN'S QUESTION.

[Written in reply to a man's poetic unfolding of what he conceived to be a woman's duty.]

Do you know you have asked for the costliest thing
    Ever made by the hand above —
A woman's heart and a woman's life
    And a woman's wonderful love?

Do you know you have asked for this priceless thing
    As a child might ask for a toy,
Demanding what others have died to win,
    With the reckless dash of a boy?

You have written my lesson of duty out,
    Man-like you have questioned me;
Now stand at the bar of my woman's soul
    Until I shall question thee.

You require your mutton shall always be hot,
    Your socks and your shirts shall be whole;
I require your heart to be true as God's stars,
    And as pure as heaven your soul.

You require a cook for your mutton and beef;
    I require a far better thing
A seamstress you're wanting for stockings and shirts;
    I look for a man and a king

A king for a beautiful realm called home,
    And a man that the maker, God,
Shall look upon as he did the first
    And say, "It is very good."

I am fair and young, but the rose will fade
    From my soft, young cheek one day,
Will you love me then 'mid the falling leaves,
    As you did 'mid the bloom of May?

Is your heart an ocean so strong and deep
   I may launch my all on its tide?
A loving woman finds heaven or hell
   On the day she is made a bride.

I require all things that are grand and true,
   All things that a man should be;
If you give all this, I would stake my life
   To be all you demand of me.

If you cannot do this — a laundress and cook
   You can hire, with little to pay,
But a woman's heart and a woman's life
   Are not to be won that way.

"THE OAKS."

A CITY FOR THE DEAD

We lay the fair foundations
   Of a city here this hour —
Not yet we see its temples,
   Not yet we count its towers.
Along the open highways
   No noisy footsteps throng,
Nor breaketh on the stillness
   Life's sorrow or its song.
Unbroken though these hillsides lie,
   Beneath these skies of June,
The city we are founding will be
   Peopled sure and soon.

We read on storied pages
   Of centuries dim and old,
When men have sat in darkness,
   Or sang in days of gold;

How they builded mighty cities
    By riverside and main,
That crowned the lands with glory
    And gave their founders fame.
The story of the cities grand
    Enriches all the past,
And gilds the record of the earth
    With wonder that shall last.

'T was something, mid her seven hills
    To break the ground for Rome —
That "Mother of a mighty race" —
    The place of Cæsar's throne
Yet all her gates were full of wrong,
    Her stones were wet with gore,
While war and tumult swept about
    Her towers forevermore.

'T was fairer work, on Zion's heights,
    To build for better things,
To rear the city of the Christ,
    The mighty King of kings.
Yet, lo ! the temple where he taught
    Is in the dust to-day,
And Old Jerusalem is not —
    Her might has passed away.
Yet still the founders' names live on ;
    Untouched by time's decay.

These mighty cities of the world
    Shine through the vistas long,
They glint the rich historic page,
    They fill the poet's song.
The homes of generations rise
    Upon our wondering sight,
The center of the nation's gone
    Before we saw the light.

In grandeur rose the palace rare,
  In grace the temple stood,
The one enthroned the power of man,
  The other, that of God.

Some of these cities grew to please
  A monarch's wayward mood,
And some were built by warriors' hands
  All stained with human blood;
While others grew beside the sea,
  Where ships came o'er the tide,
And brought the wealth of many lands,
  Then scattered it as wide,
While through their streets the restless throng
  Went beating like the tide.

These mighty cities of the past
  Were full of pride and pain,
And what has been in human life
  Is what shall come again.
And so the cities of to-day
  Are full of stir and strife,
Where busy brains of busy men
  Beat out the gold of life.
Within the quiet, where we stand,
We hear the city just at hand,
  With all its tumult rife.

But these strong cities of the world
  Are not like this we sing;
Upon these hillsides evermore
  Sweet peace shall fold her wing.
The summer sunshine and the snow
  Shall drift in silence down,
And autumn gold and spring-time bloom
  Shall bring their yearly crown
To lay them as an offering sweet
  Upon this holy ground.

Within this lovely " field of peace "
   A city fair shall rise,
One side shall touch the world of men,
   The other, Paradise.
And one by one the " low, green tents,"
   Whose curtains never swing,"
Shall open in these quiet groves,
   To shut the dwellers in.

And one by one the marble towers
   Shall cut the dainty green
Of waving grass, and swinging bow,
   With gleaming, snowy sheen.
The music of the place shall be
   Sweet bird-songs overhead ;
The rudest foot that enters here
   Shall come with rev'rent tread ;
And so the living, found in love,
   This city for the dead

The dwellers in our city fair
   Shall come with stately grace,
No longing sorrow in their eyes,
   No shadow on their face,
There never shall be hatred here,
   Nor any pain or wrong,
No hurt at noon, no cry at night,
   But peace, divine and strong,
Shall hold them till they wake to hear
   The resurrection song.

These dwellers in our city fair
   Shall be a goodly race ;
The grayhaired sire will slowly come,
   With glory on his face.
The mother turning from the work
   That loving hearts have blest,
With quiet feet and folded hands
   Shall enter into rest.

The young will come with matchless grace,
    With brows untouched with care,
And baby feet, so small and white
    Shall seek our city fair,
And by and by we'll count the towers
    Along these highways rare.

Here lonely hearts shall hide their grief,
    And ruined lives their shame;
The grass shall grow as green o'er them
    As those of honored name,
"God's acre" lies beyond the reach
    Of human praise or blame.

Above, the stately oaks shall grow,
    Beneath, the flowers bloom,
O living, loving, human hearts,
    Here for the dead make room;
The city that we found to-day
    Shall have its dwellers soon.

We lay the fair foundations
    Of a city here this hour,
We lay them in the sunshine,
    We build amid the flowers;
For since the Saviour conquered death,
    We know our city lies
Under the jasper walls of hope —
    The gates of Paradise

[For the Michigan *Union*.]

UNDER THE SNOW.

The year with its wonderful myst'ry of flowers,
Its velvet meadows and bloom-hedged bowers,
Its streams of silver, and golden glow
Of marvelous beauty lies under the snow
    Under the glow
        And under the gloom,
    Of the shrouding snow
        And the winter moon.

But whoever dreams it will always be
That the snow will cover eternally.
Who thinks it, while lily and violet sweet
With promise of spring stir under the feet.
    Under the snow,
        With a meek unrest
    And a protest low,
        Moves the year to its best.

So the heart has its seasons that come and go,
Often its summers lie under the snow;
But the bird of hope in its winter sings
Ever and aye of the coming spring,—
    Swings and sings
        Amid frost-touch and gloom,
    Of the coming of spring
        With the splendor of bloom

If under the snow for a brief day lies
All that is good, the great Father is wise;
His summer hastens, a great bird sings,
At heaven's lattice, with restless wings.
    Flowers are growing—
        God's flowers of truth;
    His day is dawning
        Upon the earth.
March 10, 1893.

[For the Michigan *Union*]

DAYBREAK

One time I stood in a valley,
  Hemmed in by its walls of stone;
The day was fair on the uplands,
  But still in my little zone
The mists and the fogs were heavy,
  The silence was dim and lone

The tree-tops were gaunt as shadows,
   And men were like ghosts in gray,
Above were the fair skies hidden,
   And the world was shut away
By the bounds of the narrow valley,
   Where darkness hindered the day.

But swiftly up to the hilltops
   In glory ascended the sun;
It smote through the fog like lances,
   And scattered the mist where it hung,
Till lifting, they fled at the splendor
   Of morning — the night-watch was done.

So truth may enter the narrows
   Shut in by rocks and the night,
And often may wait in the shadows
   The cause that is holy and right;
But God is abroad in the darkness,
   His morning comes on with its light.

April, 1891.

[Written for the Michigan *Union*]

FLOWER MISSION.

A message rings from the quiet place
   Where a soul grows white under touch of pain,
And frail, fair hands with a tender grace
   Are holding a loss that has turned to gain,—
Turned into gain for the hearts that sigh,
   For feet which stumbled and went astray,
For lives that wrecked when the storm swept by,
   Are shut from the light of the common day.

The call rings softly from gentle lips
   That ready grow for the angel's song,
Sweet as the note of the lark that dips
   Her wing at the brook, when the night grows long;
And souls that are loving, and hearts that pray
   Shall heed the message that comes to-day.

Go ye and gather
   The blossoms of June,
Rare in their glory,
   And sweet with perfume ,
Gather the splendor
   Of summer's green bowers ,
Dawns with its mission
   The day of the flowers

Stately or lowly, from garden or mead,
Lo, for your garlands the Master has need.
Not for the hall where the banquet is spread,
Not for the feast where the wine floweth red,
Not for the bridal of beauty and youth,
Not for the plighting of honor and truth,
Not for the brows of the children that play,
Not for the hands that are lifeless as clay,
Gathered to-day are the flowers that bloom,
Glowing with light, at the heart of the June.

Their splendor shall shine on an altar place
   Where even at noon the shadows fall,
Where time creeps by with a leaden pace,
   And men make moans at a prison wall ;
They come to hands that are touched with crime,
   To hearts grown weary with wrath and tears,
To lives shut in by a burning line
   That holds its judgment across the years.

The fragrance shall come with breath of love,
   To the homesick souls that went astray ;
Shall cool the fever and lift above
   The thought of the watcher that longs for day.
O God ! Wherever the shadows fall
   On any who suffer, or those that sin,
May rose and lily make plain to all,
   A path where the Christ may enter in. ·

June 10, 1891.

[For the Michigan *Union*.]

A CHRISTMAS THOUGHT.

Once more across the weary earth
Shines out the Bethlehem star,
Once more the day of Jesus' birth
Swings heavenly doors ajar;
And even lips that seldom sing
Take up the olden strain
Of, "Peace on earth, good-will to men,"
The world is glad again.

The chimes ring clear from steeple bells
Across the noise and strife,
And angel's music softly swells
The jarring chords of life;
Sweet "Peace on earth," the children sing,
"Good-will to men" — the old —
Ah! Christmas day, thy gift should bring
To earth the age of gold.

"Glory to God," the carol high
Is like a seraph song,
But ever through it beats the sigh
Of human pain and wrong
The reign of righteousness and peace
Has tarried, O so long!

'T is not enough that Christ was born,
Beneath the star that shone,
And earth was set that fairest moon,
Within a golden zone,
He must be born within the heart
Before he finds this throne,
And brings the day of love and good
The reign of Christlike brotherhood.

Dec. 10, 1892.

[Written for the National Convention of 1891.]

WOMAN'S HOUR.

Between the past and the future hangs
   A gate that so lightly clings,
It seems a breath might put it ajar,
   Yet it never stirs, or swings;
But under the arches in silence waits
A coming hand with a touch of fate.

Beyond the gate in the distance glows
   A splendor serene and high,
A fairer glory than touches yet
   Our vision of sea and sky,
And mellow and clear it softly clings
To the gateway's edge like a golden fringe.

Over the arches a perfume falls
   Like breath from the hills of balm,
And melody sweeps to a world in pain,
   As notes of an angel psalm,
The song rings out, like a prophet's cry,
And tells of a day that is drawing nigh

Beyond the portal that never swings
   Is waiting the age of gold,
The dawn of peace, on the day of God,
   By poet and seer foretold,
Who holds the key to the lofty gate?
Where lingers the hand with touch of fate?

'T is centuries now since the holy star
   Was aflame over Bethlehem,
And centuries old is the mighty song
   Of " Peace, and good-will to men,"
The wise men came when Christ was born,
   And wise men came when he died,
And wise men wandered from Olivet
   To preach of the Crucified;

But darkly the shadows are lying yet
On the world where the cross of Christ was set.
Why lingers the hope of the world so long
After the sweep of the angel song?
Why waits the dawn that shall surely bring
The reign of glory, when Christ is king?
    While pitiful cry
    And wrathful sigh
Yet enter the ear of the Lord on high.

Ah! wise men ruling in church and state,
   Where did you miss it — the Master's will?
His glory is waiting to flood the earth,
   His love is ready all hearts to thrill.
    Well may you question
      Your souls in fear,
    What hinders the day
      That should be here?
Who holds the key, since the wise men stand
Before the portals with empty hand?

   *   *   *   *   *

Behold a strong and gentle host!
They gather from every clime and coast,
With steady faith and a purpose high,
And hearts united by holy tie;
Who runneth may read — 'tis woman's hour.
The lips, long silent, are clothed with power!
    The heart of the world
      Has come abroad,
    Its cry has entered
      The ear of God,
The age of might grows old and late,
When woman stands at the mystic gate.

The wise men, toiling the world to win,
   Have sought the prisoner and set him free;
Have drenched the valleys of earth with blood,
   In giving to slaves their liberty.

They have lifted the serf to a noble place,
And wrought for half of the human race;
    But the golden day
    For which they pray
Shall never dawn upon slave or throne,
'Till woman cometh unto her own.

She has given the world the dew of tears,
    The nations are born in her cry of pain —
The nations, that after the weary years,
    Lie at her feet, the strong ones slain
'T was here they missed it — the Master's will —
And hindered the promise he shall fulfil;
But, lo! at the arch of the mystic gate
Is woman's hand with the touch of fate.

THOU KNOWEST.

Thou knowest, Lord, the things I should have chosen,
    But for thy word, "Make me alone thy choice,"
Had there not swept across my early vision
    The sweet and strong compulsion of thy voice.

Thou knowest, Lord, the way I should have trodden,
    But for thy call, "Come, child, and walk with me;"
I saw the valleys fair, the hilltops golden;
    They lie afar to-day — a memory.

Thou knowest, Lord, the treasures I was seeking,
    Until thy word, "I will supply thy need,"
Then at thy feet I left them to thy keeping —
    My heart beside them, with its eager greed

I do not know what I have missed of pleasure,
    Nor clearly see what is escaped of pain;
But only know thy will hath been my treasure,
    And all thy choosing must be endless gain

So I go onward by this way of wonder,
   And try the task thy wisdom gives to me ;
Nor praise nor blame can greatly help or hinder ,
   My soul lives only in its tryst with thee.

EASTER DAWN.

There was a night when the Lord lay dead,
   And darkness brooded o'er land and sea ;
When stars were pale, and the wind swept down
   With a moaning breath o'er Galilee.
A fateful night, in a world amazed,
   When hope fled far like a ghost alone,
And He, the mighty to love and save,
   Lay thralled by death in a grave of stone ,
        Folded and calm
        Each wounded palm,
While over his silence the earth made moan

That night the word of the prophets seemed
   To the bravest soul but a mocking lie,
While vision of faith, nor might of love
   Could tell why the Lord of life should die
        Hushed was the song
        Of the angel throng,
As they looked on the Hope of the ages then,
Wounded and marred by the wrath of men.

Slowly the night when the Lord lay dead
   Swung to the dawn of another day ,
Till a fair, sweet hue with a tender touch
   'Warmed like a blush through the solemn gray ;
But the world slept on, and no one knew
   What feet in the shadows had been abroad,
And no one heard when in heaven they sang,
   " Christ is risen, give glory to God."

Nobody knew till the women came
   And found that the stone was rolled away,
Nobody knew, till the angel spake,
   "Behold He is risen! see where he lay!
Go, tell his brethren, their eyes shall see,
   "He goeth to meet them in Galilee"

Nobody saw until Mary came,
   Mary redeemed from the loss of sin,
Weeping for love at the open tomb,
   Seeking her Lord in the morning dim.
Eager the question upon her lip,
   She spoke it out to the shining guard,—
Fearless of angels, careless of men,—
   "Where have they borne him? I seek my Lord."
Nobody heard, till the Master's voice
   Uttered her name in the silence sweet,
The soul most loving was first to know
   Death was vanquished and life complete

Then over the world the Easter morn
   Broke in its beauty on sea and shore,
"He is arisen!" the wide earth sang —
   "He is alive! and forever more!"
Swiftly the glow on the solemn gray
   Changed to the flash of an opal sky,
The shadows lifted and fled away —
   Christ had arisen! no more to die!

The sweet birds sang in the fragrant wood,
   The strong birds sang o'er the shining sea;
Out bloomed the lily and asphodel,
   And Hope came back with her melody.
      So the Easter day
         To the world was given,
       With its thrilling song,—
        "The Lord is risen"
And through the centuries yet we see
The glory that shone on Galilee.

Bring, then, the lilies
Fragrant and fair,
Wreathe all the altars
Hallowed by prayer.
Sing the high song on the first Easter given,—
"He is not here! the Lord has arisen!"

Bring the sweet roses,
In splendor of bloom,
Seek him no more
In the hush of the tomb.
Bring all your heart to his feet and adore,—
Lo, he is risen, and reigns evermore.

[For the District *Herald*]

THE CHILD AND THE KING.

I 've read of the beautiful home of a King,
   'T was a palace stately and fair,
With gleaming arches, and marble towers,
   Shining white in the upper air;
The sloping acres were thick with flowers,
Bird-songs flooded the perfumed bowers,
A vision of glory, a throne of power,
   Was this palace of the King.

Beneath the walls of the palace grand
   All lowly a cottage stood.
No royal name had the dwellers there,
   Nor a trace of the royal blood;
But only a common path they trod,
   In sight of the castle towers,
And only the perfume came to them
   From out of the castle bowers,
But a little girl in the lowly cot
   Was fair as the palace flowers.

This little maid with the shining eyes
   Was in love with the palace fair,
And wistfully watched the gleaming towers,
   Outlined in the upper air.
When music swept from the regal halls,
   And flooded the perfumed breeze,
She stood entranced at the open gates
   Overhung by the stately trees,
Until she seemed in the royal place
Herself the child of a royal race,
Upon her rested such nameless grace,
   Befitting the child of a king.

The King who dwelt in the castle tall,
   Had looked on the child one day
As she stood enthralled at the open gates,
   And he loved her tenderly;
So he waited oft for the little feet,
   And he watched for the shining eyes,
As they sought the beauty about his path,
   With a wistful look and wise;
And he said: "She's worthy crown and throne!
   I'll make the little one all my own;
She shall dwell with me in my palace home,
   And be the child of a king."

So he came one day to the lowly cot,—
   The King from the palace fair,—
And tenderly laid his jeweled hand
   On the head with its sunny hair;
So gently he spoke to the parents then,
   While they trembled to hear his tone·
"She shall dwell with me in the palace near,
   And be to me as my own;
Your love is large, but your wealth is small,
My love and wealth can compass all;
   Will you give her to me — the King?"

Then the mother bent o'er the winsome face,
    All smitten with speechless woe ,
The father weeping the slow, hot tears,
    That only the strong may know;
But the little maid, with shining eyes,
    Looked off to the marble towers,
And caught the spell of the music sweet,
    And the breath of the palace of flowers ;
Then said : " Please *mamma, do* let me go ;
    I know the palace, and love it so,
And I am to be his child, you know,
    The child of the great, good King."

So they watched her going, and o'er the cot,
    Ah me ! what a shadow fell !
Till they raised their eyes to the shining towers,
    And then they said . " It is well."
They thought of the King with his regal face,
    And the palace so grand and fair,
Then lifted their brows with a chastened grace,
    Saying softly, " Our child is there.
Our love was great, but our wealth was small,
Now into her life no want can fall —
    Our darling is with the King."

    *   *   *   *   *   *   *

Suppose it were heaven — the palace fair —
    Of which in our sorrow I sing ;
Suppose that he with a regal face
    Were Jesus, the glorious King ;
Suppose the cottage outside the walls
    Were the home that is full of woe ,
Suppose the child with the shining eyes
    Were she we are mourning so ,
O would it not help us toward the light,
To think of sweet Ella, our heart's delight,
Safe in that country which has no night —
    In the presence of the King ?

On the earthly home the shadow falls,
    But the light gleams on o'er the palace walls;
We sit in the silence and make our moan,
    But there the rapturous song goes on.
O, happy are those who thenceforth share
Her love that sought for the gateway rare;
O happy are those whom the path she trod,
Shall lure on after her, up to God;
Oh ! happy the day when hearts that break,
Shall say . " It is well for our darling's sake
That she, with her winsome, shining face,
That she, with her gentle, sinless grace,
In love with the King and his high place,
    Is at home in the palace fair."

CHILDREN'S DAY, JUNE 10, 1883.

Laughter and bird-songs and music,
    Parts of an exquisite song,
As if this old world had forgotten
    An hour, its sorrow and wrong;
June with its roses and sunshine,
    Queen month of the year, on its way
Is bringing its fragrance and beauty
    To gladden the sweet "Children's Day."

And why have a day for the children,
    When they capture all days for their own,
And govern the staid, grown-up people
    From daintiest kingdom and throne?
Children's day ! when the pink and white baby
    Decides all the days of the year,
And sets the best house "topsy-turvy,"
    By changing a smile to a tear?

Children's day ! when such elder-grown darlings
    As throng us with beauty this hour,
Upset the wise heads with their cunning
    And capture the scepter of power?

Talk of a day for the children
  Who govern us all the year round,
Who conquer with tears and caresses
  And put all our theories down!
O glad, gleeful, sunny-eyed childhood!
  Forever it weareth the crown.

Then why have a day for the children?
  A day 'mid the blossoms of June,
When the first lavish wealth of the summer
  Is filling the air with perfume?
I think 't is because of a story—
  A wonderful story and old—
Which only grows bright through the ages,
  And sweeter whenever it's told,—
Of a marvelous day for the children,
  A day with a setting of gold.

'T was far in the land of Judea,—
  The country where Jesus was born,—
When bringing to men in their darkness
  The gleam of a wondrous morn,
He carried the world with its sorrow—
  Had little to do with its song,
He sought for the sad and the lowly
  Apart from the praise of the throng.

He was busy with healing diseases,
  And opening the eyes that grew blind,
And comforting hearts that grew weary
  With words that were tender and kind.
He unfolded to wise and to simple
  The truth that was mighty to save,
And walked all the way in the shadow
  Of Calvary's cross and the grave

But he made a day for the children—
  A day of the tenderest grace,
And *they* found the June and its sunshine
  Aglow in his wonderful face.

Around him the doctors disputed,
   The rulers were there in the throng,
The scribes and the Pharisees caviled;
   The grown people's world with its wrong
Was ever before and around him,
   As he went on his glorious way;
But he turned from their praises and scorning
   To hallow a rare " Children's Day."

'Twas a time when the multitude gathered
   About him, in wonder and awe,
When the bearded disciples were busy
   With troublesome questions of law,
That suddenly into the tumult
   Broke voices, so childish and sweet,
And the crowd, with a frown slowly parted,
   Thus making a way to his feet.
Then up spoke the bearded disciples
   To mothers who smiled with delight.
" Why come ye to trouble the Master?
   Take the children away from his sight,
Behold he is weary with toiling
   And teaching from morning till night "
But sternly the Master rebuked them,
   Till every murmur was still,
Then lovingly welcomed the children,
   With words that yet tenderly thrill
Adown through the ages like music —
   The psalm of heavenly morn
To hearts of all mothers who love him,
   To homes where the children are born.

    " Suffer the children
      To come unto me;
    Better than wisdom
      Their fair purity;
Do not forbid them, to such I have given
Glory and blessing — the kingdom of heaven.

"Suffer the children
 To come unto me,
 You must be like them
 My glory to see;
Pride loses the kingdom for which it has striven;
The faith of a child wins the kingdom of heaven"

Then hands which had fashioned the world in their migh
Were laid on the foreheads, uplifted and bright;
The arm bared for conquest o'er hell and the grave,
The arm of Omnipotence, *mighty to save!*
Lifted the little ones close to his breast,
Nestled them there in a sweet baby rest;
Thus to the church in a wonderful way,
Came first the festival, sweet "Children's Day."

This is why there's a day for the children,
 When all of the world is abloom,
And breezes float over the hillsides,
 Atrill with the music of June.
We surely need beauty and gladness
 To be worthy a day so divine,
When Christ in his love blessed the children,
 And said, "They forever are mine."

I think if our eyes could be opened
 A moment, just now, we might see
The Jesus that blessed the dear children,
 And said, "Let them come unto me"
I think if our ears could be opened,
 All voices would suddenly cease,
As we listened to tones that should utter
 Their message of power and peace
I think if our hearts could be opened,
 To know all the depths of his will,
We should tremble in sorrow before him,
 Our lips growing suddenly still
As we saw how we fail with the children
 His wondrous thoughts to fulfil.

Forbid not the children !
　　O message divine !
"Bring them to me ;
　　They forever are mine."
Rear them for heaven —
　　The door opens wide.
O joy for the children
　　Since Jesus has died !
"Suffer the children to come unto me,"
You must be like them my glory to see.

I think if our ears could be opened,
　　We should hush all the songs that we sing,
To list to a gladder hosanna
　　Of praise unto Jesus, our king.
It would comfort the heart of the mother
　　That misses her beautiful dead,
Until she forgets in her sorrow
　　The words that the Master hath said.
We *might hear* the sweet voices that left us,
　　With the harps of the angels attuned,
In songs that are full of the gladness
　　Of all the unperishing bloom
Where Jesus has gathered the children,
　　In a land that is fairer than June.

O beautiful day for the children !
　　Amid the fair roses of June ;
Sing only the songs that are sweetest,
　　Bring only the choicest of bloom.
But let it all be for our loving
　　That wonderful story, and old,
Of Jesus, who gave to the children
　　A day in a setting of gold.

Jackson, Mich.

IF WE KNEW.

If we knew whose feet were standing
   Close beside the silent stream,
If we knew whose eyes were closing
   In the sleep that knows no dream,
We should be so kind and tender,
   Lightly judge and gently speak —
Let us act as if our vision
   Saw the links that swiftly break.

If we knew life's little journey
   Narrowed to a day —
If we knew our task were finished,
   E'er the flower of May —
Is there any work neglected?
Is there duty half rejected?
   Do it quickly, pray;
Near us swing the unseen portals;
   We may pass that way.

Not in gloom but still in gladness,
   Let our work be done,
Whether here or over yonder,
   Life in Christ is one,
Dark or bright the pathway endeth
   In unclouded sun

LINES HEARD AT A RECENT FUNERAL.

Rev. H. F. Spencer closed his appropriate remarks at the funeral of Mrs Dr. H S Chubbuck, with the following beautiful hymn, written by Mrs Mary T. Lathrap, of Jackson, Michigan · —

    Beautiful toiler, thy work all done;
    Beautiful soul, into glory gone;
    Beautiful life, with its crown now won,
       God giveth thee rest.

Rest from all sorrow and watching and fears,
Rest from all possible sighing and tears;
Rest through God's endless, wonderful years,
    At home with the blest.

Beautiful spirit, free from all stain,
Ours the heart-ache, the sorrow, the pain;
Thine is the glory and infinite gain —
    Thy slumber is sweet.
Peace on the brow, and the eyelids so calm;
Peace in the heart 'neath the white-folded palm;
Peace dropping down, like a wondrous balm
    From the head to the feet.

It was so sudden. Our white lips said,
"How we shall miss her, the beautiful dead!
Who 'll take the place of the precious one fled?"
    But God knoweth best.
We know he watches the sparrows that fall,
Hears the sad cry of the grieved hearts that call,
Friends, husband, children, he loveth them all.
    We can trust for the rest.

1860.   TWENTY YEARS.   1880.

TO F. M. AND VICTORIA REASNER.

Twenty winters of drifting snow,
Twenty springs when violets blow,
Twenty summers, shining and sweet,
Twenty autumns, golden and fleet,
Twenty years of sunlight and shade;
Flowers that blossom, blooms that fade,
Tangled meshes, golden and dun;
Laughter and sighing, cloudland and sun;
Under bluest of skies and stormy weather,
Dear hearts, you have traveled life's voyage together.

To-night you are pausing,
   With grave surprise,
And looking right bravely
   Old Time in the eyes;
Counting the gains and counting the loss,
How much richer for crown or cross
You are, since the olden and golden time
Your lives flowed together, as music and rhyme.

I could make a picture
   From mem'ry to-day,
Of handsome young husband
   And young wife so gay,
Fresh from the blessing
   Of parson and prayer,
With life all rose color,
   And love everywhere.
Blushing and glad in that old, silly way
Lovers have acted since Eve's wedding day;
Radiant and happy, yet ever aghast,
When caught by the world in their loving at last.

I could paint the picture
   Of bridegroom and bride,
The brown locks and bright ones,
   That gleamed side by side;
Young faces unclouded
   And eyes all agleam
With light that comes only
   Of love's rosy dream,
For I saw its sailing, the fair bark, "Delight,"
We greet after twenty years' voyaging to-night.
   But I spare you the blushes
      That swiftly would come
   If told you were foolish
      When wedded and young;
   Or, lest, scanning the picture,
      With honest surprise,
   You should tell these good people
      The artist paints lies.

What have they given, these twenty years ?
More of gladness, thank God, than tears.
What have they taken ?—Not much to mourn,
Since each has the other, with love and home.
White threads mingle with brown and fair ;
Gone the ringlets of sunny hair ;
Older the faces, where time hath wrought ;
Graver the eyes, where time hath taught ;
But twenty years out the bark " Delight,"
Bravely carries her sail to-night

What have they given, the fleeting years ?
Three merry daughters, the teasing dears ;
Filling the house with sunshine and noise ;
Gentle with girlhood, jolly as boys ;
Upsetting dignity, spoiling your frown ;
Laughing your middle-aged wisdom down ;
These are on board your bark " Delight,"
Which sailed from port twenty years to-night.

Counting life's gain, counting its loss,
God hath given you crown for cross.
God hath given you rose for thorn,
Rainbow glory for every storm ;
Richer fruitage for falling tear ;
Rarer harvest for days of fear.
O ! then be glad, dear hearts, to-night,
Bury the sad things out of sight ;
Angels, who reckon this life's success,
Count only as riches what God hath blest.

Twenty winters of sifting snow,
Twenty springs when violets blow;
Twenty summers, lavish and sweet,
Twenty autumns, golden and fleet,
Raising their frost and blossoms together
Through life's sunny and cloudy weather,
    Have left you only
    A song of praise
    To God who was with you
    All the days

1857–1882.

We were wont to dread November
With its garments gray and somber,
Trailing over summer pathways all too soon,
   With snows that fall so lightly,
   And cover, chill and whitely,
The poor, belated flowers yet in bloom,
   Till we mourn the vanished beauty
Of the sunshine and the roses of the June.

But I've seen a new November
   That was neither gray nor cold;
Not wearing ashen garments,
   But clad in cloth of gold;
Her breath upon the hillsides,
   Had the gentle grace of spring,
And the summer's wealth of color
   Did her queenly presence bring.
Beyond the spring-time tender,
   And summer's lavish wonder,
   Was the rare and finished splendor —
The rounded, grown-up beauty
   Of this marvelous November.

We are wont to dread November,
   In the autumn of our years,
When over life's bright hilltops
   Has come the rain of tears;
When the tender green of childhood
   Is changed to sober gray,
And youth, the time of roses,
   From us has passed away,
While the early frost-time lieth
   On hair that's turning gray.

We fear our life's November,
   With her chastened eyes and calm,
As she hushes gayer music,
   With the music of a psalm;

And we turn toward the pathways,
   Once thick with fairest flowers,
And listen for the voices
   Filling once the summer bowers ;
But find that over all things
   A graver hue has grown,
And hear but far-off echoes
   Like trumpets softly blown,
Till all our spring and summer
   Is seen through mists and tears,
As stately, calm November
   Comes across the rounded years,
And we say the summer's over,
   The time of frost is here

But I have seen a glory
   Break softly over life,
A mellow autumn richness,
   With largest blessings rife,
A peace beyond the battle,
   A sunshine after rain,
The sound of tear-drops melting
   In a song that had no pain ;
Sun-love, that bloomed in spring-time,
   Grown strong in summer's heat,
Pass into ripe perfection
   All glorified, complete,
Until life's spring-time tender,
   Her mid-year's wealth of wonder,
Could ever match the splendor
   Of the Beulah land, that thrills
   'Neath the light from heavenly hills,
And crowns, like any hero, life's November.

Beneath such skies of Beauty,
   To-night, dear hearts, you stand,
Where life's first ripened clusters
   Are dropping to your hand.

Small need to mourn the flowers
　　You left beside the way,
When God gives back the fruitage
　　Of well-spent years to-day.
There is no room for sadness —
For aught but simple gladness,
　　As you count the long years over
　　Since you were maid and lover,
And know that twenty-five have fled away.

Then take the long look backward
　　To-night, without a tear,
And go at memory's guiding,
　　With never thought of fear,
Across the vanished seasons
　　Whose timely sun and shower
Have brought the finished beauty
　　That crowns this happy hour.

The winsome days of childhood
　　Come back with all their spell,
The echo of sweet laughter
　　In haunts you loved so well;
Your early home, a vision
　　No other sight could dim,
Framed now like silver pictures
　　In memory's golden rim.
You remember morning greetings,
　　And evening's solemn prayer,
The touch of mother's fingers
　　On the rings of sunny hair,
The brothers and the sisters
　　That shared your love and — pie,
The sweet, immortal little things
　　That never fade or die.

And this was merry spring-time,
　　When early violets grew,
And gold-winged butterflies you chased
　　Were not so glad as you ,

And then the grasses deepened,
  More blossoms came each day,
Till laughing childhood rounded
  To youth's own perfect May.

Ah! then what starry flowers
  Made bright the path you trod,
When love came down to greet you
  From the very hills of God!
I may not tell the story
  Exactly how it ran,
With dreams, and bliss, and blushes —
  Deny it if you can!
The rapturous, sweet old story,
  Told since the world began,
And then the vow low-spoken,
That never can be broken,
  The wedding day of hearts as well as hands.

It seems no more than yesterday,
  This union of two lives,
And yet when counted slowly,
  The years are twenty-five!
But for the tall grown children,
  That came to bring you joy,
And now a wedding in your house,
  The wedding of your boy;
You could not think so many years had fled,
Since in life's rose-time you yourselves were wed

From that far land of roses
  Together you have come;
Some storm, some cloud, some sunshine,
  The will of God hath done.
You have left a path behind you
  Made smooth for other feet,
Nor spared your life's own fragrance
  In making others sweet.
You have shunned the pathways golden,
  Where worldlings seek the best,

And walked the highway olden
   Your Master's feet had pressed —
Your life's endeavor like his own,
   In making others' blest

What wonder you are passing
   Within the golden haze,
The mellow, ripened splendor
   Of your fragrant harvest days?
Not yet the snows have fallen,
   Not yet the tempests beat;
Life's gathered years are mingled
   In a beauty rare and sweet,
Where all the bliss of tested love
   Is perfect and complete.

We meet you on those golden hills
   That lie toward your west —
The hill of faith above the storm
   Where souls find deepest rest
We greet you where your lifted eyes
   Have caught the glow of light
That falls from out the " other land "
   Which has no storm or night
We greet you in the golden calm
Which is the victor's rightful palm,
Even this side the walls that bound
   The City of Delight.

SELECTED POEMS ON "THE IDEAL WOMAN."

Lo! she stands in beauty rare,
Statuesque and high and fair,
Lifted brow and radiant face,
Lips of rose and limbs of grace
  Child of earth, yet more than human;
Art thus paints ideal woman.

Lo! she comes with eyes aglow;
Cheeks where rose-tint blooms through snow,—
Queen of hearts,— yet flings her crown
With a lavish splendor down,
All for love — ah, me! so human —
Poets sing, ideal woman

Crowned afar her heart will ache;
Held in thrall her spirit break.
Whose ideal shall she be?
Art has missed — and poesy

Did you dream God's boundless thought
In our life was ever wrought?
Our ideal could supply
Every greedy human cry,
Here, where souls alert, intense,
Struggle with the bounds of sense?

Beauty fills the artist's need,
Love, the poet's eager greed.
Soul of toiler weary, long
Waits the comrade true and strong,
In the cottage, on the throne,
Where the heart comes to its own,
In that choice, from all the human,
Each shall find ideal woman.

Jackson, Mich, 1888.

LATER POEMS.

THE LAST JOURNEY.

In memory of John B. Finch who dropped dead at the Boston depot after having lectured at Lynn.

How swift was your going, my brother;
   Were all the tasks ended so soon,
Before the bright dew of the morning
   Was dried by the splendors of noon?
Did you gather the harvest of living
   From fields yet aglow with your June?

How swift was your going, my brother,
   Away from our uttermost reach;
No tender farewell in the silence
   From all the rare wealth of your speech;
No word from the lips that so calmly
   Smile on, while we vainly beseech.

How swift was your going, my brother;
   Can it be you were weary indeed?
Your voice was so ringing and steady,
   Your spirit but stronger in need;
Were you hiding the hurt of the battle,
   With no one to comfort or heed?

How strange was your going, my brother,
   What voice did you hear from afar
So urgent you paused in the conflict,
   And vanished from sight like a star?
Who sailed with your soul at its going
   Out over eternity's bar?

Are we late with our praises, my brother?
    You needed them more when the strain
Of the battle was pressing upon you.
    Ah me! with what royal disdain
Death crowns you apart in a kingdom
    Untouched by our praising or blame.

You make us no answer, my brother,
    Your silence rebukes our lament
And sends us afield, where the contest
    For truth and the human are blent.
Ah! God was anear in that shadow,
    You found him the pathway you went;
No wonder you make us no answer
    Since crowned with eternal content.

UNFINISHED LINES.

Each heart has its graveyard, each household its dead,
And knells ring around us wherever we tread,
And the feet that awhile made our pathway so bright
Pass on to a land that is out of our sight.

We fold their hands softly and fill them with flowers,
Then lay them away neath the sunshine and showers;
We fold up their garments away from our sight,
And murmur, "God clothes his beloved in white."

So they love us no more in the land where they dwell,
Did every tie break when they bade us farewell?
Has the distance no bridge over which they may come
To watch o'er the loved in the desolate home?

We listen in vain for a footfall or word;
No whisper comes to us, no rustle is heard.

LINES WRITTEN ON THE DEATH OF A LITTLE NIECE.

How did death look to you, child of our love?
   He surely was fair to your beautiful eyes,—
Fair as the wonderful angels of God,—
   Since you went from us all without fear or surprise;
      Can it be to the pure
   He ever appears in such tender disguise?

How did death speak to you, child of our joy?
   He must have been gentle, since you were so dear
That all the brief day of your sunlighted life
   Only love's music has greeted your ear
      Perhaps when he came,
   Our beloved in heaven drew suddenly near.

Where did death carry you, child of our hope?
   He left to our love but your beautiful clay,
The seal of his silence lay soft on the lip,
   His secret you kept as they bore you away,
      Do you tell it with joy
   To the dear ones you find in the light of to-day?

What did death bring you, fair child of our hearts?
   Assurance of bliss for earth's possible pain?
How quickly you won the fair pathway of life
   Some weary feet travel such distance to gain!
      Ah, never the blight
   Or the sin of the world shall thy innocence stain,
      Sweet dweller in light,
   Shut in where the angels eternally reign.

What have you left to us, child of our love?
   The memory dear of your beautiful days,
The bright sunny face and the radiant head,
   The laughter like music, the sweet winsome ways,—
      These treasures we hold,
   While chastened, we follow the white path you trod
      To the city of gold,
   Till we greet you again in the presence of God.

WRITTEN ON THE BIRTH OF A LITTLE NEPHEW.

Let the world welcome baby Hay,
Born of love and a summer day;
Child of youth in its morning rare,
Born like a prince, he should be fair.

Let hearts welcome baby Hay,
Clothe him in dainty robes to-day;
Shelter his head in gentle sleep,
Fold in comfort the tiny feet.

Let love welcome baby Hay,
What would he do without it, pray?
Cast like a mite on an unknown shore,
Sweet love guard him forevermore

Strange as the young baby Hay,
Many and many have found the way;
Angels guard you with loving care
Back to the heaven whose gift you are.

JOHN B. GOUGH.

"Him that overcometh will I make a pillar in the temple of my God, and he shall go no more out."

Like missing the delicate odors
   That out from the roses distill,
Like silence that falls on the spirit
   When quickly the music is still;
Like shadow that follows the sunset
   When golden is turning to gray,
We stand in the midst of our losing,
   In midst of our grieving, to-day.

So rare was the fragrance that followed
   The track of a wonderful life,
So thrilling the passionate numbers
   Of victory mingled with strife,

So golden the skies of the evening
  When day in its glory went down,
That, weeping for friend and for brother,
  We shout for the hero that's crowned.

O! soul that hath struggled and conquered,
  How looks the rough pathway you trod?
How seemeth the field where you battled,
  Looking down from the hilltops of God?
O! surely it pays to have borne it,
  With all of the measureless pain,
To find that the soul that o'ercometh
  Is heir of an infinite gain.

Gough dead! Say the same of the sunshine
  When evening comes over the hill,
Say music is dead, when in slumber
  The hand of the player is still.
Behold! the dimmed splendor has broken
  In morning, eternal and calm.
And listen! the player is sweeping
  The chords of an infinite psalm.

FOR THE LOYAL TEMPERANCE LEGION.

We're a temperance legion
  Singing as we come,
Soldiers of an army
  Pledged to conquer rum.
    We're for home and mother,
      God and native land;
    Grown up friend and brother,
      Give us now your hand.

We're a gentle legion,
  In our sunny youth,
Bearing as our weapons
  Only love and truth.

> We're for home and mother,
>   God and native land;
>   Grown up friend and brother,
>   Give us now your hand

We're an earnest legion,
  For we surely know
What destroys the father
  Is the children's foe.
> We're for home and mother,
>   God and native land;
>   Older friend and brother,
>   Give us now your hand.

We're an honest legion,
  Wearing colors true,
Like our country's emblem,
  Red and white and blue.
> We're for home and mother,
>   God and native land;
>   Patriot friend and brother,
>   Give *us* loyal hand.

We're a growing legion,
  By and by we'll stand
Citizens and rulers,
  Ballots in our hands;
> Then to home and country
>   We will still be true,
> Vote for prohibition
>   Grown up friends, will you?

WENDELL PHILLIPS.

Abroad were murmurs of rev'rent praise,
  And tenderest din of tears,
And suddenly then, old thoughts were stirred.
  That silent had lain for years;
Now over the place where he sleeps in peace,
  The thought of the century clears.

They brought him in state to the plain old Hall,
  Cradle of liberty's lore ;
How silent the lips, whose silvery speech
  Had filled it in days of yore !
And into that silence with blossoms sweet,
Halted the world with its tardy feet,
  And crowned him, forevermore.

Time was when the sleeping eye flamed bright
  At the wrong of an outraged race ;
Time was when billows of golden words
  With the glowing heart kept pace ;
That time, the coward world stood back,
  And left him alone — his place.

Thank God for the solemn, evening skies
  In which the stars appear ;
Thank God for the tender grace of death,
  After the toil and tears.
Thank God that looking across a grave,
  The world's dim vision clears,
Till Calvary lies in the golden glow
  Of God's eternal years.

COMPLETE.

To J. H. Pilcher, with the prayerful sympathy of his friend, Mary T. Lathrap.

It is over — the care and the watching
  That comes to the mother and wife ;
The faithful has done with her duty,
  And passed to a wonderful life.

We followed her feet, at their going,
  To the stream that we knew must divide,
At its uttermost verge we were halted,
  While she passed away — o'er the tide.

Now, here, at the marvelous crossing
   Where the seen and the unseen clasp hands,
Looking after the one who has left us,
   Forgetting all else, do we stand.

Human hands vainly proffer their comfort;
   The heart smitten sore from above,
Finds within it an infinite hunger
   That calls for infinite love.

So, often, God deals with his people,
   Shutting them with himself all alone,
Till the world slips away from between them,
   And their sad hearts lie close to *his* own

So, while 'neath our sorrow's great shadow
   In pitiful weakness we stand,
God comes, with his infinite loving,
   And shelters us close in his hand.

      *   *   *   *

By and by, we must turn to life's duty,
   Must take up its burdens once more;
And then we shall say, "How we miss her
   In ways that we knew not before."

We'll remember how patient and loving,
   How tender she was and how sweet,
Till we gather her life altogether,
   And see it, as God did — *complete*.

And then we shall say it is better
   E'en tho' the motherless weep,
Tho' the strong heart that loved her be riven,
   'T is better — "God giveth her sleep,"
Since he who hath wept with the mourner,
   Hath promised to comfort and keep.

GREETING.

Written for a little four-year-old to recite at a jug-breaking, given by an infant class in Sabbath-school.

We, the little people,
Bring you merry greeting,
We are glad you big folks came
To our little meeting.

We have songs and stories
Grave, and sweet, and funny,
And we bring our wee brown jugs
Quite filled up with money
Which we gathered everywhere,
As bee's gather honey

Then, good people, welcome
To our merry-making,
Hope you'll think it's jolly fun
Seeing our jug breaking.

THE CHANGED LIFE.

'Tis a land of old romance and story,—
   The one that slips into my song,—
As fair as a dream in its glory,
   Where nature's rare splendors belong,—
A land where wide, marvelous rivers
   Flow over gold sands to the main,
And diamonds and rubies are hidden
   In the hills that rise up from the plain;—

A land bounded north by the mountains
   Whose tops are forever in snow,
While the waves of a tropical ocean
   Lave the South with the sunniest glow,

Wide plains, at the feet of the mountains
  Where palm tree and cocoa tree stand,
And the pine-apple, lime, and pomegranate
  Drop their richness to bless any hand.

Deep forests of maple and walnut,
  The sandalwood rare, and the oak,
With greenness of myrtle and ivy
  Hung round their great trunks like a cloak.
Rare birds hide above, in their thickness,
  Of marvelous plumage and song,
And great beasts lie down in their shadows
  Or move in their might like a throng.

But alas for this land, where the sunlight
  Is yellow and rich as its gold,
Where the moonlight gleams radiant silver,
  And all things are fair to behold.
Alas! for the land of the myrtle,
  The lily, the rose, and the palm,
For here people sit yet, in the darkness,
And look in their need, for a balm.

Thank God that humanity ever
  Is filled with unrest in its night,
And struggles on upward, tho' blindly,
  Thus pleading for peace and for light
And lo! one sweet night in the summer
  There knelt, in this land of my rhyme,
A woman so young and so lovely
  Before a low, wax-lighted shrine.

On the shrine was an idol of silver,
  Before it her offering was laid,
And there, with her baby beside her,
  The young, sad-soul'd mother thus prayed.
"O beautiful goddess of mercy!
  I pray thee have pity and bless,
For I am so wretched and weary,
  Have mercy upon my distress."

"This pain of my heart and its longing
    Must come from thy anger to me,
O give my soul rest from its sorrow,
    And I'll offer a great gift to thee."
The dark eyes were woeful and tearless,
    The dusky hair swept to the floor,
And again did the pleading lips utter,
    "Have pity on me, I implore!"

She rose from her knees, but the shadow
    Lay deeper upon the young face,
And, covering it close with her mantle,
    She lifted the child from its place,
And out from her home she went softly
    And sped on, still crying for rest,
Till alone by the far-fabled river
    She stood with her babe on her breast.

One moment her hungry eyes glittered
    Over the sweet little face,
One moment the hungry arms held her
    In the closest and wildest embrace.
Then out on the deep, gleaming waters
    That mockingly slipped by her feet,
With a cry the heart gives that is broken,
    She flung all that made her life sweet.

And down in the sand by the river
    She bowed in her sorrow alone,
And listened while just for a moment
    There floated a sweet tender tone
Through the ripple and rush of the waters,
    Then died on the air of the night
And again she cried, "Vishnu! O Vishnu!
    Have pity, give peace, and give light."

At length to her home she went slowly,
    As if years had passed over her head,
And her mother's heart turned from the goddess,
    To mourn for her beautiful dead.

So back to her life and her sorrow
   She went as the dawn broke in gray,
But alas, the long night of the spirit
   Fled not with the dawning of day.

Is my picture too sad? then another
   Shall gild your sad tears with a smile,
Turn the leaf of a year, for the mother
   Who gave the dark river her child.
Another dear babe is beside her;
   Again she is kneeling in prayer,
But the shrine and the wax lights and idols,
   We look for in vain — they're not there

The dark, mournful eyes are uplifted,
   The olive hands clasped on her breast,
"O! Father in heaven," she whispered,
   "I thank thee, I thank thee for rest!
O! Jesus, thou mighty Redeemer,
   Who bore all the sin of our race,
I thank thee that one so unworthy
   Has found thee at last, and thy peace.

"Now, Father in heaven, my baby,
   I give all her life unto thee,
The other — thank God she is dwelling
   Up there where the glorified be
O make me so pure and so holy
   That, fitted to meet her once more,
We may praise the *one* God for salvation,
   And glorify him evermore.

"And Father, bless more than all others
   The one who came over the sea,
To tell, with love patient and tender,
   The story of Christ unto me.
And bless thou the hearts that were able
   To take all the world in their love,
To remember poor India's daughters
   And send her to lead us above.

"O bless them most richly, my Father,
   In their homes in a land far away,
For their prayers and their sufferings give them
   A home in thy wonderful day.
O Jesus, my blessed Redeemer,
   I praise thee again and again
For thy peace, and thy love, and salvation,
   And the way into heaven, Amen."

'T is just the old story, you tell me,
   That I have been singing to-day,
Well, what has the world worth the singing
   If that is left out of the lay?
What, indeed, since this life and the other,
   And vict'ry o'er death and the grave,
And the hope of humanity liveth
   In the power of Jesus to save?

O the lands that are sitting in darkness!
   O manhood, distorted and vile!
O womanhood, weak and degraded,
   And together they rearing the child!
God help us to publish the tidings
   Till the banner of Christ is unfurled,
And all people shall hear he has taken
   Away all the sin of the world.

[For the *Central City Courier*.]

THE PROHIBITION BLUE AND GRAY.

Sing ye a song of the Blue and the Gray,
Marching together to join in the fray —
Not as of old to the blare of the drum,
But to the battle of home against rum

Chorus,—
   Sing ye a song for the Gray and the Blue,
   Clasping their hands in a union so true;
   Sing ye a song of the Blue and the Gray;
   Victory is coming! make way, then, make way!

Sing ye a song, and yet not of the past,—
That was too mournful and bitter to last,
Bring it not back to eyes that were dim ;
Sing for the future a new battle-hymn

Sing ye a song as in triumph they come,
Shouting the cry of home against rum ,
Men of our country, united and strong,
Gallant defenders of right against wrong

Sing ye a song of our leaders to-day ;
See ! we have chosen the Blue and the Gray !
Under one banner, for country and home,
Now to the conquest the bravest are come.

Lips of sad mothers are trembling with prayer,
Lips of the children a blessing declare ,
Northland and Southland unite in the fray ,
Sing ye a song of the bravest to-day.

Chorus,—
Sing ye a song for the Gray and the Blue,
Clasping brave hands in a union so true ,
Sing prohibition for Blue and for Gray ,
Victory is coming ! make way, then, make way !

HOW LONG ?

The world is old, and time is late ;
Like silent ghosts the centuries wait
Behind the folded doors of fate,
 So close and strong ;
The years have gone, the years have come,
With bloom and snow, with cloud and sun,
And still the caravan moves on.
 O Lord, how long ?

The far-off, stable mountains hold
A record by the ages told,
But hide the lines in gray and gold,
 From all earth's throng.

The peaceful stars shine evermore,
The restless sea-waves beat the shore,
And what has been comes o'er and o'er.
    O Lord, how long?

The rivers flow toward the main,
And winds repeat the olden strain,
But all that is, has touch of pain
    That thrills each song;
Sweet hearts have broken in their trust,
Brave hearts have struggled into dust,
Yet rules the might of greed and lust.
    O Lord, how long?

How long, since earth is old with years,
And drenched with rain of blood and tears,
And thick with graves of babes and seers,
    While yet the wrong
Smites down the truth with cruel rod,
Spreads ruin in this world of God,
And hatred where the Christ has trod,—
    O Lord, how long?

Prophetic souls with purpose high,
That hear the world's unworded cry,
And plead a hope that will not die
    For all who fear;
O tell us if on any height
You see the glow of morning bright,
Or hear His footseps in their might
    Is Jesus near?

WILL IT PAY?

Out from the hearthstone the children go,
    Fair as the sunshine, pure as snow;
A licensed wrong on the crowded street
    Waits the coming of guileless feet.

Child of the rich, and child of the poor
   Pass to their wreck through the dram-shop's door;
O, say, will they ever come back as they go,
   Fair as the sunshine, pure as snow?

Out from the hearthstone, the children fair
   Pass from the breath of a mother's prayer.
Shall a father's vote on the crowded street
   Consent to the snare for the thoughtless feet?
Ah! fathers, your finest gold grows dim;
   Black with the rust of such nameless sin!
You may pave the streets with your children slain,
   And light your ways with the price of shame,
But say, will *your* dear ones come back as they go,
   Fair as the sunshine, pure as snow?

THE DEAD MARCH.

Tramp, tramp, tramp, in the drunkard's way
   March the feet of a million men;
If none shall pity and none shall save,
   Where will the march they are making end?
The young, the strong, the old are there,
   In woeful ranks as they hurry past,
      With not a moment to think or care
   What is the fate that comes at last.

Tramp, tramp, tramp, to a drunkard's doom,
   Out of boyhood pure and fair,
Over the thoughts of a love and home,
   Past the check of a mother's prayer,
Onward swift to a drunkard's crime,
   Over the plea of a wife and child —
Over the holiest ties of time —
   Reason dethroned and soul gone wild

>   Tramp, tramp, tramp, till a drunkard's grave
>   Covers the broken life of shame,
>   While the spirit Jesus died to save
>   Meets a future we dare not name.
>   God help us all! there's a cross to bear
>   And work to do for a mighty throng!
>   God give us strength, till the toil and the prayer
>   Shall end one day in the victor's song!

[The above poem was prepared for the first number of *Our Union*, the original *Union Signal*. Mrs Lathrap prepared nearly one third of the subject-matter for that number — ED]

THERE'S A SHADOW ON THE HOME.

BATTLE SONG OF THE Y. W. C. T. U.

> There's a shadow on the home, many hearts are sad to-day,
> It hushes e'en the laughter of the children at their play ,
> At its coming, want and sorrow across the threshold creep,
> And, amid their broken idols, the mourning mothers weep.

Chorus,—
>   We are coming to the rescue,— we are coming in our youth ;
>   The homes we build to-morrow shall be guarded by the truth.
>   We are coming to the battle of purity and right ;
>   And for a winsome token, we wear the ribbon white.

> There's a wrong in all the land, and the beautiful are slain ,
> Amid their graves the nation counts her revenue of shame ,
> While the price of blood is taken in legislative halls,
> A smitten manhood crouches in the gloom of prison walls.

> There's an evil in the land, and the kingdom of our Lord
> Is hindered in its coming , then arise with one accord
> And put away the wine-cup that threatens love and home;
> For the judgment surely cometh, and God is on the throne

Chorus,—
  We are coming to the rescue, we are coming in our youth,
  The homes we build to-morrow shall be guarded by the truth.
  We are coming to the battle for country, God, and right,
  And for a winsome token we wear the ribbon white.

MAPLE SUGAR AND MISSION SCHOOLS.

  My theme is full of the sweetest of things,
  Love and music and wedding rings,
  Voices of children and home and light,
  All things beautiful, all things bright;
  Mixing up morals and romance and fun,—
  Prose and poetry all in one,—
  While I, slipping loose from poetical rules,
  Sing maple sugar and mission schools.

  In a cozy parlor, one cold March day,
  Three children sat in their merry play.
  Beauty was round them everywhere,
  Books and pictures and easy chairs,
  Drooping curtains and carpets bright,
  Glowing warm in the firelight
  Mamma was sewing, and ever so snug
  Curled at her feet lay the cat on the rug.
  The little people were playing take tea,
  Their ages were seven and five and three;
  The oldest were girls, and the youngest a brother
  With hair and eyes that looked just like his mother.
  Their tiny table was all set out
  With baby china, with plates about
  The size of an old-fashioned silver dollar,
  And saucers and cups a great deal smaller
  They had water for tea and the rest of the supper
  Was maple sugar with bread and butter

  When all things were ready, each one took a chair
  With a sort of dignified, grown-up air,

And the dainty clatter, fuss, and jokes
Were only a picture of grown-up folks.
Jennie, the oldest, poured the tea,
While Baby Charlie was company,
And Nettie gravely passed sugar and bread,
And helped on the small talk Jennie led.
And thus all the waiting on properly ended,
They said the sugar was nice and splendid,
And if the girls did talk more than their brother,
His piece diminished as fast as the others
"I wonder," asked Nettie, "where sugar is made."
"Why, out in the woods," the quick Jennie said.
"It ain't made at all," said the young man of three;
"Do n't oo know maple sudar drows on a tree?"
A laugh rang out from the merry girls,
But Charley shook gravely his shining curls,
Saying, "Mamma, you make dem stop laughing at me
Do n't maple sudar drow up on a tree?"
The mother laughed, too, at her wise little boy,
While deep in her eyes lay a wonderful joy
That was born of the thoughts that had run on so free
While the children had talked of the sugar at tea.
She saw the first sunshine of spring all aglow
And violets blooming 'twixt patches of snow;
A brook just set free and tall maples,— but hold,
You shall hear for yourself the story she told.
The mother drew nearer, that wonderful smile
Coming up from her heart to her face all the while
"I will tell you the story I have in my head,
That will answer my little boy's question," she said.

"Once on a time, I know well of a home
Where a good farmer dwelt with his daughter and sons,
And his wife, a grand woman who was fitted to grace
From the throne of a queen any womanly place
'T was a little log house, with front window and door
Looking off to the east, so that over the floor
The first morning sunbeams might daintily fall
And light into glory the plainness of all.

The house was so small that almost it might stand
Right here in our parlor, and yet the deft hands
Of mother and daughter had made it appear
So cozy and neat, that year after year
It lives in my heart like a picture that age
Has softened and mellowed, but cannot make fade.
O'er windows and up to the roof the wild vines
Clambered and blossomed the long summer-time;
And round the low doorway the roses and pinks
Shed their sweet odors, and violets winked
Up in the eyes of the farmer's young girl —
Pride of the household, their beautiful Pearl.
And close by the house, slipping over white sand,
A brook cut the green like a long silver band;
But grandest of all, o'er the house and the floor,
The vines and the stream that talked on through the hours,
Stood a great grove of maples, and, shook by the breeze,
Sifted the sunlight on all through their leaves.

"And here grew the farmer's young daughter until
Childhood went by and a darker shade fell
On the clustering gold of her beautiful head;
And the eyes took the depth and the luster that's shed
Alone by the years as they touch us and pass,
Leaving beauty or ashes behind in their path.
Pearl never had been to the city to school,
Her culture was far from the popular rule,
Her manners were not of the dancing-school's art,
But grew into grace from the grace of the heart.
Her brothers declared her the lovliest girl
That ever bewitched with the flow of her curl;
Her father said, like her there ne'er was another,
And the look in her eyes told the love of the mother.

"The sunlight came out on one morning in spring,
When Pearl was eighteen; the winter's white wing
Was lifted from hillocks that slope to the south,
And all things were telling of blossoms to come.
Said the farmer, 'We must get at the sugar to-day,
The sap will run well; so we'll hasten away.

We'll go tap the trees, get the troughs all right,
Set up the kettles, and then toward night
Mother and Pearl to help us can come
And see to the boiling when that's to be done.'
All the day long shone the beautiful sun,
All the day long the sap merrily run ;
The kettles were hung, and the fires were made ;
And just as the tree-tops were filling with shade,
The boiling began, and the bright, laughing Pearl
Stood watching the steam as it rose on a whirl,
When suddenly into the frolic and fun
They discovered at once a stranger had come.

" Cousin John, from the city, so cultured and grand ;
Five years since Pearl saw him — he now was a man.
So tall and so proud   She forgot all the past now,
While the hot blood rushed up to her cheek and her brow.
He had come sugar-making on purpose, he said ;
Was going to stay till the whole thing was made
He'd carry the sap or do anything else
To help and to keep out of mischief himself

Poor Pearl ! the log house grew so suddenly small,
There came such a terrible plainness o'er all ,
The work she was doing seemed homely and mean,
But she lifted her head with the air of a queen
And gave him her welcome, but wished all the while
He looked as he did when she was a child,
That he never had come, so grand and so tall,
To make all her home seem so poor and so small.

" But Cousin John stayed till the sugar was done
And free from its fetters the little brook run,
Till the violets bloomed between patches of snow,
And then said, ' To-morrow I surely must go.'
Poor Pearl ! then she wished that he always would stay,
And thought how lonely he'd leave her next day,
While again all the house and the farm grew so poor
Because he was going ; and out of the door

She stole 'mong the maples and moonlight to think,
And seating herself by the brook's quiet brink,
She talked to the waters, and said she was glad
He was going — that she had been sad
Ever since he had come with his grand city ways.
She did not like him as she did at their plays
When they were both children; and then a bright tear
Shone on her cheek in the moonlight so clear,
And a sigh trembled up to the sweet lips that hid
The truth in her heart by that innocent fib.

"A shadow fell close in the moonlight just then,
And a voice broke the silence as if it had been
The brook that had answered. Cousin John took her hand,
And told her a story you can't understand.
But he came the next summer, and" —
"Mamma, what else?"
"Well here's Cousin John, let him tell you himself."
"Oh! mamma," cried Jennie, "'t was you all the time."
"And, papa," said Nettie, "O is n't it fine!"
While Charley just said in the midst of his glee,
"Dare, I told oo maple sudar drew up on a tree."
Then they laughed all together, but mamma she said,
"You must stop eating sugar now and go to bed."

The mother's advice is not meant for you here.
Eat all you can, for I tell you it 's clear
No one should think of dyspepsia or rule
Who eats for the good of our dear mission school.
'T will make your hearts glad and bring you no sorrow,
E'en if you do have a headache to-morrow.
But now, e'er you open your lips and your purses,
Let me put but another thought into my verses.
Our dear mission school — have you counted the worth
Of such schools as this in our dark, sinning earth?

    Picking up little ones,
      With a sweet pity,
    Out of the darkness
      And sin of a city,

Lifting them upward
　　　　From the ways trod,
　　Out into purity,
　　　　Up unto God.

　　Congress may legislate,
　　　Parties may plan,
　　Radical temperance folk
　　　Do what they can.
　　Reforms and reformers
　　　Seek to befriend,
　　They begin with humanity
　　　At the wrong end.

　　Touch you the children,
　　　Set their hearts right,
　　Set their feet walking
　　　Out in the light.
　　Human plans failing,
　　　The one Heaven gave
　　Is sure and eternal,—
　　　Jesus shall save.

Then help on the mission school, help it to-night,
Help bear their burdens and thus make it light;
And now you need listen no longer to me,
But go eat the "sudar that drew on a tree."

PHILLIPS BROOKS.

I.

So soon, away! in manhood's middle splendor,
　　While crowds hung breathless on his hast'ning word;
Lavish as ocean, rapturous and tender,—
　　A true apostle of his risen Lord.
So swift the silence on the lips prophetic,
　　So quick the feet beyond the hilltops gone;
Was any near to catch his falling mantle,
　　And send the thrilling message on and on?

II.

The tasks of God upon his Titan shoulders,
  The needs of men upon his stronger soul,
With lifted brow he breathed the life immortal,
  Until it swiftly sundered earth's control
Then place no broken column where he slumbers,
  No rifted lute, nor hint however sweet,
That such a prince in Israel "fell on silence,"
  In any hour when life was incomplete.

[Written for the *Union Signal*]

COMRADES, TWO.

WE PASS ON WITHOUT THEM.

[Written on the death of Julia Ames, associate editor *Union Signal*, and Mrs. Downs, President N. J. W. C. T. U.]

We stood in an eloquent silence
  These holiest days,
When thoughts of the Christ have been woven
  In sweetest of lays.
We came where the years were dividing
  The new and the old,
And passing 'twixt grave heap and garland,
  We counted the gold
    Of sands that, for joy or for sorrow,
    Move on where awaiteth to-morrow,
  With story untold.

All songs have seemed far in the stillness,
  Like strains of a lute
That tremble alone o'er the waters
  When voices are mute.
But years that divide do not move us
  To sharpness of pain,

So little they seem with their burdens
  Of losses and gain,
    When souls have come near the immortals,
    And treading the edge of life's portals
  Been thrilled with their strain

We heard in the circle of silence
  The falling of tears;
Have scented the fragrance of roses
  Love brought to a bier;
Have listened while low, tender voices,
  Half under their breath,
Were speaking of farewells and partings
  And talking of death.
    But out from a glory supernal
    There thrilled a great voice, "Life eternal
  I give them," it saith.

One life was a sheaf at its ripeness
  Of goldenest grain,
Its wealth had the glory of sunlight
  And sobbing of rain;
Ah! who shall dispute with the Master
  For whom it was grown,
That now in its day of completeness
  He gathers his own?
    Or who to earth's duty and sadness
    Call back the great soul from its gladness
  That heaven makes known?

One life was a flower prophetic,
  Aglow with the June;
Why tarried it not for the fruitage,
  But faded so soon?
Ah! who shall declare in what region
  Should come to its best,
The soul that so utterly loving
  Is utterly blest?
    Or who in these days of bereaving
    Would break, by a sob of our grieving,
  Ineffable rest?

Ah! comrades, we stand in the silence,
  Homesick for a day;
But how can our anguish be better?
  We follow that way
Let us lift up our hearts, our beloved
  Love on as of yore;
Who knows but in stress of the battle
  They haste to the fore?
  "Then onward, ye brave," to the duty,
    Not far, with the King in his beauty,
  We greet them once more.

AT THE GRAVE OF GENERAL FISK, COLDWATER, MICH.

I wonder sometimes that the world goes on
  Since his royal heart stopped beating,
I wonder that men can toil and plan
  And women can smile their greeting;
I wonder that even the children at play
  Do not pause as if touched by sorrow,
I wonder that any who loved him can care
  For the losses or gains of to-morrow,
Since never again, this day or another
We shall find what we lost at his going — our brother.

Sept. 1, 1890.

WHAT MEANS THIS STONE?

Written for and read at the laying of the corner stone of the Temperance temple, Chicago

Along the misty stretch of time
A million bells peal out their chime,—
A million bells of every clime,
  And silver tongue,—

They ring from steeples tall and fair,
They sound from turrets carved and rare,
And over altars steeped with prayer
    For ages long;
Till at this shrine a vanished time
    Thrills into song

The world has reared its temples old,
In ages dim and days of gold;
And evermore in reverence wrought
Its highest faith, its deepest thought,
Its strongest love and sacred pain,
In marble white of holy fane.
Then ring, sweet bells of olden years,
    With joyous tone!
A morning breaks; a promise cheers,
A newer temple woman rears
    For God and home,
And as the world's slow vision clears,
    Comes to her own.

Upon the years that are to be
There glows a radiance fair to see,
There dawns the coming century
    Of truth and right;
The clouds are lifting from the skies,
From valleys dim the mists arise,
Before the morn the midnight flies,
    And all is light.
The gate of hope now softly swings;
Above its arch a great bird sings;
The shackles fall, of might and wrong,
And all the world breaks into song
Ring, temple bells, from steeples gray,—
    In gladness ring!
Love's golden day is on the way,
    And Christ is King!

Between the darkness and the dawn,
The days to come, the cycles gone,
The age of love and age of brawn,
    Is laid this stone,
On which shall rise a temple set
Like jewel in a coronet;
In purpose high, unrivaled yet
    By shrine or throne.
Its walls rebuke the blighting shame
That, sheltered by a legal name,
Now dims a nations's fair renown
And tears her holiest altars down
Our ensign here in faith we rear —
Henceforth this place is battle-ground.

From fair foundations wide as love,
To slender turret far above,
Shall into stone and arch be wrought
The glory of prophetic thought;
And thronged upon the graceful height,
Its emblem true shall stand in light
    Serene and fine,—
A woman's figure, calm and fair,
Outlined against the upper air,
With hands uplifted as in prayer
    Who builds this shrine
    Saw age divine
Come swiftly on to human kind.

Beyond the shadows long and dim,
Upon the future's golden rim,
We lay the stone and raise the hymn
    Prophetic, grand.
Abide in strength, O jewelled stone!
For thou art set for God and Home,
For feet that stumble, hearts that moan,
    In all the land
Abide in strength before the gates
Where God's eternal promise waits.

We give thee to thy mission sweet,
With lavish wealth of love complete,
Nor count the sum
Who knows but on this altar-place
May shine the glory of His face,
When Jesus comes!

Nov. 1, 1890.

DEDICATION OF THE FIRST M. E. CHURCH OF JACKSON.

SINGING ANTHEM.

Long have we toiled with many fears,
Sometimes with song, sometimes with tears
Now, Lord, behold, this temple stands
Completed by our human hands.

Now take possession of thine own,
Within these walls set up thy throne,
Our finished work, O Father, bless,
And crown it all with holiness.

When here thy loving people bend,
Talk with them as a trusted friend;
When here sad souls their wanderings cease,
Forgive and bid them go in peace

Come in, Redeemer, King, and Lord,
Come in according to thy word;
Come in, while bending we adore,
Abide thou here forevermore

LET US DEPART HENCE.

In every life there comes an hour
Winged from on high with fearful power
Upon its trembling moments, lo!
The future's weal or woe
Is strangely hung, and as they swiftly roll,
Eternal fate is stamped upon the soul

— *D Berthune Duffield*

'T was night,—
A strangely solemn, breathless, breezeless night.
The moon half veiled her brightness and moved hushed
Along the vaulted sky, as if afraid
Her queenly robes might break the strange, deep pause
Of nature. Down from the dark blue heavens
Those holy sentinels, the stars, looked forth,
Cold, pale, and still as if afraid to shine.

No sound
Fell on the ear, no voice came borne along
The air that seemed so dense and solemn;
The restless throng that all the day had filled
The broad, paved streets and thronged those splendid piles,—
Fair Salem's pride and boast,— were gone as if
Some spirit wand had swept them from the earth.

No song
From the sweet, wild-wood warblers swept along
Through the tall trees on Lebanon's green side;
They rested all, even the sweet-toned bird,
The nightingale, poured forth no note, her voice
For once all silent in the groves that decked
The flower-twined brow of beauteous Olivet

'T was not
A peaceful calm that cometh like a spell,
Hushing the heart's wild throbbings into rest,
But a deep, awful hush, and ominous
Of some great ill to come   Upon Moriah's hill
The temple reared its lofty spires
And flashing domes, and o'er each
Marble tower the moonbeams threw what seemed
A spotless shroud of pale and misty light

The song
Of praise, that even from Jerusalem's
Cottages and halls, nightly went up
To Israel's King and God, were all unsung,

The evening prayer unsaid, or by the lips
Of gray-haired sires lisped brokenly; and tears
The while uncalled for, flowed down unconscious
Cheeks. And now the city seemed to slumber

  Knowest thou
That there are hours in the lives of men, o'er
Which Fate, the dark-winged angel, seems to rule?
And such an hour was this, the very air
Seemed dense with viewless spirit wings, hovering
Around that doomed and fated spot.

  Overhead,
Just where the bending skies met at the zenith,
A strange, bright star was hung; the light it shed
Was cold and glitteringly bright, and eyes
Gazed not upon it save to turn away
In fear. It was a sword, and seemed by hand
Of vengeance hung to tell a coming time
When in the dust Jerusalem should lie.

  Onward,
With solemn steps and slow, the moon had climbed
Up the unclouded blue. The hour for prayer
'Had come. And to Jehovah's holy house
The mitered priests went up. They spoke not as they
Solemnly prepared the evening sacrifice.
Upon the altar's holy shrine the fire
Burnt dim and low The candlestick of gold
Threw round a pale, faint glow That night, in robes
Of sacerdotal pomp arrayed, they stood,
An awestruck band. Suddenly the strange,
Dark bird of night, with long, wild shriek, that seemed
The wailing of some spirit lost, rose from
The temple's loftiest tower, and on
His midnight plume wheeled his dark flight away.

  And now
From out the holiest place, a strange deep
Murmur came Not like the sweep of angel's wings
Was it, but like the sound of many waters,

As they break in restless rushings
Upon some far-off shore, or like the wind
That makes, amid the moaning pines, its wild,
Deep, rolling anthem.

  Then were heard
The steps of a departing host, the strong
Foundations shook beneath their tread; the lights
Flickered as fanned by some mysterious breath,
The gorgeous hangings shook, disturbed by unseen hands.

  Anon,
Pealing along each dome and pillar'd court,
And echoing through the lofty aisles and
Marble halls, a voice was heard, unearthly
In its tones. Within that consecrated
Place, the Lord of Hosts had oft conversed
With man. "His stately goings" they had seen,
And there to angelic words had ofttimes
Listened with joyful awe and reverence.
But never 'neath that vaulted roof such voice
Had spoke before.

  Its words
Were few, its mission short; but on the ear,
Like the sad murmurs of a knell, they came
Low, deep, and strangely clear. "Let us depart!"
The angel's trust fulfilled,— the warning given,—
Upon the startled air their footsteps died
Away. And through the arches rang again
The echoed, "Let us depart!" Then all was still

  When years had fled,
And the proud temple lay a mournful wreck
Upon Moriah's grass-grown top, and the
Ark was far from its loved resting place,
The patriarch told with tearful eye the story of that night

March, 1858

MISCELLANEOUS.

[For the *Witness*]

THE SEEN AND THE UNSEEN.

IN any such moral struggle as the temperance reform involves, he misses the sublimest vision who sees only the human forces engaged, with the human probabilities of success, and therefore stands trembling between expediency and righteousness in chain of methods

Any contest which touches the kingdom of Christ, the welfare of humanity, and the salvation of souls must of necessity sweep out into the unseen, and lay hold of spiritual forces.

Where is the strength of the liquor oligarchy of this country? Appetite, avarice, greed of power, political policy; all these and more, are the seen forces to be overcome; but back of them is a satanic conspiracy to ruin men in this world and the other, and to overturn the kingdom of God and of his Christ. Every blow struck by this power, therefore, is in open, bitter opposition to all which Jesus came to accomplish. Not satanic influence, but Satan himself. bears rule in this gigantic national iniquity.

Wherein lies the power of the temperance movement?—Truth uttered by trenchant pen and eloquent lips, to which the world must needs pause and listen. Organizations composed of men who are willing to be counted for that truth, and organizations of women, who, by prayer and social influence, seek to advance it. All these and more; but back of them, in them, breathing through them, is God himself.

Not divine influences, but Divinity in person is on the field where eternal right is at stake, and souls are lost or won.

So this great reform, like those which have gone before it, sways not alone the armies of the earth, but other and greater armies darken the air just beyond the line of our vision, while this contest, which stirs our hearts, moves heaven and hell.

Satan cannot unconcerned look on alcohol's destruction, Christ cannot unconcerned look upon the slaughter of souls through alcohol. This puts the battle beyond "flesh and blood," among "principalities and powers."

Now set Republican and Democratic party policies, the tricks of political connivers, the value of office, and shallow sophistries of evil legislation, under the steady blaze of God's judgment, on one side, with the shadowy gloom of retribution on the other, and see how they look.

Face bravely all the truth now and here, for between that blaze and gloom every soul shall stand to give account, unless revelation is a delusion, and the gospel preached from thousands of pulpits in this Christian republic a snare and sham.

In such a realm as this, traversed by such forces, "expediency" has no place. A "choice of evils" is an impossibility. They may find room in the short-lived calculations of men, but never where the kingdom of light and the empire of darkness meet in decisive contest.

The truth admitted, then (and what Christian hesitates to admit it?), that in such moral struggles the unseen are the mightiest forces engaged, there follow two inevitable conclusions First, the final victory, however long delayed, must be with God and for the right; second, if we win in the visible and human part of the warfare, we must come to that success by the same divine principles which are victorious in the realm of spiritual powers outside our own.

"They always win who side with God" is not only the trust of the Christian heart, but is the lofty belief of the patriot and student of history.

"God is on our side," said a comforting friend to President Lincoln, in the darkest days of the civil war. "I am most concerned to be on God's side," was the solemn reply of the heart-sore, weary man, who was ahead of his country's thought, and therefore misjudged

God with man is not simply a possibility but a fact, where any evil is to be overthrown, and his power at hand makes victory assured. "What is the condition of his presence?" must therefore be the question of supremest moment to those who desire to see the temperance reform move on to the conquest.

In finding this we turn from half-truths and vain reasonings of men, to inquire what the Lord says for himself in this matter.

"Come out from among them, and be ye separate; touch not the unclean thing, and I will receive you" This is the enlistment order, if we are going with God into the war.

Absolute separation from evil, which is to go down, is the first condition —"Come out;" "be separate;" "touch not."

"The unclean thing" is in the land of judgment and destruction; like Sodom, it waits the fire of just indignation, and those who have complicity with it must suffer when that storm shall fall.

"Come out," "be separate," "touch not." Can that mean to "work with all parties"? to compromise on "high license"? to "tax and regulate"? and in order to reach the best method, and find not the right but the *attainable*, go on casting the ballot for those whose highest ideal is to "regulate" and thereby perpetuate the "unclean thing"? Remember we are seeking the divine side of the battle.

The mighty necessities of this hour and this question are not lonely in the world's history.

So Israel was separated from other nations to accomplish Jehovah's will. So Moses went to the gate with the cry of separation, when the camp was defiled by the worship of the golden calf. So Gideon found his dauntless three hundred who conquered by lamps, pitchers, and a devout war-cry In this way moral victories have always been reached.

History bears witness that the devil has never been beaten by his own weapons. From behind his own defenses, the prince of evil comes to defeat alone by the artillery of Heaven, and they who use that artillery must leave the devil's camp

There is a deal of jelly-fish talk about good people agreeing upon the principles of the temperance reform but differing about methods, as if that were a very innocent matter, to be treated with silent charity; but the sin of these good people lies in the choice of methods. The liquor traffic is a social evil considered by itself. It is a political evil through the compromise legislation which sustains it. To these propositions most good men agree. A wrong method of treating this acknowledged evil is their sin.

We are at the hour when one tremendous thing in this reform is method. "Come out," "be separate," "touch not," is the method in the unseen where the Lord of Hosts is leading to victory.

[For the *Witness.*]

A STUDY IN EBONY.

FIRST PAPER.

Whoever goes to the South with thoughtful brain and kindly heart must of necessity make a study in ebony

To the one who goes with a prayer on the lips for humanity, and a great patriotic love for his country, with its possibilities and problems, this study in ebony becomes impressive, not to say oppressive.

The Southern States cannot be traversed however carelessly, and the negro either forgotten or ignored. You ride through the level country, and there, set in wide stretches of cotton and corn, is the little cabin, and about its door is grouped the yesterday and to-morrow of your study in ebony.

You dash into a cut, and looking up to the bank above the window, you are faced again with the figures in ebony, their swaying bodies and waving hands seeming instinct with the excitement of the hurrying train.

You steam into town and step out of your car, to find five negroes, old and young, to every " grip sack," which with easy good nature they will carry a mile for a nickle.

Ebony checks your baggage, handles your trunk, drives your hack, opens the door at the hotel, builds your fire, waits at your table, until you are forced to see little and big, old and young, thus figure in our civilization everywhere Turning from these places of common toil, where a scant living is to be earned, you find the models for your study in some of the best built and equipped school and college buildings in the South.

Here with eager greed they bend over the books until now sealed to them, as if long thirst had famished their souls. You start out on a Sabbath morning, and if you would find churches crowded with worshipers, go with the ebony. What groups are there for your study! Old men, gray when freedom came , old women, who bent over the white baby and sang their heart-break out to God, when their own were sold from their arms ; men and women in the prime of life, dazed yet with all that freedom means ; then two millions born since the war — citizens by the Constitution, free men by the will of God. O there is wealth of chance for a study in ebony !

A primary thing in artistic conception is color; without it our ideal cannot be presented; so we are forced to say that in this picture "ebony" does not mean "black." Many-hued is this race of which we write. Africans, indeed! thousands of them are Americans by right of blood and birth, and lift their faces, bleached by lust, the monumental and measureless shame of the old order of things.

That prejudice, bitter as death against color, has not always made such nice distinction as it pretends, is written strong as proofs of holy writ on those light foreheads. Perspective is another important point in any picture. There are two ways to reach it in ours — first, go back thirty years and look down the narrow vista at this people

They were chattels then, bought and sold in the market. Home ties were nothing; the color they chanced to be born no praise or blame to them, the right of brain and heart denied, outraged by the white man's lust and avarice

For this state of things not the South alone, but the whole nation was responsible. Slaveships with their Yankee crews sailed from Boston Harbor, and the first prices for men and women went into Northern pockets. Constitutions sheltered the wrong; statesmanship compromised and perpetuated it; political parties fattened on its unhallowed spoils; though God was over all.

For another perspective, come to the *now* and look back at the race — free, enfranchised, outnumbering in large areas the white men who were once their masters, men and women with a destiny, asking elbow-room already for seven millions, and more to follow, and pressing the swift question to the nation's startled conscience, "We are here by your choice What will you do with us?"

Here comes the detail of the picture. Light and shade, uncertain vistas, glory on far-off hills of dreams, will not do for our study. It is crowded with throbbing human life that must have place, and race-destiny that must go into history.

To meet the problem of the black man's well-being and the country's well-being together, is too much for the South alone.

Their whole action and civilization was left by the war like a giant paralyzed, and is only now stirring to life and hope. Their fortunes were lost, the ranks of their men thinned, until family names were blotted out, and past them, thus impoverished and desolate, the proud, free North — swept on.

If one is tempted to say it was a judgment just for a measureless wrong, let him go to Arlington where lie sixteen thousand of the sons of the North,— where the very air seems crowded with souls, and across the sunniest day comes the drip of falling tears, and ask why they thus sleep, if the nation had no sin in the past, and, therefore, no responsibiltiy for the future Remember, we deal with God — and justice makes final settlement with wrong when he comes amid the watch-fires of humanity's circling camps.

It is a well-known truth, becoming every day clearer, that this great republic,— boasting of its power, flaunting its sentimentalism concerning the brotherhood of man,— has never yet come to any clearly-defined and far-reaching policy with regard to the negro race

In these last twenty-five years men of other nationalities have come to their freest own in the country. The Beer Brewers' Congress has controlled the United States Congress until the beer system, the continental Sabbath, and the party of great moral ideas, Germanized, has certainly given the German citizen not only his rights, but his own interpretation of personal liberty.

The Irishman, with his impulsive and yet imperious nature, has put his stamp of bad political notions and un-American religious faith on New England, the very cradle of the principles which built the republic, until Democracy with the Rev. M. Burchard's unwelcome definition, is at the helm of the great municipalities.

Anarchy, many-blooded and many-sided, has drilled for rapine and assassination before the eyes of Chicago's chosen city authorities, until the viper she nursed, for sake of party success and revenue, has stung her easy-going Western splendor, and wet her streets with blood.

Verily, the Republican party, in power since the war, can say, "We have guaranteed to all people the widest liberty — except these Americans in ebony."

They were made free, as a military measure; enfranchised, as a political measure, and then left for twenty years to the broken methods of changing political conditions, like sheep without a shepherd — Nay, like men without a home, and citizens without a country.

In all these years the government has never touched the race for its good, unless compelled by necessity, or moved by selfish and party interest. The negro race in American politics has been but a *casus belli* between the two great political camps which were striving for mastery.

This has seemed to go well for sefishness all the years. Denied the rights constitutionally given, they have instigated no riots, raised no mobs, purchased no dynamite, thrown no murderous bombs, but have lain docile and loyal like a spaniel at the feet of the masterful white man.

"Is this to go on?" is now the question, and history, experience, and humanity answer, "No." The church, by its missions and private philanthropy, with largeness of gift, has outstripped all that government has done for education, at least until the very recent past, and these seven millions of people, which a little while ago had only a Frederick Douglass to speak for them, have now educated leaders by the score.

These educated men begin now to measure the needs and power of a race which cannot be blown out of American politics by an oath on the lips of a politician. If the negro was not a desirable factor in our population, the time to think of it was when Boston and Charleston were agreed commercially in pushing the slave trade. They are here, and their scholars, preachers, orators, and political thinkers are beginning to bring the policy even of their Moses to the bar of the present. Once they were *commanded*, later, *led*, often by bad counselors.

The time is at hand when they will act for themselves.

We write in broadest charity for the South. "Why mention the old troubles at all?" said a Southern woman to me, with some bitterness. "Slavery was settled by the war, and we are satisfied." True, *slavery* was settled, but the negro was unsettled. When will his question be still by the present surface action of a great country?

This judgment of God *for* the colored race came two decades ago. The judgment of God *through* the colored race is yet to be. Even with his present political limitations, the ignorance and race prejudice of the negro is hindering the best thought of the South in meeting the questions, moral and political, which come with their rise of empire. In the settlement of the dram-shop and labor questions in America, these freedmen cannot be left out, and for twenty-five years to come this nation shall rock to her center with these. Both of the problems are national. Sectional politics will soon be impossible, and North and South instead of glowering at each other over the yet crouching figure in ebony, must put him from behind them, and say, "Here are seven millions of Americans not yet come to their own; what shall we do with them?"

SECOND PAPER.

I closed the first paper on this theme with the question which stands at the gates of destiny, and waits to answer, "Here are seven millions of Americans not yet come to their own; what shall we do with them?"

One of three conditions must obtain by any radical change from the present status of the black man in the South.

First, a yet more rigid domination of the white race, whereby political and educational rights shall be so circumscribed as to amount to serfdom for the negro, and thus our boast of having forever settled the principle of the brotherhood of man be given the lie before the watching world.

Two forces have united within the past twenty years to bring about this tendency toward serfdom and a demand for it on the part of the master-spirits of the South. The first in point of time, and probably of influence, was the unwise and unnatural policy of the early reconstruction days. At that time, for selfish and party purposes, the negroes were made the governing power by force, and put into a position which by every law of common sense and good government they could not long continue to hold.

In talking with the most intelligent men and women of the South, one is struck with the fact that they seem to be done with the issues settled by the war. The soldiers can meet as friends who once were foemen, but the issues raised anew by the reconstruction policy of the government have embittered all these years.

Here is the way a Mississippian told the story, with eyes that flashed beyond all control:—

"The negroes composed the legislature, and imposed upon us the jobs of their radical leaders. Men just out of slavery, who could not read a word, were elected to office, and then a 'carpet bagger' drew the salary and paid the negro ten dollars a month for sitting about, while the white man ran the machinery. We lay in our beds at night and listened to the armed negroes marching to the music of fife and drum, and did not know what wreck and shame might come to home and wife and children before the morning. We had no chance for life or property until we adopted the shot-gun policy."

Let us admit that at the bar of Northern opinion, and for that matter, at the bar of government, these men of the South were indicted as traitors deserving not only punishment, but humiliation; still the history of those days when we dealt with a smitten foe by the law of small revenge, is an eternal shame to a Christian republic.

It would have been better to have hung Jefferson Davis and a dozen others, disfranchised forever all the leaders, and then in broad magnanimity helped a stricken civilization to its feet, than to make an ostentatious pretence of forgiveness and then block the way to union by such dire insult to a century's growth of custom, prejudice, and opinion

The day of negro domination, enforced by martial law, was brief and bitter; just as the attempted domination by armed socialists, or any other class, inferior by birth or education, would be in the North. Anglo-Saxons are not to be made the stepping-stone for any race, and Anglo-Americans are intensified Saxons The uprising of the white people of the South against negro rule was in anger and anguish, not to say hatred, and its expression could neither be gentle nor just

They pushed their idea of home-rule as against national interference with such vigor that, united with the realization on the part of our statesmen that a mistake had been made, it brought the bargain which gave to Hayes the presidency, and gave the Southern States into the hands of a solid Democracy

The sun went down on the black man's kingdom when that day came. The unequaled political contest had settled no question of race, position, or destiny; it had only blotted out the confidence and love once existing between master and freedman, and left a blistering waste of distrust and fear, which lies between them yet.

The national government, with the Republican party at the helm, ruling by such majorities as to give it regal power, saw the black man's disaster and let him alone. The fruit of their policy was more than they could manage.

They enfranchised the slaves of yesterday and promised them all the rights of citizens, but the promise has never been made good. The black voter intimidated, cheated, or discouraged from his right, is a pitiable fact, after twenty years of freedom, and the party of emancipation cannot help him. The white race rule the South; they openly claim the right thus to rule. No matter on which side the majority stands, white blood *is majority*, and they freely declare it. Of course it follows: First, that in our form of government a minority cannot control a majority without hidden treachery or open injustice. Second, that a majority brought to submit to such control is already on the way to serfdom. Third, that three millions of voters, and seven millions of people denied civil, educational, and social rights must by their very existence, break down the spirit of our institutions on the one hand, and slowly breed a possible revolt on the other

First. If the South had been dealing with the slum elements of our great and small cities, she would before this have seen a baptism of blood, and found a shroud of ashes. But the docile, forgiving, loving African sings his lament to God, and waits for a better day.

It is useless to mourn over what has forever gone into history; the nation must deal with to-day as it is, and we face the fact that the Polander, the Italian, the Irishman, and the German, who landed on our shores a year ago, have a fuller and more secure citizenship than the American in ebony.

These races are strangers to our language, ignorant of our civilization, if not openly at war with the genius of our institutions; but they are free to put either ignorance, or political dynamite in their unhindered ballots; while the patriotism and Americanism of the black man has not reached its own, in government.

The negroes are held in this position by a conviction, honest and strong on the part of the white people of the South, that a negro majority holding free sway over the States, is a monstrous anomaly which should not be allowed, and must not become a fact. Their subordinate position crosses the fundamentals of constitutional law, but to take them from that State, would cross the deeper fundamentals of human nature.

Any honest mind, looking from the inside of the Southern problem, grows aghast at the conviction forced upon it that if the conditions were transferred to the Northern States, the "shot-gun policy" might be developed on the very slopes of Bunker Hill.

The continued or increasing serfdom of the negro race is therefore a national and not a sectional question. Neither delay nor cowardice will excuse from action, or prevent the hour of decision, while seven millions of Americans stand before the Constitution with its Sixteenth Amendment and pronounce it a delusion.

Second. The second change possible from the present order of things, is an uprising of the colored people in such a way as shall compel the surrender of all that is guaranteed by our post-bellum legislation, so they shall vote in freedom and win by the unquestioned right of majorities.

That such a revolt against the present may come before many years is more than probable if the negro is left to drift with the tides of thought and condition now sweeping him on.

Three main reasons are urged why the black man is forever incapable of taking an equal chance in a struggle with the white man: —

First, his indolence, which requires ownership and compulsion to bring out the elements of industry. The black race perhaps does lack the persevering force of our Northern laborers; but when that is said, it still remains true that the largest share of the labor of the South is performed by black hands. The supply makes labor cheap. The climate will not permit the sustained action of Northern latitudes. So the "dignity of labor," at the South is with the negro. This brings its own reward, low as wages are; and the accumulation of property on the part of these people, who have not owned themselves until lately, is something wonderful

It does not seem likely in a section where all life goes with a somewhat languid tread, that the indolence of the negro will seriously affect the final outcome Next, it is said that the capacity of the African for education does not reach beyond a certain limit. Southerners say that they go with a rush through school grades to the third reader, lay hold of objective things, store up nouns and facts; but when they reach the line of abstract ideas they go to pieces mentally. I took some pains to make inquiry of educators among them at this point, and the universal testimony was that a fair average of the pupils in every school and college shows as great capacity in mental and moral philosophy as white students, while there crop out in almost every such place of learning some men and women of commanding genius.

The ascendancy of white blood in many of them would do away with this theory as a check on their future All races reach their goals by following leaders, and the race of which we write has leaders to-day and more are coming.

Continued ignorance is, therefore, improbable, and the problem is not to be settled by the low content of little minds.

Again it is said they lack race-pride, and loyalty, and for this cause fail of unity in action for their own good

It is an undoubted fact that for a century the black man has found his high ideals among the white men whom he served, and his loyalty and his love were for master and master's household. They were all slaves together, with no chance for high gains in the world; but the men coming to life's destiny now will be apt to ask, "What can a black man reach in this country?" Among them are editors, like Fortune, of New York, who dare to tell the story of the "Negro in politics," as it looks from the negro's side. There are bishops and preachers not a few, who are teaching the people that instead of following a rather uncertain Moses-in-the-wilderness, it is time to cross the border to the land of race independence and nation-building. Independent political action is growing common; the negro knows he is a free man; he will one day demand the rights of a free citizen

The revolt once a fact, and the demand once successfully made by brain, or blood, or both, and several of the Southern States whose treasure and life were poured out to hold in the great union, are what Judge Tourgée calls "Black Republics," where ebony is king

Race identity is not in the centuries to be eliminated, or absorbed and lost; but come to the kingdom, who shall say thus far and no farther to the growing millions, or draw the lines of civil and political distinction before the feet of black majorities

Campaign speeches may call the slave of yesterday, "man and brother;" but are Sherman, Logan, and Blaine ready for an Africanized South?

The smoke of the conflict clears these days, the future of the republic cannot be builded on the sectional strife of the past Between the long-divided lines of Northern and Southern statesmanship crouches the yet docile negro, saying to both, since both have wronged him, "We are here by your will; what will you do with us?" If each in self-deliverance and scorn flings the question to the other, the negro will not only speak, but strike for himself.

Third The third possibility is such action on the part of the government as shall give to the black people a chance for home, country, and destiny, without putting the cotton States under their possible domination. Some territory in our national realm should by right come to these slaves of the past.

The expenditure of as much life, money, and care as has been given to the Indians, would make some domain for the freedmen a success

The negroes, in sufficient numbers to make the working force of a great people, will always be desirable at the South It is the negro in majority at the polls that hinders his civil adjustment and makes the problem so difficult.

The colony idea is old, and was discussed threadbare before the war, but it has never been tried, and, therefore, cannot be called impossible or impracticable. If the surplus negro population could be withdrawn from the overcrowded States, another day would dawn.

Progress is checked, great public questions settled in race scuffle, and nothing settled at its best. The negro vote led largely by Northern influence and allegiance, is the *bete noir* of the Southern people, and everything goes with halting tread, because these things are so.

The intense but stationary struggle is like the rope-pulling game of the college campus, where the muscle is about equally divided between the ends, and where the victory is long delayed. The white vote of a solid democracy united in the one question of preventing negro rule, is at one end. The black men — suspicious, ignorant, with race prejudice and fear — are at the other. Sometimes it swings one way, sometimes the other; but the game has not been declared "off" for twenty years, and meanwhile the years drift by a great but prostrate civilization. It is time the statesmanship of the nation dealt with this question in ebony.

AFTER TWENTY YEARS.

Twenty years since the bell outrung,
Twenty years since the song was sung;
Twenty years since the tainted air
    Of the hall of death,
    With its poison breath,
Its drunken revel, and fell despair,
Was smitten through by a woman's prayer,
When love and pain under holy spell,
Asked for their own at the doors of hell.

Beside the milestone where our forces pause to-day, stand with us both Memory and Prophecy. The hosts of reform called out by the spiritual tocsin of the Crusade, and held together by a great purpose, must after two decades feel the power of change. Bright heads are crowned with gray, young faces sobered by the touch of time; glad, hopeful eyes have deepened with the severity of the conflict, or the heart sickness of hope deferred; and ranks, however bravely filled by later comers, seem sadly thin as we count.

"The noble, great ones, gone!" What though the hope of immortality stirs our souls, that we know they dwell in fairer regions and in their joy rejoice? Still the battle seems a little sterner set since they are off the field, and between us and them lies that silence across which life's common language may not reach. What wonder then that Memory, mute-lipped and tender-eyed, holds our hearts in thrall as, pausing, we look back over the way of the years

A sadder thing must Memory note, that some have withdrawn from a yet unfinished battle, and camp to-day on the ground of ease or compromise.

Crusaders of '73, afraid of the stern issue they themselves raised, in its logical outcome in '93. *Leaders of '73*, whose trumpet-call to the defense of principles not yet victorious, rang across the world, silent and inactive in '93. *Comrades of '73*, pledged in a fight to the finish, for "God and Home and Native Land," out of the ranks in '93, or doing dress-parade duty on non-combative ground! Time makes savage analysis of character, and develops or rots the fiber of it, according to quality.

The farewells to our faithful dead are jubilant pæans, compared with those spoken to such as falter in danger or betray by any stress of temptation, a cause like that for which the white ribbon is a token.

At our stone of remembrance this year, let a great prayer ascend for a call as divine and clear, a separation as complete, daring, and unselfish, and a purpose as single and definite, as gave to us this anniversary Memory sings out of the past —

> Moved by loving and stung by pain,
> Poor with losses, from vigils vain,
> Swift from the homes whence light had fled,
> Where hope was smitten, and love lay dead,
> Women bereft went out to cry
> In the ear of the world as it trampled by,
> "We've watched and tended, have loved and prayed,
> But stronger than we are the snares they laid
> To a guilty nation we now make moan
> And seek at the doors of hell, our own."

This is the issue, and the battle-cry which, lying on the hushed lips of Memory, is taken up by the thrilling voice of Prophecy as she looks on the future into which our cause is leading, and our feet must go.

It may be counted a providence that the anniversary of the Crusade is so near the blessed Christmas time, when the heart of the world grows glad over the birth of the greatest Reformer of the ages, and the only Saviour of men. Some things we may well study anew, since they will help us to a prophetic outlook for the temperance reform, and to the right qualities in those who are its leaders.

Jesus as a reformer, had faith in his mission. He did not succeed, as men count success. He won no honors, wore no crowns. The only crowds that thronged him were those who needed his mercy, and these brought no credit to the movement, but he welcomed such to his kingdom since his mission was to "seek and save the lost"

Jesus was devoted to his Father's will. When it brought him to the shadows of the garden and the unspeakable gloom of the cross, that devotion never faltered "He gave himself a ransom for many" Jesus was faithful unto death. Nothing allured or discouraged; greater than the world for which he died, greater even than his divine personality was the unseen kingdom whose foundations he established. The shadow of the cross fell over all ways he trod, but he went on to the end and "finished his work."

Jesus was victorious It did not look so at Calvary, but light fell clear on Olivet when he said, "All power is given unto me," and entered upon his glory. To-day the thrones of evil tremble because he reigns, and all things move to his universal dominion. Since Christ marked this path, every reformer has followed it or *failed*. To be Christlike is the only way of success in moral effort The law of victory for the reform, as for the reformer, is of the greatest moment to those pledged to the world's uplifting on any great and general way.

Standing where the past and future meet, we may well rejoice at some of the winnings of twenty years. Total abstinence and prohibition, as principles, have been weighed in the balances, and tried in the fires of science and statesmanship, and have stood the test. They have come into the arena of logical debate, and no voice has been able to overthrow them. The only argument opposed is that of appetite and selfishness, and the nation's choice for bloom or blight lies between these and the truth.

The church, the home, and the public school have been permeated with right thinking and true science on these great questions. Enough of the people know the truth to make either inaction or complicity with the wrong henceforth *a sin*. The reformers who have pushed these great principles to the front have made themselves worthy of a hearing by those who mean to obey the truth, and *worthy of persecution* by their enemies. The temperance reform has won its martyrs. They lie in graves where the licensed liquor traffic sent them, and to the shame of State and nation, their unavenged blood cries yet to Heaven, while their murderers walk abroad unwhipped of justice But a government which allows truth to be slain in the streets, faces the future and the inevitable righteousness of God

The W. C T. U has won a name which has gone to the ends of the earth, a synonym for whatsoever is pure, and has translated its high principles into the languages of the world. The W. C. T. U. has developed a rounded, earnest womanhood, and brought to worthy fame some of the best known women of to-day, while its leader easily stands preeminent in the place she holds and the work she has done for her country and her time

All this being true, we should look for near tokens of ultimate victory. *But they do not appear.* The truths admitted by the brain and conscience of the nation do not get into its laws nor direct its statesmanship. The blood of souls yet stains the gold of her revenues. The actual revolt of Iowa Republicanism from the law and principle of prohibition outlines the future policy of that great division of citizens ; and the fact that bishops and brewers both rejoice in the triumph of that party which thus throws off obligation to this greatest of questions is but a token of the moral obstinacy abroad. But —

>That cry rings on and it will not cease ,
>On our borders will never again be peace.
>The voice of warning has come abroad,
>The time grows ripe for the hour of God.

What, then, says Prophecy at the gateways swinging across the path of twenty years ?—This Righteous principles can never be defeated or overthrown.

When such principles are revealed to nations, they form, if accepted, the basis of progress ; if rejected, the ground of judgment. Compromise with evil always brings disaster ; it has builded the tombs and written the epitaphs of the nations, and will while truth is truth. Well may this republic pause amid her starving and unemployed millions, and ask for diviner reasons than administrations, tariffs, and silver bills for her confused councils, financial panics, and industrial disasters. Back of them all, God reigns, and when mischief is framed into statutes, and thrones of iniquity built by law, but one of two results can follow "Repentance unto righteousness," or "Wrath unto retribution ! "

The vital question of the hour for our pledged host is this Have we in any way missed the path, divinely opened? Can we yet be trusted with the great principles so long defended? Every true reform is borne on by two lines of forces — the *subjective* and the *objective*. The subjective forces are the great, eternal, underlying truths by which it exists, through which it conquers, because of which it *must* be. These are *first*. Nothing should cloud them; no interest, no personality should divide honors, or contest with them for the first place. Every voice should be but their messenger; every worker their servant, every trumpet their battle call. Principles define the *cause;* the cause is beyond all it creates.

The objective forces are the methods by which the reform is carried on, the interests built up, in greater or less wisdom, to advance it These often express the reformer more than the reform, and may hinder rather than help the advance of principles. After twenty years the objective forces are the things to be guarded, lest they overtop, in what they ask of time and energy, the real thing involved

It takes courage and faith to stand for principles where they seem to make no progress but wait silent as the "Sphinx in Egypt sands." Workers long to show results, to say to the world, See what has been achieved! They are often unwilling to wait the triumph of conviction wrought by the Spirit of God Here lies the danger. We need a return to more spiritual weapons, a new consecration to principles which alone are eternal and triumphant. The curse is yet upon us; conscience sleeps, evil is abroad, and the God of nations at the door. We must get right or be punished.

> Set the trumpet to thy lips, O watcher
> Who heard the voice divine;
> Blow one clear strain to rouse the souls that slumber,
> This is an evil time
>
> Set the trumpet to thy lips, O watcher!
> Cry out across the night;
> Stay by the truth, wherever it may lead thee
> At last 'tis crowned in light

MARY T. LATHRAP HALL, HACKLEY PARK, MICH.

ANNUAL ADDRESSES

DURING HER PRESIDENCY OF THE STATE W. C. T. U.

[Kalamazoo, May 23, 1882.]

Sisters of the Convention :—

It seems but yesterday since, closing the convention for 1881, we turned the white page which was to receive the record that now through glow of smiles, or mists of tears, we read in our convocation of 1882. But, whether in smiles or tears, we reverently speak our devout thanksgiving to God for the grace which has been all-sufficient in trial or in toil

The changes which have come to us as an organization during the year, have been painful to all. The election of Mrs. Hudson as president was so unanimous and hearty, that she went out from the last convention with success assured to her administration, so far as a satisfied and loyal constituency could bring it, but scarcely a month had passed before she was called to her new home in Cleveland, Ohio, and we were left to miss the brave, wise, thoughtful woman who had been our leader for so long.

My predecessor needs no tribute from me in this presence, else would I give it, for no one felt her going more keenly than the one who, by the choice of your Executive Board, stands before you in her place at this hour.

The situation at the opening of the present year was not the most favorable for any conspicuous success in the temperance reform in Michigan. Our forces were depressed by the refusal of the legislature of 1881 to submit the question of Constitutional Prohibition to the people.

The previous campaign to secure this result, had been very absorbing to both the Red Ribbon clubs and the Woman's Christian

Temperance Unions of the State, and they had given themselves so fully to it, that the educational and reform work, as carried on by them since the Reynold's movement, was largely laid aside.

To turn back to what appeared to our impatient souls the alphabet of our effort, and again content ourselves with first principles, after our great hope that the final blow would be struck where it *should* and *must* be given, was no easy thing.

But ideas, like trees, get sturdier growth by cutting back, and any one who imagines that the temperance cause has weakened in the year now closing is greatly mistaken.

Checked we were, at the door of, shall I say legislative or party authority? But checked like a river, to accumulate volume and power; so, all these quiet months since we last met in convention, brains have been growing broader as they have studied the problem which concerns every department of our civil life,— education, legislation, finance, and morals. Hearts have grown hotter at the outrageous wrong which puts yearly nearly one hundred thousand of our citizens in their graves, and holds two hundred thousand more in the prisons of the country, to feed and clothe a few thousand men whom avarice, appetite, or some other form of devilishness have put into the liquor traffic; souls are growing great in an intelligent and righteous wrath, at a system of legislation that fosters such wrong, and protects it because of a solid vote that means party success.

We believe, therefore, that this "off year" in the temperance work closes with an underswell of public sentiment such as has never been known in Michigan. This is said in a general sense, as the question stands related to the outgoing of public affairs in the commonwealth as well as in the special sense in which it concerns the work the State W. C T. U. has in hand.

An honest indignation at the undemocratic action of the legislature that refused the exercise of the right reserved by the people,— to decide upon vexed and long-mooted questions, has taken possession of thoughtful men not heretofore interested in the issue itself, while disgust at those in office, who betrayed every trust committed to them by the suffrages of temperance men, and disregarded all moral obligation, has deepened this feeling.

Besides this, the alarm sounded for so long by so-called *fanatics*, has at last struck the dull ear of some, and aroused them to such action as shall protect their own best beloved from the *very legal taxpaying* and altogether *lawful saloon* of Michigan.

The spring elections have plainly indicated the spirit abroad — the temperance agitation telling on local politics in no slight degree. Many towns, like Battle Creek, put a temperance ticket in the field, and a goodly number, like Battle Creek and Whitehall, won the victory.

Since election, several towns have increased the bonds required to three, five, and even six thousand dollars, and no "straw bail." While to clinch the matter of honesty in bondsmen, some town boards have asked that a statement of the wealth of these men should be furnished the supervisors, in order that they might be properly assessed.

In the shore towns of Lake Michigan, which have never been regarded as very hopeful territory, citizens' leagues, composed of the best elements of society, are being organized for the purpose of enforcing the laws for the protection of minors, and the proper observance of the Sabbath, and already, results are encouraging.

The leading daily paper in the State organ of the dominant party, has, in the months just passed, struck sturdy blows at "Sunday Saloonism" in our chief city, and has been rewarded by the discovery of some new things concerning the strength and unscrupulous dishonor of its foe.

Decent, sober citizens looking at municipalities degraded by lawlessness, by broken Sabbaths and outraged law, and looking upon their own ruined boys, are saying, "Something must be done." So the slumbering lion of public opinion is being aroused, the lightning shaft of conscience evoked, and as sure as truth is truth and God is God, the party of to-morrow is the one that *dares* to take the Temperance Reform.

The State Alliance, in its rapid growth, is another result of this change in the realm of political thought. At first it grew slowly, even in the favor of the temperance people, but the day of doubt is past, its "enemies being the judges."

The hot attacks upon the Alliance as an organization, and upon Mr. Bontecou, its active agent, by the political press in some localities, as well as the untiring and exhaustless abuse of the organ of the liquor dealer's association, furnishes ample proof that the Alliance is not considered a bit of fancy work in the coming campaign.

Hundreds of thoughtful men who have said, "Something must be done," have also said, "This is one way to do it," and are putting *faith* and *money* into it.

Mr. Bontecou writes *The Lever*, "We shall place five thousand dollar's worth of stock for April." In a recent personal letter he says, "Before your State convention meets, we shall have over thirty thousand dollars. It [the Alliance] is going to be the most powerful concentration of money and moral and political strength, which has ever been known, inside of two years."

The relation between the Alliance and the State W. C. T. U. has been the subject of much comment, and since both are here to stay and will work side by side in the on-coming struggle, this may be a good place to set some matters right.

The Articles of Association provide for two classes of members —

1. The *Active*, who are to be voters and therefore men over twenty-one years of age. These only have the full privileges in the business meetings of the organizations.

2. Contributing members, who pay five hundred dollars into the fund, are invited to the meetings and discussions, but do not have a vote. This class is open to women, and minors who are not voters in the State.

The Alliance has been somewhat severely criticised for this so-called exclusion of women from full membership, but in the consultations between the workers in both organizations, there seemed to be two good reasons for this plan —

The one, that the Alliance faces the question *politically*. When petitions from temperance people have been sent to the legislature from time to time, the cry has been raised that they were not from the constituency of the representatives, but from women, children, and a few fanatics; and they have been of doubtful weight at the capitol. Other organizations of men for moral suasion have broken apart at the polls, but the Alliance looks not to an organized *sentiment*, but an organized *ballot*, therefore its members are *voters*.

The other reason is that the W. C. T. U. is one of the most compact and influential of temperance organizations, and cannot be spared.

To absorb our women and their money, would be in many localities to destroy the unions, a result earnestly deprecated by the men interested, as well as the leaders of our own work.

The best good of the State union was, therefore, sought in this plan, as well as the greatest power for the Alliance.

The question will be asked, Why then have the contributing membership at all? The reply is, that many women who are not, and never have been, in our work, will put their money into this form of effort, giving their means where they cannot, or will not give themselves.

There are hundreds of women who see things this way, and are perfectly satisfied with the terms, and for those who are not pleased, there is no compulsion.

We have honorary memberships at one dollar for local unions, and five dollars for the State, these being for men as well as women; but these gentlemen contributors cannot be voters in our councils. Even our mixed organizations for which we now provide, cannot be represented by a man on the floor of the convention.

Our union is a woman's union because we believe it can be most effective in that way.

The Alliance is an alliance of men, because they believe a harder blow can be struck on that plan; and let us say, Amen.

We cannot close this survey of the political situation without mention of the convention called for the 28th of June, in the city of Jackson The Northwest is athrill with the determination to carry the temperance question to the ballot box, where the clamor of the whisky ring may be silenced by the voice of the people.

Failing to reach this through the existing parties after years of patient waiting and seeking, the demand for separate political action is deemed imperative, and such action will come if the parties much longer ignore this most important moral question of the hour.

We should not, and do not forget that the Republican party of Kansas was grand enough to fight the battle for constitutional prohibition to the victorious end, and that brave St. John is a Republican governor.

We should not, and do not forget that the same party are at the front in Iowa, and stand now, God bless them, in the heat of the conflict; but the same results cannot be reached everywhere.

These States have such a party majority that they can risk the loss of a few thousand votes without defeat. In States more doubtful in the great campaigns, the parties will never take a dangerous issue until forced to do so.

These two States have no overwhelming force massed in great cities to which all else must bow; and can, therefore, be more easily brought to their present position; but in others which have these great centers and, therefore, face the danger of loss to party, the temperance victory will scarcely be reached, except by revolution, and revolution means the overthrow of the old and incoming of the new. A moment's thought will bring proof of the statement just made.

What governs the Empire State, stretching in its pride from the eastern sea to the western lakes? — New York City. What controls the Crusade State, baptized first of all into this greatest reform of our day? — Cincinnati What beclouds the vision of the average Wisconsin candidate to public honors? — Milwaukee lager. What speaks with a tone that moves all Illinois? — Chicago. What silences the voice and drags the conscience of the Michigan legislature in a great moral crisis? — Detroit and the liquor interest of the first district·

These things being so, party success does not lie along the track of a reform that cuts through the greed of avarice, appetite, and ambition for place.

The golden calf is enthroned in the midst of an enslaved and warped public opinion. What is to be done? Go in among the worshipers and bow the knee with them in the name of expediency or in hope of a far-away good? — No, never, to the gate rather with the cry of separation, "Who is on the Lord's side, let him come"

That cry is in the land, and God is in it, let all the brave remember that after that call in Israel, the calf was ground to powder.

As we stand where we mark this slow, but mighty lift of the tide of public opinion, and hear its beat on the shore that girds the tomorrow of our country's destiny, we naturally ask what of woman's work and part in the present aspect of affairs, and in that yet to be accomplished?

When one looks on the coral islands that lift themselves from the ocean, there is a voice forever in their caves that speaks of the patient toilers at the bottom that made what is seen possible; and no one may look at the temperance reform to-day and forget the women of this republic.

A song floats on the air from the Presbyterian church of Hillsboro. A psalm falls on the ear as if freshly spoken from heaven; a band of gentle women go out with solemn, but shining eyes, in the strength of God, to face, for the first time, in his own horrid lair, the hyena of our civilization. A prayer from the mouth of hell falls on the outer air, and shakes with a trembling such as came into the Philistine's camp, the moral foundations of society.

That song swelled to a chorus; that band grew to an army; that prayer brought salvation straight from heaven to hopeless souls, and a reform to the nation. In that heroic day of womanhood, kings were crowned, prophets anointed, and apostles chosen to lead in the on-coming struggle, and the temperance question was lifted on a level with the eyes of the civilized world ; and it will never down again until settled in righteousness

After nearly a decade we pause to ask, What of these aroused daughters of our people whom a saloon keeper honored by calling the " Rock of Ages Women ; " and the answer comes, " Here are we."

Meanwhile, organization has run from ocean to ocean, until there is no State or territory where their voice is not heard.

Children have listened, until boys and girls of ten years know more of the nature and danger of alcohol than their grandfathers ever knew. The church has listened, until it has declared against the wine of commerce on the table of its Lord. The nation has listened, until within two past years, nearly every legislature, State, and nation have faced the problem in some form.

Within this year the conservative South has been invaded by the matchless president of the national W. C. T. U.; and down the Mississippi, along the Gulf, and into the Lone Star State, has been carried the law and the gospel of this movement by that voice that never argues but to win, and never prophesies but to charm. The " Rock of Ages Women " still live, and this convention is only a division drill, for we of Michigan are in the army to fight it out till Prohibition or— Eternity.

Our relations with the national W. C. T. U. we should highly prize and generously meet. This work is not alone for our commonwealth, but for the country, and connectionalism is strength. We therefore urge our workers to broad views The republic is under the curse, and national life is involved in the issue

The drunkard who stumbles to your door should be helped. The child in your home or Sabbath-school, instructed ; but let us never forget in our home interests that the end to be gained, is the redemption of our common country

Our auxiliary ship with the national society and representation in its councils, is secured by loyalty to its aims in essentials, and the payment to its treasury of five cents for each of our reported memberships.

The question of the ballot for woman comes more and more to the foreground of thought in connection with the temperance agitation in our own State, as elsewhere.

Michigan women have been counted conservative upon this question which has so greatly stirred the national society, and for a truth, have moved more slowly than the other States about us. This carefulness has been the subject of some censure at home and abroad ; and we believe it is time to meet this growing idea in a different manner than we have done in the past.

It is not within the province of this address to discuss the matter from the standpoint of personal opinion, and we have too high regard for the intelligence of this body of women and those they represent, to attempt it. We deal therefore, not with particulars or opinions, but with principles and their effects.

The broad, abstract question of woman's right to the full privileges of citizenship in our form of government, which taxes, governs, and hangs her by law, is pretty well settled in her favor by the best and most unprejudiced minds in the country, and is not the question before this organization — the sole object of which is to advance the temperance cause. But the ballot in the hands of woman as a helpful or sure means to that end, is a vital question for this place and this hour. When once fairly advanced, it divides the convention and the workers they represent into about three classes.

On one hand are the women who are so radical upon woman suffrage that they believe the demand should be made at once for a right too long denied ; and even should it seem to interfere for the time with other lines of temperance effort, they believe the ultimate victory will never come until women at the ballot box first help to make the law, and then to enforce it.

To these thus fully pursuaded, hesitation is cowardice, and all expediency a delusion. They say, Let us as a State organization ask for the ballot, that we may *vote* out what we have to this time so signally failed to *pray* out of the body politic.

At the other extreme, are the conservatives upon the whole question — those who do not believe women were designed to stand abreast with men in government; that the logic of history, the very nature of things in the relation of the sexes and the word of God, are against woman suffrage These, out of a good conscience, are eager to guard what is to them a sacred Christian work, from this radical and questionable invasion

Between these two extremes is a third class, which agrees in the main with the first we have mentioned, about the *right* of woman to vote in the government, but which doubts or questions the wisdom of organized action on the part of the State W. C. T. U. to secure it, thereby making it a part of our work

The reasons for this hesitation of opinion and action are perhaps about as follows : —

1 It is a vexed question, and divides us   2 It turns attention from the main point   3. Prohibition by the vote of male citizens seems as near or nearer than woman suffrage as a means to receive it   4 With constitutional prohibition before the people, it is difficult at this time to bring to the legislature, or the public mind, another unpopular issue, with any hope of success for either. These three distinct divisions are to be found among the women of the State, and those composing them are equally conscientious, and equally interested in the overthrow of the liquor system.

For us, as a representative body, to deal fairly and wisely with so important and exciting a question, is not an easy matter, and to do so, the most radical and the most conservative must keep the good of the cause in full view, and value it above all personal opinions.

Two things are to be sought in any action upon this subject : —

One, to take just the advanced step which is necessary to meet the demands of the hour in the relations we hold to the political life of the State and the present status of the temperance reform. The *other*, to take that progressive step in such a way as shall not weaken our organization.

If the majority of the convention have reached the conviction that they ought from this place to speak in wise, dignified, and clear-cut fashion, in favor of the ballot for women, they have a full right so to speak.

If a majority of the convention really believe that at the ballot box, and in party lines, women are to be trusted more than men where great moral issues are at stake, and that therefore her vote, if summoned, would be the overthrow of the legalized dram shop, they have the fullest right to express that conviction.

If a majority of this convention believe that great good will result to the temperance reform in Michigan if the women of the State W. C. T. U. shall not only *declare* but *work* for the ballot both through the next legislature and among the people, then they have a right so to *order* and so to *plan*   But as such a new departure in methods would involve more than a mere expression of opinion by resolutions, it should be remembered that a majority vote, which divides hearts, interest, and opinion upon an essential point, and fails to carry a loyal acquiescence of the minority, is never a safe victory in an organization like ours ; so our hope lies in reaching the ideal so beautifully expressed by another, "In essentials, unity ; in non-essentials, liberty ; in *all* things, charity."

In closing, it remains for me to congratulate you upon the work of the year, so well and faithfully done in the midst of much that would dishearten all but the brave souls who see the triumph from afar by the eye of faith.

Some of our number, since we last met, have laid down the toil of life and entered the rest and reward of the faithful. Others that are here have passed under the rod of sore trial, and have been giving to the world in loving ministry the crushed-out fragrance of their own chastened lives.

Now, together we lift our eyes to the open doors of opportunity that shall lead us out into usefulness, or into heaven, in the years to come. It matters little who shall praise or blame us, if at last the "Well done" of the Master shall baptize our souls into infinite calm and satisfaction.

Some one has told us of a carver in stone who worked on that poem in marble, the cathedral of Milan. The work he was doing was to go high on the turrets, and when once in position no human eye would ever see it again. "Why are you so careful in your work?" said a looker on. "No one will ever see it after it is once in place."

"I am not making it for men," answered the artist, solemnly, "I work for the eyes of God and the angels." If such reverent words were fitting one who only carved in marble, how much more for those who work on deathless souls.

[Adrian, May 24, 1883.]

' Only another Convention,"—
    The looker-on may say,—
A thing of noise and pretension,
    With method, plan, and invention,
  So much in fashion to day ;
A parliamentary redemption
    For souls that have gone astray,
And, "Roberts' Rules of Order,"
    For feet that are out of the way.

Such words might be spoken from the *outside*, in this day of reforms for the million ; but I, who am permitted from the *inside* to greet this goodly company of royal women, know that the noisy theorists are not here; but a part of the bravest and most patient army that ever did battle for God and humankind.

When, ten years ago, women, carefully sheltered and tenderly reared, went into the saloons of this country, making their plea to God and men from the very lair of the tiger, and singing their songs made sweet with many tears, as near the threshold of hell as those in the body ever come, the world stood aghast for awhile — and, when its brain cleared, said "The crusade is heroic."

But since that wave of enthusiasm passed by, we have had nine solid years of the *dead level* of conflict, about which the world has thought and cared but little. Years of hope and fear, success and defeat, patient toil against wrong thinking, wrong living, wrong preaching, wrong voting, and wrong legislation; and these have called for more heroism than the brief days of marvel, that have passed into history as the "Woman's Crusade."

The Woman's Christian Temperance Union confronts a vice as old as humanity, entrenched in blood, poisoned by centuries of hereditary transmission. It confronts a traffic, made powerful and respectable by law; a traffic which has its defenders not only in the saloon, but at the bar, in the pulpit, in legislative halls, and the belated schools of science; and yet, without money, political influence, or votes, it fights the foe which has them all. But, thank God, in these years of ceaseless struggle it has never retreated from a position taken, never gone into winter quarters, and never once pulled down the banner lifted — for God, and Home, and Native land

THE SITUATION IN MICHIGAN.

When we separated at the close of the Kalamazoo Convention one year ago, we had two main desires so far as temperance legislation in our State was concerned, and for the fulfilment of these desires we have labored during these months

The first was the submission of the question of Constitutional Prohibition to the people. We had reasonable expectation, even at that date, that the State Convention of the Republican party would favor such a measure, and that if such expression were given, the legislature of 1882-3 would not fail to carry out the party pledge

In this trust in "princes and the children of men," we have been sorely disappointed. The Republican State Convention, under severe pressure from its strong temperance element, did put a plank in its platform which pledged the party to bring this question to the ballot-box, where the voice of the people might decide it. We do not say that such expression was dishonest, or that they did not intend to keep the pledge they made ; but this has been a year of cyclones, not only in the physical, but in the political world ; and in the autumn a cyclone struck the party which has held the dominant position for twenty-two years in the nation, since which the world is a bit "topsy turvy" to their vision,— Michigan Republicans not excepted.

It is a little curious to watch the later action of this party concerning temperance reform. When Kansas won the victory for prohibition through the Republicans, their most progressive journals and leaders said to the temperance people: "Now, what need have you for another party? do n't you see you can soonest win your cause through the existing and victorious organization?"

When that fire ran over the border of Kansas and set Iowa aflame, until the Northwest and conservative East were lighted with the signal fires of a new legislation, the Republican press and leaders grew suddenly silent Kansas was a "feather in the cap" to attract the gaze of temperance men and hold them in party lines ; but that which followed was the "trump of doom," and something must needs be done

On the 27th of last June the people of Iowa, by thirty thousand majority, after a splendid campaign, declared for Constitutional Prohibition, and the State rang with jubilant songs Two months later, the Republicans assembled in State convention, but they uttered no word, and made no sign that they shared the enthusiasm of the people What was the matter? Is it not just possible that, even at that early date, the national party managers had spoken?

When the autumn campaign was fully inaugurated, they withdrew temperance speakers from the canvass in some States, and in others talked beer and water from the same platform. In Michigan, the temperance question was squarely out in the submission plank; but which of all the speakers discussed it in their campaign oratory? The silence was significant. What was the matter? Is it not just possible that the national party managers had spoken?

Now the legislature of Michigan has failed to redeem the pledge made in party conventions, and the voice of sovereignty in Iowa is hushed by a technicality. What *is* the matter, if the national party has not spoken? The mother may forget her child, but the Republican party will not forget the Raster resolution, and the bargain made for a solid beer vote in 1872.

We speak no hard words against them for any or all of these things. To throw away *success* for a fine moral point, is not a thing done by political parties, especially when they are twenty years old, and have grown accustomed to the crown and scepter. We desire in calmest and gentlest speech to say that it seems settled that the party of moral ideas intends in no way to imperil its interests by any serious legislation against the liquor traffic.

To say that it is far ahead of all other political organizations, that it shows a *clearer* sentiment than they, while it is true, does not meet the case. The party *does not* and *cannot* favor prohibition. The logic of the situation is as inevitable as it is serious. There is a chance just now for patriotism, conscience, and heroism — to choose righteousness instead of success.

The Republican party was grandly born of a great principle, in an hour heavy with destiny to the country. Such another hour is here. The prohibition principle demands a Prohibition party, and the voice of God speaks to-day, as it spoke of old to Samuel the prophet, concerning Saul. —

"And the Lord said unto Samuel, How long wilt thou mourn for Saul, seeing *I* have rejected him from reigning over Israel? Fill thine horn with oil, and go; I will send thee to Jesse, the Bethlehemite, for I have provided me a king among his sons."

There may be many to make lament, as the prophet did for the King, but when the God of all the earth rejects a man or a party, they gather up their feet in death.

One grand victory we gratefully record as we close the work of the year. The same legislature that could not see its way clear to declare for the prohibition principle in government, has granted our petition for scientific instruction in the public schools upon the physiological effects of stimulants and narcotics.

We remember yet across the twelve months, the eloquent words of Mrs. Hunt at our last State convention, as she held before our minds the "key to the situation." At that time it was resolved to enter upon this work, and Mrs. M. J. C. Merril was appointed to take charge of the department. The task then undertaken has been well performed, and the toil well rewarded.

No petition ever circulated by the W. C. T. U., except the one for the Girls' Reformatory, has met with such universal approval. Men who were not total abstainers themselves signed it, with words of praise, and said that our public schools *should* teach all scientific truth needed for self preservation and right social conditions

The vote in the legislature was equally satisfactory. Only two votes were recorded against it in the Senate, and but twelve in the House. After the victory, your president and corresponding secretary decided to present, in the name of the State W. C. T U, a bouquet of flowers, with thanks, to every member who voted for the bill This plan Mrs. Porter, with the aid of the Lansing union, most gracefully carried out.

The papers reported the scene as most beautiful, and even touching, and said that eyes were moist with tears as the grateful acknowledgment was made.

Scientific education is not now, even after so favorable an issue, to be considered an accomplished fact, and so left to take care of itself. We have need of great energy and wisdom in the future of this department.

To make the law a reality in the State, it becomes our duty to become familiar with the text-books now approved, and those which shall appear under this new and growing demand. We must work through school boards, teachers' institutes, and the State board of education. Prizes may be offered for the best essays on the effects of alcohol and tobacco, in the several grades, until, by such intelligent and persistent agitation, the time may soon come when scientific truths, which shall correct old errors, break down wrong education in our foreign population, and lift us to higher views and a better civilization, shall surely be a part of the knowledge gained in the schools of Michigan. Nor is this all for which we are responsible in this hour of new opportunity.

The school ballot is in the hands of the women of Michigan. Every woman over twenty-one years of age, who is the owner of taxable property, and every one who is parent or guardian of a child of school age, is a legal voter on school questions. This ballot decides all matters pertaining to public education, and elects the inspectors and district boards. These boards, when elected, have the management of the schools, employ and dismiss teachers, and decide upon the courses of study.

Since our attempt to introduce the science of temperance into the public schools, and bring its importance to the attention of our educators, we have found our Gibraltar in the district board. You appear before the ordinary superintendent of the city school, and respectfully ask him to examine Dr. Richardson's text-books, or "Alcohol and Hygiene," and give at least an occasional oral lesson upon this live subject. The superintendent listens with a bland smile, says he should be most happy to comply with the request, etc., etc., but all lines of study are decided by the board of education, that he is not allowed to introduce anything foreign to the regular order of things, and you would better see the board.

You go and seek the gentlemen to whom is entrusted the intellectual training of the youth, and when you reach them, you are among all the ins and outs of politics. These gentlemen are respectful to the voting and tax-paying power which elects them, as well as being often personally astray on the temperance question, and thus a solid wall has been found, especially in the cities.

There is a chance to change all this, right early, if half the dreams about woman's influence in politics are true.

The legislature has settled it that instruction shall be given with special reference to the physiological effects of stimulants and narcotics. The school boards carry out this law. The school ballot creates the board The ballot is in the hands of the mothers whose children are to be benefited by this knowledge. It is easy then to see who holds now the "key to the situation," and where the responsibility lies.

We have about one hundred and thirty Woman's Christian Temperance Unions in the State, with a membership approaching four thousand. Of these, probably three thousand are voters under some one of these qualifications, each of these should be able to influence at least one more to vote right for the sake of the best education; that will give six thousand votes from the temperance sentiment of these one hundred and thirty towns, and will make a decided change in matters in many of them.

I desire seriously to recommend the unions to take this matter in hand, and act, because by so doing a direct blow may be struck in the interests of your children, and the better education of the public mind on the temperance question. In the city of Flint this has been already done. Three women were put in nomination, and women went to the polls and voted, and the three were elected. One of them is Miss S. A. Rulison. Please, beloved, do not longer resolve, argue, and demand, but vote.

The question of prohibition in the constitution, by the voice of the people, is by no means laid in its grave by the late action of the legislature The temperance forces will rally under a standard which represents their own idea, and legislators can be sent to Lansing with such an idea before them, and such a constituency behind them as shall make it certain that the greatest of questions shall be constitutionally settled. But in the meantime it is manifestly the duty of temperance men and women to ask what can be done for the enforcement of law as we have it

The tax law, with its police provisions, is susceptible of enforcement, in the present state of public opinion. A lawyer, who knows whereof he speaks, says it is now much easier to convict a rumseller for violation of law than it has been for years. There are several reasons for this encouraging state of things : —

1. That although the idea of license, which is at the foundation of the law, is the child of the liquor dealers themselves, the statute has been so watched and amended by temperance men in the legislature, that, well enforced, it can be made to work for righteousness.

2. There is a growing and indignant sentiment against the saloon and its results, as more and more the light of truth, moral, scientific, and statistical, is turned upon it ; and —

3. Although we are often disappointed in the action of politicians and parties, so far as the ultimate idea of prohibition is concerned, yet in many ways they do show a recognition of the growing power of the temperance reform, and those in office dare not lawlessly disregard the rights of the sober and honest citizen.

It is to be remembered that a more intense and focalized public sentiment is required to change an established order of things and create new lines of legislation, than to enforce a law approved by the judgment of the people, and tested in their experience So while for the present we fail to reach our highest ideal, I desire to urge upon your attention the advantage of enforcing the present law.

This law is absolutely prohibitory on the Sabbath, legal holidays, elections, and upon every day between the hours of 10 P. M and 6 A. M. It is also prohibitory for minors, common drunkards, and for those concerning whom special warning has been given by friends.

The work of detection and complaint is laid upon the police officers in cities, and upon constables and marshals in smaller towns, and the duty of executing the law, upon the prosecuting attorney. I know how many stories could be told of treason, trickery, and rascality, upon the part of sworn officers of the law ; but even in face of these facts, something can be done, if it is only to convict the officers themselves at the bar of public opinion. Officers are sometimes intimidated, because the friends of sobriety leave them without support, and then abuse them for failing in the unequal contest with the most unscrupulous forces in society.

We have now in our statute books another troubler of the liquor dealers — although the "weakling" is not likely to cause much destruction — and that is the Local Option law, which gives to incorporated villages the power to suppress saloons

Not far from a hundred villages in Michigan come under the rights thus conferred, while some one was "napping" in the "third house" at Lansing.

While this statute is not to be considered as a slice from a political millennium soon to be here, the saloon can be outlawed by it in towns which have the sentiment or back-bone to do it. It is well known that the real victories of the old prohibitory law were in towns like those named in this provision, and many of them were free from the saloon curse. There is a chance now to return to the same high order of things.

In connection with this subject of the enforcement of law, I desire to call your attention to the plan of the citizens' league of Chicago. The point aimed at by them is such use of the police regulations of a law not so good as our own, as shall protect minors and suppress the sale of liquors to common drunkards. The league have had no mean success in this work. Juvenile arrests have been diminished one third, and many saloons closed, which lived by *breaking* law instead of observing it

Shortly after the protest about the management of the State Fair was published in *The Lever*, I received a letter from Mr. Paxton, general agent of the league, with some reports of results accomplished by this style of effort, and after a careful examination, I open the question before you.

The unions of the State spend a good amount of money each year in temperance platform education. The lecturers of *The Lever* course and those outside of it are put before the public largely by the efforts of the women Let some of this money during the coming year be put into the work of the Citizens' League. It does not begin by calling out, first, last, and only, those who are total abstainers in habit, and prohibitionists in sentiment, but stands with the law, and asks all who believe in wholesome restraint to come forward.

If Mr. Paxton could plan for a campaign through Michigan, going into every district and touching at least its centers, great good might be accomplished, and many who turn from mere temperance sentiment, however good, could be moved to protect their children.

We turn now from the political situation to the moral and educational side of the question — the side with which we are more closely allied in our own organization. Sometimes the temptation comes to our long-toiling and weary women to think the work of the W. C. T. U. is finished, and we must now look to other agencies for the carrying on of that which we had the honor to begin ; but any such idea is a great mistake. The groundwork of all right thinking and living, and so finally of right legislation, is laid by the hands of women, and a civilization never rises higher than its mothers.

Other modes of temperance effort have come and passed, and other organizations run their course, since the women of this country heard the call to the crusade , but we are here still in the good providence of God.

Our mark was set pretty high, but from it we have seen no reason to decline

Redemption for the *individual, education* for the *masses, prohibition* for the *State*, and to bring these, Christ, science, and law have been constantly invoked. We are here to thank God for the past, and take courage for the future.

On her way to California, Miss Willard wrote me these words: "Although we have not gained much by legislation, this has been one of the best years for extending our organization. North and South the W. C. T. U. is taking stronger hold on the faith and hearts of the people."

Senator Blair wrote me from the senate chamber at Washington. "There is hardly anything possible at all which the W. C. T. U. cannot perform, provided it continues to maintain its unity and to put forth its strength. I consider it the most powerful organization in the country — not *apparently*, perhaps, but *really* — and its future will be one of blessing and redemption to mankind."

So much for the general outlook. Then we turn to our own Michigan, which has no mean record.

1. The Red Book of our State Union shows the part taken in the crusade, which stirred the whole of Michigan as by breath divine.

2. The Reynolds Reform, the first fire of which was kindled in the city of Adrian, and the campaign largely conducted by the woman whose voice has bidden us welcome ; that reform was largely carried on by the Woman's Unions

3. The Girls' Reformatory. It was thought out and wrought out, by the State W. C. T. U. It matters not that this fact seems to be forgotten and ignored, the institution is an accomplished verity all the same, and is doing its work.

4. Scientific education in the public schools, which we hope soon to see translated from a *law* to a *reality* in the educational system of the State.

The present need of our organization is broadening at the base. The danger is in running to showy and public convocations, which deal in the theory and oratory of reform, without much behind and below them which either benefits humanity or glorifies God.

Let our aim be for *real* workers, in *real* unions, carrying on with zeal *real* warfare for the truth, and accomplishing *real* victories. Organize, strengthen, perfect; for we are here to stay, as was said last year, until *prohibition* or *eternity*.

The Gospel Temperance Reform was first laid upon our hearts by the Holy Spirit, but there is cause for fear that it may go from our hearts to our heads, and leave us mere humanitarians or theoretical reformers The safeguard is the study of God's word, and keeping our own hearts aglow by the power of prayer. Anchored here, we shall exult in God, and not in circumstances, and have a victorious faith in the darkest day.

We are to remember that the children of God are not in this world to reform human governments, but to set up a new and spiritual kingdom. The works of the flesh and of Satan are not reformed, but destroyed by the coming of the will of our King who said: "I come not to send peace, but a sword." So faint not, beloved, when legislatures refuse your plea, and the world's great machinery of government goes over your desire for purity and righteousness.

This heavenly kingdom is built in loyal, ransomed souls, and not in legislative halls, and its King is crowned in contrite hearts, and not in palaces,— so Christ for the individual, is a most important part of our work

Joseph Cook has several times since his return to this country, reminded us that this enthusiasm for the salvation of the victims of strong drink is greater in England than with us. He would not have said that, looking upon a meeting in the Reynolds or Murphy revival. The reform was on our hearts then; we did not *plan* so much as we *prayed*, and we were satisfied only when souls were brought to sobriety and Christ.

"Shoot lower, if you shoot to kill," was the stifled command in a deadly battle, and the whole line of men dropped on their knees and "shot to kill."

I feel like speaking solemnly the same words to you this hour. We have been aiming at men's heads, and the temperance reform is brilliant but cold. Let us to our knees, dear fellow-workers, and "shoot lower," till we find the hearts of men.

Bible readings, cottage prayer-meetings, house-to-house visitation among drinking people, jail, prison, and poor-house visiting, and evangelistic services of ten days' or two weeks' duration, so arranged as to reach the great outlying masses that flee the churches, should be part of the work of every temperance union. It is here we may "shoot to kill."

The Sunday-school work needs more attention then we have given it in Michigan. The proofs are ever before us, that a mere head knowledge of truth, however important, does not control life, until there is added to it the voice of authority from the conscience. The public school educates the mind. The Sunday-school educates the conscience, and herein lies the great importance of temperance truth in its teachings.

We have met, strangely enough, with much difficulty in securing anything systematic and thorough in the way of gospel temperance training in the schools of the church.

The great universal lesson system is in the hands of men who have their eyes on the whole world when they arrange these Bible studies, and in that world is beer-drinking Germany, wine-drinking France, ale-drinking England, and *everything-drinking* America. We live among ourselves so much that we do not realize how many Christian people regard alcoholic beverages as at least an occasional necessity, and total abstinence as a fanaticism.

In these truths lies the need of effort. Our Sunday school conventions should be visited by a superintendent who could urge the matter upon them in such a way as to win a hearing. Circulars to ministers and superintendents of Sabbath-schools were sent out, and the subject constantly pressed upon the attention of the Church of Christ of every name.

I am satisfied that not much is to be gained by effort with the national committee who prepare the lessons. They are too much occupied with the greatness of *their* international *idea* to pay any attention to so small a matter as the salvation from the saloon, of the children and youth about whom they say such eloquent things !

When I was a child, I often heard it said that those who attended Sunday-school rarely found their way into the prison. But a study of statistics to-day shows that a large percentage, and often a majority of criminals, in a given institution have been Sabbath-school scholars. And as half of our prison population are under twenty-one years of age, it seems a short cut from the modern Sunday-school to the jail and penitentiary. There is an awful logic in the fact before which the Church of God should tremble. Three fifths of those are felons because of drunkenness. If there were right teaching of conscience in the Sabbath schools, such a dire calamity would be impossible. We certainly have a duty in this direction to which we should at once address ourselves

Standing between the years, looking forward at the greatness of the opportunity and need, and backward at our strength as measured by our past doing, an oppressive sense of the incompleteness and poverty of our efforts is sure to come upon us

The world, to our human vision, goes on very much as if we did not toil or pray against this monster wrong, and we say in half despair often · —

> Only weak women to stand
>   And speak 'gainst a wrong that lieth
> Like a bitter curse on the land ,
>   To voice the strong man's groaning,
> The broken heart's sad moaning,
>   That ceaseless chorus intoning,
> A dirge for the thousands slain
>   By the monster scourge that worketh
> Its wreck in liberty's name

But as this sense of incompleteness reaches the heart, I am reminded of a sweet, ancient legend I found not long ago

It is said that a monk in one of the old convents was constantly painting pictures of "saints, martyrs, and the sweet Christ face crowned with thorns." But his paintings were mere daubs, never allowed a place on the chapel walls, and laughed at by those who understood art.

At last the poor monk grew disheartened, the dream of his soul was so far beyond the work of his hands, and one night he said · —

> "My life's work is all valueless!
> To-morrow I'll cast my ill-wrought pictures in the fire."

But as the words of lament left his lips—

> "He raised his eyes within his cell,—a wonder!
> There stood a visitor, thorn-crowned was He,—
> And a sweet voice the silence rent asunder,
> 'I scorn *no work* that's done for love of me.'"

Then upon the poor, worthless paintings fell a resplendent beauty; such light, such shade, such coloring had never been known before,—because divine; and the poor monk learned that in God's sight—

> "'Tis pure intent gives to the act its glory,
> And holiest purpose makes the grandest deed."

The world may not prize our work more than his brethern did the poor, love-wrought paintings of the monk, and we may ourselves grow discouraged at its imperfection. But I pray that the Christ for whose sake we love humanity, and labor for its salvation, may appear unto us until all incompleteness shall be lost in the glory of his coming, while every comforted heart hears for itself the benediction—

> "I scorn no work that's done for love of me,'

and catches the light of victory sure to come.

[Flint, June 4, 1884]

The circumstances of this hour permit me to speak to you, dear fellow-laborers, rather than to the general public, as I have done in other years.

I greet you therefore in Christ's name, whose love constrains us to the work which has filled our thoughts and hands in the months gone by.

Since our last annual convention God has been very kind to us. All who were chosen last year as officers and superintendents have been spared to undertake the duty placed in their hands; the ranks of the district vice-presidents — the women without whose zeal, sympathy, and wisdom the work could not go on — remain unbroken, and we are permitted to meet once more together.

I greet you joyfully, therefore, in this loving unity, born of a great endeavor for home, country, and for God.

As you sit in this annual gathering, you represent over five thousand women in Michigan, whose hearts are as your hearts in this great matter, and for whom you speak. You are allied by community of organization and effort with every State and territory in this vast republic, and constitute a part of the blessed company that makes up the national W C. T. U., that grandest organization of women the world has ever known.

What manner of persons ought we to be, beloved, in consecration to God, in love for each other, in the lofty spirit and method of our ministry, when in our power all these are honored, and in our failures, all these are made weak. God give us each the Might of His Spirit, and the Beauty of His Holiness.

THE BACKWARD GLANCE.

It is natural, and therefore fitting, in these annual conventions, to set open the doors leading toward the past, that, warned by defeats and encouraged by success, and seeing both in that softened light which falls upon what has passed us forever, we may better be fitted for future labor and achievement

As we open these doors to-day, the vista lengthens, and there come trooping toward us the sandal-footed memories of ten years; for here we round up as an organization our first decade. Already our "Historical Meeting" has gathered up these memories and put them in proper setting of graceful speech, so I need not further record them.

The past year has been one of labor along our usual lines without any one conspicuous effort engaging all the unions throughout the State The refusal of the legislature to submit the question of constitutional prohibition to the people and the granting of our petition for scientific temperance instruction in the public schools seemed to settle for the time the two prominent questions before us, and leave the unions to local work.

This fact has been considered by some a misfortune, and the State Executive Board has been appealed to during the year to create a "boom," for the reason that the unions were dying of inaction for lack of some great and special aim.

I have not been ready to believe that the women who compose our unions act only upon the excitement of some special and showy effort, and fail in a steady and quiet endeavor for the same great end. But if this is true in any degree, there are some things we need always to remember —

First, that the local union with its local influence and success, is at the very foundation of all we do. If the women in these unions are not moved by the swift degradation of the children on their own streets; the failure of the Sabbath-school in which they sit as teachers to educate the conscience in the gospel for the body; if they are not stirred by the ruin of men who are their neighbors, and the smothered sob of women and children within reach of their own finger tips, if they are not drawn with quenching interest to the weekly meeting for prayer and mutual enlightenment; if they fail to help in the circulation of temperance literature that brings to the masses about them the living truth concerning this great evil and its cure, then a few large gatherings like this will never bring the victory for which we work and wait. I stand here to-day, therefore, to *glorify the Local Union,* to give it not the *lowest* but the *highest* place in our chain of organization; for without this, glowing with zeal, and full of power, all other gatherings are but a glittering pageant, with no force beyond the hour when materialized in brightness, and vanish in — air.

Let me repeat the thought once before expressed,—that more unions in more towns, with more women in them, working out our social, educational, and gospel plans among the people, is the urgent need of the hour.

Our success the past few months has been in this direction. Some of the county presidents have honored that misused office by doing grand work in organizing and building up. The district vice-presidents with renewed zeal and success have been enlarging their borders, and without being specially in that work, I have since January organized five unions, while at some public meetings recently held, the membership of some older unions has doubled. The people are asking for our organization. A business man wrote me from a town in the third district· "We have had other societies, and they have gone down; now we want the Woman's Christian Temperance Union;" and they have one of fifty members.

The new basis of representation has been helpful not only to the State but to the local treasury; bringing a business-like collection and remittance of dues which has made our financial condition better than ever before.

I magnify the local union for its influence wherever it has a place. I found one town during the year where its power had destroyed the cider mill and cider drinking, setting new fashions for a rural population.

I found another where three men, husbands of women who went into the work only three months ago, had become sober, and who were looking to God for help to stand, while some of the dear workers themselves were feeling their own need of personal salvation through Christ. Because of these facts and many more, please take some suggestions for the greater strength and usefulness of our local organizations —

First, organize wherever possible; do not let other societies stand in the way, for the W C. T. U. does a work, has an influence, and reaches unforbidden a larger class of people than any other agency possibly can.

Second, choose godly women for officers and leaders. Others may work with us and do honest service, but let the leaders be women of faith and prayer. Ours is a *Christian* Temperance Union, and Christ taught us that this world is to be saved from the heart-level of love rather than the brain-level of logic. Keep the local union, therefore, steeped in the spirit and breath of prayer.

Third, be sure to seek and hold the most friendly relations with the churches. You are at this question all the time, with quick conscience, and sharpened senses, and it comes to pass that the hardest thing, sometimes, is to be patient with the poor, belated people, who open sleepy eyes, and utter opinions about the temperance reform, which, like crawfish, back up to us out of the middle ages of darkness. But still be patient. If pastors are not ready with help, remember that brain-work is costly, and they have the care of all the churches.

If the Sunday-school is too busy with the "high art" of its method to see the children of its church dropping into gulfs of shame unwarned, while they understand the sins of all the Canaanites, knock patiently again and again at its door.

If the church trustees are yet allied to the old political parties, and are a bit afraid of such clear-cut prohibition sentiment as our writers and speakers proclaim, so that union meetings and open churches are harder to secure in these sensitive days, consider that opinions held for years, and party associations made strong with memories and achievements, take hold of the life, and color the medium through which men see In spite of much that we might criticise, our hope for the final victory is the church of Christ. Let us therefore keep close step with it.

Fourth, let every officer do her own work; do it faithfully and fully, or else resign. It is the weakness of many a union that a few women are overworked, and so yield under the pressure to weariness or discouragement. Let the president lead, the treasurer collect and guard the funds, the secretary use her pen for the good of the work, each one meeting her own responsibility

The members are under an obligation as solemn. Officers, however faithful, cannot succeed without a loyal, willing-hearted constituency at their back. I have been often asked to tell a company of women what they could do to make the union meetings more interesting and the work more effective; but when I began to unfold plans which meant personal effort and individual responsibility, the "pray have me excused" came in the way of all success. Such unions die, not for lack of work, but lack of willingness to do it.

Fifth, don't attempt too much. Make yourselves familiar with all lines of national and State work, but attempt first the *one thing* which in your own locality will hit hardest and make sentiment most rapidly, taking others as you can.

Sixth, make the union meetings a power. Let it not be said that with thirty departments leading out into the greatest reform of the century, the meetings so lack intellectual food, that some other means must be sought to reach women of mind. Let no leader of a devotional hour open the Bible haphazard. Send to Hannah Whitall Smith for her Bible-reading helps, and make the prayer-meeting interesting and spiritual. Spend part of every meeting in real study of the aims and method of work undertaken by the W. C. T U., until each department is understood. Take, for example, Hygiene, and think of the possible questions that may be propounded. What is the relation of hygiene to the reform we seek to accomplish? What is the aim of the department? When was it created? How can we practically apply it in local work? These and kindred queries will open the whole matter of right living, and disclose the fact that underfed bodies demand stimulation, and overfed stomachs are the dens of morbid appetite. Go through the list that way, and it is worth a year in college to women willing to read and think.

Do your business by proper "rules of order" Have a tea-party talk over business, and then you will be at home in larger gatherings.

Eighth, have a little library which belongs to the union. "The Annual Minutes of the National and State Unions," Miss Willard's "Hints and Helps," Dr. Jutkin's "Hand-book of Prohibition," Miss Coleman's "Alcohol and Hygiene," and a catalogue of the National Publishing House, will do to begin on. Art, science — and religion, are bringing gifts to this altar to-day. Write the State superintendents for information in their lines — they are supposed to know *everything*, and some of them do.

Answer every letter. Read every circular. Fill every blank report Keep step with all the army, and may God bless the local unions. From our fundamental organization we naturally come to consider the county work.

I wish to call attention to the fact that the county president is largely an unknown quantity in our polity. She is appointed to "make bricks without straw," and has not much place anywhere, but a few women are proving that even this office can be magnified.

I was "put through" by such a worker in Gratiot county, with good results. In order to place the county work where it belongs I wish to urgently recommend that the presidents of organized counties which have within their limits four auxiliary unions shall by virtue of their office be full delegates in the annual convention.

The burden of some of the districts is now very heavy, and relief to the presidents of these must come from improved county organization.

The congressional district speaks for itself in our State I have this year attended the conventions of the first, second, third, sixth, eighth, and ninth. These are coming to rival the State meeting in interest and value, indeed they can give time to papers and discussions which the crowded hours entirely forbid at this gathering. It will greatly aid our work and workers to make these district annuals more and more like institutes, rather than conventions.

The district unions in Michigan, by our present plan, stand next not only to the State, but to the national organization, and the women who lead these, mold State policy and represent us in the national convention. It is therefore needful that they be wise and thoughtful.

The financial basis of these varied organizations is perhaps their weakest point, especially is this true of the county and district.

A majority of our district presidents could go into any town, address an audience acceptably upon the work of our society and the great end it seeks, and then organize. But they are not rich women; and the cost of travel must be met, and they are delicate about taking collections for their own expense in their own territory.

Each of these delegations would be glad to see the numbers greatly increased another year. The constitution gives your president charge of that work, but she needs the cooperation of the working unions; the same is true of the county, so once more I magnify the local union because it is our hope for a broad and business-like financial policy. The new Southern and Western States this year organized, have seen this need and placed the dues of the local unions at one dollar, and some at two dollars per year

By a clause in the report of the finance committee, adopted at the meeting of the national union in Detroit, last fall, each State was asked to consider the propriety of making the dues to the national *ten cents* per member instead of five. There is little doubt but this will be done at St. Louis, and we need to be ready for such action.

Our State receives from the unions ten cents per member, and pays one half of that sum into the national treasury, leaving the other half as our only settled income to support the work at home. If we have more for headquarters, lumberman's papers, etc, it must be raised by special appeal, and such appeals reach generally the interested few, so the burden is not equal A financial change between the State and national is surely impending, and in view of this fact, and our home need of more money, I wish to recommend that we so educate sentiment in the local unions as to place the dues at one dollar per year; that of that amount twenty five cents per member be paid to the State, fifteen cents to the district, and ten cents to the county treasuries, leaving fifty cents for local work. I urge this increase beginning at the local treasury, because they with their present income cannot increase dues to the State without discouraging depletion of their own resources

We cannot, of course, legally fix the dues of the local societies, but we can agree upon a universal financial plan, which shall lift us altogether. The arguments for such a liberal policy in our State work need only briefest mention to impress you.

We need more printed matter, constitutions, helps to organization, and other State leaflets, to meet our requirements The State minutes never pay for themselves, but take from our treasury every year, because we sell for ten cents what it costs twelve or fourteen to print. I would be glad to have them *free*, at least one copy to every union, if our working capital made it possible. With more money we could put a paid organizer in the field independent of collections, or have a paid secretary, and thus greatly strengthen the work. Give this plan your earnest thought, and let us build for the future.

We now turn from forms of organization to our lines of work.

The superintendents are charged with, and each is just as responsible for, the growth of her department, as the vice-presidents are for the growth of their district.

Our departments are the result of the study and thought of ten wonderful years

We have been blessed in this national union with women of one idea, in each of these realms of education, and the fruit appears. There is a call for this one-idea zeal in our State superintendents.

The movement inaugurated by the Michigan women, at the national convention at Detroit in behalf of the "woodsmen among the pines" has resulted in a new department — work among the lumbermen — with Mrs. Evelyn Peters of Manistee, as superintendent, than which nothing could be more fitting.

We probably never expended eighty-three dollars in our work, which brought immediate pleasure and permanent good to more human hearts than this venture on the liberality of the unions. I am sorry that every union here represented has not had a part in putting this cup of cold water to thirsty lips.

I called your attention last year to the aim and effort of the Citizens' League, for the enforcement of law as we have it, and am glad to note that in several important points in the State this movement has been inaugurated. This organization began its career in the one idea of the protection of our youth from the degradation of the saloon, and surely no work is more urgently demanded

There never was a time in the history of this country when young boys and girls were going headlong to ruin as to-day. Little boys of ten to fourteen in "Jesse James Bands," "Burglars' Dens," and "Cow Boys' Ranches," bound together by secret oaths and with the vile literature of to-day as their teachers, are being initiated into the depths of vice, on the very border of babyhood.

Little girls in widest freedom are thronging the street, the depot, the post-office, and that latest "general insanity," the skating rink, where all ages, classes, and kinds mingle together

Then the news stand is becoming the ally of the saloon, with the dime novel, which opens innocent eyes upon a life not else dreamed of, inflaming curiosity and passion into a fever which burns the purity out of childhood Alas for a country that sets a trap for the feet of the children, and allows the blight of hell to fall upon their young souls, for the sake of votes and revenue!

When Mr. Paxton, agent of the Citizens' League of Chicago, came to Jackson to organize, he said in a public address, that at the time of the riots a few years ago, when the streets of our western metropolis were thronged with armed men, when the days were full of anxiety, and the nights of horror, some thoughtful citizens went forth to see who composed these hordes of lawless rioters, and found that *eight* out of every ten were minors.

When the mob despoiled Cincinnati of its peace and fair fame a few weeks ago, some one observed how many very young men were in the throng. At first that uprising may have been, as it was declared, a burst of indignation at defeated justice; a few hours later it was a carnival of communism, and a jubilee of the "apostles of dynamite."

Such a fuse of death, leading to destruction, lies hidden under the tumultuous, ungoverned life of our great cities — and we do not import all the dangerous element by any means.

Boys brought up to despise labor as a degradation, or to hate it from sheer laziness, and coming to a practical world where honest bread must be earned by toil of hand or brain, are well nigh sure to take to living by their wits, which means crime against their fellowmen and their country; and such get easy education and shelter in the saloon.

To the enforcing of such police regulations as shall protect and reform the youth, the Citizens' League is pledged. When organized under the right conditions, and composed of men of weight and influence who have the courage to stand up and face the devilish modes by which the saloon defends itself, the League is a power; but it is no child's play, as can be easily found by trial. Some things it will assuredly accomplish.

One, is to enlist men who are not prohibitionists or pronounced temperance men in a trial of a law, which they say is the *best* way of dealing with the liquor traffic.

Another, is the swift enlightenment of these men as to the size, color, and habits of the animals they license. I have listened to temperance speeches recently, which remind me of the story of the Frenchman who was asked to prepare a critical essay on the mule; and never having seen the animal he sat down to evolve a mule from his own consciousness.

Such a mental performance is an address upon the saloon and its keeper by gentlemen who think moderation is true temperance, license the highest art of dealing with drunkard making, and that most of the men in the business are greatly misrepresented and needlessly condemned; but let them try it awhile — the saving of their own boys — and their vision widens. A young man came once to President Finney, and criticised a sermon which he had preached upon the responsibility and power of Satan. "I do n't believe in a personal devil," said the young fellow. "O, you do n't," replied Finney, " well, fight him awhile and you will."

The Citizens'-League is sure to find the " personal devil " in the liquor traffic, consequently it benefits the men who compose it, and may succeed in guarding the children from the foe that watches for their innocents.

The reformatory work has had new success in Michigan during the last winter and spring. Hughes and Ward have been working under a pledge which opens with the words, " Christ for all the world, and all the world for Christ," and for the first time, in any pledge we have seen, acknowledges the power of Jesus to save us from appetite. As a result of this thought, I have heard only good of their work.

From several places reports have come of the excellent service in the cause of total abstinence and prohibition done by Hon. Ansel Gray; and the songs of rejoicing over the great good accomplished by the world-known Francis Murphy at Manistee, has made us all glad. I desire to urge upon the unions anew the use of the total abstinence pledge, and the employment of at least one speaker during the year, whose special mission it seems to be to reach drinking men. It has seemed to me for many months that we might recall Dr. Reynolds to our State for a campaign, which, if not so startling as the first, might be as great a blessing.

The political situation was never so stormy, and never so hopeful as now, since we began our work, ten years ago. When God works out the great purposes of his righteousness for any people, he sets the battle in array first of all in the individual conscience. Such conviction brings unrest, and often anger. This is what Christ meant when he said, " I come not to send peace but a sword."

There is a solemn though fretful underswell of opinion and anxiety beating up from the homes of the people against the saloon; and the voice of love, duty, and right, breaks with stern rebuke across the smooth-spoken arguments of custom and political policy. Such stern rebuke once grew to the sharpness of the bayonet in this country, but slavery perished at its point.

The present protest of heart and conscience shapes toward the ballot, which shall speak the death sentence of the legalized saloon.

Our opposers tell us that public sentiment is not yet ripe for prohibition; we point to the year's record in answer.

There was public sentiment enough in Ohio to cast and count three hundred and twenty-three thousand votes for prohibition in spite of fraud and wrong on guard at the ballot box.

There was public sentiment enough in Iowa to give to her legislature what Talmage called the "swarthy courage" to give the people what they voted for — Prohibition.

There must be public sentiment for enforcement of law in Kansas, for within two months, in one of her towns two churches were fired and one burned to the ground, a dwelling destroyed in the same way, and an orchard ruined, because those who owned them were standing up for law against the saloon power.

What but public sentiment defeated the bonded whisky bill, and made money and argument alike powerless to move a Congress that felt the world's eyes upon them, and heard the voice of conscience within them?

What but public sentiment has set nearly every legislature in the country wrestling with this reform, which will not lie still? Closer restriction, scientific education, statutory or constitutional prohibition, are the questions often held in abeyance at the party conventions, but coming up through all barriers to the gates of legislation.

It was public sentiment that spoke with such trumpet tones in the great church gatherings of the past month, and made the national convention of Greenbackers, at Indianapolis, say, "We are in favor of submitting to the people the question of equal suffrage without regard to sex, and the prohibition of the liquor traffic."

Public sentiment to-day, in Michigan, upon this question, is the most troublesome problem the parties have to deal with. It has organized the union party, and is shaking loose from old ties the men who, by-and-by, shall speak in the majorities of righteousness. It has carried the war into Convention and caucus, and stirred at the spring elections nearly every town and city in the State.

It has seized the local option law, enacted by the last legislature and signed by Gov Begole, while the lobby were napping, and has put Decatur, Tekonsha, Sturgis, Otsego, Union City, and Portland under prohibition

It has given backbone to town boards, until bonds have been placed so high, and such sharp attention paid to their quality, that as a writer said of Elm Hall, in Gratiot County, "Whisky has to pack his grip and go."

PUBLIC SENTIMENT.

Why, thanks be to God, there is more pressure to public sentiment to every square inch of the party press, party platform, party convention, and party manager, than they know how to bear. And this underswell from the hearthstone is the knell of the "Monopoly of Abomination."

The combat deepens! The hatred of the saloon guard against those who work in this reform, strikes deeper, and takes in its hand more offensive weapons. Assassination and the torch are not new to them, and words of scorn, sharp as the knife and bitter as gall, are ready even for women, who hold up only hands of pleading and prayer against the monster that lays their household idols in the dust. But, sisters, the State! the republic! the whole round world shall see it yet!

There died this very year a man who trod the lonely road of moral martyrdom for conscience' sake and for an outraged race. It was in Boston, too, the city upon whose rocky coast the nation was born, and that hears forever the cradle song of freedom, coming up from the lips of the sea

A half a century ago, Wendell Phillips stood, as Elijah did on Carmel, and said to this nation, "God alone is God, and truth is truth;" and then lived up to his preaching.

He was mobbed on the Common, and hissed in Faneuil Hall, but he stood still and let the battle break, sometimes around him, and sometimes over his head. But he came to his own at last. They laid him in state in the old hall which had seen the long struggle for right and freedom, and a century with its *living* and its *dead*, pronounced judgment on that finished life.

> Abroad were murmurs of rev'rent praise,
>   And tenderest din of tears
> And suddenly then old thoughts were stirred,
>   That silent had lain for years,
> Now, over the place where he sleeps in peace,
>   The thought of the century clears.
>
> They brought him in state to the plain old Hall,
>   Cradle of liberty's lore.
> How silent the lips, whose silvery speech
>   Had filled it in days of yore,
> And into that silence with blossoms sweet,
> Halted the world with its tardy feet,
>   And crowned him, forevermore.
>
> Time was when the sleeping eye flamed bright
>   At the wrong of an outraged race,
> Time was when billows of golden words
>   With the glowing heart kept pace,
> That time, the coward world stood back,
>   And left him alone — his place
>
> Thank God for the solemn, evening skies,
>   In which the stars appear,
> Thank God for the tender grace of death,
>   After the toil and tears
> Thank God, that looking across a grave,
>   The world's dim vision clears,
> Till Calvary lies in the golden glow
>   Of God's eternal years

The last year, the last ten years of work for conscience' sake have not been all sunshine and ease. The future may be yet more stern, because nearer the end of the desperate struggle. But, dear fellow-workers, often weary, often discouraged, if only across our graves, the world shall see truth, and victory shall come.

[Albion, May 19, 1885]

Notwithstanding that words of welcome have been already so well spoken, I cannot refrain from saying that to no one heart can these women from the four quarters of Michigan be so *welcome* as to mine

These are they who have stood about me, with holy zeal, unfaltering courage, and a mighty faith, during a year which has tried the gold and discovered the dross in the great temperance reform ; as our question passes every day nearer to the fiery rain of the final and decisive conflict.

I speak my welcome, therefore, to the general officers who have borne with me the honorable responsibilities laid upon us by a noble constituency at that never-to be-forgotten convention in Flint, where every hour was made bright by some new ministry of love.

Out of an abundance of personal care, and from under the shadow of personal sorrow which has come to some of them, our secretaries and treasurer have guarded all interests with fidelity, and wrought with brave trust in our cause and rare faith in God.

I speak my welcome to the State vice-presidents, who each in her own field, has been indeed a leader. Under their patient and often unnoted toil, our organization and its work have grown and strengthened, until all along the line we lift our heads from the wave of opposition and blame which went over them, with hearts united, ranks unbroken, and souls glad in what God hath wrought.

Some new comers are among these district leaders to-night, and we give them our hands, asking the blessing of Heaven upon them in their new responsibility.

I speak a welcome also to the department superintendents, our "one-idea" women, who each with a golden key stands before her door of hope for the temperance reform, and makes the W. C T. U. tell upon the class she represents.

JUVENILE WORK ; SUNDAY-SCHOOL WORK , KINDERGARTEN , SCIENTIFIC TEMPERANCE INSTRUCTION IN THE PUBLIC SCHOOLS.

These departments sweep around the childhood of the State, whether neglected or fortunate, and so far as we can secure the co-operation of the home, the church, and the great public, teaches them the truth, and warns them, from the high ground of moral and scientific law, of the dangers lurking in alcoholic poisons, however deftly clothed by commerce, or daintily named in good society.

Lumbermen and miners, soldiers, sailors, and railroad employees have been touched on the shoulders by hundreds, and personally appealed to by tender and thoughtful letters prepared especially to meet their needs, while general literature by barrel and bale has been sent into the northern pine woods, to cheer and help the lonely toilers in the forest.

Special meetings at forts, bethels, and missions, have turned many discouraged and sinning men to higher thoughts, and not a few to wholly ransomed lives.

Our evangelistic and reform work has kept up the watchfires of gospel and moral-suasion meetings, until by the power of the pledge and the cross, there are hundreds of happy homes in Michigan this hour that were dark with want and sorrow one year ago.

The flower mission and prison and jail work reaches the men behind the bars, whom the world calls criminals and then forgets, taking to them the story of the Christ who was crucified between two thieves, and out of his own suffering gave eternal life to the one who repented.

The department of Heredity and Hygiene opens the volume of God's law written in our bodies, and preaches from the standpoint of science that awful truth of revelation, "The wages of sin is death."

Through the department of legislation we have asked the legislature of Michigan to submit the question of Constitutional Prohibition to the people, believing as we do in the right of the homemakers to speak against this great home-destroyer of our age, while our Franchise department has sought to persuade women to use the school ballot, a right already in hand; while they look for the wider privileges of full suffrage as a protection to their threatened hearthstones.

Two hundred regular prayer meetings a week; scores of Sabbath gospel meetings; lectures by the hundred; newspapers circulated by the thousands; temperance leaflets by tens of thousands; bands of hope; industrial schools; newsboys' meetings; soup houses for the poor in the bitter weather of last winter, all this is but a scant summary of the good things set in motion by the department work of the W. C. T. U., to the superintendents of which I now add this word of personal greeting.

Last but not least, I speak my welcome to the delegates from our local unions. These are the rank and file of our army, without which, brave leaders could make no advances, win no laurels, and achieve no success. The annals of the heroines are written in the local unions.

Money given from scanty purses, time given from crowded lives, toil given from hands made weary with household care, self-interest forgotten, criticism falling powerless at their feet, praise and blame alike harmless, as these listen through their loving mission to the voices of other women who moan for their slain, and the sobs of outraged children, whom this Christain nation lays in the fiery arms of the liquor Moloch for Revenue.

In that marvelous poem, "The Light of Asia," the poet tells of Buddah the prince, who gave his life for the world. He dwelt in a marvelous palace in the midst of fabulous magnificence, only beauty before his eyes ; he had for his bride the fairest among women ; joy, power, and security swept around his life like the full tide of the Southern seas ; but up through the music, across the royal splendor, there came ever to his ear the moan of the world out-side — a world that sinned and suffered, and needed help, strong, changeless, and tender So he turned away from ease, luxury, and beauty, and went out to suffer with humanity and help it. These women here to-night have learned this lesson, not from the rare story of Buddha, but at the feet of the Christ of Christianity, and I welcome these toilers for the endangered and lost, in his sweet name.

Shame on the men and women who have met such as these with the shafts of blame, because salvation to the right must always mean destruction to the wrong Shame on the man. the party, or the clan, who is wounded by the same blow that strikes the legalized liquor traffic, or cries out against the hurt which comes from any source to this gigantic iniquity

REFORM WORK.

Any review of the year would be incomplete which did not record the great good resulting from the visit of Dr. Henry A. Reynolds. His reform work in Michigan in 1876 lifted the temperance question to the level of right thinking as no one instrumentality has done since the crusade One year ago at our convention, it was decided to invite his return for a new campaign this winter Our invitation was accepted, and he entered upon his work in December. The hard times, and most of all, the feeling following the November election, seemed to place well nigh insurmountable barriers in the way of continuous and successful labor , but since January his work has been such as to cause great rejoicing The newspapers have not given publicity to it, as before, but there are hundreds who follow him with thanksgiving, and call him blessed

Strange as it might seem, the northern part of the State engaged most of his time. The smaller towns and smaller unions entered upon this method of work, while the larger towns and stronger unions have for some reason failed to use their opportunity.

There is much stronger temperance sentiment in the new towns along the lines of the Grand Rapids & Indiana Railroad and in Traverse county, than along the line of the Michigan Central, or in the more southern counties. They need temperance evangelism very badly. These towns were lifted to the interest and zeal for the temperance cause in the first half of this decade, but outraged law, which has given a free lance to the saloon element, has stricken down righteousness in the streets, and our hands are full of blood.

Dr. Reynolds's work is on the old line of earnest appeal to manhood, only touched into greater depth by the chastening which has fallen on his own heart and life. He will work in Michigan until August 1, and every day should be full.

Captain Linscott and John R. Clarke have also done excellent work, mostly in the northern counties, and entirely under the auspices of the W. C. T. U.

We are asked often, and with great emphasis, "Why don't you temperance people work on the practical lines of reform and gospel work, instead of forever going off into the unattainable realms of prohibitory law?" We would like to ask from this place another question: If these non-partisan temperance people, who give us so much advice, believe that the only way to reach the best results is through reform and moral suasion work, why don't they do a little of it, and invest some of their money in the salvation of the drinking classes? For it cometh to pass that all, or nearly all the direct effort for saving the victims of our American liquor system, and our Michigan tax law saloon, is made by "unpractical" people who believe in prohibition.

LITERATURE.

One very encouraging sign of progress is the increasing number of our people who are reading temperance newspapers. In city and country homes, the journals devoted to this subject are to be found, and are doing their steady work. The *Union Signal*, the official organ of the national W. C. T. U., has been, and is behind none in this warfare of principles. It is not only a woman's paper, devoted to our "ways and manners," showing as a mirror the many-sided and womanly work of our temperance hosts; but it has discussed the great civil problem of the saloon in politics, with masterly skill, and is growing in influence as it meets the need of this mighty hour in a great reform. Nearly every district in the State has a share of stock in the paper, either fully paid up or partly provided for, and the Fifth District has two shares, while the list of subscribers in the hands of Mrs. Benjamin is growing larger. We have no need to blush for temperance journalism to-day, while we have the metropolitan *Voice;* the able *Reformer;* the *Sixteenth Amendment*, with its national issue of the wrong constitutional attitude of the government to the liquor crime; the *Weekly Witness*, which threw the power of an old, established name into the struggle; and the fresh *Pioneer*, issued from the same office. All these are Eastern, while at the West we have the never-to-be-forgotten *Lever*, which fought our Michigan battles on poor rations, small pay, and no bounty, before it went to Chicago and took a wider command, and last but not least, the *Center*, published at Detroit, by Rev. Frank Cressey, a man well known to us. This paper should be speedily made the organ of intercommunication between State temperance organizations and workers. Let me urge upon you the importance of the regular temperance newspaper among the people The *Union Signal* first, for our women, and all we desire to instruct, after that, the political paper for the voters of the State, until this truth for which we struggle finds expression at the ballot box

AT THE EXPOSITION

No achievement of our organization within these last months has been of greater social and educational power than the W. C. T. U. booth at New Orleans. It was decided last fall at St. Louis, that we should attempt to speak from that gathering of the people, for God, and home, and native land. Accordingly Mrs. Nichols, national superintendent of temperance at State and county fairs, undertook the World's Fair also. She was aided by Mrs Judge Merrick, of New Orleans, whose social influence set before us an open door. Application was made to the commissioner for space for the W. C. T. U., and the chief man of affairs said wonderingly: "Woman's Christian Temperance Union! what have they to exhibit, unless it be their women?" But he yielded nevertheless, and with his own hand measured off the "space" in the gallery of the government building, just by one main stairway. We might have filled that space with women worth going across the continent to see,—some rare specimens could have been furnished by Michigan,—entirely worthy of contemplation in this easy going age when compromise is chosen instead of truth, and policy instead of righteousness. But it was our *work* and not our WOMEN that was to be exhibited at the Exposition.

Imagine our space, twenty feet one way, forty the other. In the center an eight-posted pavilion, with canopy-shaped top, wreathed with grasses, grains, and flowers. The floor beneath carpeted and made comfortable with chairs and tables, while in the center stands the great victory, a fountain of pure filtered water. I call it a victory, because when we began to exhibit our work at New Orleans, there was not a place on the ground where filtered ice water could be obtained. There was beer to the right; beer to the left, beer at every corner; and it came out in the effort to secure our first exhibit of pure cold water, that nature's beverage had been excluded in the interest of said beer. The fountain in our pavilion was completed two weeks before permission was secured to tap the main pipe, and then it was done by catching them with guile. The water came, however, with the Mississippi back of our purified rill, and an abundance of water coolers with drinking cups were ranged alongside the pavilion and kept supplied with ice by the contributions of the unions all over the country. Then the world was invited to come and "take a drink." The quaintest of the water-tanks was from Louisville, Ky., the merry thought of Colonel Bain and wife. It was a huge inverted jug with a faucet, and duly inscribed "The way of the wicked he turneth upside down."

You must now imagine a shield from every State and territory. Decorated wood, battered brass, embroidered velvet, hand-painted satin, and from Colorado one of solid minerals, gleaming with gold, silver, and copper. Among them was our own, and I assure you it did not suffer by comparison even in that goodly company. Beside these, were banners, placques, and devices representing the department work of the W. C. T. U., until the place was brilliant with a many-sided interest.

Temperance literature, religious, scientific, and general was on sale, while newspapers and leaflets were as free as the ice-water.

Amid all these reminders of our aims and methods, the temperance people of every State clasped hands, and here a reception was tendered Miss Willard, some of us lesser lights sharing the honor, and ice-cream.

The meetings held in Exposition Hall and in the city during temperance week arrested the attention of thousands, and moved hearts and minds before untouched. In these gatherings, men and women, Northern born and Southern bred, looked into each others' eyes, as they only can on the temperance platform, where the old bitterness is laid down, and even the color line drops out of sight, in the presence of a great, new issue, over-mastering enough to unite all sections and move all hearts,— the issue of everybody's home against the dram-shop.

THE WORLD FOR TEMPERANCE.

Another far-reaching mission, to which you have been asked to lend your aid, is the world-wide tour of Mary C. Leavitt. The organization of an international W. C. T. U. was projected as early as the Centennial year, and a skeleton plan adopted. Imperfect as the shaping of the thought was, it brought about a community of interest between our national organization, the British Woman's Temperance Society, and the workers in Scotland, as well as introducing gospel temperance work in the mission stations of heathen lands. In most of the missionary lands, even in native churches, the pressing need of the hour is a total abstinence Christianity. The example of Americans and English people abroad, not excepting Christians and missionaries, is one of the worst influences which come to the heathen in an effort to found among them a pure church. It will be remembered that the eloquent Raus Chandra Bose, of India, said with fine scorn, speaking of his past life, "I never drank intoxicants as a Hindu, I had to become a nominal Christian before I found that degradation."

England, one Christian nation, has defiled India with drunkenness and China with opium; while America makes a hundred drunkards with her whisky, where she makes one convert with her missionaries. The Woman's Christian Temperance Union needs therefore to go abroad.

I desire here to quote from a letter written me by the wife of a missionary in Cawnpore, India, which may serve to open your eyes to the relation of the temperance question to the evangelization of the world. She says:—

"You know we are in the English-speaking work. Part of my husband's charge is the chaplaincy of about two hundred soldiers. He at once began temperance work among them; they became interested and many signed the pledge. We then appealed to our church to help in the work, when lo! it was found nearly all used wine on their tables, supplying it for guests if they do not drink themselves. Not long ago George Muller, of Bristol orphanage fame was here, and we were invited to dine with him at the home of an English missionary. Wine was at all the plates, and even George Muller himself drank his wine. I can safely say there is an utter absence of temperance sentiment here. We need literature, temperance papers — even old ones would be welcome. I could use tons if I had them. Another missionary, recently from China, told me that missionaries themselves, when dining with aristocratic families, often yield to the social custom of wine drinking."

Some years since an American bishop went around the world with quite a large party of ministers, and only *one* of all the company was true to his total abstinence principles to the end. My informant was one of the party. I mention these things because we are told, often with some severity of rebuke, that the church is all-sufficient as a temperance organization, and nothing more is demanded. The facts just cited prove that the church has not carried total abstinence principles to the heathen, and they often fall under this curse after leaving a heathenism which forbids the use of all that intoxicates. The missionaries from this country are nearest right, but not all the representatives of American Christianity are clean in this matter, nor is the American church yet abreast with this hour.

Our government is also guilty of a false representation of Christianity abroad. I presume you read with a blush of shame of the man just appointed minister to Japan. A few days before he was thus honored, he was the center of a drunken brawl in Washington and in charge of the police. We were told that family influence did it; and for so light a reason, such a man is to stand before the keen, shrewd Japanese, and say "Behold a typical American." O Christian republic, thou art a whited sepulcher to the pagan peoples of the earth!

To carry our principles to these far-off lands is the object of Mrs. Leavitt's tour. She went without purse or scrip, first to the Sandwich Islands, and beyond to the other nations, seeking to reach all women. Let us pray for and help this world-wide evangelist of gospel temperance.

GOSPEL POLITICS.

I should be false to the interests that center in this hour, if I failed to speak frankly and without fear, of the relations of the Woman's Christian Temperance Union to the political situation of the country. The relation of our organization to the home, the church, and social life is pretty well assured. No society has been more praised than we, as we have taught the truths of total abstinence, and moved along educational and religious lines. Even our petitions to municipalities, legislatures, and Congress have brought no censure except from the allied forces of rum. Indeed, for ten years we have walked with our Master in his triumphal entry to Jerusalem, treading a path of palms and hosannas Suddenly we found ourselves in the hall of Judgment, with a possible Calvary before us, and we may well pause and ask why?

Last November the great majorities that shape destiny in this free republic, changed their minds, and a party with a glorious record, regnant for twenty-five years, lost the scepter of national empire, and came into authority in States where it is still dominant with greatly reduced power. As might be expected of human nature under such circumstances, the defeat brought great bitterness and wrath, and as might be expected, instead of looking within to see whether the people had cause to change their minds, they looked without for those on whom the blame might be laid, and in the distribution of wrath, our organization did not escape.

Not a soul of us was among the majority at the poles, not a name of us counted in the result. No finger of ours touched the omnipotent ballots which told the final verdict. Yet we were counted worthy to suffer with others.

Ministers of the church of Christ, preaching "righteousness and temperance," agreed together that no notices of temperance prayer-meetings should be read from the pulpit. Boards of trustees shut the churches against all services of the W. C. T U. In a city in Missouri, the officials voted to exclude all women from church membership who belonged to the society. Actual threatenings were made to burn our gentle national president in effigy in her own town, and everywhere the W C T U. was denounced as a political party, and guilty of aiding in the defeat of the one retired from power.

Two questions face us at this point : —

First. Are we guilty of the charges made against us, viz, of being a political party and helping to the political results of last November?

Second. Are we right and consistent in our present position, even if that position did work harm to a great political organization?

The Woman's Christian Temperance Union from the outset had three distinct aims set before it. Whatever line of work has been taken up, or new departures made, these have ever been in view. First, The reformation of the drinker. Second, The salvation of the children and the youth from the possible degradation. Third, The final banishment of the dramshop by prohibitory law.

The first years of our more than a decade of organized effort were spent for the drinker; pledges, prayers, songs, appeals, gospel meetings, all sounded up to one invitation, Come to the pledge and to Christ. And they did come, by hundreds, throughout the land. Eighty thousand drinking men signed the pledge during Dr. Reynolds's first visit to the State. But the years went by, and the percentage who under the old temptation went back to their cups, was appalling. The church stirred into interest by the first wave of this new revival, grew dispirited and impatient with the many failures, and faith for the final perseverance of reformed men died out of her altars. We temperance women saw these failures and felt them keenly. Why should we not? Every fallen man was the wreck of our hope and our endeavor. Then with sorrow for these, we turned to the youth and children, with the cry, "It is easier to prevent the evil than to save these lost ones." We organized young people's societies, bands of hope, and temperance schools. We knocked at the doors of the Sunday-school influence, and besought for definite work in the nursery of the church. We finally asked the State to provide for scientific temperance instruction in the schools of the people. We had victories that looked like real success, but in the face of our efforts, drunken children were being arrested in Chicago at the rate of more than a thousand a month. The quantity of liquor consumed was on the increase much faster than the increase of population, and our prisons were full of young men. City councils were lenient, police power was intimidated or traitorous, laws made for the protection of the young and tempted were disregarded; the very hand of empire, State, and nation seemed palsied before the legalized liquor traffic.

What destroyed our reformed men, honest in a weak intention? What tempted the children, and filled the saloon ranks from the home and the Sunday-school?—Of course the dram-shop did it. This was its legitimate work; and yet the institution was permitted by public opinion, licensed by majority vote in both political parties dominant in the States.

These facts, hard, stern, undeniable, brought us face to face with our third aim, the destruction of the dram-shop by law. Our work was well nigh futile while it stood in every town to destroy. What enginery should we turn against the fountain of all the evils we had sought to cure? The gospel methods, Bible, song, and pledge, would not do here. What touched the drunkard did not reach the drunkard-maker. Our educational method did not avail. What cared the saloon power about the action of alcohol, except upon their coffers filled with the price of blood? Where was the saloon that we might reach it? My friends, it was not in morals, not in the educational realm. The saloon was in government, solidly settled upon the foundation of State and national law, and it came into the realm of government by the path of party politics, as all things must in a government by the people. Finding these things so, we followed our question where it led us, just as we had said, We will go after the drinker to his temptation, after the outcast child to his danger. So we follow our principle to the end of our duty, God helping us. The liquor system was created at the ballot box, it has seized every new lease of power by making not *one* but *all* parties do its bidding. No question can come fairly to the people without the aid of a political party, and seeing all this, we went to these same political parties with our question.

We have been to legislatures, and won here and there a victory, but the attitude of the government was wrong, everywhere the effort was to regulate and perpetuate the evil. We sought for a party willing to take the prohibitory principle, and so change the trend of political action. We petitioned; they refused. The Democrats dashed all our hopes with that hoary-headed resolution about sumptuary laws. The Republican party held their peace until our president turned away, then in Tallyrandish language talked about " promoting all American industries " We did not understand these words even then, until the party journals expounded their hidden force. Remember, we were at the end of the ten years of toil, with sharpened sense, and souls alive to a growing need. We were looking for help to overthrow the dram-shop by prohibition, and these were the words we found to comfort us : —

"So far as the Republican party is concerned, its course is clear. Let it be distinctly understood we have no terms to make with the Prohibitionists, that we believe that the legislation they seek is a gross, an unwarranted outrage on the liberty of free citizens, and that, as Republicans, we shall oppose them to the end." — *Brooklyn Times (Rep).*

"The quicker that he (Neal Dow) and all others get it out of their heads that the Republican party is a Prohibition party, the better " — *Ill State Journal (Rep.)*

"Prohibition must be prohibited in the Republican party." — *Chicago Tribune (Rep)*

"There is one mistake that some of the temperance men who are sincere and honorable are liable to make. It is that of insisting that the Republican party must adopt their great and only principle, or brave their steady animosity. The Republican party is not going to adopt their great and only principle, and that is all there is to it. The Republican party has its distinct work to do, and that of the Prohibition party is not a part of it. This might as well be recognized now as hereafter, and action taken accordingly." — *Cincinnati Commercial Gazette, Jan. 14, 1885.*

"There are hundreds of saloons in Cincinnati and other Ohio cities, that are substantially Republican club houses." — *Commercial Gazette.*

"Our national organization is twenty-four years old. During all those years the Republicans have been in power in national affairs, and I submit to every candid brewer, be he Democrat, or be he Republican, if the brewery interests of our country have not grown to immense proportions, if our rights and our interests have not been protected, fostered and encouraged by our government." — *Secretary Outhout, of Brewers' Congress, Rochester.*

"We utterly condemn and denounce as a measure essentially unrepublican and despotic the adoption of Constitutional Amendments prohibiting the manufacture and sale of fermented or distilled beverages." — *Resolution of Cook Co., Ill., Rep. Club, 1882.*

The Republican candidate for governor, Joseph B. Foraker, before the Lincoln club, at Cincinnati, June 23, said : —

"We know that the principles of regulation. . . . are eternal and will stand. And to those principles of regulations and taxation of the liquor traffic, be it known to all men, the Republican party is unalterably committed."

You will see by these things that our principles were homeless yet.

I have purposely up to this point avoided all allusion to any other body of temperance people. The W. C. T. U. trod their own unique path to all these conclusions. We were not theorists, crooning over illusions and delusions. We were discoverers, and were on the spot where these facts were to be found. Moreover, we were desperately in earnest, not to run a showy moral reform, but to destroy the dramshop.

But these underlying causes which had so forcibly impressed us, struck with still greater emphasis a large body of men in this country, who need not petition, but who could speak at the ballot-box for themselves. You see, my friends, we could not be a party, any more than aliens, minors, or idiots could come to that high estate, for we were not citizens. But these men could and did organize a political party. Long before the Crusade, there were prohibitionists in the country, who believed the only way to get the saloon out of government, and prohibition in, was to organize and vote to that end. This prohibitory organization had sometimes made a respectable showing, but nationally it had not been of rapid growth, mainly because of the war issues yet unsettled and the lack of proper temperance sentiment among voters; with another hindrance lying in the hope cherished by multitudes of the best citizens, that the Republican party, born of *moral* rather than *political* forces, would finally take the issue. These men to whom the abolition of the liquor traffic was the commanding question, preferred to be right, rather than to be in the majority, so they stood like an "ensign on a hill," witnessing against a wrong they could not remove, and would not fellowship. They boasted such names as Judge Black, Gideon T. Stewart, A. A. Hopkins, and John Russell. These men have waited long — as they must wait, who think ahead of their times.

Lately, the rising tide of temperance sentiment on the one hand, and the impudent greed of the liquor oligarchy for political power on the other, has called attention to the warning ensign on the heights of moral right, and a revolt of conscience struck the old parties. By Nov. 4, 1884, one hundred and fifty-two thousand voters, who were a political party, said, "By God's help, we will make a way for prohibition to get into government."

The Woman's Christian Temperance Union, which was not a political party and could not be, but was looking for one to espouse its cause and carry it to the proper realm for settlement, saw the battle put thus in array, and was glad.

In 1883, at the national convention in Detroit, the following resolution was passed: "Resolved, that we lend our influence to that party by whatever name called, that will furnish the best embodiment of prohibition principles and will most surely protect our homes."

In 1884, the test had been applied, and in the full knowledge of the position of all parties, the following solemn declaration was made at St. Louis: —

"We refer to the history of ten years of persistent moral suasion work, as fully establishing our claim to be called a non-political society, but one which steadily follows the white banner of prohibition wherever it may be displayed. We have, however, as individuals, always allied ourselves in local and State political contests with those voters whose efforts and ballots have been given to the removal of the dram-shop and its attendant evils, and at this time, while recognizing that our action as a national society is not binding upon States or individuals, we reaffirm the positions taken by the society both at

Louisville in 1882, and at Detroit in 1883, pledging our influence to 'that party by whatever name called, which shall furnish us the best embodiment of prohibition principles and will most surely protect our homes' And as we now know which national party gives us the desired embodiment of the principles for which our ten years' labor has been expended, we will continue to lend our influence to the national political organization which declares in its platform for National Prohibition and Home Protection. In this, as in all our progressive effort, we will endeavor to meet argument with argument, misjudgment with patience, denunciation with kindness, and all our difficulties and dangers with prayer."

To have done less than this at such an hour, would have been to turn our backs upon the results of our own endeavor, and refuse to accept the answer to our own prayers.

We are ready now for the direct answer to our questions.—

1. The W. C T. U. is *not* a political party any more than when we worked in this State with the Republicans for the submission of constitutional prohibition and the temperance educational law, passing resolutions of thanks for the work they did. The organization stands where it has stood for ten years, so far as principles and aims are concerned; the only difference being that the battle deepens and has moved on, and we must go with it, or turn deserters.

2. We are consistent in doing what we may, with the social and moral influence women possess, to help those who can carry the struggle beyond where we may go.

One question still remains: Did we help to defeat the party retired from power last November?

I think our work for all the years, has tended toward the defeat of any party, that cannot, or will not, take the temperance question. We have labored incessantly to put not only the vice of drunkenness on the public conscience, but the national sin of the legalized system which creates drunkenness. The boys gathered into the bands of hope ten years ago, voted for St. John last fall, and the men who get right on this great question, cannot travel long with political organizations that are "unalterably committed to regulation" instead of prohibition, because the political parties of the past have protected this crime, and think only of protecting it. Therefore, every prayer, every leaflet, every address which tends to the final overthrow of the liquor traffic must defeat those who thus aid it and give it power.

If you ask whether the passage of our resolution at St. Louis helped to the final result, and made us worthy to suffer the things to which I have alluded, I reply, No; that resolution did not weigh a feather in the final count. It was passed only eight days before the national election; the papers were crowded with the conflict, and it scarcely came abroad, until after the great contest. That action and its fruitage belong to the future. There is much that comes to the front to be spoken as we consider the temperance reform in politics, and the present status of the old parties. It seems best, however, in this presence, and amid these surroundings, to deal only with the facts which had to do with the political expression of the W. C. T. U., which grieved and even angered those who had been our friends

Two results were predicted as sure to follow our so-called partisan position. One was a serious "set-back" to our work. We can reply, looking over the past winter, that our general work has received no perceptible check. Organization has gone on, and the past months have been characterized by great activity in all our moral, evangelistic, and reform lines of effort. There has been no winter in ten years when the temperance question has been in legislation as in the one just past. Several States have submitted the question of constitutional prohibition to the people, and nine States have passed the scientific temperance educational law, so that henceforth in fourteen States the school-house is arrayed against alcohol, and old sophistries concerning this once named "good creature of God" are to be dispelled by the unanswerable demonstrations of science. Even where our cause has for the time been defeated, the vote has been startlingly close for the other side God is in this reform, and it will not down.

Again, we have been told that we have left all possible success to follow a forlorn hope; that the flag that we hailed in the fight can never lead to victory, because it represents but one idea, and gathers but a mixed and fanatical multitude under its folds. We pause to count some of them over as samples. Joseph Cook, Rev. Dr. Deems, Theodore Cuyler, President Seeley, David Preston. But I am not here to speak of the Prohibition party or defend it, I wish rather at this point to quote from the author of the "Letters to Cleveland, the Man of Destiny," which appeared in the *Inter-Ocean* and aroused an interest which was phenomenal. In speaking of "what anvils rang, what hammers beat," in the formation of the Republican party, he says: —

"It was the most amazing piece of political conglomeration which the history of parties reveals It had at first no politicians in it. Its differential idea had been gathering strength in the popular mind for a score of years Neither party would give it lodgement or countenance, though both had used it for their own advantage. . . . So obscure was its birth, that of the half dozen claimants for the honor of its paternity, not one of them had more than a limited local reputation . . It was anomalous also in the contrariety of its elements. It embraced a vast preponderance of the active, aggressive thought of the day. The extremes of political faith were found within its ranks, — Whigs and Democrats, federalists, and state-rights, theorists, protectionists, and free traders . They were banded together by the one common idea that whatever might be done, must be done to restrain and effectually eradicate American slavery. Of party discipline there was not a trace, but there was an instant and universal subordination of all other political purposes to the promotion of an 'irrepressible conflict,' which most of its members no doubt supposed it would require generations if not centuries to decide "

"Siva" then goes on from the birth to the death, writing as one does of those who lie in their own sepulcher. Speaking of these elements, he says . —

"Whether they will again unite in the near future depends entirely on the question whether an issue shall arise sufficiently momentous and engrossing to absorb and unify these elements. At present no question stands in the foreground which is at all capable of accomplishing such result Some think the regulation of the civil service has taken the place of the old question of individual right, and is to be the absorbing impulse of a grand to-morrow Thus far it has shown none of the elements of a popular issue. Unlike all great questions of the past, it has started from the top and seeks to make its way downward to the masses . . . So far as present appearances indicate, the Republican party has before it one of two prospects "

The deductions from this elegant putting of the case are plain · —

1. Victorious parties are born of many elements in citizenship, gathered about one great issue of paramount importance.

2. Parties die when they lack an issue that stirs the conscience and sounds the bugle note of progress for a free people.

Friends, the issue is here. The gathering has begun ; the victory comes to-morrow. The legislature of Michigan has been no exception to the general rule in the pressure brought to bear upon it for changes in existing statutes, or the enactment of new laws regarding the liquor traffic. It is estimated that one third of all the legislation of the country pertains to this pet evil of civilization Revisions of the tax-law, local option, the question of submission, and the Ann Arbor bill providing for prohibition within a radius of five miles of the State University, have all been before our law-makers, but as yet nothing worthy of note has been reached. The Ann Arbor bill was defeated, the bill for submission passed the house, the Republicans and twenty-three Democrats and fusionists voted therefor. It was defeated in the Senate by a strict party vote, lacking four of the necessary two thirds. The measure is likely to come up again, but a senator friendly to the bill wrote me a few days since that no change was expected

This gives our Republican friends a chance to say that if the Prohibition vote had not spoiled their majority, all might be different. But we remember the magnificent chances of six, four, and two years ago, when the women of our unions walked literally hundreds of miles to secure great petitions, and feel that the thing they seem now willing to do, has been too long delayed The past winter we circulated no petitions, but the following memorial was sent to Lansing: —

To the Honorable, the Senate and House of Representatives of the State of Michigan —

We gratefully note the fact that the bill providing that the question of constitutional prohibition of the liquor traffic shall be submitted to the people of Michigan, at the next general election, has been taken from the table and is again before your honorable body.

We, the officers of the Woman's Christian Temperance Union, representing more than five thousand of the women of Michigan, heartily petition for the passage of the bill.

First Because we believe that prohibition put by the will of the people in the organic law of the State, is the only adequate remedy for an evil so great.

Second. The people have the right to defend themselves at the ballot-box, from a system which wounds morally, destroys physically, burdens financially, and harms the righteous powers of the government under which they live.

Your petitioners also pray that a joint resolution be passed requesting the Michigan representation in the Congress of the United States to vote and use their influence for the prohibition of the importation, manufacture, and sale of alcoholic liquors, whenever this question comes into the realm of the national legislature

For the State Woman's Christian Temperance Union,

MARY T. LATHRAP, *President.*
EMMA A. WHEELER, *Cor. Sec*
JULIA A. UPTON, *Supt. of Legislation and Petition.*

This memorial was handsomely received, spread on the journal and printed, on motion of Senator Belknap, for which courtesy we are very grateful. If the question should be submitted, we are pledged to do our utmost in the campaign. If again disappointed, we shall still work on until the legislature which fails to reform the law, shall be itself reformed.

We turn in closing this general outlook, to our own lines of effort again, and in doing so, it is well to consider the causes of the vice we deplore, and whose ravages we seek to stay, and some of the hindrances to be met.

Among these we name, first, carelessness with regard to the morals of children. The streets of towns, large and small, are crowded with boys and girls whose freedom from restraint is likely to prove their ruin. In a recent report of the Woman's Prison of Massachusetts, it appears that ninety per cent of these criminal women came to their loss through drink, and a very large majority began to get their first appetite for liquor between the ages of ten and thirteen years, by drinking cider and beer at the solicitation of older women. These traps are everywhere for the unwary feet, and yet parents let the younger children go beyond their care, thinking their very innocence a safeguard against sin Alas! how many find too late that childhood may be despoiled. At fourteen comes the danger line to youth. I have wished sometimes I could take some careless and overtrustful mothers with me for a month's trip, to see the young miss of to-day, over-dressed, over-aged, over-vain, in company with empty-headed, bold, bad boys, or older men who flatter to destroy.

Another cause of the drift toward drunkenness in the youth of to-day, is idleness in the hours outside of school, and after they have left school altogether. A sad wreck is going on in homes that should produce an intelligent and virtuous citizenship, and any system of home and public education that fails to produce noble citizens, is a bad thing for the republic. Consider for a momont the school days of average boys and girls who need to learn how to be practically useful because they must make their own way in the world. About five hours and a half are spent in the school room, the rest of the day largely on the streets or in some out-door life This superabundance of mere play is allowed because it is said that the brain work required demands such reaction. But is idleness necessary for the reaction needed? There is wood to cut, coal to bring, an occasional pail of water for mother, the lawn to be trimmed, the weeds kept from the garden — exercise which brings every muscle into play and relieves the brain. Indeed such work as this is recommended to preachers, lawyers, and brainworkers generally But the boy of to-day must play! One of our humorous writers has said that "a boy whose back would be broken by pulling a few weeds out of an onion patch, will willingly dig all over a ten acre lot to get angleworms for bait."

What of the girl? — There are dishes to be washed, sweeping and dusting to be done, clothing to be kept in repair, and the art of cooking mastered. But these are too hard for the little woman of these times I know school girls whose tender mothers would hesitate to ask them to do up the tea dishes, for fear it would be an over-exertion, who will put on rollers and skate for four hours on a stretch in the unwholesome air of a crowded rink. Now all this might be amusing but for the outcome in "good-for-nothing" young men and women who live by their wits or their vices.

Suppose the boy thus idly reared, to graduate at the high school at seventeen Commencement is over, and the world before him. What can he do to earn his dinner? — Nothing, until he gets some hard knocks from this practical world. He has used a gimlet to put on skates, a saw to make stilts, a hammer to crack nuts, but that does not make him a mechanic. Bookkeeping is a conundrum in a school-book, but he knows nothing about it His head and his hands are his capital, but he cannot touch the practical world with either to earn his first loaf of bread. Some boys at this point go to college and into a professional life a few years later on, but the student life of the masses ends with the common school.

The girl must meet life the same way What can she do? Sew? — No, her mother or dressmaker did that Cook? — No indeed; she never learned. Teach? — Just barely, but an undisciplined girl makes a poor teacher. If marriage offers a way out of the wilderness, her husband will need the digestion of an ostrich, or another cook to begin housekeeping with.

Do you question the connection between these things and the reform which brings us to this meeting to day?

It lies in the fact that the greatest danger of this country is in a degraded, non-productive citizenship. The road to that is a childhood warped by a false education, and an open saloon to receive the drifting, idle life.

The most hopeful field we have is among the children and youth. Agitate on these questions in all your unions by holding mothers' meetings, securing the statistics of school attendance, and looking into the provisions of the compulsory education law. Much can be done to save from vice and bring intelligence to the future citizenship of the State in this way.

Another cause for evil, which is also a hindrance to its overthrow, lies in the apathy of women, or, at least, their inactivity, in the threatening presence of the greatest foe to a woman's treasures. We are prone to talk so much among ourselves of the interest of women in total abstinence and prohibition that we forget the mass of women are as alien to the spirit of this great movement, as if they never heard of it.

The reasons for this strange neutrality are two. 1. I believe a majority of women yet believe that alcohol is a safe and often necessary thing in proper quantities, and have no fear or compunction in using it as a family remedy, or to add flavor to an extra dish for the table; and this belief, which generally has an appetite more or less strong back of it, is sufficient to keep any one from decided ground. Within a week a Christian woman said to me with great earnestness, that the best way to do temperance work was to get drinking men soundly converted, and then they would be all right without prohibition; and before the conversation ended, she said she believed liquors were necessary, and often the best remedy, and she had as "soon take brandy as salt and water."

Within a week I heard two ladies talking together of the effects of the first warm weather upon the system, and one said, "I am taking beer, I always do when I feel bad" We need to talk total abstinence among the people. Science is with us, appetite is against us Let us thunder into the ears of fathers and mothers the awful consequences of hereditary taint and bad home example.

The second cause of inactivity, is the unpopularity of our question, and the many ways in which it strikes personal interest Not long ago, in a Western city, a banker's wife joined the W. C. T U, and became active. Upon one occasion her name appeared in the papers in connection with the work; immediately a liquor dealer who was a heavy depositor at the bank, called on her husband and told him his wife must get out of the union or he would withdraw his business. In a few days that Christian woman had left the temperance work, and put her efforts somewhere else. This is a hint of the cause why so many Christian women give all their energies to the Indian, the heathen, the freedmen — anything, but to throttle the serpent that hisses at their very door. It takes grit as well as grace to do duty in this cause, and the husbands of some of these radicals belong to the "noble army of martyrs."

We have no cause for discouragement. God is for us, and who can prevail against us? With cheerful courage, confident hope, and all-conquering love to those who are with us, and those who are against us, we work toward a sure victory.

"Fear not, let not thy hands be slack. The Lord thy God in the midst of thee is mighty."

[Manistee, Mich., June 8, 1886.]

The majority of the world is asleep when a great reform is born. Custom, ambition, appetite, and the moral inertia of humanity are all opposed to a fresh thought of God when launched upon the world. It is, therefore, not the many, but the few, who are prepared for the self-consecration and self-sacrifice necessary to meet the early conflict of the right against the wrong. It generally happens that the laggard, sleepy world when first aroused by the earnest cry of awakened souls, is far from being good natured. Startled from easy indulgence, set face to face with wrong which demands redress, the first burst of indignation is against the reformer, instead of against the evil which he combats. For this reason, the Bethlehem song which announced Christ, was not sung in the palace halls of the old rulers, but out on the Judean plains, to the wandering shepherds, who were fresh-hearted enough to want God and a new order of things, in a land made sad by many wrongs.

Ever since that day, when the unwelcome Prince of all kingdoms was crowded to a manger for his birth-place, truth has sung its electric anthems to those made ready to hear. When I speak then, to-night, first of all, to my comrades of the W. C. T. U., I speak to the prepared souls who have heard the Bethlehem song of a new redemption. This melody which is burdened with "peace on earth," "goodwill to men," and with promise of coming victory, brings us together year by year, as the silver trumpet's blow from hill-top to hill-top summoned old Israel to war against her enemies.

You are drawn, dear sisters, by the impulse of a noble endeavor; held by a bond which toil, sacrifice, and a freshly awakened world in its twilight temper can never break or weaken. Women. On guard over the home kingdom, already degraded and desecrated by that outrage to love's treasures and its purity, Intemperance. Christians: Holding through all to the Christly spirit, while insisting on the Christly power which is to destroy "the works of the devil," instead of compromising with them. Temperate: No poisoned blood, no pulses fevered with alcohol, no cup of danger lifted to your own lips, or pressed to the lips of others, thus holding your own bodies as temples of the Holy Ghost, and thus guiltless of a brother's blood. These in union so strong that about this idea, women of all denominations, all nationalities, all colors, clasp hands,—union so wide it touches already, or is on its way to touch in the world's W. C. T. U the peoples of the earth. Pure women, true Christianity, real temperance, close, far-reaching union,—W. C T. U. It might be translated, "Woe Cometh To Unrighteousness" that protects the rum traffic in this republic of Christian homes and Christian mothers.

Born in a crusade at which the world yet wonders; organized into a great connectional society, coming with gentle but unfaltering step across the years, this largest of all unions of women, in one endeavor, stands to-day victorious instead of defeated, and gives notice to the world in the name of the Lord of Hosts, who is with us, that the saloon system must go down. In every State and territory the watchword has been spoken. From height to height floats the white symbol, and North and South clasp-hands, since Frances E. Williard bore the first real lilies of peace across the red line of the old carnage

There is no organization to-day so truly national as the W C. T. U. You will excuse me if in the name of the Michigan division, I pause to shout for the whole Grand Army to-night We have been called hair-brained, fanatical, useless.

The question comes. What have you done after all? We invite the real seeker after the truth to go and ask why Lucy Hayes's portrait is in the White House? Why the girls' Industrial School is at Adrian? Why intoxicating wine is banished from the communion table? Go read the record on Constitutional Prohibition in Kansas, Iowa, Maine, and Rhode Island, and of Local Option in Atlanta and through the Sunny South land. Search the statute books of fourteen States and one territory for laws compelling the study of temperance physiology; stand by the presses pouring out books to meet the demand of these laws. Then go to Washington and ask why Congress has just passed the first temperance measure since we had a country, and you will find that Mary H. Hunt and the W. C. T. U. are a very clearly defined power to the men who voted for the National Temperance Educational bill. You will excuse us for shouting, since we usually work more than we shout. All honor, to the non-partisan organization that educates. Double honor to the Prohition partisan who votes. But I tell you, friends, when this great-crested, red-breasted Cock Robin of the liquor traffic is dead, and the question is asked: Who killed him? may some one of our host be there to answer:—

> "We of the Union,
> With our faithful women,
> We killed Cock Robin"

The claim often made that the temperance reform is the foolish dream of narrow souls, has been given most emphatic refutation, by the breadth and character of the work attempted by this organization. Its thought and effort touch humanity at every point, beginning in the cradle, nay, before the cradle, in the solemn laws of heredity, and widening until they reach not only every relation of the individual life, but the aggregate of lives when they compose society and nations. Every department is founded upon some truth of science, morals, or experience. On such truth, demonstrated to the intellect, taking hold of the convictions, and so governing the life, rest the fundamental principles of this reform; viz., total abstinence for the individual and total prohibition for the State. These principles need no explanation, no apology, no defense; they are safe, pure, right,— and must come to victory in habit and in law. To secure such victory, education and legislation are both demanded. It has been charged that the W. C. T. U., have left the high ground of moral and religious education and become clamorous only for political remedies for a great evil. We deny the charge. · of the events of the past year was the centennial jubilee of the temperance reform For a whole century, from Dr. Rush to Frances Willard, the reform has been in the moral and educational realm, and in this moral reform we have held no mean place. But the law of progress in this movement is like all that has gone before it: First, education, second, agitation, third, legislation. Some, indeed most people, believe in education This has made the work for scientific temperance instruction the most popular in our history, but many are unwilling to go farther.

"Tell them the danger, and then let them take care of themselves," cries selfishness; "don't stir up the world because a few are doing wrong." Others go to the second step of agitation. Looking on the work of the dram-shop, they speak out in indignation against it Its cruelty, its lawlessness, its wickedness, they see as the reformer does, and make indignant protest. But, strange to say, the men and women are comparatively few who are fully abreast with the third step in the contest — prohibitory legislation. At this line our forces divide to-day, but let no one rejoice, the division is only for a season. Some weeks ago in the city of Baltimore, I listened to Senator Colquitt, of Georgia, as with an honest and sturdy indignation, which could not fail to be eloquent, he arraigned the saloon for its iniquity. As we returned to the hotel, I said to him, "Senator, when you travel back to the wrong attitude of government where the saloon is intrenched, then will be a chance to get under conviction about its political supporters." This free land will never educate and agitate, so arraigning brain and conscience against wrong, without finding the hour when it must legislate that wrong into the dust Be patient, friends, who believe in all three We are on the ground a little early; put down your ear, and you will hear the tramp of the coming millions — and the saloon must go.

LEGISLATION AND PETITION

There are several important matters which should be reached by this department, through the legislatures of 1886 and 1887. In order that it may be more effective, I would recommend the appointment of a secretary at Lansing, that we may have such assistance as can only come from one residing at the capital. I would recommend a popular petition asking for local prohibition within a radius of five miles of the Michigan University, at Ann Arbor A petition asking for such legislation was quite widely circulated two years ago, and sent to the legislature, but the prayer of the petitioners was denied A movement of this kind should be started early and made as influential as possible. The reasons for the people asking such prohibition of the saloons, are many.

1. It is a State institution supported by public money paid by the people.

2 The boys and girls from the homes of the people are sent there for education, and should be protected from unnecessary temptation.

3. Ann Arbor has forty dram-shops made especially attractive to lure the bright, ardent, student life, besides the billiard halls and pool rooms.

4. It is becoming a positive injury to the good name and high standing of our Western Athens that these saloons do tempt to dissoluteness some of the students coming from all parts of the country. From one letter recently received from Ann Arbor, I quote : —

"I have been wondering for a long time what could be done to remove the forty saloons from the college town, and it has entered my mind to appeal to you. Can you not instruct the unions to circulate petitions in every town? . . . If these could pour into our legislature this winter, the great work might be done."

Another, equally earnest, after speaking of the effort two years ago, says : —

"I believe there is no more important work for the women of the State. There is not a woman but should be deeply concerned about the welfare of this university. Hundreds of young men and women are coming and will continue to come to Ann Arbor, and money from the State is being appropriated and will be in the future. This, apart from mere selfish interests, should induce our workers to turn their attention to banishing the sale of intoxicating liquors from the vicinity of the University. Will you not bring the matter before the ladies and tell them we have here forty saloons ; tell them to imagine the temptations in connection with these ; ask them to tell the people of Michigan about these things, for if judiciously brought before them, they will rise up and remedy these great wrongs." It may be objected that the citizens of Ann Arbor ought not to have their "personal liberties" invaded in the interest of a company of non-resident students who choose to go wrong We reply, that it appears that the saloons are there largely to entrap the students , and from these they seek their gains. A Citizens' League was recently organized for the better enforcement of the law, and they sent out a circular setting forth certain facts concerning the saloon influence in Ann Arbor. Within a few days, the following communication has appeared in one of the city papers, which speaks for the need of some action. It is signed by "An Old Citizen" and speaks as follows : " The circular sent out by the Citizens' League some months since, has been bearing its legitimate fruits, but fruits different from what its authors doubtless intended. One of our prominent business men received a letter a few days since from a Western friend. This business man had written his friend, using one of the envelopes that set forth Ann Arbor's attractions on its back ; and his Western friend in answer said, in effect: 'I have read with deep interest the many advantages of Ann Arbor as depicted upon the back of the envelope sent me But there is one thing according to your own citizens' admission that you neglect to mention, viz, your saloons My boys are at Oberlin where they have no saloons.'"

A systematic examination of our laws, reveals a deplorably low state of opinion as to the crime which hurls a woman into the abyss of an irredeemable ruin. The "age of consent" as known in law, in many States is at ten years, almost back to the line of babyhood, and Michigan, to her shame, is among the number. After her tenth birthday the child is counted a woman, where the priceless dower of her virtue is concerned. She cannot control her property or her residence, she is not of age in any sense until she is eighteen, only in presence of the act, or lust, that would destroy her I have scarcely dared to trust myself to open this burning question, but when the penalty for luring a young girl to her ruin is lighter than for the theft of a horse, it is criminal not to speak.

The White Cross army with which we cooperate, is composed of men who work with men for their own manly well-being and the defense of women Its principles strike at once to the root of certain opinions that promote licentiousness. First, it takes the same high ground for personal purity in men as in women, and admits no physical or moral necessity, or excuse for them, that could not be held for mother, sister, or wife Second, it strikes a blow at the assumption that while women are called the weaker sex, and put under limitation of citizenship, and otherwise, because of that claim, the demand is made that they always be morally the stronger, and stand guard over their own weakness and man's assertive nature together. The whole high theory of the "White Cross Army" calls manhood to the defense of womanhood, from himself first; and if necessary from her own weakness which may be her danger.

A man who would strike down a woman on the street, or leave her defenseless in a burning house or sinking boat, would be hissed at as a coward. But the man who lays womanhood in the dust of life's most unmerciful disaster, goes scott free in his sinning. There are at this hour three young girls in the reformatory at Adrian, the eldest not yet eighteen, all victims of one gay young man *They* are criminals, in keeping of the law; *he* is a gallant, in society

It is a piece of drivelling and hypocritical cowardice for men to stand up and claim superior strength of muscle, of brain, of courage, of nerve, of self-command, and then go all to moral flinders before any temptation where sex is concerned, and say to a yielding woman made weak by her very loving, "You must be strong for us both, or we shall go to ruin, and on you will rest the blame." It is the thinnest possible sham, to hide the grossest possible wrong

GIRL'S INDUSTRIAL SCHOOL.

The temperance women of Michigan must always be interested in the prosperity of the institution at Adrain for the shelter and reformation of young girls, because it stands as a monument of their endeavor.* It was my pleasure to visit it on Monday morning, May 31, and hold a brief service in the beautiful chapel. The room was quiet and empty as we entered, and the sweet May sunshine came in floods of glory through the stained windows. Soon the sweet-toned organ filled all the place with melody, and into the sunshine and music marched nearly two hundred girls, from ten years old up to the line of twenty-one Dark and fair, merry and sober, pretty and plain, they were like any company of girls, one might say. But I remembered a blight was on them; more sinned against than sinning, mostly; they can never know a day henceforth without a clouded sun. Robbed of innocence, despoiled of life's very morning, I watched them come in, and by the time they were seated, tears were in my eyes, and a sob at my lips, as the woe of their early blighting reached my own heart.

What could I say which had the music of hope in it, to these who were looking back to an abyss where virtue went down, and forward to a world's savage scorn? Ah sisters, it is a place for tears O ' men is it fair? Do you protect women, after all, either by love or law? Miss Scott, the superintendent, had said to me, "There is not a girl here but is trying to do right ; they really want to be good, but they have never had a fair chance, and it is hard for some of them." I ignored the past, and tried to begin where Jesus does, with the soul at the point where it makes choice of God and a better way, and from thence goes toward the victory. During prayers at the close, I felt that heaven drew near. God pity us ! The angels minister to a good many people we are too fine to associate with

Why have I told you all this ? — Because I want you to pray for the unsheltered girls of the State, and work for them too You would

---

* This institution was established directly through Mrs Lathrap's influence.— ED

shudder with unspeakable horror if I should tell you why some of them are there, the angels must have wept over such losing. For its larger usefulness the institution needs now two things: One is, more room. The accommodations are limited, and further aid for the present is denied So necessity and sentiment outside crowd the girls out, before the influence of the place gets much hold upon the character. The ideal of the projectors of this enterprise was that it should be reformatory and educational, that those who entered should remain a sufficent time to change, in some degree, at least, the tendencies of life, while the moral character is being strengthened and the unskilled hands taught useful domestic industries. Surely it is not waste.

Another need is a good, devout woman for chaplain and religious instruction. The pastors of the city go out and preach to them, but more is demanded. These blighted lives need to be led with a mother's tenderness to the pitiful Christ. They cannot *grow* to him, they must *go* to him and find strength and peace

> Wandering feet that went astray,
>   Who shall lead thee home,
> Far in sin's delusive way,
>   Who shall lead thee home?
> Who shall softly at thy side
> Whisper hope since Christ hath died?

EVANGELISTIC.

Let me press upon your attention and faith, dear workers, the value of human souls. There are many remedies for the evils of society, but only one remedy for sin, the groundwork of all evil I urge then that you make the evangelistic work more prominent. No union should feel satisfied if the year goes by and no one really converted to Christ. We have members among us without a Christian's hope and joy, children old enough in our bands of hope to begin the new life, and the whole world in its want before us Whatever other success we covet, let us seek this best gift,— the salvation of souls.

Let us, having chosen the right, not be impatient It always pays in great moral revolutions to go the long way round with God, instead of any short-cut of expediency. Judge Tourgée in his Appeal to Cæsar, when speaking of the attempt of the nation to settle the negro question, suddenly, says. "Time! What has God to do with time? Shall we not attempt a great work because we may not live to finish it?" Let us, dear comrades, work on, ready to see the victory or die before it comes, but work patiently as if we were to be here forever.

A railroad over the mountains of western North Carolina has a wonderful triumph of engineering at a place called Round Knob. You come down the rugged steeps by many a curve, and into dark tunnels, then out through a narrow cut, where a long, deep valley is to be crossed. It is only a mile to the other side where you must go. But the train sweeps around the gorge nine miles to make it. That was the civil engineer's long way around with God, and when he laid his track on the strength of the eternal hills, he did better work than he could have accomplished by any short cut on a creaking trestle-work. Human expedients may be offered: short, easy ways across the difficulties, the truth is content to go the long way round with God.

We stand between the years with thanksgiving for the past, and courage for the future. Our cause will triumph; the light of morning is on the hilltops, its victory in our souls.

> Little by little the skies grow clear,
> Little by little the sun comes near,
> Little by little the days smile out
> Gladder and brighter on pain and doubt.
> Little by little the seed we sow
> Into a beautiful yield will grow.
>
> Little by little the world grows strong,
> Fighting the battle of right and wrong,
> Little by little the world gives way,
> Little by little the right has sway,
> Little by little each longing soul
> Struggles up nearer the shining goal
>
> Little by little the good in men
> Blossoms to beauty for human ken;
> Little by little the angels see
> Prophecies better of good to be;
> Little by little the God of all
> Lifts the world nearer his pleading call

[Port Huron, May 31, 1887.]

It is said that when the decisive hour in the battle of Waterloo was near, the English troops were lying on the ground in columns four feet deep under the very guns of the enemy. The command had been given to wait until the French were close upon them before opening fire. During these moments of awful suspense, Wellington rode up and down the lines repeating over and over, in tones of suppressed excitement, "What will England say to you if you falter now? What will England say to you if you falter now?" An old officer made the statement that he repeated it thousands of times Anyway, the question was burned into the waiting, silent ranks, until they felt as if they were lying under the walls of Parliament, and when the order rang out, "Now, up and at them!" each soldier felt the honor of England was in his hands, and his spirit was simply invincible.

Do you think, my sisters, the battle is done, and we are assembled to adjust ourselves to the conditions, and learn the lesson of defeat? — Nay, verily, the Waterloo of the liquor traffic is afield in State and nation, the contest is begun, but is not finished, the decisive hour waits a little farther on, and we are of the silent ranks who may meet a sterner shock of battle than has yet been What will the world say to us if we falter now? What will the Christ of the world say to us if we falter now? I would like to repeat it over and over until I feel and you feel that we sit under the light of the judgment seat, with its glow upon the decisions we make.

They are shortsighted indeed who underestimate the gravity of this hour. Truths insisted upon for a century have taken root in the consciences of men and women. The wrongs and sorrows which result from the legalized liquor traffic grow too bitter for longer endurance. The dangers that thicken about our free institutions become more alarming every year. Meanwhile the liquor oligarchy increases its impudent demands, intimidates or buys its political servants; threatens or murders its moral and political opposers The pitiful truce of compromise to secure a false and transient peace cannot last. Righteousness abides. Truth is abroad. Conscience is awake. God is on the throne, and the liquor traffic is going down.

In spite of the Upper Peninsula with its imported voters, and the "broadcloth and slum combination" of Detroit and Grand Rapids, the saloon is going down in Michigan and in the Republic. The victory will not come in some half holiday of parade; the silent ranks this hour wait the hot struggle under the guns of an enemy taught of hell. What will the world say to us if we falter now?

One of our women, writing me just after the election, said · "I am satisfied we need to learn a new lesson of dependence on God. We are trusting too much in our own wisdom and methods; we talk of this as *our cause* when it is *God's cause*, and in him is all hope of victory." They were wise words, fitly spoken, and have come often to mind in these weeks

Sisters, before we enter the history of the past year or discuss principle and method, let us sit for a few moments with the disciples at the feet of Jesus while he teaches them how to pray A civilization once approved of God, and the special object of his divine care was in the throes of revolution. The proclamation of a new truth was stirring the hearts of the people as the winds stir the forest leaves. The footfall of a new king was shaking the throne of the Cæsars, and what was older and more sacred, the proud Jewish ecclesiasticism Old customs tottered; old rites grew hollow; old parties were dying, and these long regnant forces contended with the new. The old had numbers, thrones, armies, and traditions, the new had truth and the Messiah of the coming dispensation. The one trusted in the old order of things, and said, "We have Abraham to our father" The new forsook the past and with spiritual vision said as they looked on Jesus, "Thou art the Christ, the son of the living God."

This state of things brought a revolution that by-and-by blotted out a nation and made its citizens sojourners in strange lands until now The revolution was in the realm of human policies and dominion greatly honored of men, the power was of God and came from above. It was not strange, as the contest deepened about them, that the old, stately supplications of the temple did not fit the sharp, new needs of the hour, and the disciples came to Jesus, saying, "Teach us how to pray." Nor is it strange that the prayer he taught should be the key of the future kingdom to which the old must give place. My soul has stood in silence before its meanings for many a day.

"Thy kingdom come." After Calvary, on a purchased earth, over a redeemed race, the right of Christ to rule was established. His kingdom set up at such a price was to grow in human hearts; so ever since and henceforth, the warfare is with anything and all things which stand between Christ and a human soul. "That is right," says some conservative listener, "I always thought the Woman's Christian Temperance Union forsook its true mission when it left the gospel line and invoked political forces."

Wait, my friend. "Thy kingdom come" has demolished thrones, uprooted dynasties, and buried powers under the dust. One hundred years ago we were praying it in the Christian churches of the North, and the slave was sobbing it out in the rice swamps and cotton fields of the South. By-and-by a law of Christ's kingdom stood in judgment at the gates of this government and condemned the man who sold his brother. Then the struggle began; parties were disrupted; churches were rent asunder; treasures were poured out, and hill and vale were wet with blood, but finally the prayer, "Thy kingdom come," had its answer in new laws that acknowledged the brotherhood of man. The Christ of peace was on his way to the manhood of the negro race and righteousness in government, but his chariot wheels' shook the very foundation of this great country before his kingdom came.

"Thy kingdom come," we pray it again before the mocking, scornful power of this legalized infamy, the liquor traffic. Custom, fashion, appetite, political party, and policy, all enter into its armor of pride; but it stands in the path of Jesus to human souls, and it will go, while the stroke which destroys it will wound those who on any height, or in any depth, give aid or support to the gigantic crime.

> "Thy kingdom come" Upon the hilltops glistens
> The morning glow, for which we wait and long
> "Thy kingdom come," O true hearts, pause and listen,
> Around you soon shall sweep the victory song
> Short is the work when God puts forth his power,
> Then, patient, watch with Christ this twilight hour

"Thine is the power." This is the lesson we need now to learn from the lips of Him who gave the prayer as a key to unlock the doorway between our weakness and the strength of God. We might well be discouraged if the power were with us, but it is not. Our organization is strong and growing, our national leaders wise and influential, our methods, the marvelous outgrowth of consecrated brain and heart, while God has put the fear of us upon our enemies. But let us look ever away from all these, saying, "Thine is the power," and then keep our hearts so pure, our organization so free from selfishness and guile, that the divine power may have its way

"Thine is the power." We give to Thee glory,
  Since for our strength the work were all too great.
"Thine is the power." Beneath the mighty shelter
  In solemn gladness we may toil and wait
Sure is the end. True souls that watch in sadness
Shall sing some golden morn the song of gladness.

THE AMENDMENT CONTEST.

Before beginning the preparation of this address, I thought to say but little concerning the contest through which we have so recently passed, but the intense interest felt over all the country, in the true history of our campaign, and its results; the fate of other States which at this time are in a like struggle; and the fact that the history of the year past and work of the year to come is so interwoven with it, has changed this first decision, and leads me to say some things which are waiting to be said.

The Woman's Christian Temperance Union is fully committed to constitutional prohibition — State and national. We believe the only right thing is an entire change of the theory and attitude of government toward the liquor system, and that such change can only come by the expressed will of the people put into fundamental law, and to this end we work, as individuals and an organization. That we did not last winter circulate petitions to the legislature, asking for the submission of the amendment, was not because we had abated in the least our desire for this form of legislation. The action of the State Executive Board at its meeting in December, 1886, exactly expressed our position at that time

Resolved, That while we are unalterably committed to the principle of constitutional prohibition, we do not see the necessity of petitioning the legislature of 1886–7, for the following reasons: First, that we have already twice done this work; and second, the party in power has recorded its promise of such action.

Resolved, That should the Constitutional Amendment be submitted to the people, we will use our utmost effort to secure its victory at the ballot-box.

This pledge we fully redeemed

When the November election was over and it was found that the Republican party had come into power with increased majorities, a leading paper said editorially: "The people of Michigan have chosen to give the temperance question into the hands of the Republican party for the next two years;" and later in the same article, "The Prohibitionists have little reason to expect favors from the present legislature." The radical temperance people therefore quietly waited the action at Lansing. It is well the world should know that with the dominant party in the State of Michigan rests the honor and responsibility of submitting the amendment, as well as the entire control of the method of that submission.

The text of the amendment was one of the earliest and gravest difficulties in the way of success. It has been widely criticized for its intricate and bungling wording, and we believe justly so. If our legislators had been traveling a new path, there would have been excuse for such a mistake, but Kansas, Iowa, Maine, and Pennsylvania had all furnished models — the amendment which the Pennsylvania legislature adopted being so nearly perfect in form as to avoid the difficulties met by the other States

The sweeping and indefinite phraseology concerning property rights in liquors, furnished one argument for the enemies of the amendment, while the failure to except sacramental wine, arrayed against it the ritualistic churches and those of our foreign citizens. When the discussion upon church rights had just begun, a friend of the amendment met a member of the legislature, who voted for submission, and said to him : "It is unfortunate that you failed to make an exception of sacramental wine, for it will array the whole Catholic Church against it, as well as other religious bodies." "That is just what we want," said the honorable gentleman; "that will defeat it." The proofs are many that some of the difficulties which hindered the campaign were prepared with malice aforethought.

When the contest opened, less than ten per cent of the newspapers of the State, including the religious and prohibition press, were for the amendment, and all the daily papers in the State save one, were arrayed against it. The leaders of the old parties, with few exceptions, were openly opposed, or silent as the grave, while the battle went on, and when the decisive day came, party leaders, party servants, and members of the legislature who at Lansing had voted to submit the question, stood side by side with saloon men at the polls and worked to defeat the amendment. The party whose measure it was ; the party that demanded the withdrawal of the Prohibition ticket, out of gratitude for its action, elected its State ticket by increased majorities, but the amendment was defeated. That it was counted out by fraud (if it was so counted out) does not change one jot the responsibility. The people made a magnificent fight, but party machinery, set to run in harmony with the demands of the liquor traffic, defeated them.

We bring our meed of honor to the few leaders from the old parties who stood out for the truth, and whose voices were heard in its defense. We honor also the citizens of all parties who voted for the home and against the saloon. We speak our earnest words of praise for the newspapers which voiced the people's best thought in their struggle; but now that the smoke has cleared away, some things are as clear as noonday.—

First, if the Republican and Democratic organs are reliable exponents of party sentiment and attitude on this question, then both these parties in Michigan are opposed to prohibition Second, if Republican and Democratic leaders represent the position and intention of the organizations that put honor upon them, then both these parties in Michigan are opposed to prohibition. Third, the only difference between these political parties is, that one believes in license and the other in higher license. Fourth, that the only hope for prohibition lies in a revolt of citizenship from standards that perpetuate the saloon, and the lifting of a new standard, for absolute and unqualified prohibition. Fifth, that while the relations between the ruling political parties and the liquor traffic remain as close and friendly as at present, a free ballot and a fair count for Prohibitionists is as doubtful at the North as a free ballot and a fair count for the negro at the South

I need not tell you that with all the forces, open and secret, arrayed against prohibition, with intimidation at the polls, and treason at the count in Detroit, with the Upper Peninsula mapped out for fraud, that the 4th day of April was not a day of defeat but of victory, and the end is not yet. This marvelous expression of the people's will on the temperance issue, has given the politicians and our present legislature a more knotty problem than was the campaign which went before.

What do they offer to a people cheated out of a well-earned victory? What do they propose to the forty-nine counties which gave majorities for prohibition? What do they propose to the American population, who said by their votes, "We believe the saloon to be un-American, and dangerous to our free institutions." Low license and township option, says the Democratic press. High license and county option, says the Republican press. And the legislature goes to

Wayne county, the stronghold of the anti-amendment un-American vote, for the ideal of a new legislation.

The newspapers have been telling us with great earnestness that the policy of prohibition cannot be forced upon centers of population like Detroit, Grand Rapids, and Saginaw Valley. The graver question seems to face us: Shall these centers, with their low sentiment mold legislation for the remainder of Michigan? The local option phase of legislation as at first proposed by our law makers and the Republican press, seemed attractive even to many of our temperance people. The possibility of putting the magnificent sweep of counties in the Southern Peninsula under prohibition, looked like the next best thing to victory in the whole State. Even our W. C. T. U. women wavered, and three letters came to me inside of twenty-four hours asking that the influence of our organization be put on this line. After thought and prayer, we sent out the "No Compromise" leaflet. The positions there taken against local option will bear repetition here, with additions growing out of later developments. We are opposed to local option, because, First, it secures the consent of the State to the perpetuation of the saloon. Second, it does not settle the attitude of the State, but turns a great moral and political question over to the recurring chances of bitter local contests. Third, it is only helpful to the cleaner sections, leaving the city centers to an ever-increasing evil. If there is any locality which needs law, it is that where the crime is rampant against which the law is made. Fourth, local option has the license-principle and possibility, and secures the consent of the State to the existence of the saloon where the local majorities so elect. Fifth, it leaves license in force to be applied outside of territory put under prohibition by option, and receives of such localities a revenue from vice; because of this fact any State law of this kind must unite license and local option together.

Then the statement is superficial and misleading, that we should secure the same results by counties as on the fourth of April in the vote for constitutional prohibition for the State. To vote the saloons out of one county and leave them in the next, disturbs the balance of trade, and into this question, which appeals to the consciences of men, come other and local arguments that grow out of business relations, and an appeal to self-interest. Local option is therefore no substitute for constitutional prohibition. Now some will be ready to say, "Local option has been a great success at the South," and so it has. But the conditions are very different from our own. They have an American population, black and white, we have a large foreign element. Their dangerous classes (largely negro) are docile and subservient from nature and long training. Our dangerous classes are turbulent and imperious, and "boss" the political situations. They have practically one party, and the question is one of opinion inside the party line. We have two opposing parties so equally divided that each has hope of success by winning the shifting and purchasable vote

One of our representatives said to me recently, "We really desire to lessen the evils of the saloon business and make law that can be enforced" I said, "Why then do you not amend the penalty end of the law instead of the tax end?" The penalties for disobedience of our liquor laws have never been adequate to the crime; and here lies their weakness Suppose the only penalty for stealing one hundred dollars was a fine of twenty-five dollars; you see the thief could make seventy-five dollars, and work into a respectable and paying business. Saloon men sell liquor on election day or Sunday in disobedience of law and make one hundred dollars, they are fined but twenty-five dollars, and of course can afford it. The laws at the South are a success, largely because strong at the point of penalty. A gentleman in my own city has just returned from Georgia. During his stay there in a local option town, a man was arrested for selling liquor in defiance of law, and was sentenced to the chain-gang for four years It is safe to say he won't try it again.

Watch carefully our liquor legislation and its enforcement, and you will be driven to decide that it is not the intention of the average law maker or officer to hurt the saloon men or cripple their ruinous work The tax or license, with the legal status and power it gives, is not a burden to the saloon; it is hush money to quiet the *good men*, who think something ought to be done, and are not ready for the only right thing The twin of the local option method — and it is a "Siamese Twin," for the one cannot exist without the other — is high license. In its old familiar garb it needs no arraignment in this presence. We are all familiar with this false principle in government, that under pretense of regulating and controlling the liquor traffic, has fostered and given it power, until after eight years of license legislation, the National Anti-Saloon Republican Convention declared as follows —

"The liquor traffic as it exists to day in the United States is the enemy of society; the fruitful source of corruption in politics, the ally of anarchy a school of crime; and with its avowed purpose of seeking to corruptly control elections and legislation, it is a menace to public welfare, and deserves the condemnation of all good men"

How does the liquor traffic exist to-day? It "exists" by sanction of the State, and compels protection through laws which, while they vary in method, all have the license quality and power. What remedy is proposed for an evil declared to be so great? What "practical and progressive measures" to meet this "menace to public safety?" — *More license*, a higher price for legal status and governmental sanction It makes one's blood grow hot with indignation that such a state of things can be, and we recall the time when the acknowledged evils of African slavery were met by *more compromise*.

In Michigan we have had ten years of this kind of policy. The liquor traffic has been paying the tax required into our city treasuries, and then laying its greedy hand upon the lines of municipal power We have literally "builded our towns with blood, and established our cities with iniquity;" have —

> "Paved our streets with the children of slain,
> And lighted our ways with the price of shame,"

until Christian conscience has been silenced, and the *revenue* has been put above the *human*. What but this could have given us such a spectacle as the "Business Men's Anti-Amendment Movement"? Think of men living in wide houses, driving fine equipages, and enjoying the luxury that money brings, standing up to plead that the rumseller might remain as a tax gatherer, to pick out of the pockets of the laboring classes that which should lessen their own righteous obligations to the civilization which brought all the chances of wealth. Good men pleading for the perpetuation of the saloon, with the wrong, the sorrow, the sin that flows from it, when they know the money coveted must largely come from want in other homes, and the enforced starvation of women and children! O friends, cannibalism is decent to it! I can respect a savage who with the approval of a rude conscience and the demand of a depraved appetite picks the bones of his fellow-man *to live*, but I have only solemn condemnation for an intelligent man who asks us to believe him a Christian, while he deliberately supports, for his own advantage, a system that picks bare of hope and joy and peace the lives of the helpless and defenceless

I never hated the whole license system as I do to-day, since this revelation of its poisonous effects upon the consciences of otherwise good men   But the wrong cannot abide

> "Somewhere beneath the vaulted sky,
>   Somewhere beneath the slumbering sod,
> Wrath broods her thunders ere they fly,
>   Pale Justice steeps her chastening rod,
> When Wealth and Power have had their hour,
>   Comes for the weak, the hour of God"

The question likely to be asked is, "Would the Woman's Christian Temperance Union oppose local option if that were the law, and the contest was on in any town or county?" — *Certainly not.* As between license by any authority and prohibition through any power, we are always on the side of the prohibition forces

Why then oppose the action of the legislature? — Because our law makers are not on prohibition ground, but are skilfully avoiding it. The measure commits Michigan still to the tax law, puts the authority of the State behind the tax principle, and relegates prohibition to a recurring and unstable chance in localities

I have gone thus fully into this question because we go out from here to meet it. Already the issues of the presidential contest loom up on our political skies. The great contending parties are practically on the same ground concerning the perpetuation by law, and for purposes of revenue, of the great liquor system of this country, while they are amusingly busy just now seeking a difference of method and expression This political sham-battle has had its center in Albany during the months just passed. New York is the pivotal point next year; there are fifty thousand Prohibitionists who will not go back to the fold; there is a respectable body of Mugwumps not yet laughed out of existence. So in this great fight for the crown of national power, the scales swing dangerously even for the contending forces.

One of the first discoveries made in the recent struggle was that Christian conscience is not yet clear upon this great question How strange it seems yet that the first sharp shot against the amendment came from the church. After all the teaching we have had on the sacramental wine question, after all the testimony from Jewish history and customs which should convince the uttermost doubter that during Passover week Jesus could not have instituted the sacrament with fermented wine, many ministers rushed to the saloon side of the contest in defense of the so-called " rights of the church " Of course these rights were never in danger even by the unfortunate wording of the amendment, but it is a pity that so large a percentage of the great church of Christ should have given even temporary moral support to the wrong side.

For several years, comparatively little has been said on the question of unfermented wine at the sacrament, but manifestly educational work on that line is yet needed. When we began agitation upon this question, it was largely because, following the crusade, many men who had been confirmed drinkers were converted and came into the church Some of these were tempted to their fall by the fermented wine they found on the Lord's table, and others in self defense refrained from it altogether. This led to a new position, for the sake of the weak who might stumble, but soon it was found that unfermented wine had higher claims than its harmlessness.

Some scholarly men have severely attacked the temperance people for bringing their "fanaticism" to such sacred places, but we believe it easy of proof that the passover wine of the Jews was unfermented; that Jesus never spoke of the contents of the cup he offered his disciples when he instituted the sacrament, as wine, that much of the wine of commerce found on the Lord's table has not a drop of grape juice in it, and is therefore unfit for such use; that unfermented wine, being the pure juice of the grape, fills both letter and spirit of Christian obligation; that alcoholic wine may be a source of temptation to the weak, and is therefore a danger; that as long as fermented wine is used by the church in its most solemn sacrament, the liquor traffic will claim the custom in moral support of its iniquity If this be fanaticism, let it be proven If we are right, then when another contest comes, as it must, let us hope for the honor of the church this question may not again arise

Sadder, if possible, was the position of many Christian men on the main question. That the tax system should have its defenders in pulpit and pew, was at once a sorrow and surprise, while the arguments were unworthy such moral heights We believe largely it was from lack of thought and education. Much has been said about the propriety of taking such questions as those involved in the amendment contest into the church for discussion. Our Circular No. 1, to ministers, was criticised in some quarters for this reason, and in many places church doors were closed even against ministers who were speaking for prohibition. We have only to say in defense, that had the amendment been in any sense the issue of the Prohibition party, or any political organization, if the discussion had involved the interests of candidates, or the success of men, we should not have asked what we did. But a great moral question was sent to the people for decision through constitutional methods.

Everything on which Christ's kingdom is to be built is menaced by the dram-shop. Has the church then no place in the contest? Has it become so dainty it can only build tabernacles on the mountain, but refuses to go to those possessed with devils below?

Ah, friends, in this country just now with its mighty problems that shake society to the center; with the nations of the earth pouring their untaught and discontented thousands in upon us; with the old landmarks of Christianity being tampered with by vandal hands; there is little use for a religion so sacred and so ethereal that it cannot bear the sharp, awful, human battle-grounds where life meets death, and heaven meets hell.

The growth of Christ's kingdom means the overthrow of all human government not built in righteousness. God help us! What we need is *more* instead of less discussion in the church concerning this great question. The liquor traffic abides to-day by the consent of the Christian church of America. A liquor dealer said to me recently: "What we have most to fear is the awakening of the right wing of our army, the Christian high license men, for the church holds the balance of power, and if it turns against us, we are gone." I tremble sometimes as I think of it. What will arouse us? Haddock at the North, Gambrell at the South have gone down, from the very heart of the church, in this contest for truth, others have suffered many things, and yet the great forces sleep on, or awake to defend the murderous rum power and plead for its life.

It is my desire, however, for a moment to touch the other and hopeful side of the question of our foreign citizens and the problem of prohibition. The first great cause of their attitude is ignorance, not about everything, but about the one vital thing to us: the relation of dram-shop to government. This is their first experiment with a republic where every man is as good as the next one because he votes, and it is also their first experience with a country where the ruling power is in the dram-shop, instead of on the throne or in the House of Parliament. The foreigner is shut away by the bar of language from the American religions and the Prohibition press. But temperance, according to political parties, and, worse, according to the saloon, is translated for him into his own tongue ; while with it come the customs and habits of thought, brought from civilizations of a different type than ours. And such influences as these shape his thought, and prepare him for civil life.

What wonder that we reap what thus is sown. The mass of foreigners reach their first knowledge of our institutions through the saloon and its political and social environments. The result is, they are worse men when they have been here five years, than at their coming.

The thing demanded for them is another view of America, its foundations and possibilities, then these men will cease to tear down the house that shelters them and their children

I have heard of a little girl, the daughter of a minister, who was put safely to bed and told to say her prayers She went all through with the children's petition, and then the "good-night" was spoken ; presently the mother heard the sweet voice taking up a new and strange supplication, and it ran thus : "O, Lord, I saw a little girl on the street to-day, it was very cold and she had no shoes on, or stockings and — and," hesitated the petitioner over the problem that seemed too great, "and — and — it isn't our business, is it God?" Alas! how many of our grown-up prayers go that far — bemoaning an evil before God without going to the rescue with a devout, personal consecration

Dear comrades of the white ribbon, the past is with God; the future, longer or shorter, as he wills, is ours. Forget that bitter April day with the driving storm, to-morrow is June, glad, sunny, glorious June, when God makes all things new. So, sooner or later, to the world come the promised fruit and flower. Forget that sad April day when evil seemed to triumph, or remember it only for the lessons that make stronger and wiser for effort yet more sublime.

The foundations of truth are secure, no matter how shifting may be the clouds and shadows that often shut us in.

I shall never forget a ride I took one time through the valley in Wisconsin, where, hemmed in by the hills, lies the beautiful sheet of water known as Spirit Lake. It was early morning, the valley was still in the shadow, and a light cold and gray lay on the water. The mountains were literally hidden with the mists that hung about them until they seemed an unstable thing soon to melt away

By-and-by the sun came over the hilltops, and touched the mists with a glory rarely seen. It tore them in rainbow scarfs ; it piled them into temple and palace and tower. Finally, they lifted slowly, and it seemed as if the mountains themselves were departing; but it was only the transient, misty splendor which was lifted and lost in the blue above, while rock and crag and hilltop *stood*, as they had for ages, with the crown of the sunlight upon them. "The strength of the hills is His also." We shall know it and rejoice

> "When the mists have rolled in splendor
> From the beauty of the hills"

[Coldwater, May 22, 1888.—Extracts]

A great evil is always entrenched in a wrong order of things made possible by the consent or acquiscence of the majority. A reform takes issue with the order of things; a reformer takes issue with the majority. Before victory is reached, the reform with its declared principles must compel a new order of things, and the reformer must call about the truth he proclaims, a new majority. When one contemplates the radicalism of all this, he ceases to wonder that the battle is long and weary, and that often in the stress of the conflict it is difficult to see which side is winning or which is losing. It is not the heroic and decisive hours, crowded with assault, carnage, and surrender which test the loyalty, courage, and patience of the soldier, but the weary marches when no results are apparent, the slow days and nights of camp life when the army must be alert but cannot strike a blow, and victory yet lingers on some distant dawn.

I have thought these days, of a time in the journey of Israel to the promised land. The golden calf had been set up in the camp and worshiped with showy honors, but, suddenly, into the midst of the unhallowed feasting, came Moses from the presence of God, his very face bearing the light of the heavenly world upon it. It was only an image they worshiped; they had seen the Egyptians do the same thing and caught the low ideal from another people.

Moses was out of sight and some substitute for a higher religion seemed necessary. Even Aaron stood by in acquiescence. You see popular opinion was at the level of the golden calf, and the ten commandments were Utopian and impractical. But out of the shadow of Sinai came Moses, with the tables of stone, and calf and worshipers went down before them. Evil was slain by the righteousness of law. There were tumult and pain and blood, before truth triumphed, but when the chastened nation again took up the march, it was on the level of the moral law I have thought of Moses in that hour of supreme loneliness, driven apart from the people, taking issue with the aggressive and consequential majority, standing alone for God's will. It was no wonder that he pitched the tabernacle "without the camp afar off," and through the pillar of cloud sent his cry, "Show me now *thy* way that I may know thee," and the Lord answered · "My presence shall go with thee, and I will give thee rest."

Rest! it must have been the last thing the great leader expected. There was no rest from the weary and complicated journey, no rest from a turbulent and faithless people, no rest from the care of a great soul with a divine commission yet unaccomplished. It was rest in spite of all these. *Rest* in the presence of God.

Sisters! the "golden calf" is in the camp of our people, the song to its praise will ring all through these months; Aaron the priest, even, will stand by saying weakly, "The people are set on mischief." Be it ours to stand in loneliness if need be, with the prayer, "Show me thy way," and thus find the rest of His presence.

> Truth never comes by flowery ways
>   Unto its own,
> But wakes the world by trumpet blast
>   All rudely blown.
> Right bares a sword two-edged and strong,
> And through the ranks of vanquished wrong
>   Ascends the throne.
> And yet brave souls afield with truth
>   Abide in calm,
> The battle roar shall change at last
>   Into a psalm.
> Truth sends a sword for its increase,
> But after comes the Prince of Peace,
>   With crown and palm.

What is the Woman's Christian Temperance Union? is a question often asked, even in these days, when it has reached proportions that should gain recognition from fair-minded and generous people. The answers are so varied and so often untrue that they admonish us that we are yet unknown to many people, while some, perhaps, know us better than they desire. It is often asserted in these days that we are a political organization, the sentimental annex to an impractical party. It may be worth while to deny it, and since the W. C. T. U. is on the field of progress in connection with some of the largest questions of the hour, to say what we are.

First. The Woman's Christian Temperance Union is evangelical. No revival of religion lifting the world to a higher spiritual plane and saving the multitudes, has surpassed the great awaking known as the Woman's Crusade. No church known to history, was ever born in a whiter heat of the Holy Spirit, or baptized with a more divine courage. No body of believers ever held the faith of God's word in greater purity, as they went on with their appointed mission. Let me say in gentlest warning to the women later come to this work, and who inherit its precious and hallowed past, " Other foundation can no man lay than is laid, which is Jesus Christ."

Repentance, faith, salvation through Jesus is the hope of the drunkard, consecration and the baptism of the Spirit, the preparation for the worker, the will of God the guide to method, in answer to the prayer, " Show me now thy way " has made us all what we are.

Whatever, comrades beloved, shall be the achievements of the future, we may never get beyond these fundamental principles which are the reasons of our prosperity. As well may the mariner repudiate the polar star, as for the W. C. T. U. to sail by any but the Star of Bethlehem. The evangelism of the organization therefore is not, and should not be shut up in a single department that by distinctively religious means seeks to win souls to Christ. The evangelical spirit must pervade all departments and rule in all methods.

I solemnly say to the church, often tried with our radicalism and not always helpful to our need, that the truest ally of the church of Christ in the world to-day is the W. C. T. U.,— abreast with her doctrines, her ideals, and her efforts, surpassing her in brave condemnation of evils which make our Christianity a hissing and by-word among the heathen. We claim that those who make war on our principles and their active outworking, are contending with the vital truths of the sermon on the mount, and the quick, eternal forces of Pentecost. Again I repeat, the organization represented here *is evangelical.*

Second. The Woman's Christian Temperance Union is a moral organization. Certainly, my listener will say, if thus evangelical, it must be moral. But the distinction we desire to make is, that the union stands for the wider morality that pertains to a high civilization, as well as that which narrows to individual life.

No body of men or women has ever put forth and maintained cleaner standards, or sought more persistently to make such ideals real. The sanctity of the Christian Sabbath; the Bible in the public school; the sacredness of the home; an open and earnest demand for social purity; the recognition of God in government, are some of the moralities involved in the new crusade. Many of us never dreamed how far this Christian nation was from high morals in law and habit, until these students and workers assailed the iniquity of both.

It was but an embodiment of our organization and its principles to see Miss Willard stand on the platform at the woman's council a few weeks since, and in face of Washington society, gay and sensuous as it often is, attack the dance, the ultra-fashionable dress, and all that frivolity at the top of good society, which makes the mournful wrecks at the bottom possible. Church members dance, play cards, frequent the theater, dress in a way that outrages modesty, while the pulpit is dumb, or timid, and the discipline ineffective; but you will search in vain in the ranks of our two hundred thousand effective workers for these things, so they have the right and courage to rebuke them.

This stand for good morals widens from individual life to the purest patriotism. There is no need greater to-day than that this nation should be recalled to its early spirit and ideals. Our civilization is being wrenched from its old and stable foundations and built on the shifting debris of other lands. Boston is Irish, New York is everything but American, Cincinnati and Milwaukee are German, Chicago is Communistic. The great West, Indian, Mexican, Chinese, Mormon — everything. The need is true Americanism — more of the old ideals everywhere. The home, not socialism; the free, not the parochial school; the Christian, and not the continental Sabbath. If America for Americans "is too narrow a cry," as Mr. Depew says, then surely Americans for America must be safe. For all this high morality in the individual and the republic, the W. C. T. U. is bravely pledged, and for it, before all men as bravely speaks.

Third. The Woman's Christian Temperance Union is intellectual. I use this word rather than educational, because describing what the organization is, rather than the work it does. It is often said that the union does not win the higher circles, but strikes the great middle class. Very well; perhaps it is true that neither the foam nor the dregs of society are with this army, which is organized to pity the one and help the other, but do not forget that twice the White Ribbon has presided at the White House; that it sits at the tables of senators, and walks every whither in pretty good society. The claims we make, however, are for the intellect behind it. There has never been such an array of genius brought together in any one work. I know something of woman's organizations,— educational, benevolent, and religious,— but challenge them all to match the unity, method, and intellectual force which has revolutionized the nation's thinking in fifteen years, and is on its way to the world's thinking.

Leaders, orators, authors, editors, poets, educators, preachers, physicians, lawyers, artists, and then between two and three hundred thousand of such a rank and file as keeps the beacon lights glowing from the Atlantic to the Pacific, and from the blue lakes of our Michigan to the sunny waves of the gulf!— do you count me a "fool in my glorying"? Very well; the glory belongs unto God, who has called and anointed such a multitude. "The Lord gave the word, and great is the company of women who publish it"

It is both cheap and easy to call this company fanatics, but the W. C. T. U. has made its assault upon the wrong by way of the world's brain. It never has taken a position without a, Thus saith Reason, thus saith Science, and thus saith God. It has touched society, and put the social glass at the bar of conscience; touched the church, and taken the wine of commerce from the communion table; touched the public school in twenty-four States and all the territories, and let in the light of science on the alcohol question; touched legislatures, until a great advance has been made in law concerning moral questions; touched political parties, until in growing perplexity,

> "They wriggle in and wriggle out,
> Leaving the watcher still in doubt
> Whether the snake that made the track
> Was going in or coming back"

This consecrated brain and heart force has created an organization so democratic and so thoroughly national that under its banner sit North and South, white and black together; so far-reaching that its nerves of power extend into every State and territory; so connected that an order from the leader thrills all these nerves to united action It has developed specialists in science, education, and religion, until each fraction of our many-sided population has been fitted with the thought most needed. It has created a literature so unique, so fresh, so pure, that the leaves are for the healing of the nation

Fourth. The Woman's Christian Temperance Union is political. The claim is often made that great changes have come in principle and method since the beginning of the association of women, but its earliest declarations were as unequivocably for prohibition as for total abstinence, and prohibition of the dram-shop meant in the past what it must mean in the future, political action. At first, less was said about it, and all plans and toil centered in the salvation of the drinker, and the preventive agencies that should guard the young and innocent. But could we make our constant fight for the man who was ruined by drink, without coming at length to take issue with the man who sells the poison? Could we censure the man who sells, without a word of blame for the Christian government that licenses that sale, and shares the profits of the price of life? Could we arraign the government, without attack upon the dominant political party that declares for this infamy in its platform, and when lifted to power, keeps its pledge to this "gigantic crime of crimes"? Could we attack the attitude of the political party, without a word of condemnation to the voter who willingly stands on a platform that perpetuates the saloon, and with his ballot at one end of the combination of iniquity, drives his fellow-men into the gutter at the other end, while the voter lessens his municipal taxes? The party saves its guilty life, and the government gets the revenue by this legalized wreck of the human soul and body. It is often urged, to our condemnation, that the W. C. T. U. has espoused the cause of a political party. It is a truer statement to say a party espoused our cause. No class has the monopoly of a great reform when God sets his forces in motion for the overthrow of evil and the triumph of some great truth. There was a party making ballot-box testimony for political prohibition, long before the Crusade. Constitutional prohibition was not the thought of the Woman's Christian Temperance Union, nor of any of its women, no matter how earnestly any of them may have espoused it. It was B. F. Parker, of Wisconsin, grand secretary of the lodge of I. O. of G. T. who in 1876 first suggested the present well-known form of prohibition by constitution, and the methods for securing it. The first State legislature before which the non-partisan petitions came was that of Wisconsin in 1877. The work was done by the Good Templars, and the petitions contained fifteen thousand names. From thence the idea spread over the country, until, before the liquor power was awake and had made bargains with party forces, Kansas and Iowa came into the kingdom of Constitutional Prohibition. The early political history of the W C. T. U. is one of close affiliation with the party dominant in the section where its work was done. At the North there was intense sympathy with the Republican party. At the South, as intense sympathy with the Democrats. Through these great parties it sought to carry out its "do everything" policy for one whole decade. The winnings were worth the effort, and were honorable to the parties who sometimes heard our petitions and granted our requests But the saloon, untouched by these little side victories, yet stood entrenched in government, and our enemy divided its strength between the two great parties, and compelled their protection. In 1884 we learned wisdom from our enemies, and followed the liquor traffic to the political conventions where platforms are made and principles are declared. Our cause was laid before them in the memorial for sale in this convention, and now historic. We plead through the eloquent lips of Miss Willard, "Choose ye this day whom ye will serve," the home or the saloon, a righteous cause, or this aggressive, insolent evil, and they made their choice.

If all this be true of the W. C T. U., then such an organization is worthy our sustained enthusiasm and effort Its meetings should not be the chance entertainment of an hour, when nothing else is upon our hands, our prayer for its prosperity should not be a chance impulse, caught from some unusal circumstance, and it should not stand a doubtful beneficiary at the end of all other giving.

No tree, however grand its visible proportions, can be strong with decay or weakness at the roots, and the State and national conventions are not so true an index of our power as is the condition and usefulness of the local union. Because of its importance, I take a moment for the thought of *organization*. Let it be remembered that ours is a connectional organization. The local exists because of the State and national, and these because of the local. The wide plan and purpose, however, comes to the local union from outside, and for that reason, this fundamental organization should be loyal to its auxiliaryship.

Two notable events as related to womanhood and our society have recently transpired. The first was the council of women at Washington. Never in the history of the world has a like body assembled. The diversity of nation, language, type, and life work made the personnel of the council a marvel, and the review of the doings of women for forty years, in which each presented the outgrowth of her own "heavenly vision," was just as great a wonder.

One missed the enthusiasm of comradeship found in our national gatherings, as well as their warmth and spiritual power. The Christian element, however, was quite dominant. Nothing could have been more fitting and orthodox than the opening sermon by the Rev. Anna Shaw, and whenever one of our sisterhood appeared, Christ was not forgotten. The radical woman's rights' leaders were at the front in the meeting, and naturally honored as those who blazed a way for the later comers. There was to me sad pathos in the present religious attitude of these women; some of them were born of orthodox ancestors, reared in the orthodox faith, and once in the communion of the orthodox church. You must go back forty years to find them fighting the old order of things, appealing first to the church in hope of justice for women, under the law of freedom in Christ. You must think of them repulsed, sneered at, preached against, before you wonder that both soul and faith revolted from what they thought to be a bitter wrong. We came to our broad thinking in kindlier time, made possible by their "cry in the wilderness," and it is not yet easy to "keep sweet" in presence of remnants of barbarism still remaining.

I looked at Susan B. Anthony, a strong but gracious personality, and thought how upon her had been heaped the polite contempt of women too small to understand her long self-sacrifice; the slander and bitterness of men whose selfishness her ideal womanhood assailed, and grew sad, that looking as she is toward the sunset, she will die too soon to be understood or set right I do not wish to be understood as endorsing their revolt from the faith we cherish, but speak of their work as it stands apart from all else, and of the bitter struggle of forty years as a reason for the development of what the religious world continues to flippantly or viciously condemn. The council was a milestone in woman's history. The world has moved in forty years, and will move until there is "neither Jew nor Greek, neither bond nor free, neither male nor female, but all are one in Christ."

The second event is the Council of men in New York — I mean the General Conference of the M. E. Church, and its exclusion of the women sent as delegates. There is strong temptation to say things not altogether gentle concerning this latest injustice perpetrated in the name of law; but women are growing too wise and strong to use either tears or tirade as weapons of defense. There are some points, however, that all Christian women should know and consider. First, the women sent as delegates were peers of any of the men in ability, in the record of Christian usefulness, and in devotion to the church. Second, they were elected by the constitutional method provided, and as representatives to a body, the votes of women as well as men had helped to create. Third, they were rejected solely because they were women, and upon a law always until this hour interpreted in an exactly opposite sense. How was it accomplished?— First, a protest was sent out from the bishops, or by their advice, against the admission of women, and signed by the ministers and laymen. This protest made excuse for the bishops to prejudge the case by instructing the secretary to omit the names of the women from the roll. Second, with swift haste, after this high-handed and previous action, the bishops declared with a show of impartiality as follows: "The bishops have no jurisdiction in the matter of eligibility of the classes of persons in question, and General Conference can only act upon it when properly organized." Already they had exercised "jurisdiction" and just as effectively excluded the women as did the final vote. Were they afraid to accord such women as Frances Willard and Mrs. Ninde the small justice of pleading their own cause? Third, the bishops again proceeded to argue the question in their address, without giving it unbiased to the forum of open discussion.

This was the way the case came into court. Was it any wonder such verdict was reached? The law by which the case must be tried was made to depend on the "intention" of those who framed the provision for lay delegation. The women had voted then as laymen, and have sat ever since in lay conferences unchallenged. Now we are told that it was never the "intention" that they should be admitted to General Conference. All acknowledge the law did not exclude them in its language, but its "intention" and "interpretation" was made the bar. This interpretation was not the province of the General Conference, it was decided, but must come in local option fashion from the annual conferences. It did not seem to strain constitutionality when interpreting the law to shut the women out, but dire results might come if interpreted so as to admit them, and they were excluded. Lastly, the case thus prejudged was sent back, not to the court of the people, whose vote men and women together created the lay conference, but to the ministerial fraction, where by ecclesiastical agreement, or pressure, defeat is most certain and easy. There are a few questions which now greatly interest three fourths of the Methodist Church; viz, if the church is a "congregation of faithful men," and the word "laymen" does not include women, where are we anyway? — the three fourths, I mean. If the annual conferences, which represent a membership composed of two women for every man, shall vote to forever place the minority over the majority, will it be our duty as self-respectful women, simply for a Methodist law, to any longer lay down our cash, our toil, and like Priscilla, our necks, for their sakes? If it were God's law, we might do it willingly, but we are dealing with the "intention" of a Methodist law. If our brethren stand simply on that law, and are anxious only for constitutionality in the question, as they declare, they are guilty of such injustice over a voiceless majority as, practiced against men anywhere, would lead to open revolt If that law and its interpretation is but a shield for a deeper conviction, or a deeper prejudice, let us have the argument upon the *real reason* why men are opposed to admitting women to General Conference.

I had a talk with Bishop Ames upon the subject of licensing women to preach, just after his famous decision against them in the Detroit Conference. In answer to my serious plea he said, "I do n't object to women's preaching, God bless them, I wish a hundred in Michigan were talking for Christ, but as the law of the church is, we cannot license them." I replied, "Bishop, there is a moral quality in this question; it is either right or wrong for women to preach; if right, the church should sanction her; if wrong, all your law cannot make it right" The same is true in this matter, and I hand to these fathers and brethren the problem to solve. It is enough for the liquor traffic to juggle in intimidated courts, and prolong infamy by a technicality, but in Christ's name let us have honesty and religion in the court of the church.

The national outlook was never so stormy and never so hopeful. The failure of local option in Atlanta broke the hope of Georgia, and indeed of all the South, and that section is stirred by the forces of prohibition as never before Everywhere the battle lines are being drawn. God is on the field — compromise is past, and the saloon curse is going down!

I leave much unsaid because already I have gone beyond the proper limits of this address. I welcome you all, welcome our sisters, gray-haired and gentle-hearted, who hold the sweetness and courage of the years; I welcome you who stand in life's storm-center between the sunset and the morning, giving the best of all your years to this great struggle; I welcome with choicest thought, as I would with choicest word, the girls of the Y's; our reinforcements to-day, our successors to-morrow.

> Clothed with brave and gentle grace,
> Looking with prophetic face
>   Across the years
>
> They shall toil as we have done,
> Finish what our thought begun,
> Sometimes singing in the sun,
>   Sometimes hushed in tears

It does not seem much after all. If we toiled for the winnings we can tabulate year by year, we should get out of all the struggle and sit down in life's quiet, easy places, but the path we go leads on to the golden sunset and up to a golden morning, where under the eyes of the Master we serve, we shall have kindlier judgment than the world ever gives, and in nowise lose our reward. For these few days together we "pitch our tabernacle afar off" from the camp defiled with the worship of a "golden calf," and like Moses make our petition, "Show me thy way," and we shall hear in our comforted hearts the answer, "My presence shall go with thee, and I will give thee rest," as we return to our task. The work is for each, the promise for all, no matter how the duties may differ, and the "well-done" waits not for the great deed but for the small one faithfully performed. In the old days in Switzerland, sentinels were stationed along the mountain tops to watch the approach of enemies, and when danger was near, to light the beacon fires. When these flashed out from peak to peak, the brave Switzers went forth to the defense of their country I have heard the story of a little lad, crippled by a fall, who mourned always that he never could be like other boys, or by-and by do a man's work in the world. In such dark, mournful moods, only his mother could comfort him, and she often prayed, "Show my poor lad, that he may do something for thee." One day, in restless temper he climbed the mountain, at the foot of which his cottage dome was nestled. The enemy was near, but the beacon fire was not lighted, and the sentinel was absent from his post. With struggling breath he piled the fagots, lighted them, and aroused the valley as the foe came piling in through the passes of the hill. The invaders fired upon him, but wounded as he was, he kept the fire glowing until help came. Strong men bent over him in wonder and said, "Boy, you have saved your country! do you know it? You have saved your country!" They bore him tenderly to his mother, and laid him on his little cot to die, but the light of heaven was on his face as he said, "I did not live in vain, mother, I lighted the beacon. I saved my country." Sisters, the enemy is at our door, light the beacon and keep it aglow.

[Bay City, Mich , May 28, 1889.— Extracts]

In these recent days I have thought much of the story of a lonely man in a beleaguered city, surrounded by a strong and bitter enemy seeking for his life.

The only crime chargeable to him was that of living so near to God that he had an open revelation of the divine will, which he used for the defense and deliverance of his people

It was told the haughty king who opposed Israel that the prophet knew the things "he spoke in his bed chamber," and fear, that hound that follows the track of cowards and evil doers, came upon him.

It came to pass, therefore, that to destroy a great people, the monarch decided one man must first be slain, since he stood as their defender. So, in the night, an army clothed with the cruel splendor of war, silently hemmed in the city where the prophet abode. In the morning the servant of this lonely and defenseless seer brought the tidings to his master. His answer was as full of peace as a psalm: "Fear not, for they that be with us are more than they that be with them," and then he prayed : " Lord, open his eyes that he may see, and the Lord opened the eyes of the young man and he saw, and behold the mountain was full of horses and chariots of fire round about Elisha." Another prayer, and the enemies were stricken with blindness and led in helplessness into the camp and power of the king of Israel.

If I do not find each year the strong and supreme message for you, my fellow workers, it is not that I do not seek it. I know your self-devotion and sacrifice , I feel the weariness of spirit which often overtakes you and makes the grandest endeavor, for the time, seem cheap and common. We need therefore to seek the heights when we come thus together, and get a vision of the divine side of our toil, and its sure promise of reward.

It is for this reason I would have our united and constant prayer in these days be for an open revelation of the heavenly forces which are with us in the contest that grows graver with every hour.

The prophet's servant had the human vision only — he knew his master; was familiar with his past history and achievements; had seen his supernatural life; but here was a strange and most alarming combination of forces to crush him. Now, at least, there was no way of escape when the power of a mighty army was pledged to his capture and his destruction.

Elisha had the divine vision — he was not lonely, nor weak, nor defenseless. He counted the larger and mightier host, invisible to mortal eyes, and knew himself defended.

The prophet, a man like others, was thus supported because he stood for the truth, though standing alone. The invisible army of horses and chariots of fire that crowded the mountain were the defenders of God's right. In the nation he had chosen, the King of all kingdoms was afield to take care of his own, as he ever will be.

> "Not alone in far-off story
>   Do such mighty hosts await,
> Coming in a rush of glory
>   Through the swing of heaven's gate;
> God can marshal yet his armies
>   To decide a nation's fate.
> On the hills his great encampment
>   Gathers at his high behest.
> White the tents, and strong his legions,
>   But such majesty and rest
> Broods above, we miss the vision,
>   By our human fear oppressed"

The heavenly outlook which came to the prophet's servant was never more needed by our patient hosts than now. We look back two years, to see Constitutional Prohibition slain by a dishonest array of political forces, and an equally dishonest ballot, and look back one year to see local option, on which many hung their hopes, laid low in the supreme court. Out of this trifling with what we believe to be the people's will if its expression could be unhindered, we expected a mighty uprising of the conscience vote in Michigan, but when the chance came to rebuke those responsible for the history of the past two years, we find our hopes betrayed. Now, as we turn toward the capital, where the law makers have for months trifled with this imminent question pressed upon them by fifty thousand petitioners, we learn there is little or no chance for any of the proposed methods of dealing with the saloon except high license, which every honest man and woman has come to know is the liquor dealers' best defense from prohibition

The Woman's Christian Temperence Union represents two lines of power: First, organic; second, ideal, or educational. Our battle is within these, and only by a faithful use of our tactics can we succeed.

These expressions of power have two orders of leaders. First, the official, which begins with Miss Willard, at the head of the national organization, and runs an unbroken chain to the president of the smallest union, in the most out of the way locality.

It is no mean thing, therefore, when a woman is elected to any office in a local union. If she is careless of her trust, or imperfect in her fidelity, it harms the whole unity of our forces. Organic power, at its best, gathers up individual force of numbers, belief, enthusiasm, and effort, and puts to the work in hand organic aggressiveness. It is the foundation for the ideal and educational; it is the body to the soul of our endeavor. We have five distinct combinations of organic power, under the same forms, and acting in perfect harmony, viz., national, State, district, county, and local unions, and each is dependent on the other.

The second line of power is the *ideal* and *educational*, and its leaders are the superintendents of departments. Organic power means women. Educational power means *ideas*. Wendell Phillips once said, "Agitation is the atmosphere of brains," and agitation is impossible without ideas, the size and loftiness of which usually measure their usefulness to the world.

What are our ideals? — Briefly, an individual, *self-governed*, with brain, blood, and nerves, that are not steeped in poison. A home, *love governed*, where the curses of the alcohol maniac, and the pitiful moan of his hapless wife and children are never heard. A church, *Christ-governed*, that stands with God for the prohibition of evil and the salvation of men, and dares rebuke sin in high places by ballot as well as exhortation. A State, *justice governed*, that scorns to fill its coffers with the price of virtue and of blood, through high license on an acknowledged infamy. A nation, *God-governed*, the commerce and civilization of which can touch heathen nations without sending them to lower savagery, and meet the stranger within its gates with other welcome than the open doors of the legalized saloon.

Are these ideals high? Friends, they are possible, and the height has attainable is more than an ideal; it is duty, and goes before the judgment

OUR IDEAS ARE MANY

"Science is finding the truth," said a bright woman in a recent institute, and we come to the world with discovered truth, and only ask for it an honest hearing.

Many of us remember when Christ and science spoke a different gospel to us, but we know now it is one, and that to "love God with all the heart, and our neighbors as ourselves" can never mean to prostitute the forces of government for the perpetuation of a system that tramples on God's law and defies his power, while it poisons the body and wrecks the soul of our brother.

I was startled a few days since to hear a Christian woman gently and sadly urge greater effort along the evangelistic lines of the W. C T. U., for the reason that "the church was not in a position to do such work for drinking men and those who suffer with them." I listened to the awful judgment on the church, and asked, "Will you please tell us why you say so sad a thing?" The reply was: "How can the church do this work when a majority of its members believe in the license system, and a majority of its men vote for a perpetuation of the evil?" Then some one told of a drinking man recently converted, who said, in giving his experience, "I walked the streets on Sunday mornings lonely and full of want, but no one asked me to enter the church, and their bells did not ring for me."

I have thought of it often since then; possibly, my sisters, we are trying to grow in the wrong way, and while we wish for the strong and influential to come to our numbers and give us influence, we are neglecting the fields white for harvest, and the fainting souls that need and want our help. Let us go to these,— the poor, the weak, the erring. We may not always take the Master to the high places of society, but he will be near us as we minister to souls in need

I fear we are often betrayed into thinking our ideas so long clear to us are accepted by most of the world; but if you could have heard Kate Field tell a Boston audience "that alcohol is both a food and medicine; that total abstinence is a fanaticism, and prohibition a tryanny; that the wine-drinking promotes temperance, and the most sober people are the wine-making nations; that the Bible is on the side of moderate drinking; that the viticulturist is the greatest moral, physical, and intellectual benefactor of his kind, and that 'prohibition is a failure,'" and have heard the applause ring out at these exploded falsehoods, you would know your ideas are not yet conquerors, even in Boston, and need pressing yet upon the thoughts of the people.

There is no doubt but that the relation of the W. C. T U. to the Prohibition party has been misunderstood by those interested, and overstated for wrath's sake by a partisan press.

Meanwhile the W. C T U., rightfully abroad in a holy and peaceful war, refuses to die or be driven from the field, and this puzzles some onlookers as the turtle did the Irishman.

It is a well-known fact that a turtle will live some time after its head is cut off. An Irishman once caught a turtle and, to kill it, cut its head off. A man who saw the body moving, said: "Why, Pat, you did not kill that turtle." "And sure I did," said Pat. "Now, come here and see if he is dead," said the man. When Pat saw the turtle moving, he exclaimed . " Sure, I killed him, and he is dead, but the crature is n't sensible of it." Only in this case the " crature " is not dead.

Constitutional prohibition is under sentence of death, and will die in every Republican State, unless a miracle interferes with the party ax. As in New Hampshire and Massachusetts, so will it be in Pennsylvania. The Republican party has struck its highest intent in the high license method, which now holds above all others in every legislature it controls, and in every State where it is dominant.

The Warner-Miller campaign with its argument was the supreme expression of party will; the terms of contract fully stated. The price was high, but the brewers and whisky trust did not stand for a few dollars, when putting their shackles on the party which, from its place of power, should in turn shackle the nation, and he who runs may read it.

What was the motive of the Warner-Miller campaign as he himself stated it?

"I did not expect to win," said he, "but thought I could hold down the prohibition vote, and give the State of New York to Harrison, and save the party."

Is the intention of the high license bargain and method to restrict the saloon and protect the home? Nay, verily; but to save the party.

Some of us have mourned even to tears over the result in New England, and mourning, we have wondered why such an hour had come to the great cause of constitutional prohibition. Let a whisky

paper answer this question. Speaking of the late defeats, it says.
" For this outcome the temperance people have themselves to thank.
The meager vote cast for Gen. Fisk at the presidential election shows
how little in earnest Prohibitionists are. When it comes to a
question of building up a national party that will give cohesion and
backbone to the movement everywhere, the vast majority will not
respond. When prohibition was the issue in Michigan two years
ago, one hundred and seventy-eight thousand six hundred and thirty-
six votes were cast in its favor, but at the election in November only
twenty thousand nine hundred and forty-two votes; so in other States
in the same proportion. Now, if Prohibitionists were in earnest and
really believed their cause to be of more vital import to the nation
than any other, they would have turned out and voted for Gen. Fisk,
and built up a party that would have had some power. They evidently wish to serve two masters, and it was written long ago that
this cannot be done."

We commend this judgment of our enemies to those who profess
prohibition, and vote high license, and especially to Prohibition party
men who last fall deserted their colors in the hour of supreme need,
and voted for the protection of everything but immortal values.
Sisters, be it ours to stand when days are darkest for the cause we
love; as God is true, the judgment draweth on.

> "Through all the long, dark night of years
>   The people's cry ascendeth,
> The earth is wet with blood and tears,
>   But their meek suffrance endeth.
> This wrong shall not forever sway,
>   Tho' many toil in sorrow,
> The bars of hell are strong to-day,
>   But Christ shall reign to-morrow"

[Jackson, May 20, 1890 — Extracts.]

I have tried heretofore in my annual message to touch the foremost lines of thought in this great temperance reform and bring you
the beaten oil of my best endeavor. This year the entertainment of
the convention, and my personal desire to fill these days with comfort
and pleasure for all, has made such demands on time and strength
that I have gathered but fragments of the many things which have
been in my mind to say.

There never has been a time when a wider and more inviting field of discussion was spread out before us, and I longed to enter it fully.

During the past year the temperance question has been forced to the front by both the friends and the foes of prohibition, and stands to-day revealed in its relation to great public interest and political methods as never before

There is divinity in the principles upon which this reform rests. It lives by the truth, and the truth will not down at any man's bidding and cannot be bought by any man's gold. We are therefore a year nearer to victory than when we last met in convention.

The success of prohibition in the two Dakotas and their coming to Statehood with this principle fixed in their fundamental law, and the sharp contrast of the defeat of the same philosophy and method in New England and Pennsylvania have brought the battle afield, until we see as never before inconsistencies of conflicting policies in State and nation, and the irrepressible conflict that can only be settled in righteousness, and not much longer can such settlement be delayed. It is a serious hour, my sisters, but full of hope, since God is on the field.

A great and unusual pleasure is mine this year; in that I am permitted to welcome you, my sisters in Christ, and comrades in a great cause, to my own home, and to the city where my husband and myself have resided since the close of the war.

It was here I first learned the art of public speech in the prayer and class meetings of this church It was in one of the rooms in this building I read my first missionary essay on the "Women of India" and was unwillingly "tugged" out on the seas of all lands, thus entering on my work for the Woman's Foreign Missionary Society in which many of you were my helpers.

Within four miles of where you are now sitting I preached my first six sermons in the little Congregational church at Michigan Centre. It was in this building I was licensed to preach the gospel, after such profound religious experiences as yet lie in the great silence between God and my own soul.

It was here that I took up the temperance work, and from these ways to which all true hearts bid you welcome, I have come and gone for all the years.

I might tell you how at the beginning of these things, the minds and lips of my fellow-citizens bristled with interrogation points, not to say criticism and condemnation, because of the unusual path in which my feet were set, and that because of this, here have grown some of the strongest friendships of my life, and here some of its bitterest antagonisms. To-day this past, which has not been without its conflicts and shadows, lies under the softened glow of memory It does not sadden me as once it might, but I do not care to go over it again; enough for me are the years yet to be traveled to that clearer light where we shall know as we are known, "when the mists have rolled in splendor from the beauty of the hills"

For nearly nine of these years, you have honored me by your choice of leadership. I thank you to-day, as I often do in my heart, for your confidence and love, and yet more for your faithful toil in the midst of the deepening problems of the greatest reform of our day

Womanhood has moved to wider fields and better recognition since first I shocked many good people by preaching the gospel. It seems a century ago that some of the bitter things were thought and spoken about woman's right to live and speak for herself.

There is hope for the future if we prove worthy, for judgment grows kinder, and the demand braver, for all that is best for the feminine half of the world

It is for us I plead for a better chance to plead, also for a nobler womanhood to meet that chance and take it, not for self, but for humanity and God.

I have carried a prayer in my heart for months that this gathering might be a pentecost to us and to this city. Let all our hearts say, Amen, while we seek it together.

From the human side the outlook for the temperance reform is not as bright as some times it has seemed, and often we may feel like sending through the darkness the old cry of the Orient, "Watchman, what of the night?" It is only faith that can answer with steady tone, "The morning cometh," and yet God's morning often waits close by the darkness of human wrong and sin.

We are but playing to-day with the solemn problems that stand at the doors of the present in this great republic.

Easy luxury sleeps on silken couches, conscienceless ambition bargains the country's weal for place and power; unsatisfied greed trades in the bodies and souls of men, and turns every legitimate trade into a robber, cowardice lays finger of silence on lips that should speak, and binds hand and conscience in the slavery of partyism; while under the glittering show of commercial and political power burn the volcanic fires of vice, poverty, and lawlessness, false religion and irreligion that now and then speak from hot lips their warning of danger near.

The labor problem is difficult and dangerous, and breathes the discontent and tumult of all lands. Communism, anarchy, socialism, and nationalism, each have a center in the great bodies which make up the impervious labor movement, and shade off from these centers until when they meet even in softened sentiments, the trend is not wholly safe, nor the demands founded in justice and reason.

The "strike" is near to revolution, speaks the language of threat, and often has the color of conspiracy. Intelligence and humanness settle difficulties by arbitration; ignorance and savagery by force of some kind, and more and more the labor problem tends to force of necessity, if not of arms.

The prime danger is in its roots, which sink in soil of religion and government wholly alien to our own. The veins of our civilization are gorged with the blood of many lands, and the poison brought from far has touched the heart of a nation founded on the home, the school, and the church, and safe only while the character, intelligence, and conscience these represent are on the throne.

True hearts in this free nation must stand for the real rights and sure uplifting of all men, but among the questions of the hour are two: First: Shall a growing division of classes and wealth finally degrade and rob labor of all its rights and chances? Then another. Shall labor by un-American thinking and un-American voting, enslave and degrade the political forces of the republic and pull down the costly structure that shelters it? and there is danger of both. Labor not only represents the industry and wealth-producing power of the country, but it represents the majority, the imperial force in politics. There is therefore no excuse for the red flag and the brutal threat it represents. The ballot-box in a government by the people is an ever opening way to peaceful revolution. Monopoly and monopolsts could not exist without a certain order of things fixed in the financial and business methods of the nation; this order of things could not exist but for the choice of the majority, either intelligently or ignorantly expressed.

If monopoly is created and enthroned by the votes of laboring men, why then should they complain of the master they have chosen? Representing majority, the labors of this country represent all possible reform, and if they fail in the needed intelligence and moral heroism, they can look for nothing but the growth of the wrongs they approve or permit. Of what does labor complain? — First, Of class distinctions and democratic institutions, and yet labor draws the severest lines, and in the world of industry and politics declares for class, and makes its war from a class standpoint. Second, Labor cries out against the tyranny of capital, and yet organizes a tyrant which touches even liberty and life, against all men who do not choose to enter this organization and pronounce their shibboleth until "union" and "scab" have become the watch-words of injustice. Third, Labor professes to abhor monopoly, and yet stands for the liquor monopoly, and with nickles and votes pours into the coffers six hundred million dollars a year earned by sweat of brow, and sets its worst enemy on a throne of iniquity created by law. Labor can, if it will, make degradation and tyranny impossible, rebuke injustice; lift the tariff tax from the nation's toilers, who pay the cost of protecting its monopolists, and thereby stop the main cause for the unequal distribution of wealth. Labor can strike down the saloon which degrades boyhood, cheapens and destroys manhood, beggars the wage worker's home, and is the fruitful source of half the evils from which the bitter discontent of the present arises.

The temperance question, which brings us together, stands not only in our midst like an unsolved riddle, seeking solution by the moral and educational forces we represent, but it stands with stern face and impervious gesture, in the halls of legislature, in the dignified presence of supreme judges, and the wider court where the people speak at the ballot box.

In a superficial study of the present, it would seem that all which represents power is on the wrong side. The saloon is the enemy of the home and of all good and righteousness; smitten manhood, walking abroad in noisy shame, or crowding in the shadow of prison walls, condemns it; pale, broken-hearted women robbed of children, husband, and home cry for, its destruction; children wronged and outraged in this Christian land lay their pitiful sobs in that scale of justice where the sob of a child curses deeper than a strong man in his wrath; and yet to set this iniquity on its licensed seat of power, the bribes of the liquor traffic cross the palm of not only the ignorant voter, but of the Senator, the office-seeker, and party manager, until all the power they represent is given to perpetuate it. The ballot-box is no longer the defense of the nation but the open shambles of political hucksters where its honor, its interest, and the bodies and souls of men are sold for a longer lease of power. The recent disclosures of the methods by which prohibition was defeated in Pennsylvania, Massachusetts, Rhode Island, and Michigan should arouse the conscience, the patriotism, and fear of our people, and bring a revolution. But this liquor traffic not only climbs to high places of legislative and executive power, but lays its hand on the judicial court of higher appeal, and binds that to its greedy self-interest.

The better sense of the people has recently been startled by a decision of the supreme court, in which the police power of the State has been put under another limitation in dealing with the saloon business. How well we all remember the cry of the campaign of 1884, that the prohibition of the liquor traffic was not a national but a State question, lying within the province of the State, and to be finally decided in the smaller tribunals of county and township; now the supreme-court of the federal government crosses this line of State rights, reverses its own decision held for forty years, and opens a legal way for the alcohol pirate to prey unchecked on prohibition territory. The right to ship liquors into prohibition States in unbroken packages has always been held, and has been the largest hindrance in the enforcement of the law, but heretofore the police power of the State could arrest its sale and make such shipment unprofitable. Now this right to thus ship liquors is extended to the first sale, and the State is powerless before a liquor agent with a supreme-court decision as his backing. This sword, however, over which the liquor dealers and their organs set up howls of delight, is two-edged, and cuts high license more deeply than prohibition. A decision on a case carried up from Michigan, involves the same point; viz., that a wholesale dealer who sells in first packages needs no license other than the federal, thus all protection is taken from the high-license-regulated, thousand-dollar men, and will certainly bring trouble into the camp of the enemy. But the devil was never a good lawmaker, and his kingdom is built for destruction.

Another court decision which has shocked the conscience of the nation is the one from the supreme bench of Wisconsin, excluding the Bible from the public schools as an improper book on account of its sectarian character. The warfare against proper ethical and religious teaching in the schools has been hitherto covert and local; this shows what may be after a few more millions of beer-drinking, Sabbath-breaking, church-hating, God-defying foreigners who are made citizens with dangerous haste, are given the liberty to rule to its ruin this American and so-called Christian nation.

All these things which for the present are reverses, bring us face to face with certain conditions: —

First. An apathy among good people which comes from real discouragement, and a belief that these evils are inevitable and that there is no use in keeping up the battle.

Second. A relaxed sentiment which affects individual conviction and action, and in a wider way serves to tone down public morals.

Third. A growing boldness on the part of those who oppose temperance principles and legislation, which shows itself in all those familiar forms of persecution which have followed the track of reforms from the preaching of Noah until now.

Fourth. A division of sentiment and heart even among reformers, who in human discouragement and blindness find the cause of present defeat in the unwisdom of methods which they condemn, and call out again in this time of offence and bitterness the question once on the lips of Christ, "Will ye also go away?" These conditions we are to deal with, my sisters; are we ready for the contest?

The W. C. T. U is a unit for total abstinence and prohibition. Beyond this we do not care to discuss the non-partisan movement. The arguments have been fully answered; let us meet all these things with gentleness and faith. Why should the great work stop while we come down to hold parley with any? It is for us to be the more earnest, and try to extend our organization until it is more and more a power.

It is not strange that the radicalism of the W. C. T. U. is often called in question, for the reason that the principles back of that radicalism are so little understood. Distinctions are being clouded by the sophistry of the hour. Men profess to believe in temperance, and yet put wine on their tables, and drink socially before others to their harm, and these moderate users of alcoholic beverages insist that only excess is wrong. A political party may declare belief in temperance and morality, and yet stand for the perpetuation of the saloon by law. The principles represented here this hour sweep far beyond these positions, and there is present need of an aggressive promulgation of the things we hold, and our reason therefor.

We are more than temperance people. *We are total abstainers.* That means an utter banishment from our lips and homes of any beverage of which alcohol is the center, and with a large majority of our women it means its banishment even as a medicine. This is not the result of a prejudice narrow and unreasonable, for years of earnest study have cleared away the mists, and science is with our position. It is the man who drinks that is shut up to the ignorance of the past. Doctor Benjamin Richardson, of England, was a drinker when the London physicians assigned to him the task of investigating the action of alcohol on living tissues. He took a year for his experiments and came out a total abstainer; his science had convicted his conscience and controlled his life.

What are the steps to a radical total abstinence? These are some of them: Alcohol is a poison. It is never a necessity in health, is of doubtful utility in medicine. It creates an appetite for itself by its effect on the body. It breaks down the physical nature, poisoning the blood, unsettling the nerves, wearing out the heart and making the drinker liable to disease. The la grippe during the past winter has been especially severe among drinkers and tobacco-users as is every epidemic yet known. Alcohol goes farther and attacks the moral nature. The gnaw at the stomach conquers the will and enslaves the victim. The husband grows brutal, the father cruel, the son forgetful of his gray-haired sire. Not a relation in life can be thought of which is not marred and dishonored by the victim of drink. Then the poison in the blood of one generation goes on to the next, until even a nation comes to stagger under the burden of inherited appetite. These disasters are not simply possible, but probable in the case of all men and women who trifle with this danger. It is not with us a question of wine *vs.* whisky, or beer *vs.* brandy, not of quantity, but of the choice of the moral nature in face of a monstrous evil. We believe in presence of the light of to-day, that drinking is a sin *per se*—breaking God's law of personal safety and the sacredness of the body which is the temple of the Holy Ghost, and doing harm by example in all relations to other lives, thus touching with blight common weal.

Appetite, dainty, well dressed and well bred, stands a link in the whole dark misery that to-day curses the nation, and calls for the visitation of God. With such reasons for being total abstainers, we must be prohibitionsts. We believe that which is harmful and wrong for one human being to use, is equally harmful and wrong for another to sell for his own advantage. We believe the license system is a throne of iniquity set up by law, and that in making legally right a thing that is morally wrong, the nation becomes partaker of the sins and infamy of the liquor traffic. It is not drunkenness which is our national sin; drunkenness is the ugly outbreak of human weakness and appetite. It is licensing a sin by choice of the imperial power of government, with which God takes issue, and on which his judgment waits. The nature of alcohol and its effects on the human system, its blight on the whole manhood of the victim and its entailment on those who come after him, have gone beyond sentiment, prejudice, or fanaticism; to question it, is to confess ignorance or dishonesty. When such a scientific truth is thus demonstrated to the intellect, it should take hold of the conscience and regulate the life, and God holds us responsible for sin against his law written in our bodies as well as those engraved on tablets of stone. We are often told that very good people differ in opinion about total abstinence and prohibition; as well might we say that good people differ in opinion about stealing, or treason. The saloon is the organized expression of Satan's kingdom on earth. It breaks all the commandments and teaches men so to do. To protect and perpetuate it, is to defy God, to ruin men, and to be a traitor to the State by aiding and abetting its worst enemies. "No drunkard shall inherit eternal life," is the creed of the Christian, yet we license three hundred thousand men to make drunkards, put their gain in our coffers, their servants in power, their greed into government, and this is made possible by the ballots of Christian men.

The day of ignorance is past, and in the light of these times the drinker and the seller are sinners before God and men, and the voter who consents is "partaker of their crimes." There is need for fresh statement of these fundamental truths. We are facing relaxed sentiment in habit and law. A reckless spirit is abroad on these vital questions, and as sure as God is righteous, we shall not go unpunished unless we repent. I have been studying recently with renewed interest the story of Belshazzar's feast, and seeking for the offense which brought the hand from God to write upon the wall. It was not the feast with its reckless and licentious splendor, all that had been before, it was not the wine drinking and the debauchery, the revel was nothing new. What was it brought the hand with its sentence upon the wall? — It was taking the costly vessels that belonged to the King of kings, and prostituting them to the base uses of the hour and his own heaven-defying ambition. This moved Omnipotence against him and his crumbling throne. God allows men and nations to use their own values in sin's service, and fill up the measure of iniquity, but where they lay sacrilegious hands on that he calls his own, the *Mene, Mene, Tekel, Upharsin*, rings through palace halls, and thrones and kingdoms slip into dust. There is something like this going on in our own land ; a revel of power and splendor is on ; our lords are drinking wine and praising the gods of high license and of revenue, but at this feast I see some vessels sacred unto God — the *home* he has ordained, the Sabbath he has hallowed, and the bodies and souls of men. Men may smile and revel in their places of power, but the handwriting will come, and God will rescue his own

In presence of these truths touching the value of individual life and the cost of a great civilization, we can be nothing else than radical. Between right and wrong there is no ground save a battleground

[Grand Rapids, June 2, 1891 — Extracts]

For the tenth time it is my honor and pleasure, as it is my duty, to come before the annual convention of the Woman's Christian Temperance Union of Michigan with a president's message, and speak such words of review, encouragement, and suggestion, as may aid the great work in which we are united.

It is fitting, my sisters, that first of all we make loving and devout acknowledgment to God for his guiding hand and manifest care. He has given us through the years, remarkable oneness of purpose and harmony in our ranks. In a wide knowledge of our work and workers, I know of no State union made up of more independent thinkers than our own, and yet how slight and few have been the differences which have marred our councils , and in such discussions our lines have never wavered nor been broken. Let us then be thankful that through the changing fortunes of the cause we love, and amid honest differences concerning methods, we have held unity of purpose in the bond of peace. We have had also unusual immunity from *change and loss* in our official ranks.

None of us believe in a life-tenure of office in this society, and yet our loyal constituency in district and State has seemed to appreciate leaders trained by experience, and made wise for service.

We believe a comparison of our own with other State unions would reveal the fact that no similar group of executive officers has remained so long with as few changes. This has given generalship at home, and such influence as knowledge brings to the national councils.

I am not pleading for our policy as superior to all others, for it has its objections. Under the long stress of responsibility, brain and heart sometimes grow weary, and the company of women on whom you have put this care from year to year exhaust ingenuity, and would often gladly give the task to fresher hands. These words, therefore, are spoken only for the purpose of calling attention to a fact, in order that we may rejoice in the long-tested unity of true hearts, and the preserving care of our heavenly Father, over useful and valued lives.

We may also be thankful that the figures from convention to convention show a *steady and substantial growth* in unions, and financial income. The treasurer's report, at the convention of 1881, shows unions, 133; dues, $329 36; total income, $773.11 In 1891, the record shows, unions, 365; dues, $1764, total income, $4252.37, which is the largest in the ten years.

When we consider the stress of adverse influence which has been upon us in the more recent past, and the present status of the temperance and prohibition problems as related both to social and political conditions, this is indeed cause for thanksgiving, yet I am compelled to say that we might have pushed farther on if we had been stronger of faith, and more liberal of policy, and laid foundations in the past for which ground has never yet been broken.

We have set up some modest monuments while passing on, but our own abode has been in tents, and we have never dared any official dwelling for our State organization, or undertaken to support a permanent philanthropy, and here less able States have gone beyond us I feel impelled to say to my sisters of the executive committee that when we grow too conservative or timid to lead the brave constituency represented here to better thinking and new achievements, we have outlived our leadership, and should make room for braver souls I believe the local unions are generally more ready to advance than we to lead.

The work of ten years cannot be represented by results and victories easily pointed out, much of that which makes for sustained consecration and power, lies out of sight, where hearts keep tryst with God, and make such sacrifice of self as has no annals save in the books above.

Among achievements honestly coming from our work we may point to the Girls' Industrial School at Adrian, with one of our own number, well known and loved, at the head of its board of control; to the Scientific Temperance Education law which, without the opposition such measures have aroused in other States, has been steadily influencing the studies in the public schools; and the law raising the age of consent to fourteen years, which although far below our ideal, marks an uplift in morals applied to statutes.

It is beyond any power of language to speak the best thought of my heart to you, my comrades, as we close a decade of this relationship in a difficult but sacred warfare. You have been gentle with my faults, patient with my mistakes, and kind and loyal beyond expression.

You have taught me many valuable lessons since I came to be your president, and I bless you from my heart to-night. If I needed defense in this presence, I could say as in God's sight, that with all my work with you I have tried to be true, not only to the organization, but to its individual members, and have been single in my purpose to advance the cause we represent and make the Michigan W. C. T. U. a foremost power in that advance.

If your heart is as my heart to-night, there is no need of further speech.

> Beyond the rim of the sweetest sound,
> Are silences yet unbroken,
> Below the line of the deepest word,
> Is a deeper yet unspoken;
> After the holiest prayer is breathed,
> A holier still must linger,
> And strains divinest within the soul
> Touch never the lips of the singer.

The losses and gains of ten years are ever impressive; many feet that once kept step with ours have reached the end of the journey; and many voices we long for are silent forever. Who shall say they come not nearer than we think as we gather here, and are of that innumerable company of which Paul speaks · "Wherefore seeing we also are compassed about with so great a cloud of witnesses, let us lay aside every weight and run with patience the race that is set before us." Others, once of our company, have turned back, and walk no farther with us, thoughts of these sadden us more than the memory of the white-robed victors who were faithful unto death.

We have gains of wisdom, patience, and experience, and gains of blessed friendship that enrich our lives, and we hold them as the golden harvest after toil. Our hope for the ultimate victory of the great truths for which we stand is not less strong, if it rests in these days more on faith in God than on the force of any human endeavor or the fidelity of men. This firm foundation for our trust is a blessing truly when we remember that after these years of prayerful purpose and high endeavor, the State of Michigan stands in the same relation to the liquor traffic as ten years ago. During that time both political parties have been tried by State and nation, side movements, industrial and monetary, have disturbed for a time the lines of policy and citizenship, some forced moves have been compelled by the issue of prohibition, which will not down; but all these have been made to *escape*, and not to *answer* the question, What shall we do with the dram shop?

It is here still, legalized and aggressive, the camping ground of evil forces, the political pawn shop where honor is given in pledge for place and spoils; the market house of a vicious, debauched, and un-American ballot, that, ever increasing, already threatens the safety of our free institutions, and smirches executive, and even judicial honor

Setting here a tenth milestone, I would speak no word colored by loss of faith, or toned to sadness by discouragement, for, searching my own soul, I find neither; indeed, I grow more sure every day that the battle will be fought to the finish, and the saloon driven from the throne of law.

It may not be done by a great uprising of moral and patriotic sentiment, as once we hoped, as always we pray, but this government by the people is coming to its death struggle. Majorities that rule get final power from the worst populations of many lands, brought up and hurled against all righteousness. The nation is reaching its dead line, and there must be reform, or destruction A vicious and brutalized majority is bound to be a tyrant, and the solemn testimony of history is that the sun of all tyranny sets in blood.

I say frankly I am more puzzled at the present situation than in any of the years past. If I should analyze that situation as it appears to me, I should grieve and perhaps offend some of my own brave comrades in the battle; but complicated as relations seem, my faith never wavers, since the battle is not ours, but God's

Of three things I am well persuaded: First, that there has been no hour since the Crusade, when the W. C. T. U was more needed among our moral and social forces than it is to-day. Second, It should be our first thought at this convention to strengthen every weak point, fling aside every hindrance, and prepare for more effective service than ever before. Third, We are of no earthly, or heavenly use either, unless we dare the farthest battle line in this contest, fling our banner where the smoke is thickest, and are faithful to the most aggressive truth and method. Far from us be the day when we shall have only a "name to live," and content ourselves with past achievements, or sentimental dreams.

I have chafed for many months over a certain lack of sharp effectiveness in our work. We are building forts, as if for long quarters, putting up earthworks, and laying out camps, as if there was a pause in the battle; we are shooting at random many times. My sisters, let us this year "shoot to kill," in our warfare on rum drinking and rum selling, and find the heart of the enemy. To this end, will you give thoughtful attention to some things which will make for the efficiency we so much desire. We need for ourselves a *great, new conviction* concerning the blighting curse we face, and the principles without which this reform is meaningless. It is the law that human energy in the best channels of endeavor sometimes flags; human strength weakens or wearies; great truths once burdened as with fate, grow threadbare and cheap in their seeming, from long and constant use, until even strong and inspired souls find themselves under the juniper tree with Elijah.

It is at this point the true reformer stands revealed, and the chosen are fed from heaven. Let us not be greatly disturbed then, when in stress of battle mere camp-followers fall out, and false motives break like reeds. The divine feeding at the brook, in the solemn silences of the wilderness, is the only cure for the kind of discouragement the prophet felt, and the ravens always find the chosen of the Lord. The only source then of this great conviction which stirs all powers to untiring zeal, and leads the way like a pillar of fire, is with God.

It is quite the fashion to exhort each other to personal consecration, to earnest evangelism, and to prayer for the old Crusade fire, but, my sisters, God never repeats himself. The Crusade was only the dawn notes of the reveille — his way to arrest the thought of a careless and selfish nation, to a mighty struggle.

We need a higher faith, a stronger courage, and a more prophetic vision than the Crusade women ever knew. Many who prayed in saloons are out of the contest to-day, because unwilling to go with God to the answering of crusade prayers. Divine power was not exhausted in 1873. God's to-morrows are ever greater than his yesterdays. He has gifts and revelations for the temperance hosts they never yet have known, and greater than any past must be the future before the victory is won.

> "There is a fount about to stream,
> There is a light about to gleam,
> There is a warmth about to glow,
> There is a flower about to blow,
> There is a midnight darkness changing into gray,
> Souls with vision of the morning, clear the way."

On the foundation of this high faith we must do better building in our local unions; our need is not so much *more* members, as *better* members, much of our weakness is with ourselves. I would like to see a new pledge presented in each local union which should read something like this. —

Believing, as we do, that the triumph of our principles would make for the peace of the home and the coming of Christ's kingdom, we hold our obligations to the Woman's Christian Temperance Union as solemnly binding upon us, and promise to faithfully attend its meetings, sustain its work, and pray for its success.

The whole situation has grown graver with each day since our last convention, and the only unclouded vision is upward where God reigns. Amid contending forces we pause to ask, Who are with us for a battle without compromise and to a finish, for temperance and prohibition. As we look about for allies, we find that the most advanced science is on the side of our principles.

Demonstration of the nature of alcohol and its effects on living tissues has arrested attention and compelled belief. The medical profession has agreed in many of its large and influential councils with the verdict of abstract science, and has written down alcohol an irritant poison, to be dealt with as such in the treatment of disease.

This scientific position has in ten years gone into effect in thirty-eight States and territories, and more than three fourths of the children in the public schools are within the circle of this radical teaching.

Does science then stand for the destruction of the poison shop? Let us see. After the amendment campaign in Massachusetts, Joseph Cook declared that Harvard College was one of two great forces that defeated prohibition.

In Connecticut, all Yale with her science was aggressively on the wrong side, as I myself know. And our own University has never been known in this reform. *Science* is doubtful when we come to prohibition.

Next, the church is with our position, North and South, colored and white; nearly every denomination has spoken in disciplinary law for total abstinence, and in strongest condemnation of the liquor traffic They have gone farther, and declared for political prohibition in such language as this : " Legalizing the liquor traffic is sin ; " " License is vicious in principle and inadequate as a remedy." Some branches of the church have even advised their members to withhold their influence and votes from parties that are controlled by the saloon.

A collection of these resolutions hurled at this business of drunkard-making ought to annihilate it ; conference, synod, general assembly, association, all unite; they approve our science, declare our principles, and hurl anathemas at the foe we fight.

Do they mean it, these Christian churches of the Republic? Do they really mean it? or are these expressions ecclesiastical dress parade?

Let us see · After the amendment campaign in Massachusetts, Joseph Cook was quoted as saying that Phillips Brooks's church, with Harvard College, were the two great forces that defeated prohibition In 1889, the highest council of the Congregational Church declared . " That the saloon is so great a menace to the peace of society, and so great a hindrance to the cause of our divine Master as to demand the employment of the wisest and most efficient means for its removal."

But within the past two weeks the Congregational ministers of Chicago took the question of the "removal" of the saloon into their meeting, and passed a resolution asking the legislature of Illinois for a one-thousand-dollar high-license law.

In May, 1888, the General Conference of the Methodist Episcopal Church declared the liquor traffic "cannot be legalized without sin " Two distinguished laymen, Gen. Clinton B. Fisk and Hon. Warner Miller, sat in the conference and voted for that resolution. Four months afterward, Warner Miller was stumping the State of New York as a high-license candidate for governor, on a high-license platform, and Gen. Fisk, as candidate of the Prohibition party, was standing for the professed and expressed principles of his own and other churches. Warner Miller and high license received 631,293 votes in New York, while General Fisk and Prohibition received but 33,621, and in the whole nation but 249,945 votes.

It was stated in the public press that leading Methodists and saloon keepers sat together on platforms in that high license campaign, and at a banquet given Mr Miller after his defeat, he was eulogized as one of the noblest laymen of Methodism.

Did they mean it when in May they said, "It cannot be legalized without sin," and then voted high license in November?

In 1890 the M. E. Church South, at their general conference, resolved; "The license system is a sin against society, its essential immorality cannot be affected by whether the license is high or low," and called on its ministers and members to agitate the question

During the same year, Dr. D. C. Kelley, of Tennessee, was suspended from his pulpit work in a most partisan and unjust way, because he felt it his duty to illustrate the resolutions of his church on the Prohibition platform; and although the ruling of the presiding bishop has recently been reversed, he has suffered till the pathos of it will go with him to his grave.

In 1889, the general assembly of the Presbyterians met in the church of which Dr Howard Crosby was pastor, and after a splendid contest over the report on temperance, passed the following: —

"We earnestly recommend to ministers and congregations in our connection, and all others, to persevere in vigorous efforts until laws shall be enacted in every State and territory in our beloved country, prohibiting entirely a traffic which is the principal cause of the drunkenness and its consequent pauperism, crime, taxation, lamentations, war, and ruin to the bodies and souls of men, with which the country has so long been afflicted."

In 1890, the general assembly again adopted a strong and vigorous report, submitted by its standing committee, in which was the following: —

"We enjoin our ministers and people to abate nothing in their zeal and effort in and out of the churches, to check the drinking habits of society, and by effort, voice, and vote, to oppose the traffic in intoxicants as a beverage."

Recently the most distinguished Presbyterian in the country, the president of the United States, set an example from Washington to the Pacific Coast and back again, in direct antagonism to these utterances of the church of which he is a member; we quote but one of the many things in proof: —

"PRESIDENT HARRISON PROPOSES A CHAMPAGNE TOAST IN SAN FRANCISCO.

"SAN FRANCISCO, Cal., May 14 (Special Correspondence).—During President Harrison's visit to this city, he was invited to attend a banquet given by the recent Phi Delta Theta College fraternity, of which he was once a member. After a few remarks he lifted a glass of champagne and said:—

"'I propose that we drink to the order to which we have given our allegiance and our love'

"The spectacle of the president of these United States inviting the citizens of this wine and rum-cursed city and State to indulge in intoxicating drinks, will no doubt be highly edifying to those Republicans who voted for him because of his reputation for temperance and piety."

We pause for very sorrow and shame at these examples in high places, and ask once more, "Do they mean it, our more than three million Methodists, nearly three million Baptists, another million of Presbyterians and Congregationalists, and many other churches from whose records we might quote hot condemnation of the liquor traffic? Are they really in the battle to the finish?"

Now, consider the attitude of these churches toward the Woman's Christian Temperance Union. Our battle is their battle, if Christ's kingdom comes; our faith their faith, our principles their confessed belief; then why are we so often denied sympathy and help? why shut out of church buildings, and sometimes denounced as disturbers of the peace?

In my recent trip through the South, the State conventions of the W. C. T. U. were mostly held in courthouses and halls because of the attitude of the church, and the bitterest criticism was found in the religious press. We ask them for the why. At the South they answer, "We object to you because of your position on Woman's Suffrage."

In this latitude they say, "You are a political society, and we will have none of you."

As non-voters we are not in politics, and cannot be, are we then to be persecuted for saying *that if we were in, we would vote as we resolve, and as we pray?*

Who is with us to fight this battle to the finish? The church seems a little uncertain.

Next the legislative forces of government seem with us, for by State statute, and local option method, the powers that be have endorsed the prohibitory principles.

The people are with us, for in many a hard-fought battle they have put county and commonwealth under prohibition, and carried it into fundamental law.

Judicial decisions are with us. The United States Supreme Court has declared against, "the right of the citizen to sell intoxicating drinks," against the right of government "to bargain away public health and public morals," has given testimony that the traffic is a "danger, and the source of our greatest evils."

All these seem with us as we look for allies. A great tidal wave has been gathering year after year and stands to-night off shore, a mile high, and wide as the horizon. Science, religion, morals, legislation, law, are its threatening forces; why then, in God's name, does it not come over and sweep the saloon from the face of our country? What holds it back? There is but one answer — *Party Politics.*

What makes a conductor for the lightning stroke of science? — *Party Politics.*

What keeps the Sinai thunder of the church resolution out of the ballot-box? — *Party Politics.*

What weakens law by half enforcement? — *Party Politics.*

What makes void the highest judicial decisions? — *Party Politics.*

The temperance reform to-day stops short of political action and ballot-box decision, so the curse and guilt abide.

This is a solemn hour. God never allows for very long the gathered forces of truth and righteousness to be the playthings of either cowardice or dishonesty. That wave of power must come onward to its mission by the action of citizenship, or it will recede, leaving us to darkness and confusion, a deadened moral sense, and the retribution of heaven. Every question that shakes the country to-day and threatens its life, has root in our religious and moral conditions; we can only settle them by righteousness, or revolution.

The political parties in power for thirty years are both in the grasp of the liquor party, and yet they hold the vote of the church, as well as the beer brewers' congress, and do what Victor Hugo charged on Napoleon — "hinder God."

Finally, my heart turns with longing to the strong men and women who kindly listen this hour to a discussion of themes of less interest to them than to these delegates gathered from all parts of the State. Some of you are in sympathy with our principles, but to you has never come the great conviction that calls to personal consecration and self-sacrifice; or coming, it has been put away, and so you stand apart, thinking of us kindly, but let this work cry in vain for your help.

Some may agree with our principles, and take issue with our methods, and not only withhold kindly help, but discourage and weaken by criticism of minor things, this greatest reform of the hour.

Others, still, are opposed to us altogether; do not even accept the truths for which we make our battle. May I ask you to consider some things? You find fault with our radicalism. Are we, then, more radical than the truth? You criticise what you call our obstinacy. Are we more persistent than the evil we fight? Will you consider as Christians, that "no drunkard can inherit eternal life" That God says, " Woe unto him that giveth his neighbor drink, that putteth thy bottle to him and maketh him drunken also"? And when He says woe, it means *woe*.

Will you consider that this bottle is not only a saloon bottle, but a governmental bottle, set out to tempt by law, and that every man who votes for license has part ownership in the bottle, and employs a saloon-keeper to hand it out?

Will you consider that God's woe covers the results of vice, crime, and blood, and you are in the count, if by your example or consent, the bottle goes to a neighbor's lips?

Men often object to this view of the case, but will you call to mind the judgment that fell on David for the death of Uriah? David did not kill him, he was miles away when Uriah fell, but he organized the conditions that slew him.

May I ask voters for license if you do not organize the conditions for all we deplore, when you set up the dram-shop and give it legal sanction?

Let me ask you to consider as *patriots* that the saloon is the most un-American and dangerous thing in the country, and that in giving it the very key of political power, we hand not only our sons but the republic to the destroyer.

May I plead, friends, that you no longer meet this reform with the cry of fanaticism, but ask for one honest hour, Are not these reformers right? And if right, why am I not with them?

One word more to you, my sisters. Even reformers have no light for the world, except it be given them from above; and the shining of that light is dimmed, or darkened, except we walk with Christ.

He was the truest reformer of the ages; the truth he proclaimed was at war with his times; the principles he advocated cut like a knife into the evils of his nation, and neither guilt in purple nor in rags escaped. He trod a lonely path, and was never popular from the manger to Calvary, and at the cross it looked as if not only the Reformer, but his cause was slain. But beyond Calvary was Olivet, and after crucifixion came victory.

In our humble way we follow him, but when we lose his spirit, we miss the divinity of our mission and the power to bless the world.

Our divine Leader had faith in his mission, made absolute self-surrender for others, was in perfect harmony with his Father's will, was patient with the slow faith of his chosen co-workers, and lived and worked and died because he loved.

May grace be given us to follow in his footsteps, for yet the world is weary, and hearts wait for the morning. Be it ours to say, before other eyes see the gold across the gray, Behold the morning cometh.

[Detroit, May 23, 1892 — Extracts]

There comes to me to-night a tender memory of years ago when a quiet and rather sober girl, I daily trod the long stretches of Larned street or the more fashionable ways of Jefferson avenue to the old tenth ward schoolhouse, where for three years I sought as a teacher to add to the sum of intelligence in Michigan and the sum of wealth in my pocketbook. I remember also the Sabbath days in Dr. Hogarth's church, when sermon, prayer, and psalm charmed the fret of the week out of my spirit and fitted for the duties yet to come; almost across the spaces of experience and years I touch once more the rim of that unforgotten time.

Here, too, was spent the first weeks of my honeymoon with my soldier husband, when the tide of warlike preparation beat along these streets, while at depot and wharf were the sounds of martial music, and the fall of woman's tears.

Since then I have wandered far, have seen all the large and many of the small cities of the country, and speak from knowledge when naming Detroit the "Pearl City of many States."

She has never boomed, flared, and fizzled, but stable and elegant, has sat at the gateway of our inland seas, a city worthy of our pride.

She has been charged with being a trifle slow, but if the cable and trolley-cars have not roared along these broad avenues, they have been the more homelike, and some of the citizens may have missed what Chicago often furnishes, a too "rapid transit" to immortality.

It is truly a joy, dear sisters, to be welcomed in such royal fashion to this beautiful city, let us so pray and work through these days as to leave behind a blessing when we depart.

For eighteen years we have kept step with the ever growing and progressive host of women who have temperance, purity, and prohibition as watchwords, and the white ribbon for their token, in a battle that has been no gala-day or dress parade.

We do not gather here in these pleasant places as veterans at a camp-fire, to talk over the scenes of a finished battle and rejoice in victories won or dangers past; we are yet on the field, facing an enemy never more bold or aggressive than to-day; while oh! the pity of it, the "fire in the rear" and "you can never do it" people, are thicker than they were in 1861, when that other great conflict of the century was on.

We gather for better preparation; the work of the days is to rub off the rust and grind away the dulness from every weapon of truth, to bring the new recruits to the firm step of regulars, and all to a nobler courage, a finer motive, and a better trust in the God of battles.

With us are the "Daughters of Veterans," our gentle Y's not here to listen to a thrice-told tale of how their father saved the country thirty years ago, but to get ready for the conflict as their elders fall, and gird on the armor that must be worn by those who save the nation of to-morrow from the evils that threaten

Almost I hear some of my comrades who have fought so long and bravely, sigh, Shall we soon or sometime shout the victory? Nay, dear hearts, many of us never. It remains only to be faithful until death, unless the Lord comes soon, and after toil sing the song of joy with the glorified.

We are told that Gideon, Barak, Samson, David, Samuel, and a host of the elders, "subdued kingdoms, wrought righteousness, obtained promises, stopped the mouths of lions, quenched the violence of fire, escaped the edge of the sword, out of weakness were made strong, and turned to flight the armies of the aliens." But "these having obtained a good report through faith, received not the promises," the "better things" being left to us who live in later times. So to the end it may be ours to find in faith the "evidence of things not seen" and bequeath to those who follow us the triumphs our unrewarded toil shall help to bring.

I am conscious of a degree of hesitation as I begin to urge you onward to new effort and fresh conquest. In the quiet place where these words were written, my heart said solemnly, What have these women not dared and sacrificed to help banish the saloon and save the home?

The beaten gold of time from crowded lives, the beaten oil of thought from tired brains, the costly percentage of gifts from narrow incomes; all these have been laid on this altar of reform, and when all was done, it has been left them to stand in silence and pain while criticism and opposition swept over, and blame often instead of praise was their reward.

But I know we seek together the wisest method and the best equipment, so have thought for many days that there comes a stage in every great work where it is profitable to consider some reforms for reformers.

In the first intense days of our history, we had perfect unity of heart and action, the methods were few, the purpose one, and baptized into the same spirit, "the watchmen saw eye to eye."

In that early time no one came to us whose heart God had not touched, and with the saloon floor as an altar place and the rescue of the lowest as the aim, there was no room for personal ambition.

When organization followed the first great impulse of baptized souls, there came into it only those whose feet touched the rock of evangelical faith.

Christ for the reformer, a living, vital force within, the Holy Spirit as a conscious power, with God and men and the Bible as the textbook and guide,—these were the foundations on which the work stood, while the law of the spirit and the sword of truth guarded the doors of the W. C. T U

The sweep of power in those early days, who that was in it can forget? I remember one night during a summer meeting at Ocean Grove when more than a hundred knelt at the altar seeking Christ, and it was said three hundred were converted during the ten days. That was a "School of Methods" in salvation, and we had many of the kind

But organization widened conception and study until our energies found new channels not purely spiritual, and science, sociology, and law brought new methods Humanitarianism came to stand with Christianity in shaping the work of reform, and brain power in some degree supplanted heart power.

With the broader creed came other thinkers whose souls had not been touched with the old fire, and the Woman's Christian Temperance Union needs to-day what the church needs, a baptism from on high of evangelical faith and pentecostal power. I say this because it needs to be said, and we of all others should be reckless for the truth's sake.

Sometimes these days our unions are dominated by ambitious spirits, who misrepresent the genius of our mission I said to you long ago, elect only godly women to office," and plead for Christian leaders everywhere. The question was raised then in criticism, as it will be now. How can we judge who are Christians? Let God and the Bible judge.

"Other foundation can no man lay than is laid, which is Jesus Christ." No man cometh to the Father but by me; "he that hath not the spirit of Christ is none of his," and "by their fruits shall ye know them."

You will remember that when Moses was to build the tabernacle for God's abiding, he was shown the pattern of it in the mount, every post and curtain, the holy of holies, the home of cherubim and seraphim, and the place of worship and of sacrifice. The command to the builder was, "See that ye make it according to the pattern shown in the mount."

I presume Moses had advisers who thought they could improve on the pattern, but he built it to the end, by the upper vision shown him, and when it was complete, the divine presence crowded the place until Moses stood outside to worship.

'Dear sisters, it was given us to see the pattern in the mount; are we building by it in our own lives and in our organized work? O, let us have a care, since we so need the coming of Him who alone can give the victory.

We have appealed to the drunkard and the saloon-keeper, to the voter and the legislator, to the court and the jury, to the church and the preacher, but still the curse abides on all the land, and often we seem hedged in on every side.

Shall we not seek the hidings of God's power, as we have not in all our past? for, as I said to you one year ago, we need a higher faith, a stronger courage, and more prophetic vision than the crusade women ever knew. We could afford to give up all methods of our own, all human friendships and human trust, to find the "what next" lying in the will of God.

The Woman's Christian Temperance Union has made some history the past year. The meeting of the world's and national unions at Boston brought together an assemblage of women the like of which was never known before.

The press was generous and impressive in the story it told of those days at Faneuil Hall and Tremont Temple, but no words could do them justice.

The visit of Lady Henry Somerset has been a great blessing to the white ribbon women, and we believe to many yet outside our ranks. How impressively this daughter of an earl, in her finished elegance of culture and wealth, has rebuked the cheap assumption of some of our American ladies who consider the temperance reform very far beneath their attention, and taught the lesson of service for Him " who came not to be ministered unto, but to minister, and to give his life a ransom for many "

Several large questions involved in our work, have, during the past year, been pushed to the height of national recognition, and lift like mountain peaks from the plain of ordinary effort ; one is the Sunday question, as related to the life of our Christian nation and the Columbian Exposition.

The *reckless mood* of our people was expressed by a Chicago business man when interviewed, as follows —

" I believe in opening the gates on Sunday and granting the sale of liquor under proper restrictions; the people of the world are coming to see us and must have what they want."

The *thoughtful mood* is expressed in the three thousand petitions which have gone to the directory, and many to Congress, happily not without effect.

Among the petitions are the National Farmer's Alliance and some divisions of the Knights of Labor, who thus make answer to the plea for open gates, in the interest of the working people. Ten States have acted upon the question of closing their State exhibit, and nine of the ten have voted to close them.

A determined anti-Sunday-closing movement has gathered into the brotherhood the infidel and lawless, with certain devout people who do not believe in the first day of the week as the Biblical Sabbath. These, under a taking name, in which, as usual, " liberty " figures, are distributing tracts and making argument wherever an opportunity can be found.

The old "Church and State cry," the lament for "working men," and several other moldy pleas are brought forward to sustain their ungodly demand.

But in this Christian land Sunday stands not only for God's right to rule according to Christian belief, but for man's right to rest according to everybody's need, and we should push the battle for the American *vs.* the Continental Sabbath.

The sale of liquor at the Fair has also stirred the pulses of our people and is yet a very live question. The recent discovery of a bulwark against such sale in parks or fair grounds among the laws of Illinois, seems to turn the victory to the side of righteousness, but the fact that the final vote by the general directory is postponed until after election, so as to trim between beer and Bibles, makes one doubt the final outcome.

The Social Purity department has been making warfare on certain literature yet sent through the United States mails, and on impure trade marks and advertising cards sent out by tobacco firms.

A great many very respectable men use tobacco, and many sell it; can they do it without knowing that the trade in the vile stuff is made the agency for an influence equally vile on manly purity? We are not half awake to the infamy of this twin of the liquor traffic, in its direct effects and its indirect education in other lines of vice. While Christian men smoke and chew, and sell tobacco to feed the same vice in others, they will have the mixed and smoky conscience that enables them to vote a license to the liquor traffic, and the twin curses will blast the boys.

I used to think, before my experience as a reformer, that even a moderately good father would do anything to defend his household and save his boys from evil things, I have given up that idea long ago; the average man will do *nothing* that will hurt his business or his political party, and the home and children may look out for themselves.

About the same verdant period I thought men reverenced and protected women because of their womanhood, but I have changed my mind about that also. Men in a certain jealous fashion protect and defend the women who belong to them, lest their own happiness or honor suffer, but manhood in this country ignores the cry that comes from womanhood as such, and leaves it defenseless before the law, while the scum of every land except China is welcome to the place of power, and allowed to dictate a system that lets the saloon loose upon all that women love and prize.

If self-respecting women make protest against these things, they are met with the cry that the political and ecclesiastical progress of women will destroy the family. So Church and State unite in one thing if in no other; viz., in defining a position for women, and so far as possible keeping them in it.

Lady Henry Somerset made a very bright retort on this kind of sentiment the other day in her London speech, when she said, "They tell us the cradle stands between woman and the ballot-box I would that the cradle stood between man and the public house"

We are often told that good motherhood is the need of the hour and the country, but as I look at it, the saloon, the brothel, the tobacco counter, and the demands of men that invoke and support them with the laws on the statute book which legalize and defend them, suggest the greater need of good fatherhood to rule in home and State Would it not be well for preachers and editors to turn their guns in that direction?

But the woman question, which is the center of the human question, will not down

In the House of Commons the other day, in spite of Mr. Gladstone's pamphlet, the vote against woman suffrage was a majority of but twenty-three in a total vote of three hundred and twenty-seven.

The House of Representatives in New York voted to give woman the full ballot, by a vote of seventy to thirty-four

In the discussion one man said "The House should not fritter away its time with such a silly measure; women are not fit to vote."

Then General Husted sprang to his feet and said: "My God! women not fit to vote! The wisest statesmen of the world have been women, from the Queen of Sheba down to Victoria The bravest persons in the world are women; they were last at the cross and first at the sepulcher, while men slunk away in cowardice. Women now vote on school questions; I do not see why they should not vote for State officers who tax them."

The women of Wyoming will this year help to elect the president of the United States, and two will sit as alternates in the Republican national convention at Minneapolis.

The Methodist General Conference now in session seems more afraid of women than any other class of persons with whom they have to deal.

When the "heathen Chinee" came up, they discussed him and grew eloquent over his rights. When the negro came up, they lamented, because he suffers in the contest of races at the South; but when the women of Methodism are hinted at, they are smuggled off into a committee, while the conservative brethren button up their coats to keep from a chill. Go on with your statistics, brethren, we are three-fourths in the figures and are still here.

> The wise men, toiling the world to win,
>   Have sought the prisoner and set him free;
> Have drenched the valleys of earth with blood,
>   In giving to slaves their liberty,
> They have lifted the serf to a noble place,
> And wrought for half of the human race;
>   But the golden day
>   For which they pray
> Shall never dawn upon slave or throne,
> 'Till woman cometh unto her own.
>
> She has given the world the dew of tears,
>   The nations are born in her cry of pain —
> The nations that after her weary years,
>   Lay at her feet, her strong ones slain;
> 'Twas here they missed it — the Master's will —
> And hindered the promise he shall fulfill;
>   But, lo! at the arch of the mystic gate
>   Is woman's hand with the touch of fate.

The human question stirs like the swell of the tide, and beats against every shore line of injustice and wrong, with a threat at the edge of the surf.

The need of the hour is a moral conviction, an organization of forces on the basis of the ten commandments and the golden rule, not to array industry against wealth, but to unite them both in a warfare on all that is wrong and dangerous to the whole country.

Wanted, then, a moral issue. Where shall we find it? Four years ago the Republican party said in an appendix to its national platform, "The first concern of good government is the virtue and sobriety of the people and the purity of the home." That statement is true, and it is only another way of saying that in the nation's life the moral forces are imperial, and in our form of government these forces can only be conserved through the integrity of the individual citizen. Another thing it says by inevitable logic; viz., that "government has to do with the virtue and sobriety of the people," indeed, that is its "chief concern."

If the Republican party was honest in this expression, then the temperance question is its chief issue. If it was dishonest, the truth remains the same, and the citizen should leave the party and follow the truth.

Let us locate the responsibility for this "chief concern." In the current number of the *North American Review* is a discussion on "The man or the platform," in which several politicians from both camps take part. In one thing they practically agree, that the *platform* and not the *man* is regnant, for the declared principles of the party become the methods of empire. Says Mr. Quay "The chief executive is to carry out the principles enunciated by his party simultaneously with his nomination. Thus once in four years is presented to our people a choice not only between men, but between policies of government.

So long as boys are wrecked and mothers weep, so long as homes are ruined, and the sob of unsheltered childhood finds the ear of God, so long as the gospel lets in the light for the lost, and Christ alone is king, there will be a fight on this temperance question, until victory. So long as this Christian nation sanctions the destruction of its sons for revenue, and sets on a legalized throne "that scum of all villainies," the saloon; so long as "the wicked are justified for reward," "cities are built with blood" and the Lord Jehovah reigns, there will be a prohibition issue, and one day the right will triumph.

> When wealth and power have had their hour,
> Comes to the weak the hour of God.

[Muskegon, May 9, 1893.—Extracts.]

I realize to-night, as often before, that a feeling of sadness is inseparable from every milestone at which we pause to take reckoning of our yesterdays and peer with prophetic vision into the future; for the past comes not back, and carries not only its record but its opportunities into eternity.

This year is especially full of historic memories, as all the world lingers with us to look over our marvelous track of four centuries of human achievment on this continent. We enter as a State W. C T. U the twentieth year of our organized history, and it may be well for us, also, to remember and to ask, Are we worthy of our past and ready for our possible future? Often I fear we are neither as great, generous, nor brave as we should be. We climb the heights of duty with lagging steps, or, caught in the mesh of easier things, sit down with the rest of the world and let the curse against which we are pledged to make unceasing warfare move on to new victories. I have felt this in an unusual way during the last few months, when with impaired strength I looked toward the western skies of life, and said, "The way grows short, and the evening will soon come down." Then, sisters, I called for our work's sake, and when you did not quickly answer, I wondered with a sadness and disappointment which lingers yet.

The past year has not been all to our organization and its achievments that could be desired. For this reason we have tried to put aside mere reports, and call live women out in plan and purpose in these convention days.

Our machinery runs too much on theories, which have from their familiarity palled on our senses. We need live women with sharp convictions, to do hand work at the present hour of this reform. I saw once a water-wheel in the mountains which ran an ore mill in the valley below. It needed no attention, I was told, but the water fell, the wheel turned, and the mill ran, with no human nigh. It looks sometimes as if we supposed our work to be so adjusted; that cold water ideas will run the wheel of the temperance reform, if we sit down and never go near; but while we thus act, it is not our mill that is running, but the gin mill.

We represent a level of conscience, and are charged with the propagation and defense of certain principles beyond even the stand ards of the church. Total abstinence is not required as a test of membership in any church, it is a test with us, and for good reasons, both scientific and moral. Out of the four millions of Christian men in the evangelical churches, but two hundred and seventy thousand have hands that are clean from the license ballot which gives the saloon system its legal security and hellish power. *We* are forever anti-license On the question of social purity the church is well nigh dumb, while the innocent and unwary drift to their doom, and guilt goes on unrebuked. " We ask for a white life for two'"

Charged by the Holy Ghost with these truths, are we doing our best to bring them to those around us whose convictions are not yet stirred? They do not read our literature. They are beyond the range of ordinary influence, and we must carry the truth to them by the living prophetic voices called for this time.

The church resorts to the protracted and special service to secure the conversion of men and women who are in the weekly congregations, as well as those outside, how much more must we, to interest those who stand so far off from what we desire them to believe.

Another thing to be striven after is *effectiveness in the local union*. Often I have urged upon you this necessity as the primary one, and yet the question is forced upon us, Is the local union an educational, moral, and social force, which makes for the new era about which we dream? Let us settle it forever that the local union will not be a force until it compels respect from the community in which it is set by its associated aims and organic strength. To reach this place of honor, two things are necessary. One, to do our work in a businesslike way and accomplish as a fact what we hold as a theory and profess as an object. Another, to stand by our principles — "Sink or swim; live or die; survive or perish," to unfalteringly contend for the faith delivered to us at the beginning.

First Total abstinence for the individual. How much this gospel needs yet to be proclaimed! The great civic displays of this Columbian year from inauguration on, have been object lessons to teach the youth of our land that drunkenness is glory, and not shame. The wine-glass gleams on social heights, surrounded by such glamor as hides the bite of the serpent and sting of the adder. The beer bucket finds its way often borne by the hands of children, to the homes of the poor, and drenches with stupid misery the present and coming generations.

A Wall street man who knows the world well, said to me the other day, "Do you know what stands in the way of such teaching as yours, and the end you seek? It is the habit of all kinds of men to drink, at least a little, so few are total abstainers, and willing to have it put entirely away." This is a rock against us. Principle, truth, conscience, are all on our side, but the objection of appetite is our foe.

It is like the Frenchman at the church wedding, when the minister said, " If any one present has a reason to give why this man and this woman should not be joined in wedlock, let him now speak or forever after hold his peace." A little Frenchman arose, and lifting both hands exclaimed, "I object, I object." The minister was astonished and said, "State your objection, sir." "I want the young lady myself," was the quick reply. This illustrates the foundation from which many an objector speaks. The battle for sobriety is not yet won.

Second. Total prohibition, the ultimate law of righteousness for the State. Look over the field; the flag we proudly call "Old Glory" waves over a liquor oligarchy more aggressive and better entrenched than ever. This power has planted seventy thousand more saloons than we had at the inauguration of President Harrison. It throttled the general commission and local directory of the World's Fair, as well as the citizens who are supposed to rule the township environments of Jackson Park, and put eighty-seven drink-shops inside the Exposition grounds on prohibition territory. It elected Carter Harrison to the mayoralty of Chicago against the best elements of that great city. It is sapping and mining under every prohibitory liquor law in the country, and has the help of both political parties in its work; so the legal battle is as yet but a skirmish to what *must be* before victory. Am I wrong in saying that at this point we have faltered a little in action, if not in faith? It costs us something personally to meet the condemnation of husband, brother, and friend, but were we right when we stood for political prohibition, and the only men who represent it at the ballot-box? If so, why should we be any less decided than in other years since the curse of the rum traffic, and the still greater curse of the civil legislation which sustains it, is yet on the nation? We should hesitate long in these days of indecision before getting together "with so-called reform forces" which refuse to attack the saloon, or do justice to woman. Equal suffrage, although not a test of loyalty in the W. C. T U., has come with good reason to be part of our faith. A few evenings since, at the close of a lecture, I met Aaron Powell, well known to you as one of the leaders in the National Temperance Society. He said to me, "The way of hope was illustrated the other day in Kansas Men will never deliver themselves from political bondage to the saloon until women reinforce them at the ballot-box." The great principles of total abstinence and prohibition were the reasons for our organic being. Let us stand to them though the stars fall. These are enough to quicken the pulses of this generation and bring a new day to the world. Why need we fear, or be confounded, since the battle is not ours, but God's?

The departments are ideally great; we can only make them really effective by putting into the special lines they suggest, more money and better activity. To secure the first, every union must meet its obligations, and to bring the second, our consecration of time and talent must be greater. I am sorry for our superintendents; they are not rich women, they have not all their time to devote to this work, and we respond so slowly to their call Can we not begin to do better with these specialists who have filled the world with better thinking? I have been greatly disappointed that a larger sum was not contributed to the missionary fund, which was to help some of our most important departments, such as work for lumbermen, foreign-speaking people, etc.

The national union has passed through some trials this year. The death of Madame Willard, and its effect upon the health of our national president, as well as her official relation to the world's union, has kept Miss Willard in England for many months, and we cannot do else than feel her absence. This is intensified by the fact that she is not likely to return until late in the summer, and we shall miss her and Lady Henry Somerset, for the great congresses, where they were expected to shine as bright stars as any other body of men or women could produce.

This delay in their return is due to the evolution now going on in the British Women's Temperance Association, the pending contest in England over the district veto, or local option act of Parliament, and greater still the fact that a longer sojourn abroad is considered necessary to restore Miss Willard's strength to where she can once more safely take up the burdens of the national work The W. C. T. U. has a day in the Woman's Congress, which comes next week at Chicago; a day in the Temperance Congress, June 9; and a part in the World's Temperance Congress, held also in June — the World's and National Conventions coming on in October.

It is very wonderful in how many ways the advancement of women to equal place in the world's work and rewards is being emphasized by the events now passing. Mrs. Potter Palmer, in her address at the opening of the Woman's building, May 1, said that one of the strangest things in history was the persistent injustice which had been done to women, and coolly done as if in righteousness. The long night of that injustice seems past, and morning dawns. The place accorded to the women of our own land, in the great work of preparation for the Exposition, is without precedent in history, and the coming out of the women of all lands to activity on entirely new lines, is a marvel. The womanhood of the world is to-day in a wider sphere than ever before, and from the heights of vision reached this year, can never go back. It behooves us to grow grander in these grander times, for the battle of the ages seems gathering in our day and on our shores.

Four hundred years lie between us and the Spanish keel that touched this continent's outlying islands, and gave to the world the grandest domain, and at length the most wonderful civilization known to history.

Whether Columbus was saint or pirate, Protestant or Catholic, has little to do with the present. He was but the servant of the future when he pushed open the narrow door-way to the West for the mighty populations that have followed. Our republic, which this year honors the discoverer, and shouts over the progress of four centuries, was not, however, born under the flag, nor after the ideals of the daring Spaniard, nor the people he represented. America was discovered by Columbus, but the nation was born at Plymouth Rock in the high, white faith of the Puritans.

The two ideals are on the battle-field of destiny to-day, and undertoning the pæans of our great jubilee, the thoughtful will hear the slogan of two camps, and through the garlands, see the gleam of a sword which may flash in deadliest contest, before it is decided whether Christ or Antichrist shall possess ultimate America.

Happy will it be for us, if Christian liberty and a pure faith shall triumph.

Let the shout ring on, I would not stay it. My pulses beat quick as I read of the great naval review at New York, when the war-ships were hung with the garlands of peace, and the nations of the earth turned out for a play-time together. My heart thrilled at the journey of the Liberty Bell from Philadelphia to Chicago. God grant that the broken circle that silences its music may not be the token of a possible time when the nation, whose new song it led, shall send out only broken strains, or be silent as are the nations of the past.

A crisis draws on, unless all laws of cause and effect fail, and the Judge of all the earth has vacated his throne. Let us glance at some forces which are hastening this crisis —

Now, remember that behind nearly every licensed bar stands a foreigner; that nearly all the great breweries are owned by foreigners; and in order to find the men who represent this aggressive political power, you must dip down below the level of the American, the Protestant, the educational and moral ideals of this civilization, and drag up the worst, and you can easily see where the nation is drifting, and what the end must be.

My friends, you who sometimes blame the reformer for what you call his fanaticism, how will you save your country from the grip of these forces? Have you a better way than by the awakening of the conscience of the people, until conviction shall sharpen to action, and we shall at the ballot-box strike down the foe that threatens us?

In view of these problems, we face what is our chief danger,— the saloon. What upholds the saloon?— The license system. What creates the license system?— The ballot of the majority. Who is in that majority?— Bishop and brewer, preacher and saloon-keeper, deacon and drunkard, good and evil. The conscience and conviction that must save are abroad and find expression elsewhere, but never reach the ballot-box, and the curse goes on. A beer-brewer in Pennsylvania said during the campaign in that State:—

"The music of bands on the way to picnics and in beer gardens, will soon drown the voices of the muckers droning in the churches." (Muckers is the German for hypocrite.) Such is their aim, and such their contempt for those who " drone in the churches," and vote with them at the polls. I spoke, a few evenings since, in a town in New Jersey. At the election a few days before, the license men had won a great victory. The minister gave out the hymn, " Onward, Christian Soldiers" When the choir reached the words,—

> "Like a mighty army
> Moves the church of God,
> Brethren, we are treading
> Where the saints have trod,"

I could hardly keep from crying out, for two of the ministers sitting inside the altar-rail stood openly for high license, and a majority of the men in the large audience had voted, directly or indirectly, for license.

"Treading where the saints have trod!" Think of such slander of Moses, with his cry of separation at the gate of a defiled camp. Of Gideon, with his three hundred and his conquering cry, " The sword of the Lord and of Gideon!" Of David, with his faith in

Jehovah, and his smooth pebble from the brook! Of Elijah, on Carmel, with the question of the ages, "How long halt ye between two opinions?" Of the saints, who counted not their lives dear unto themselves, and were slain for devotion to a holy name and holy cause!

Nay, beloved, the church of to-day is *not* treading where the saints have trod, or the saloon and the legal iniquity behind it would go. We are "building towns in blood, and establishing cities in iniquity," and the woe of the Lord Almighty is upon it. It is righteousness or revolution, Christ or blood, for this beautiful land of ours, unless the light of history is false. Who of us are "treading where the saints have trod?" Are we in the fight to the finish, without wavering or fear?

I believe the conscience of the nation is stirring. What if those to whom we have called and for whom we have waited, awake to find us sleeping, or prophesying smoother things? Let us pray for a new anointing, that we may bring no vain oblations, utter no prayers, sing no hymns, and profess no faith to which we will not pledge our money, our lives, and our sacred honor. Citizens of our fair State and country who listen here to-night, with more or less of interest, to this setting forth of the work and principles of the Woman's Christian Temperance Union, you may stand afar and call us fanatics, but the battle is around you, and you may not escape. The highest civil power has invoked and established the liquor system, and set up a "throne of iniquity by law," and the cry of it goes up to God.

Lean out your souls, and listen to a chorus that goes ever upward, — at noon and midnight, past the altars where we worship, and the places of governmental power,— the groan of a father, the cry of a mother over the boy that went astray, the moan of a wife as her heart was broken, the sob of a baby, under the blow of a hand brutalized by rum,— then the jingle of our blood-stained revenue, that is the purchase price of souls, and the stake we play for a nation's life. Where is the remedy? I open the Bible and read the law of national deliverance : —

"If my people that are called by my name shall humble themselves and pray and seek my face and turn from their wicked way, then will I hear from heaven and forgive their sin and heal their land."

Beloved, who will stand for God and truth, for home and native land?

> "They are slaves who fear to speak
> For the fallen and the weak,
> They are slaves who will not choose
> Hatred, scoffing, and abuse
> Rather than in silence shrink
> From the truth they needs must think,
> They are slaves who dare not be
> In the right with two or three
>
> Is true freedom but to break
> Fetters for our own dear sake,
> And with leathern heart forget
> That we owe mankind a debt?
> No! true freedom is to share
> All the chains our brothers wear,
> And with heart and hand to be
> Earnest to make others free"

[Ann Arbor, May 22, 1894]

Some weeks ago the injunction of my physician and the kind co-operation of those who assisted in the arrangements for this State convention, released me from writing the usual annual address. This decision brought quite as much regret as relief, for never during the years in which I have held my present relation to the Woman's Christian Temperance Union of Michigan, has there seemed so much to say that demands speech.

We are making history so fast on the one hand, and on the other are reaping the ripened grain of destiny sown in the years now gone, that this is a day prophetic for all who are given to see the signs of the times. Some reaping is being done in our own State since Governor Rich has compelled the retirement from public office of men who have been robbers of the people's rights and traitors to the people's will. These men, with cheeks hot with shame, with blighted names and bartered honor, are gathering a harvest of disgrace. Yet, as we read the swift condemnation of leaded headlines in the press, and hear the expressions of hot and shocked displeasure, we remember the campaign of 1887 for prohibition, we think of money, effort, and prayer to bring the conscience of the voters of this State where the choice should be for home and purity against the saloon. We remember that so far as honest men can decide, the choice was right, but in two counties the tally sheets were made to lie instead of telling the truth; and at the bidding of the rum power, officers whose hands were on the ark of constitutional rights, played false and sold out our fair commonwealth to the basest of men and measures. We remember that when such men as David Preston and Samuel Dickie, in behalf of the best citizenship, sought redress, the party press, so shocked to-day, sneered, and the legislature said, "We cannot go behind the returns." So fraud crystallized into history, and the imperial powers made choice of a lasting lie. Since then the harvests of political corruption have grown, and tally sheets are no longer sacred. The highest officers are on the political counter, tagged with the dollar mark, and Michigan's political record is a sorrow and a shame. We are being taught, however, that the executive power of the State can "go behind the returns," and that back of false counts is the saloon power.

Looking the republic over, we find that, following on the glitter and music of our Columbian year, came soon the cry for work or bread, and the growl of discontent, which bodes no good, while the shambling regiments of the Coxey army will not be sneered down, but stand at our gates of power, like a judgment Why all this in a country like ours? Because we have counted the gold of our revenues above broken hearthstones and ruined souls, and God awakes to take account of the values that bear his image.

Writing into the heart of these times, W. T. Stead, of England, has recently angered sinners and saints alike with his book of startling title, "If Christ Should Come to Chicago" The sinners cry, "Fanatic," and the saints solemnly say, "Irreverent," but we can see no ground for criticism in raising the most pertinent question of the hour. If Christ ever comes, as the church believes he will, there will be a day when he draws near. If it were now, what would he find in this so-called Christian country? If but one question could be impressed on our own great organization in State and nation, I should choose this: If Christ should come, would he find faith in us? We have dared an unpopular cause, do we dare still after twenty years? And are our faces set patiently toward the battle that shall help on that kingdom to which in his glory Christ shall one day surely come?

There are some tokens of discouragement, some faltering because the victory waits. O sisters, if Christ should come to this convention, would he find us faithful of heart in this evil time?

As helping the line of advance, will you notice the following weak points in our work: 1. We are not organizing new unions with persistent method. 2. We are not winning new women to the old unions as we should. 3. We are not putting our meetings at the intellectual level necessary in these days of women's clubs. 4. We are not keeping up the broad agitation necessary to awaken thought. 5. We are not careful enough to make all departments and methods lead up to, and teach our first great principles,—total abstinence and prohibition. 6. We hesitate to broaden our plans and push to prominence our State interests. To correct these and other tendencies, I respectfully offer the following recommendations: —

That we put in the field one or two State organizers, who shall stir the old unions, bring to pass new ones, and reach the public with the principles which we advocate. Part of the money coming from increase of dues should find its way back to the field and build up the organic forces. That so far as possible, the district presidents attend the county conventions to meet the workers and get insight into the territory they have in charge. That the district convention be, so far as possible, so arranged that the State president may attend them, not so much as a speaker for the public, as a worker with the women That a system of half-yearly reports on postal cards be inaugurated in the districts, in order to convey to the president the condition and needs of the unions midway of the year.

We advise State superintendents of departments who carry on general or county work, to avoid duplicating superintendents in the local unions, but work through the county and district. Imagine a small union of say fifteen busy women, carrying forty departments, and you will see the reason for this method.

*OUR HALL AT HACKLEY PARK.

From my heart I commend the grand loyalty which, finally aroused in the hearts of a large majority of our women, has carried this enterprise to completion.

The deed of the hall runs to the State Woman's Christian Temperance Union. It is your property, and you must care for its interests. By our articles of incorporation, the executive committee are the trustees, and a separate board is not needed. I recommend that you set apart each year seventy-five dollars as a provisional fund for insurance, improvements, care of the building, etc. This

*Lathrap Hall.

money, we believe, will not nearly all be used; for as our women find their way to that beautiful spot, the income of the hall will pay its expenses, and the school of methods is carried on by the assembly.

Believing that every token of God's providence points to the speedy enfranchisment of woman in church and state, let us stand in our place fearless for the truth; and, as an organization help on every wise plan that looks to the ballot for woman in Michigan. Thus, "forgetting the things that are behind," let us reach forward unto the victories yet to be, since the battle is not ours but God's.

ADDRESSES BEFORE THE WOMAN'S COUNCIL.

THE NATIONAL WOMAN'S CHRISTIAN UNION.

[Delivered at First Triennial Meeting of the Woman's Council.—Washington, D C., February, 1891]

Without controversy the National Woman's Christian Temperance Union brings to the galaxy of organizations which compose this Council a character and history at once unique and impressive. No association represented has touched so many springs of praise and blame, of love and hate, and become equally distinguished for the friends it has won and the enemies it has made; proof of the effectiveness of the mission undertaken lies easy to find on the very surface of things. Cursed at the bar of the legalized saloon ; hissed on the floor of the Beer Brewer's Congress, scorned by conventions of political parties, misrepresented by the all-powerful press, denied its prayer in halls of legislation ; sneered at in places of fashion, where the wine-glass tempts to destroy, criticised by conservative pulpits ; and unwelcome often even in the Christian church, it has been left to this organization of ballotless women to arouse all classes of opposers and find for themselves the hate of hate. Then, on the other hand, blessed by the fevered lips of the drunkard ready to perish ; sought by the wandering feet of the boy or girl who went astray, hallowed by loving thought at thousands of firesides ; baptized with holy tears by the mothers whose battle it wages, perfumed by the stainless prayers of the little children, endorsed by the expressed principles of organized Christianity ; sustained by the highest and freshest authorities in the scientific world, praised by lips grown careful through statesmanlike speech, believed in by the best, trusted by the most needy, it has been granted them also to find the " love of love." We may ask therefore, the uttermost doubter and strongest opponent to acknowledge in all fairness that the society at this moment represented has been and is a force in the nation's life worthy of candid consideration. It has touched the home, the school, the church, the political and legislative powers of the whole country, until the shore-marks of its influence are wide as the republic. Born an evangel to the abject, the smitten, and the broken-hearted, the first songs of its holy crusade were of Christ and a better life, and were sung by sweet voices that never wavered, and at the very "jaws of death and the mouth of hell" To-day this gentle evangel has come like Elijah at the court of Ahab, to be the severe-browed prophet of an evil time, when a guilty nation sets up a throne of iniquity by law, and gathers her revenues from the slaughter of her people

No one can understand a great moral, intellectual, and patriotic force, such as is the Woman's Christian Temperance Union, without considering the conditions which demanded its being, and the power which controls and gives method to its actions.

Real reforms are always more divine than human, and are ushered in by revelation to souls prepared to understand, and heroic enough to do the will of God

Less than half a century ago Wendell Phillips stood in his lonely place, which no man coveted, and said to this nation, "God alone is God, and truth is truth," and then lived up to his preaching. When he was mobbed for opinion's sake, and hissed in the forum of public debate, he stood still and let the battle break, sometimes around him, sometimes over his head, but he came to his own at last You remember how he lay in state in the historic hall which had sounded to the notes of that long struggle, while a century with its living and its dead pronounced judgment on that finished life.

> Abroad were murmurs of reverent praise
>   And tenderest dew of tears,
> While suddenly, then, old thoughts were stirred
>   That silent had lain for years;
> Till at the shrine of a dead man's face,
>   The thought of the world grew clear.
>
> They brought him again to the plain old hall —
>   Cradle of liberty's lore,
> How silent the lips that with golden speech
>   Had filled it in days of yore!
> And into the stillness, with blossoms sweet,
> Halted the world, with its tardy feet,
>   And crowned him forevermore

Of the divinity which bore him through the struggle of the great anti-slavery reform his own lips testified, when only a few hours before his death he said, "Nothing but the spirit of Christ has enabled me to suffer and endure what I have."

It is in vain to attempt the explanation of certain lives, or certain great movements which lift humanity to higher levels and leave out the supernatural, and no observer, however thoughtful or kindly, is prepared to judge fairly the beginning and evolution of the society of the White Ribbon unless he understands the word enthusiasm according to the Greek, which means, "God in us," and not according to the German, which signifies "A swarm of people with us" Given then the "divinity which shapes our ends, rough hew them how we will," the conditions which have ripened for this peculiar work and agency are of great interest.

A decade after the close of the Civil War the Woman's Crusade startled the nation, compelled attention, and defied ridicule For many years before that first shot at Sumpter which "hurtled round the world," the entire attention of the country had been engaged with the great discussion which led up to the final conflict, and other reforms had been forgotten in the one absorbing theme The doctrine of total abstinence for the individual, which is the foundation of the temperance reform, had not been largely brought to the attention of old or young by any authoritative and universal agency. The scales had not yet fallen from the eyes of science, and moral standards were not sharply defined, even by the church. Into this somewhat loose drift of opinion broke the Civil War; money grew plenty and moved rapidly; blood was hot, and society disorganized, while camp and field life benumbed the tenderness of conscience, broke up the niceties of education and habit, and opened to the flower of a nation's manhood the doors of recklessness and self-indulgence. What wonder, then, that appetite often conquered the conqueror, until at the very feasts where we celebrated our victories, there stood with muffled face another problem.

Before the war was finished, the government seized upon the commodity of the saloon, and the drunkard, figured its percentage on the gains from the vices of the people, and in 1863 the liquor traffic climbed the throne of revenue. Ever since that day this cruel, vicious, and un-American power has held in its hand at once a scepter and a lash For those who bow to its demands and do its bidding, the extended scepter of money, preferment, and power; for those who hesitate or resist, the lash of its scorpion-like vengeance. During its legalized elevation it has whipped political parties, like spaniels, to its feet, scourged good men out of their places, from the United States Senate down; driven official representatives in other nations to act as drummers for the commerce of ruin; cowed some pulpits and the majority of the Christian manhood of the country into silence or subserviency, cracked its whips over press, legislative hall, and an outraged ballot-box, until to-day it is the tyrant of our civilization.

It was near the beginning of this reign of iniquity that the Woman's Christian Temperance Union took its place among the moral and social forces of the century. It is to be noted, however, that the legal status of the liquor traffic was not for a long time closely related to this new movement. The blow which aroused the womanhood of the country was struck farther back, in the most sacred places of a nation's life. At the altars of home manhood lay smitten, the fire went out on the hearthstone, the light of hope and love died in the heart, and mothers and wives and little children paid the revenue in hunger, tears, and often blood. No strong voice from its high places rebuked the republic for its growing shame, the war debt must be paid if drunkard's graves *were* hollowed, and hearts made desolate. It was these awful results of the liquor traffic which first aroused our women, the great hurt of drunkenness was the misery they sought to heal,— a hurt wide as our populations, the moan and pain of which were everywhere. It is not strange, then, that the first work of this organization should have been intensely evangelical. The saloon door was besieged with pleading and prayer; the drunkard was sought and drawn from the very verge of ruin, neglected childhood felt the mother-touch long denied it; while the pledge, the reform club, the friendly inn, and the ribbons — white, red, and blue — were the tokens of a marvelous faith, the center of which was Christ, the hope of the drunkard.

This holy crusade into the slum kingdom where King Alcohol held his court, was thought by most of the world to be a somewhat heroic and noble thing, if people's taste ran that way. But the years went by, and drunkenness was not cured; indeed, the pro rata consumption of intoxicating drinks increased, and, although a few were saved, the great tide of destruction swept on. Dealing with a result, while a cause which may be touched remains unrebuked, is the work of the foolish or insincere, and the temperance women were neither; so patriotism came to stand by evangelism in the great contest.

It must be remembered that at no previous time were the women of the nation so well prepared to study political conditions and form political opinions as in the years just after the war. The doors of a higher education had been thrown open, giving to them the outlook of cultured minds. With the going of the men to the battle-field and to death, the farm, the shop, and the store, as well as the home, were left to the hands of women, so they were thrust by thousands into business life; then when the cost of the nation's struggle came to be counted, it was found that its women had freely laid on the altar such costly gifts that all past relations were changed.

Thinkers, tax-payers, and unwilling partners in the cost of evil legislation, the women of the country could not stand idly by when another danger was being grown by law, and not rebuke it. Patiently these women sought to solve in the realm of morals and religion, the problem of the drunkard's relation to his own overwhelming appetite, and to cure the land of drunkenness. But ten years of experience, from the drunkard to the saloon, from the saloon to government, from government to the political party, and from the political party to the voters whose choice is law, brought these gentle reformers to the yet more difficult problem of the relation of the powers that be, to the drunkard's legalized temptation. Who is responsible? Where is the guilt? were the questions pressed always to an answer, until it was found that the saloon, the government, the party, and the voter were all in agreement. We do not mean agreement of character, these were often wide apart, but they were agreed upon success; the saloon to perpetuate itself, the government to get the revenue, the party to get the government, the politician to secure the spoils of office, and the voters to shout on the winning side.

While the Woman's Christian Temperance Union was the evangel of the slums, it won the praise of the world; since it stood a prophetess at the gates of the palaces and legislative halls of the nation to rebuke the powers that be, from the ballot-box to the Senate, for legalizing that which created the slums, it has been counted worthy of thorns and stripes.

I pause at the threshold of the great discussion concerning the political attitude of this organization; but here within sight of the white shrine of the Capitol dome, I say solemnly, "God dealt once with this nation for the sin of enslaving the bodies of men, and the scars of that smiting are yet upon us; how much more shall he come from the hidings of his power when our sin is the enslaving of souls!"

"Somewhere beneath the vaulted sky,
　Somewhere beneath the slumbering sod,
Wrath broods her thunders ere they fly;
　Pale Justice steels her chastening rod;
When wealth and power have had their hour,
　Comes, for the weak, the hour of God."

ELEMENTS OF POWER.

From this review of conditions which called for the rise and progress of the organization, we turn now to certain elements of power which make it notable. Without controversy the greatest has been its evangelism, of which mention has already been made; but as women are yet on trial in some fields of endeavor, we wish especially to note certain other forces which have made for achievement and success in seventeen years of endeavor "for God, and home, and every land." First are the exceptional principles espoused, and held with rare and courageous fidelity. It is not strange that the radicalism of the Woman's Christian Temperance Union is often called in question, for the reason that the principles back of that radicalism are so little understood. Distinctions are being clouded by the sophistry of the hour. Men and women profess to believe in temperance, and yet put wine on their tables and drink socially before others to their harm, and these moderate users of alcoholic beverages insist that only excess is wrong. A political party may declare belief in temperance and morality, and yet stand for the perpetuation of the saloon by law. The high creed of the White Ribbon sweeps far beyond these positions. We are more than temperance people. We are total abstainers. That means an utter banishment from our lips and homes of any beverage of which alcohol is the center, and with a large majority of our women it means its banishment even as a medicine. This is not the result of a prejudice, narrow and unreasonable, for years of earnest study have cleared away the mists, and science is with our position. It is the man who drinks that is shut up to the ignorance of the past.

Dr. Benjamin Richardson, of England, was a drinker when the London physicians assigned to him the task of investigating the action of alcohol on living tissues. He took a year for his experiments and came out a total abstainer; his science had convicted his conscience and controlled his life. What are the steps to a radical, total abstinence? These are some of them. Alcohol is a poison. It is never a necessity in health, is of doubtful utility in medicine. It creates an appetite for itself by its effect on the body. It breaks down the physical nature, poisoning the blood, unsettling the nerves, wearing out the heart, and making the drinker liable to disease. Alcohol goes further and attacks the moral nature. It gnaws at the stomach, conquers the will, and enslaves the victim. Not a relation in life can be thought of which is not marred and dishonored by the victim of drink. Then the poison in the blood of one generation goes on to the next, until even a nation comes to stagger under the burden of inherited appetite. These disasters are not simply possible, but probable, in the case of all men and women who trifle with this danger. It is not with us a question of wine *vs.* whisky, or beer *vs.* brandy, not of quantity, but of the choice of the moral nature in face of a monstrous evil.

We believe, in presence of the light to-day, that drinking is a sin *per se*, breaking God's law of personal safety and the sacredness of the body which is the temple of the Holy Ghost, and doing harm by example in all relations to other lives, thus touching with blight the commonweal. With such reasons for being total abstainers we must be prohibitionists. We believe that which is harmful and wrong for one human being to use, is equally harmful and wrong for another to sell for his own advantage. We believe the license system is an iniquity, and that in making legally right a thing morally wrong, the nation becomes partaker of the sins and infamy of the liquor traffic.

It is not drunkenness which is our national sin, drunkenness is the ugly outbreak of human weakness and appetite. It is licensing a sin by choice of the imperial power of government, with which God takes issue, and on which his judgment waits. We are often told that very good people differ in opinion about total abstinence and prohibition; as well might we say that good people differ in opinion about stealing or treason. The saloon is the organized expression of Satan's kingdom on earth. It breaks all the ten commandments and teaches men so to do. To protect and perpetuate it is to defy God, to ruin men, and to be a traitor to the State by aiding and abetting its worst enemies. "No drunkard shall inherit eternal life," is the creed of the Christian, yet we license three hundred thousand men to make drunkards, put their gain in our coffers, their servants in power, and their greed into government, and this is made possible by the ballots of Christian men.

In presence of these truths touching the value of individual life and the cost of a great civilization, we can be nothing else than radical Between right and wrong there is no ground save a battle-ground. We are often told that principles have cost us popularity; very well, such a result was expected. When the reformer grows popular, he has missed his mission, and made terms with the enemy. Next in elements of power, we name organization; its methods run in connectional lines, from the local union through county, district, and State, to the edge of the republic, then afar to the world outside

This was the first organization sufficiently national in spirit to cross the sword line between North and South, bearing the lilies of peace to homes and hearts on both sides of the line, until the past was beguiled of its sting in the high endeavor of a common cause. Every State and territory in the union is now within the circle of crystallized power. To make this an accomplished fact has taken such courage, patience, and self-sacrifice as will never find proper record, save in the story of eternity. This nation-wide movement is much more than local associations of women bound together by a national tie, although that were enough to rejoice in, it means also the organization of ideas and ideals vital to individual and public well-being, and the organized forces are but the living home of another power mightier still; viz, the great truths for which they exist.

Wendell Philips once said, "Agitation is the atmosphere of brains," and agitation is impossible without ideas, the size and loftiness of which usually measure their usefulness to the world What then are the ideals for which battle is made? — Briefly, an individual self-governed, with brain, blood, and nerves free from poison; a home, love-governed, where purity glorifies life and the curses of the alcohol maniac are never heard; a church, Christ-governed, that stands with him for the prohibition of evil, and dares to rebuke sin in high places by ballot as well as exhortation; a State, justice-governed, that scorns to fill its coffers with the price of virtue, by license high or low, on an acknowledged infamy, a nation, God-governed, the commerce and civilization of which can touch heathen peoples without sending them to a lower savagery, and meet the stranger within its gates with other welcome than the open doors of the legalized saloon. Are these ideals high? — Nay, they are possible; what is possible and right, is duty, and duty brings us to judgment.

These allied forces are not only nation-wide but earth-wide, and the gracious woman who presides over this Council is the president of a federation of the world. For swift vision of growing domain I quote from Miss Williard's address before the Atlanta Convention. Speaking of the World's Woman's Christian Temperance Union, she says : " Twenty-one countries have translated our motto, ' For God and Home and Native Land ', it was seen in Chinese, Japanese, Siamese, Norwegian, Dutch, French, and Maori, at the World's Exposition. Seven sacrificing years have strewn the earth with local unions, thirty-four different nations are now federated against opium, alcohol, and tobacco." My pen falters at the outlook, add to this in every land the Young Woman's Christian Temperance Unions which are training the true succession of these older apostles of a new dispensation; add the children, — thousands upon thousands of the Loyal Temperance Legions with the pledge in the hand, a reason in the head, and a conviction in the heart,— think of such wide influences and answer if the day of redemption from appetite has not dawned It seems to me the sunrise gun was fired last year by the Arabs, when in an anti-rum congress they passed the following : " Resolved, To surround the entire coast of Africa with a cordon of armed ships to confiscate every European vessel containing liquors, and sell the crew into slavery." No wonder Miss Williard says of this action, " Would that some of the Boston ships that carry rum might fall into the hands of these righteously indignant Arab heathen."

The third element of power I shall call Harmonious Individuality. Miss Williard's vivid and impressive personality has been photographed not only on the hearts of her co-workers who love her, but on the history of her time, in lines that shall never be effaced; and some of the sharpest shading which makes for this noble immortality has been done by the hands of her enemies in their jealous but impotent rage. But strong as she is in her own place, it is one of the marvels of her leadership that she has drawn about herself other women, in their way equally strong.

What a temptation in the council of women to eulogize the heroines of the White Ribbon ! Some are the fearless path-finders of new empire, some are separated agitators who allow no hand to be laid upon them which brings obligation to be silent, some are statesmanlike, to whom the great truths of this reform are so clear that their very might holds them calm, some are the singers of song, even in the night; some are prophets with a long vision for the morning;

some, like priestesses, learn in secret places the will of God. I hesitate to name any, because of necessity forbidden to name all. My work, however, would not be complete if I did not record the fact that science and not fanaticism has fixed the standards for total abstinence and against intoxicants ; that these advanced scientific positions are to-day acknowledged in the laws of thirty-seven States and Territories, and in the text-books studied by three fourths of the children of the republic. Can this he said without writing the name of Mary H. Hunt? The school of the church, that temple of childhood and youth, where brain and conscience are educated together, has been also reached, until the high moral philosophy of scientific truth is being brought to ten millions of the people's children in their Bible studies. How can this be written and no mention made of Lucia Kimball? The great outside world of childhood so often denied all careful training has been partly gathered, and the carefully reared called out for a special purpose, until the "marching songs" of the Loyal Legions are sung around the world. Who can tell the story of these heirs of to-morrow and not write the names of Helen G. Rice and Anna A Gorden ? One day of every year the prisons, jails, and almshouses of the country are filled with the fragrant gifts of the flower mission, and many days of the year the gospel of love and hope is preached to those whose feet have gone astray into crime, which shuts them from the common brotherhood of men. Who can make report of such a ministry and withhold words of reverent praise from Jennie Cassidy, whose years of invalid life have blossomed into a benediction on those who most need it ; and Mrs. J. K. Barney, who believes in Christ for criminals? The Woman's Christian Temperance Union has kept abreast of all right thinking on the woman's question, and the story of its evolution along the line will always suggest with a thrill of enthusiasm noble Zerelda G. Wallace, with her fine gray head, the statesmanlike speech, which disarms the doubter and wins the opponent in spite of their prejudice, and her younger and gifted associate of other days, Dr. Anna Shaw.

These in department work are but examples of the fine individuality which runs through all classes of toilers in this many-sided society, organizers, evangelists, lecturers, a great company, but each an intense personality, while the State presidents with their real zeal, tempered with wisdom, compose for its president a cabinet worthy of her peerless self. You might as well try to sneer down the sunlight in the interest of darkness, or scold down the bolts of God's lightning, as to use these impotent weapons against such inspired and intrepid souls, intent on a divine mission.

Finally, in representing this society, we wish to call attention to certain great facts which have been demonstrated, and large interests which have grown out of its life and work.

Among these facts are: First, The friendship of women for each other Second, the capability of women to become leaders in the world of thought and action as soon as the opportunity is presented. Third, the genius of women for compact organization and sustained endeavor, under either the smile of prosperity or the fire of discouragement and criticism Fourth, the moral strength of women when related to public as well as private questions, which indicates what will be their value when endowed with the full rights of citizenship. Fifth, the capacity of women for business life and the successful management of large and important financial concerns.

This thought lies at the threshold of certain great interests which have grown out of, and become part of, the history of the N W. C. T. U.; viz., The Woman's Temperance Publishing House; the National Temperance Hospital, and the Woman's Temperance Temple. It must be remembered that the effort of the years has been to win the world's heart by the way of its brain, so a special, critical, and unique literature was demanded

When the work began, no such literature was in existence; but it has been created, so choice, so versatile, so wide in range, that its leaves are literally for the healing of the nations; and this comes to our great populations in seventeen different languages.

Of the beginning of this notable publishing house in Chicago, I quote from Miss Willard's "Women and Temperance," and it introduces to you another remarkable personality. Miss Willard says:—

"Mrs. M. B. Carse will perhaps longest be remembered as founder of the *Union Signal*. I shall never forget the look of exultation with which she came to me at Old Orchard Beach, in 1879, when we were both attending the gospel temperance meeting in that lovely seaside resort, and with look inspired she said to me, 'I could not sleep last night. I had a waking vision of a paper we must have at the West to represent our broad and progressive work. It will not do to wait a whole month for news from our work. We must pass the word along at least once a week. Nothing will help the movement like this frequent interchange of thought, purpose, and sympathy!' and with beaming countenance and earnest words she laid her plan before me, adding impressively, 'I have prayed much about this, and it is going to be.'"

Those who know her magnificent energy, winning manners, and undoubted faith, will not wonder that Mrs. Carse raised five thousand dollars to serve as a nucleus for the new journalistic enterprise. It was not long until we had a weekly paper, the name of which was *The Signal*, and the motto, "Thou shalt give a banner to them that fear thee, that it may be displayed because of the truth" (Mary Bannister Willard, our first editor, gave us this significant and beautiful motto); and we had wider space and fresher news. In 1882, *Our Union* merged its destiny with that of its wide-awake sister of the West, coming with the headquarters of the N. W. C. T. U., to the city of Chicago. From this junction of force has resulted the largest temperance publishing house ever known to the annals of the great reform.

This publishing association is now ten years old. It started with five thousand dollars; now its capital stock is one hundred and twenty-five thousand dollars,— over seventy-five thousand dollars of which is already sold to White Ribboners,— and pays a yearly dividend of seven per cent.

The National Temperance Hospital, located also at Chicago, was undertaken by some women of wealth who were willing to invest largely in order to demonstrate that alcohol is not a necessity in medicine. The unions in the whole country were interested; beds were endowed, rooms furnished, and supplies sent in to help on the work. The Hospital and its method of treatment have had the active sympathy and help of some of the best physicians of Chicago, among them N. S. Davis, M. D., LL. D., who easily stands at the very head of the profession in the country. Mrs. J. B. Hobbs, of Chicago, is president of its board of managers. The Hospital is always full, and would be if twice the size. A new building is demanded, and will come in the near future; so the enemy is dying in the scientific ditch as the light of demonstrated truth is dawning.

The last and greatest venture of the W. C. T. U. is the Temperance Temple, the corner stone of which was laid with most impressive ceremonies, Nov. 1, 1890. Three thousand children marched through the crowded streets of Chicago to the platform prepared for them on the wide foundation. Never will any who heard it forget the song from those musical throats.:—

> "Little eyes will watch you grow,
>   Rise, Temple, rise;
> You are built for us, you know,
>   Rise, Temple, rise"

Back of this great enterprise— its inspiration and its hope— is the woman who was the projector of the W. T. P. A., Matilda B. Carse.

It is to be hoped that in five years the Woman's Christian Temperance Union will come into full possession of their building. They have already given and pledged in gifts to the building fund, about two hundred thousand dollars, and money and pledges are coming in daily with increased rapidity.

This great enterprise has been too great for the grasp and faith of some of the women. They were not all born in Chicago and built on the large prophetic pattern of that marvelous city, but they do have faith in the woman who said, "Arise and build;" so, stone by stone, it grows and is already complete in its beauty to the lifted vision of Mrs. Carse. All this is but a glimpse unworthy of that which I have tried to represent. Let us not miss the secret of such sustained and glorious endeavor.

In that marvelous poem, "The Light of Asia," the poet tells of Buddha, the prince who gave his life for the world. He dwelt in a stately palace in the midst of fabulous magnificence; he had for his bride the fairest among women; joy, power, and security swept around his life like the full tide of the southern seas, but through the music, across the royal splendor, came ever to his soul the cry of the world,— the sad world that needed help, strong, changeless, and tender. So one night he stole out in the silence, away from sleeping wife and child; turned his face from ease, ambition, and royalty, and gave up his kingdom to hush the moan that called him to self-sacrifice. The women for whom I speak to-day have learned this lesson, not from Buddha, but from Christ. When you read the letters of the Woman's Christian Temperance Union, say gently, "These are they who hear the cry of the world."

WOMEN IN THE METHODIST CHURCH.

[Delivered February, 1891, in Washington, D. C., at the first Triennial meeting of the National Council of Women — in the absence of Jane M. Bancroft and Franc Elliot, who were to take this subject.]

MADAM PRESIDENT, LADIES, AND GENTLEMEN: It is fair to say that I did not expect to represent the Methodist Church until coming on this platform a few moments ago; and while I have many things which I might say, I expect to refer to a subject that just now has prominence not only in the minds of Methodist people but in the minds of people throughout the world. It has been recognized for a long while that the women are banging away at the doors of the church for admission. I desire to say that under this movement of the women for recognition there lies a philosophy that is wide and deep.

It is now about forty years ago since Professor West, living in this city, wrote out the first curriculum of college study for women, and it raised a great storm of abuse about his ears. He was told that women were incapable of higher education, and that if women could master mathematics they ought not to be allowed to do so, because it would make them strong-minded. The fact is, that to-day many schools are open for the education of women; as large a percentage is open to them as to their brothers, and it has proved to the world the fallacy of the idea that women are incapable of higher education. Our girls go to school, and come out and love and marry and make better wives and mothers, which proves that after mastering mathematics they are but women still.

Forty years ago there were less than half a dozen avocations into which women could go and earn a scanty livelihood. Now there are more than three hundred. The women are entering the learned professions, and are sweeping through the arts and sciences, and also reaping the golden rewards of the business world. Woman's altered relation to the world of education, and her changed relation to the material world, the money world, and the responsible world, shows that she can take care of herself, and this has within twenty-five years changed the relation of women to all things in this world. That is the philosophy which underlies this condition, and if you cannot stand this urgency of womanhood everywhere, for a recognition among the powers and responsibilities and developments of the world, you would better move into a more solidified world than this.

Now let us apply that philosophy to the church. The business world has recognized women, and opened its avocations to them. General Spinner recognized women, and pushed open the doors of these departments to them,—doors that had never been opened to them before. The business world has recognized the women, and it seems strange that the church should be surprised, not to say embittered, in this discussion about women's right and power under these new conditions. Women have got their brains broadened by the same studies, demonstrations, and investigations that the men have.

You have opened the doors of your colleges to the girl, and she has come back educated. What are you going to do with her after she comes back? Do you suppose that she is going to sit down and crochet impossible dogs on tidies? The women of to-day remind me sometimes of the scientific and humorous picture of a chicken which went round in the illustrated papers some time since. This chicken had just pecked its way out of the shell and stood with a piece of shell on its back; shaking its wings, it began to look back at the little shell, and, stretching itself up, said, "Nobody can ever convince me that I have been in there."

Brethren, we have pecked our way out. You might just as well be good-natured about it and help us along. Why should not the church feel this same recoil and change that the business world has felt? It should, for this reason, that three fourths of the church are women; two thirds of the Sunday-school teachers are women; they are doing its work as teachers, and supporting the church, paying its bills and elevating its societies; and you, brethren, would not have enough church to be buried from if it were not for the efforts of the women.

Now think of this little male contingency in the church, this little company of men in the official corner of the Methodist Church,— or in any other church,— considering themselves to be the whole church, suddenly saying to the Methodist women that they have not belonged to the laity all these years. Imagine them saying to us, "You do not belong in any regular way to the laity of the Methodist Church at all."

Now look for a moment or two into the history of the Methodist Church. If it had not been for the mother of Wesley, we never would have had any Methodist Church. I do not mean simply because she was the mother of the founder of the church; because if I used the remark in that sense, it would mean everything on the face of the earth; but I mean that Wesley was tied up in his narrow ecclesiastical surroundings. Somebody was preaching a more wide gospel, and one that resulted in redeeming England. His mother said, "You would better go and listen and see what there is in it;" and so that great man, brought up in the English Church, was converted, and his glorious work for the Lord Jesus Christ generated the power that was so grand and glorious that its influence has been heard around the world. When Methodism was transplanted from the old country, it took root and divided the people in this country, and to-day the Methodist denomination is the largest Christian denomination in the United States of America.

In Wesley's time, in the societies and class-meetings there were religious exercises in which women were sometimes asked to open their lips in prayer and speech. It is true that women in Wesley's time were not licensed in an official capacity to preach, but they were called upon to do so sometimes. Upon one occasion they were warned not to preach near where a brother was preaching, for fear they would draw away his congregation. I was astonished when a reverend gentleman in the city of New York said to me that we have only a single church in this country that is American in its polity; that the churches had all borrowed their ideas and polities from Europe.

I thoroughly offended some of my friends by saying that the Methodist Church was but a second remove from the Roman Catholic Church, and was almost as close in its method of organization as even the Catholic Church itself. I am not saying anything in the way of criticism of the Methodist Church. I am only stating what is a fact and cannot be disputed. The Methodist polity in its early day was the willingness of the men who had hold of it; and in those days Methodism was a great propaganda that was seeking the salvation and redemption of souls. It means more than that to-day. It means great book concerns, valuable literary works, and great editors; and it means a great many things it did not then mean. It means power and life.

The women of that church in 1871 organized the Woman's Foreign Missionary Society, and have carried it on with marvelous success. Following that came the Woman's Home Missionary Society, which looked to the help of the Indians and the negroes, and the evangelization of the cities. I do not just now recall its date, but there came a time — and I want you to notice this particularly — when the Methodist Church came to such a position that the laymen made a demand for representation in the General Conference. The Methodist Church has always been an ecclesiastical body The brethren composing the laity began to knock away at the doors and say, "We think we ought to have representation in the conference as the lay body of the Church"

Why did they do this? — Bishop Simpson had said that they gave the money and they supported the great institutions of Methodism, and he thought they ought to have recognition in the main body of the church in order to say where and how their money should be expended. The laity said, "We do the work, and we furnish the money to carry it out, and we think we ought to have something to say." At first the ecclesiastical board was unwilling to let the laity in, but finally they knocked so hard that the board was obliged to do so, and submitted the question of the admission of lay delegates to the conference of the church in this country.

I thought I was one of the laymen too thought when the doors of the General Conference were open, that they should be opened to the female laity too. So, about this time the women began to act, and five women were elected to the last General Conference, and among them was the honored president of this council, Frances E. Willard. I was honored by being one of the alternates. I saw Miss Willard, and asked her to come to the State of Michigan, and she said, "I am not going, because that is the month in which the General Conference meets." I said, "O, do not be alarmed, you cannot get in The brethren will not let you in." She said, "Why, Mary, do you think the brethren will shut us out?" I said, "Yes." And so they did. How was that accomplished? — The whole case was prejudged in the first place, and the most remarkable things were done in order to prejudice the case against us. Usually, bodies of men are organized at the outset, and the credentials are considered before the organization is perfected. The result in this case was that those five women, just as devoted and brainy and useful as any of the men that stood upon the floor of that conference, were shut out solely because they were women. The brethren did not say that, but they said the "law of the Methodist Church was not in shape at present to admit them;" and the women were voted out on that technicality. I am glad they did it.

Now face to face with this unusual organization of that General Conference, that body, by its action, declared that women were not full members of the Methodist Episcopal Church, and were not in the same relation to it as the men. A new law was put through to define the subordinate relation that we should henceforth hold in the Methodist Episcopal Church. I wish you to fix that clearly in your minds, because there are women going around, saying, "I don't want to be admitted to the General Conference." I want to say that the women are fully aroused, and tha when the laity in the Methodist Church deliberately declare in the face of the historical past of the Methodist churches, that women are in no full sense members of the church, when they were converted and baptized and were taken into the church, and that a new law must be made in order to define woman's subordinate relation, or to lift her up to the privilege of full membership in the laity, is it any wonder that the world is astonished, — as three fourths of the membership of the Methodist Church are women, nine tenths of its work is done by them, and seven tenths of its charity is being done by them? I say, is it any wonder that the world expects to see the women admitted into the higher ecclesiastical council of the largest Christian denomination in the United States of America? What did this conference do when it organized in this extraordinary manner? It organized the order of deaconesses! They said the women should sit in straight gowns and plain bonnets and do their work for nothing. If I have gotten clearly before you two things, I will sit down, as the bell has rung. Two things I desire to fix in your minds. I am a Methodist and love my church, and I want to see it go on and forge ahead. Three fourths of its membership to-day are women; and women always bring to the altar of Christ their best efforts and their love. I want you, if you are interested in this question, to understand that the women by the usual method of getting into the Methodist Church are in every full sense members thereof, and that just now the church has enacted a new law to define their subordinate relation, or to lift them up to the privilege that womanhood has had in the Methodist Church since its organization in this country.